THE NIGERIAN LEGAL SYSTEM

AUSTRALIA
The Law Book Company Ltd.
Sydney : Melbourne : Brisbane

CANADA AND U.S.A.
The Carswell Company Ltd.
Agincourt, Ontario

INDIA
N. M. Tripathi Private Ltd.
Bombay
and
Eastern Law House Private Ltd.
Calcutta
M.P.P. House
Bangalore

ISRAEL
Steimatzky's Agency Ltd.
Jerusalem : Tel Aviv : Haifa

MALAYSIA : SINGAPORE : BRUNEI
Malayan Law Journal (Pte.) Ltd.
Singapore

NEW ZEALAND
Sweet and Maxwell (N.Z.) Ltd.
Wellington

PAKISTAN
Pakistan Law House
Karachi

THE

NIGERIAN LEGAL SYSTEM

by

AKINTUNDE OLUSEGUN OBILADE
LL.B. (Hons.) (Lagos), LL.M. (Harvard),
Legal Practitioner, Senior Lecturer in Law
at the University of Lagos

LONDON
SWEET & MAXWELL
1979

Published in 1979 by
Sweet & Maxwell Limited of
11 New Fetter Lane, London.
Photoset by Inforum Ltd. of
Portsmouth and printed in
Great Britain by
Fletcher & Son Ltd. Norwich

ISBN Hardback 0 421 23920 4
Paperback 0 421 23930 1

PREFACE

THE primary purpose of this book is to satisfy the basic needs of students of the Nigerian Legal System (or any other subject relating primarily to legal institutions and administration of justice in Nigeria, by whatever name it is called) in universities and similar institutions.

The latest comprehensive textbooks on the entire subject were published in 1963. They are T.O. Elias, *The Nigerian Legal System* (2nd ed., 1963) and B.O. Nwabueze, *The Machinery of Justice in Nigeria* (1963). The latest comprehensive works of aspects of the subject are A.E.W. Park, *The Sources of Nigerian Law* (1963) and E.A. Keay and S.S. Richardson, *The Native and Customary Courts in Nigeria* (1966). Since 1966, important reforms in the legal system have occurred. For example, the native courts of the northern part of the country have been replaced by a new type of court known as area courts, and customary courts in parts of the southern portion of the country have been abolished. In addition, there have been constitutional changes facilitated by the military revolutions of January, 1966, July, 1966 and July, 1975. Such changes including the creation of States have had important effects on legal development in the country. Owing to the multiplicity of enactments now being made with comparable ease in this military era and also to lack of textbooks relating to legal development effected during the era, the student of Nigerian law does not find it easy to trace the development of the law in the several jurisdictions in present-day Nigeria. Thus, the need for a new textbook is greatly felt.

It is hoped that this book will be useful not only to the student of Nigerian law and the law teacher but also to the legal practitioner as well as the curious general reader interested in having more than a smattering knowledge of the administration of justice in Nigeria.

In many parts of the book detailed factual information is given in order to enable the reader — in particular, the student — to understand the law fully, to trace readily the materials needed for legal research and to provide him with the basic tools of constructive criticism of the law. But notwithstanding the usefulness of the detailed information, it is hoped that the law student will be encouraged to pay greater attention to those parts of the book containing a critical analysis of the law and that the information will be used principally as essential raw material of legal research and criticism. Such encouragement may be reflected in university examination question papers in the Nigerian Legal System consisting mainly of questions requiring the opinion of the student rather than mere factual information; for in my view proper law study does not consist in memorising a large mass of factual information.

Treating in detail all the various aspects of legal institutions and administration of justice within the confines of a textbook of this size is a stupendous feat which I have not achieved. Accordingly, I have treated some topics in outline only — particularly, civil and criminal procedure, the chapters on which are almost entirely expository.

In general, for the purpose of clarity, the jurisdiction of origin of legislation cited in this book is indicated in the footnotes. But where such jurisdiction itself indicates its origin, mention is seldom made of the jurisdiction of origin in the footnotes. In citing cases, I have tried to follow the method of citation prescribed or suggested by the law report publisher, but where the method is not uniform with respect to the same series of law reports, I have tried to adopt a uniform system of citation.

In general, the law is stated as at May 1, 1977 but a few of the changes in the law which occurred after that date have been mentioned briefly.

I am grateful to the following persons for the encouragement which they gave me during the preparation of this book: three of my colleagues in the Faculty of Law of the University of Lagos, E.E. Uvieghara, Esq., Dr. M.B. Oyebanji and C.O. Olawoye, Esq., Dr. J.O. Ogunlade of the Continuing Education Centre of the University of Lagos; D.V.F. Olateru-Olagbegi, Esq., of the Nigerian Law School; F.S. Ogundana, Esq., of the Nigerian Bank for Commerce and Industries; my sister, Miss Yemisi Obilade of the Faculty of Arts of the University of Ife; and my wife. I am also grateful to Professor L.C.B. Gower, formerly Dean of Law of the University of Lagos, now Vice-Chancellor of the University of Southampton, for his criticism of the first draft of this work; officials of the various Ministries of Justice in Nigeria who gave me useful information and to several other people who responded favourably to my request for interview with them on aspects of the legal system. I hereby express my thanks for secretarial assistance to members of the secretarial staff of the Faculty of Law of the University of Lagos, in particular, E.A. Saiki, Esq., who typed most parts of the first draft of the manuscript.

I am also grateful to the University of Lagos for a research grant it gave me in connection with this work; to my little daughter, Titi, who occasionally broke my solitude while I was trying to untie the Gordian knot in the course of my preparing this book, in order to remind me that I needed some recreation; to my former teachers both at the Faculty of Law of the University of Lagos and at the Harvard Law School for encouraging critical analysis of the law and thus contributing indirectly to my inclination to write this book; to my parents, S.O. Obilade, Esq., and Mrs. Folasade Obilade, both of whom contributed immensely to the success of my early education and thus, like my teachers, contributed indirectly to my inclination to write this book; and to all others who have contributed directly or indirectly to the success of the preparation of this book.

Faculty of Law,   AKINTUNDE O. OBILADE
University of Lagos,
Nigeria.
June 29, 1977.

CONTENTS

PART 4.   THE ADMINISTRATION OF JUSTICE

TABLE OF CASES

xii

TABLE OF ENACTMENTS

TABLE OF STATUTORY INSTRUMENTS

ABBREVIATIONS

A.C.	Law Reports, Appeal Cases
All E.R.	All England Law Reports
All N.L.R.	All Nigeria Law Reports
A.L.R. Comm.	African Law Reports (Commercial Law Series)
App. Cas.	Law Reports, Appeal Cases
B.P.S.	Benue-Plateau State
Cap.	Chapter
C.C.C.H.C.J.	Certified cyclostyled copies of High Court (of Lagos State) Judgments
C.C.H.C.J.	Certified copies of High Court (of Lagos State) Judgments
Cmnd.	Command Paper
Co. Rep.	Coke's Reports
E.C.S.	East-Central State
E.C.S.L.R.	Law Reports of East-Central State
E.N.	Eastern Nigeria
E.N. Laws 1963	Laws of Eastern Nigeria 1963 revised edition
E.N.L.R.	Law Reports of Eastern Nigeria
E.R.	English Reports
E.R.L.R.	Law Reports of the Eastern Region of Nigeria
E.R.N.	Eastern Region of Nigeria
Fed. and Lagos Laws 1958	Laws of the Federation of Nigeria and Lagos, 1958 revised edition
F.N.L.R.	Federal Law Reports
F.S.C.	Selected Judgments of the Federal Supreme Court of Nigeria
J.A.L.	Journal of African Law
K.B.	Law Reports, King's Bench Division
Lagos Laws 1973	Laws of the Lagos State of Nigeria, 1973 revised edition
L.L.R.	Law Reports of the High Court of the Federal Territory of Lagos (1956-1966)
	Law Reports of the High Court of Lagos State (since 1967)

L.N.	Legal Notice
L.S.L.N.	Lagos State Legal Notice
M. & W.	Meeson and Welsby's Reports, Exchequer
	Judgments of the High Court of
M.N.A.L.R.	Midwestern State, Annual Law
	Reports
M.N.L.N.	Midwestern Nigeria Legal Notice
M.N.L.R.	Midwestern Nigeria Law Reports
M.S.N.L.R.	Mid-Western State of Nigeria Law
	Reports
M.W.N.	Midwestern Nigeria
M.W.S.	Midwestern State
N.C.S.	North-Central State
N.E.S.	North-Eastern State
Nigeria Laws 1948	Laws of Nigeria, 1948 revised edition
Nig. J. Contemp. Law	Nigerian Journal of Contemporary Law
Nig. L.J.	Nigerian Law Journal
N.L.R.	Nigeria Law Reports
N.M.L.R.	Nigerian Monthly Law Reports
N.N. Laws 1963	Laws of Northern Nigeria, 1963 revised edition
N.N.L.R.	Law Reports of Northern Nigeria
N.R.N.L.R.	Law Reports of the Northern Region of the Federation of Nigeria
N.W.S.	North-Western State
N.W.S.L.N.	North-Western State Legal Notice
Q.B.	Law Reports, Queen's Bench Division
Q.B.D.	Law Reports, Queen's Bench Division
Ren.	Renner's Reports
RSLR	Law Reports of Rivers State of Nigeria
S.C.	Judgments of the Supreme Court of Nigeria Reserved Judgments of the Supreme Court of Nigeria
S.E.S.	South-Eastern State
S.E.S.L.N.	South-Eastern State Legal Notice
U.I.L.R.	University of Ife (Nigeria) Law Reports
W.A.C.A.	Selected Judgments of the West African Court of Appeal
W.L.R.	Law Reports, Weekly Law Reports
W.N.	Western Nigeria
W.N.L.N.	Western Nigeria Legal Notice
W.N.L.R.	Western Nigeria Law Reports
W.R.N. Laws 1959	Laws of the Western Region of Nigeria, 1959 revised edition

W.R.N.L.R.	Western Region of Nigeria Law Reports
W.S.	Western State
W.S.C.A.	Judgments of the Court of Appeal of the Western State

Part 1

INTRODUCTION

Chapter 1

INTRODUCTION

A. The Nature of Law

In a wide sense, the term "law" may be defined as a rule of action. In this sense, one may talk of laws of science, for example, Ohm's Law of Electricity. This book does not deal with law in that sense. It deals with law in the strict sense, a narrow sense — law in relation to human actions. In such sense, law is a complex phenomenon. A good definition of it must, therefore, be complex. Although there is no universally-accepted definition of "law," it is clear that law consists of a body of rules of human conduct. Every society, primitive or civilised, is governed by a body of rules which the members of the society regard as the standard of behaviour. It is only when rules involve the idea of obligation that they become law. When they merely represent the notions of good and bad behaviour they are rules of morality. But law is most effective when it conforms to the moral feelings of the members of the community. Mere coincidence of patterns of behaviour does not indicate the existence of law. Mere habits are, thus, to be distinguished from obligatory rules.

Although, practically, obedience to law is usually secured by sanction there are people who obey the law merely because they believe that it is in the best interest of society to do so. Sanctions, however, serve the purpose of protecting the general community against persons of defiant behaviour. Without sanctions, the continued existence of society would be in danger and society would ultimately disintegrate.

In primitive societies, the obligatory rules of human conduct usually consist solely of customs — rules of behaviour accepted by members of the community as binding among them. Customs are usually unwritten. In a primitive society, there is no centralised system for the enforcement of rules; self-help is usually resorted to. Notwithstanding, the obligatory rules constitute law.

Some people consider law as a command. Although there are examples of rules of law couched in terms of a command given by an authority and directed to an individual, most legal rules are not in that form. For instance, rules relating to the making of wills do not command any person to make a will. A command involves an order like that given by a traffic warden or policeman to a motorist to stop.

There are people who think of law as only what the officials do. They argue that what is stated to be law by the legislator is not the law because it is subject to interpretation and that it is the interpretation given by the judges that constitutes the law. Admittedly, there are sometimes in written rules vague words the practical meaning of which may depend on the opinion of the judge. But most rules of law are seldom the subject of litigation. Moreover, it is impossible to identify judges except by reference to law. Therefore, if law is simply what the judges say, it would be impossible to know it.

Some people say that law is normative in character. They contend that law states what people ought to do, that it prescribes norms of conduct. Others argue that law is imperative in character — that it states what people must do and what they must not do. On the other hand, some others see law as a fact. Clearly, the existence of law may be considered as a fact and law cannot be understood except by reference to facts. But law is applied to facts and can, thus, be distinguished from fact.

The opinion one holds about law may depend on the angle from which one views it. For instance, the ordinary citizen may think of law simply as a body of rules which must be obeyed because he sees it from an external point of view and the judge may consider law simply as a guide towards conduct because he sees it from an internal point of view. Neither of them has a complete view of law. Thus, law is indeed a complex phenomenon.

B. Characteristics of the Nigerian Legal System

One of the notable characteristics of the Nigerian legal system is the tremendous influence of English law upon its growth. The historical link of the country with England has left a seemingly indelible mark upon the system: English law forms a substantial part of Nigerian law. Another characteristic feature of the legal system is its complexity. Nigeria consists of a federal capital territory and 19 States.[1] Each State has a legal system. The capital territory, too, has its own legal system. In addition, there is a general federal legal system applicable throughout the country. The complexity of legal systems is further revealed by the application of local customs as law in each State. A small town in a State may have a system of customary law different in some respects from the customary law system of a neighbouring town even if all the indigenous inhabitants of both towns belong to the same tribal group. Thus, within the legal system of a State, there may be a multiplicity of legal systems. There is such multiplicity in the southern parts of the country — in Anambra, Bendel, Cross

---

[1] The States are Anambra, Bauchi, Bendel, Benue, Borno, Cross River, Gongola, Imo, Kaduna, Kano, Kwara, Lagos, Niger, Ogun, Ondo, Oyo, Plateau, Rivers and Sokoto States.

River, Imo, Lagos, Ogun, Ondo, Oyo and Rivers States.[2] It is therefore clear that there are several legal systems within the complex
legal system of Nigeria.

In spite of the diversity of legal systems, history has contributed to
a measure of uniformity of Nigerian legislation. On some matters the
laws of the various States are almost identical. The main reason is
that Nigeria had a unitary government from 1914 to 1951 and some
legislative measures passed during that period continue to apply in
the various territories in so far as they are not repealed by the appropriate legislative authorities.

Mention should also be made of the legal profession. As a general
rule, every legal practitioner is eligible to practise as barrister and solicitor. But a person who has been appointed to the dignified rank of
Senior Advocate of Nigeria is not permitted to practise as a solicitor.
Moreover, in special circumstances, a person who is not enrolled as a
legal practitioner in Nigeria may be permitted by the Chief Justice of
Nigeria to practise as a barrister, but not as a solicitor.

C. THE DIVISIONS OF NIGERIAN LAW

Criminal Law and Civil Law

Criminal law is the law of crime. A crime or an offence is an act or
omission punishable by the State.[3] Civil law is the law governing conduct which is generally not punishable by the State. No clear distinction can be drawn between a crime and a civil wrong in terms of the
quality of an act. An act may be a crime as well as a civil wrong.
Thus, a motorist who, as a result of his negligent driving, injures a
pedestrian, has done an act which may constitute a crime as well as a
civil wrong. Criminal proceedings are instituted principally for the
purpose of punishing wrongdoers. Civil proceedings are taken
mainly to enable individuals to enforce their rights and receive compensation for injuries caused to them by others. Criminal proceedings
are controlled by the State although private persons may sometimes
institute such proceedings. Civil proceedings are usually taken by
individuals but the State may be a party to a civil proceeding. As a
general rule, an act or omission is not a criminal offence unless its definition and the punishment for it are contained in a written law. The

[2] In some States in the northern part of the country, the diversity of legal systems is
minimal because Moslem law of the Maliki School constitutes the only body of
local customs there. At present, the States in the northern part of the country, that
is, the northern States, are Bauchi, Benue, Borno, Gongola, Kaduna, Kano, Kwara,
Niger, Plateau and Sokoto States.

[3] See for example Criminal Code (Lagos Laws 1973, Cap. 31), s. 2; Penal Code (N.N.
Laws 1963, Cap. 89), s. 2; Criminal Code (Fed. and Lagos Laws 1958, Cap. 42), s. 2.

only exception is contempt of court. On the other hand, many civil wrongs are not governed by written law.

Classification of crimes

Criminal offences are classified in terms of seriousness in the southern States (States in the southern part of the country[4]) as follows: felonies, misdemeanours and simple offences. A felony is an offence which is declared by law to be a felony, or is punishable, without proof of previous conviction, with death or by imprisonment for three years or more.[5] An offence which is punishable by imprisonment for a period less than three years when committed by an offender on the first occasion and punishable by imprisonment for three years or more when committed by him on a subsequent occasion is not a felony for proof of previous conviction is necessary before the offence is punishable by imprisonment for three years or more. A misdemeanour is an offence which is declared by law to be a misdemeanour, or is punishable by imprisonment for not less than six months, but less than three years.[6] An offence is a simple offence if it is neither a felony nor a mideameanour.[7] The distinction between felonies and other offences is important in relation to power of arrest and bail. For example, under section 12 of the Criminal Procedure Law of Lagos State,[8] a private person is empowered to arrest any person in the State whom he reasonably suspects of having committed a felony by day or by night. Such power of arrest does not extend to other offences in so far as the suspicion relates to daytime. With respect to bail, under section 118 of the same Law, a person charged with a felony other than one punishable with death may be granted bail at the discretion of the court but a person charged with an offence which is not punishable with death and is not a felony must be granted bail unless the court finds any good reason to the contrary. Formerly, in all the southern States, under an English rule known as the rule in *Smith* v. *Selwyn*,[9] in general, no civil proceedings could be taken against a person on a wrong which constituted a felony unless criminal proceedings on the wrong had been taken against him and completed. Civil proceedings on such wrong might be taken against the offender before the criminal prosecution only if the proceedings could be taken without a disclosure of the felony or

---

[4] The States are Anambra, Bendel, Cross River, Imo, Lagos, Ogun, Ondo, Oyo and Rivers States.
[5] See *e.g.* Criminal Code (Lagos Laws 1973, Cap. 31), s. 3.
[6] *Ibid.*
[7] *Ibid.*
[8] Lagos Laws 1973, Cap. 32.
[9] See *Smith* v. *Selwyn* [1914] 3 K.B. 98; *U.A.C.* v. *Taylor* 2 W.A.C.A. 67; *Ojikutu* v. *African Continental Bank* [1968] 1 All N.L.R. 40.

if there was reasonable cause for not prosecuting the offender — for instance, if the party bringing the action had reported the matter to the police and the police had decided not to prosecute the offender. The rule was applicable in the southern States by virtue of various High Court enactments which provide in general for the application of the rules of "practice and procedure" for the time being of the High Court of Justice in England (in the case of Bendel, Lagos, Ogun, Ondo and Oyo States[10]) or rules of practice and procedure observed in the High Court of Justice in England on September 30, 1960 (in the case of Anambra, Cross River, Imo and Rivers States[11]). The rule was abolished in England by section 1 of the Criminal Law Act 1967. Accordingly, the rule does not now apply in any of the southern States except Anambra, Cross River, Imo and Rivers.

In the northern States, that is, States in the northern part of the country, there is, at present, no express classification of offences into felonies and other offences but offences fall into two categories there too with respect to power of arrest and bail.[12] Moreover, notwithstanding the absence of any express classification of offences into felonies and other offences in those States, the rule in *Smith* v. *Selwyn* applied there by virtue of the High Court Law of Northern Nigeria which provides in general for the application of the "practice and procedure" for the time being of the High Court of Justice of England.[13] Today, by virtue of the Criminal Law Act 1967 (of England), the rule does not apply in any of the northern States.[14]

There is no doubt that the rule in *Smith* v. *Selwyn* contributes to delay in obtaining justice. It is therefore suggested that it be abolished in Anambra, Cross River, Imo and Rivers by appropriate legislation.

In terms of procedure, crimes are also classified in the southern States into indictable and non-indictable offences. An indictable offence is an offence:

(a) which on conviction may be punished by a term of imprisonment exceeding two years; or
(b) which on conviction may be punished by imposition of a fine exceeding 400 naira; and

---

[10] See, for example, High Court (Civil Procedure) Rules (W.R.N. Laws, 1959, Cap. 44), Ord. 35, r. 10.
[11] High Court Law (E.N. Laws 1963, Cap. 61), s. 16.
[12] See Criminal Procedure Code (N.N. Laws 1963, Cap. 30), ss. 26, 28 and 34.
[13] See *Nwosu* v. *Chima* 1966 N.N.L.R. 155. There was an express classification of offences into felonies and other offences in the northern part of the country until September 1960. Thus, the rule in *Smith* v. *Selwyn* applied in that part of the country until that date. See *Ibekwe* v. *Pearce* 1960 N.R.N.L.R. 67.
[14] See *Oyewale* v. *Okoli* (1975, Suit No. NCH/137/73 (unreported), a decision of the High Court of the North-Central State (Uwais J.).

(c) which is not declared by the written law creating it to be punishable on summary conviction.[15]

All other offences are non-indictable offences. Magistrates' courts in the southern States try indictable and non-indictable offences. The usual procedure followed by the High Courts of those States in the trial of indictable offences is elaborate. In the northern States, there is no classification of crimes in these terms. The magistrates' courts in those States, too, try offences summarily and, as in many of the southern States, they generally hold preliminary inquiries into serious offences before the trial in the High Courts. The High Courts in the northern States, like their counterparts in the southern States, generally use an elaborate procedure in the trial of offences.

Classification of civil wrongs

The commonest classes of civil wrongs are contract, tort and breach of trust. A contract is an agreement enforceable at law. A breach of it by a party entitles the other to compensation as damages. A tort is a civil wrong which occurs independently of an agreement and leads to the award of damages to the party wronged. An act may constitute a breach of contract as well as a tort. For example, a builder who erects a building negligently may be liable for a breach of contract and he may also be liable in tort for his negligent conduct. The only interest protected by the law of contract is interest in the performance of agreements but the law of tort protects several interests, for example, interest in the person, interest in property and interest in reputation.

A trust is the relationship which arises when a person who holds property has an obligation in equity (the law developed by the old English Court of Chancery) to deal with it for the benefit of another. The person who gives the property is the settlor; the person who holds it is the trustee; and the person for whose benefit it is held is the beneficiary. Generally, there is a breach of trust if trust property is dealt with by the trustee improperly, for example, if the trustee who is not also a beneficiary uses trust property for his own purpose.

The law of contract, the law of tort and the law of trusts are found mainly in judicial decisions.

Public Law and Private Law

Public law is that part of the law which primarily involves the State. It regulates the relationship between the organs of government and the relationship between individuals and the State. Private law is the

---

[15] See, for example, Criminal Procedure Law (Lagos Laws 1973, Cap. 32), s. 2.

law which deals primarily with the relationship between individuals.

Public Law

The main branches of Public law are criminal law, constitutional law, administrative law and revenue law. Criminal law has already been explained.[16] Constitutional law is the law which regulates the structure of the principal organs of government and the relationship between them and determines their principal functions. Administrative law deals with the functions of government agencies. Revenue law governs taxation and other sources of government revenue.

Private Law

The main sub-divisions of private law include the law of contract, the law of tort and the law of trusts all of which have already been explained. Other main branches include the law of property, company law, partnership law, commercial law, family law, law of succession, private international law, law of evidence, law of remedies and law of procedure.

The law of property governs title to or interest in property. Property may be classified into real property (realty) and personal property (personalty). Real property consists of all landed property excluding leases and tenancies. Property other than real property is personal property. Personal property may be divided into two classes, namely, tangible property (tangible chattels), that is, property that can be touched, and intangible property. Tangible chattels are called "choses in possession." Items of intangible property excluding rights relating to land are choses in action. Examples of choses in action are stocks, shares and copyright. Leases and tenancies of land are termed "chattels real." Property may also be classified as movable property and immovable property.

Company law is that part of the law which governs associations of persons having a common object, usually a business undertaking. Partnership law governs agreements between two or more persons to carry on a business and share the profits and losses of the business in determined proportions. Commercial law is the law which regulates trade or commerce. Family law deals with the family. The law governs such matters as marriage, the relationship between parent and child, custody and guardianship of children and adoption of children. The law of succession governs the devolution of property on death. Private international law or conflict of laws is the law which deals with cases involving more than one legal system. A conflict-of-laws case arises, for example, where a Nigerian goes through a ceremony of marriage in France with a citizen of Ghana and the court

---

[16] See p. 5, above.

has to determine what legal system governs the validity of the marriage.

The law of evidence relates to proof of facts before the courts. The law of remedies governs remedies given by the courts. The remedies include damages (a remedy at common law — the law developed by the old English common law courts) and two equitable remedies, namely, injunction and specific performance. Damages are awarded as monetary compensation. There are two types of injunction, namely, mandatory injuction and prohibitive injunction. A mandatory injunction is an order of the court given in equity directing a person to do an act. A prohibitive injunction is an order of the court given in equity directing a person not to do an act or to stop doing an act. Specific performance is an order of the court compelling a person to fulfil an obligation.

Substantive law is that part of the law which directly creates, defines and regulates rights and duties. Examples of branches of the law that are mainly substantive are the law of contract, the law of tort, the law of trusts, the law of property, company law, partnership law, commercial law, family law and the law of succession. Adjective law or the law of procedure is that part of the law which governs the method of bringing judicial proceedings as well as the method of obtaining a remedy through such proceedings and prescribes the course of the proceedings.

Common Law

The term "Common Law" is used in several senses but as a division of Nigerian law, it means the law developed by the old common law courts of England, namely, the King's Bench, the Court of Common Pleas and the Court of Exchequer. There were originally several systems of local customs in England. But under the guise of enforcing the customs of the realm the common law judges developed a system of law known as the common law of England. Rules of the common law are, therefore, found in judicial decisions. The rules cover criminal law and civil law. But with the exception of the law on contempt of court the common law of crime is not part of Nigerian law.

Equity

Equity is the law developed by the old English Court of Chancery as a result of the rigidity of the common law. Whenever the rules of the common law worked hardship or injustice, the litigant sent a petition to the sovereign as the fountain of justice and the Royal Council. The Lord Chancellor granted relief on behalf of the sovereign and the Council as he thought fit. He followed no established principles in dealing with such matters. His intervention was, however, always made on grounds of conscience. Only when such grounds were present would he interfere with the rules of the common law. The principles of equity developed in a piecemeal manner because equity presupposed the existence of the rules of the common law and had to act upon them on grounds of conscience in order to achieve justice. There developed a dispute between the Chancellor and the common law judges who frowned upon the interference of equity with the common law. The Chancellor maintained that he did not deny the right of the litigant at common law but acted only to avoid the hardship of the law. The dispute was referred to King James I for settlement and resolved in favour of equity. Accordingly, whenever there was a conflict between a rule of equity and a rule of the common law on the same matter, the rule of equity was to prevail. Since equity recognised some rights unknown to the common law, for instance, rights under a trust, the Chancellor and, later, the Court of Chancery gave judgment overriding the judgment of the common law courts. In particular, in cases where a person had obtained a judgment at common law by fraud, the Court of Chancery often gave relief by ordering the person not to enforce the judgment. Moreover, the Chancery could order a litigant not to proceed with a common law action. The Judicature Acts 1873-1875 fused the administration of the common law and equity in England and provided, as James I had decided in 1615, that whenever there was a conflict between the two on the same matter equity was to prevail. Common law and equity, however, continued and still continue to exist separately in cases not involving a conflict. For example, the legal interest in property may be owned by a party and the equitable interest in it may be owned by another. The equitable owner may bring an action against the legal owner to enforce his equitable right. Finally, it should be mentioned that because equity was developed by a court, its rules are found only in judicial decisions, except that there are many equitable rules that have been incorporated into statutes.

D. TERMINOLOGY

The terminology used in criminal proceedings is different in many respects from that used in civil proceedings. A party who institutes criminal proceedings is a prosecutor or the Prosecution. A party against whom the proceedings are instituted is an accused or defendant. But in civil proceedings, the plaintiff sues the defendant. In some civil proceedings, the party who brings an action is not called "the plaintiff." For instance, in divorce proceedings, the party who brings the action is the petitioner. The action is brought against the respondent. In criminal proceedings, the accused is *charged with* an offence;

he may plead guilty or *not guilty* and if the Prosecution succeeds the result is a conviction: the accused is found guilty, that is, convicted. He is, thus, criminally liable or criminally responsible for the conduct in question. The sentence imposed by the court as punishment may be mandatory, for example, a sentence of death in general in murder cases. The accused may be *sentenced* to imprisonment for a term of years, months, weeks or days, or to a fine. He may be bound over to be of good behaviour for a specified period. If the accused is not found guilty, he is discharged or discharged and acquitted. One result of an acquittal is that the accused cannot be charged with an offence again on the same facts. In civil proceedings the defendant may plead *liable* or *not liable*. If the *suit* succeeds, there is judgment for the plaintiff. The judgment may, for example, contain an order that the defendant should pay damages to the plaintiff or an injunction compelling the defendant to do an act or ordering him to refrain from doing an act.

In both civil and criminal proceedings, the party who brings an appeal against the decision of a lower court is the appellant; the other party to the proceedings is the respondent. Where an application for an order is before a court the person who applies is the applicant and the person on whom the application is served or who opposes it is the respondent.

In criminal proceedings before a court of first instance, the name of the prosecutor is written first in the title of the case. Thus, in *The State* v. *Appoh*,[17] the State was the prosecutor and Appoh was the accused. In all criminal proceedings, the "v." between the names of the parties which stands for "versus" (against) is rendered as "against" in speech. There is a growing practice of referring to a criminal case, no matter by what court it is decided, simply by the name of the accused. In civil proceedings before a court of first instance the name of the plaintiff is written in the title of the case before the name of the defendant. Thus, in *Alli* v. *Okulaja*,[18] Alli was the plaintiff and Okulaja was the defendant. The "v." is pronounced "and" in all civil proceedings.

Titles of some cases begin with the expression "In the matter of" (*In re* or *Re*). In civil proceedings involving the interpretation of wills and trust deeds, this expression followed immediately by the name of the testator or settlor usually constitutes the title of a case.

Some case names include the term *ex parte* (on the application of). In such cases, the name of the person upon whose application the case is heard is stated immediately after the term thus, *The State* v.

[17] [1970] 2 All N.L.R. 218
[18] [1972] 2 All N.L.R. 35; (1971) 1 U.I.L.R. 72.

President, Grade A Customary Court, Oyo, ex parte Atoke.[19] Applications for the writ of habeas corpus and for the orders of *certiorari, mandamus* and prohibition are usually entitled in this form. In admiralty cases, the name of a ship may constitute a case name.

In an appeal case, the name of the appellant usually appears in the title of the case before that of the respondent, but sometimes the order of the names before the lower court is simply reversed.

A court overrules its previous decision or that of a lower court when it holds in another case that the previous case was wrongly decided and, accordingly, gives a judgment opposite to that given in the previous decision. If a court hears an appeal from the decision of a lower court and gives a judgment opposite to that of the lower court it is said that the judgment of the lower court has been reversed. A court distinguishes a previous decision when it holds that the issue involved in the previous case is different in some material respects from the issue involved in the case now before the court.

E. Law Libraries

Law libraries are very essential to the proper study of law. A law student should be familiar with the cataloguing and shelving systems used in the library to which he has access. Usually, university law libraries classify books by subject and shelve them in accordance with that classification. In order to enable the reader to find easily books required by him, a law library usually has at least one general card catalogue. A general card catalogue lists all the books in the library. There is at least one card in the catalogue for each book. If only one card catalogue is available it may be arranged by author or by author and title or by subject. In an author-title catalogue, there are at least two cards for each book — one for the author and the other for the title of the book. There may be two general card catalogues — one an author-title catalogue and the other a subject catalogue. In addition to general card catalogues there are, usually, special card catalogues which list books of a special class. For instance, there may be a separate special catalogue for each of the following classes of materials: law reports, periodicals, legislation and microfilms.

In general, books other than textbooks may be classified for shelving purposes as follows:

A. *Legal Periodicals*
   1. Nigerian legal periodicals,
   2. English legal periodicals,
   3. Other legal periodicals arranged by country.

[19] 1967 N.M.L.R. 267

B. *Statute Books*
1. Nigerian statute books,
2. English statute books,
3. Other statute books arranged by country.

C. *Law Reports*
1. Nigerian law reports,
2. English law reports,
3. Other law reports arranged by country.

D. *Digests*
1. Nigerian law digests,
2. English law digests,
3. Other law digests arranged by country.

E. Encyclopaedias.

F. Reference Books.

Generally, textbooks may be similarly divided into three classes, namely: (a) Nigerian law textbooks; (b) English law textbooks; (c) other textbooks. The textbooks within each group are usually arranged by subject. For example, textbooks on the law of contract are separated from textbooks on criminal law.

There may be in a law library a reserve section containing rare books in very high demand. Normally, books in a reserve section are not to be borrowed. Some reserve sections are open to only a restricted class of readers.

A good study of the cataloguing and shelving systems used in a law library is only a starting point in legal research.

Part 2

AN OUTLINE OF
THE HISTORY OF THE LEGAL SYSTEM

Chapter 2

AN OUTLINE OF THE HISTORY OF THE LEGAL SYSTEM

A COMPLETE history of the legal system of Nigeria must include an account of the administration of justice in the various territories which together ultimately constituted Nigeria. But for the purpose of this book, that account will not be detailed.[1] One obvious reason is the need to avoid substantial repetition of an account of the pre-existing legal systems when the administration of justice in Nigeria as a political unit is ultimately examined, for the modern legal system is based mainly on the legal systems of the various territories. All that is intended to be stated here with respect to the territories is an outline of the history of the pre-existing legal systems emphasising those aspects of the systems that are features of the present legal system in order to enable the reader to trace clearly the origin of those features. Accordingly, an outline approach will be adopted here. The history of the legal system will be examined under the following six heads: the period before 1862; 1862 to 1899; 1900 to 1913; January 1914 to September 1960; October 1, 1960 to January 16, 1966; and January 17, 1966 to the present time.

A. THE PERIOD BEFORE 1862

Historical records show clearly that long before the nineteenth century each of the territories which together now constitute Nigeria had a system of administration of justice. In most parts of the territories now constituting the northern States,[2] the principal law administered by the courts was Moslem Law of the Maliki School the main sources of which were, and are still, in writing.[3] In the territories now constituting the southern States[4] and in some parts of the territories which now form the northern States the law in force was unwritten customary law.

Before the nineteenth century, British and other foreign merchants had started to trade with the indigenous people on the coast

---

[1] For a detailed account, see T. O. Elias, *The Nigerian Legal System* (2nd ed., 1963).

[2] The northern States, that is, the States in the northern part of the country, are Bauchi, Benue, Borno, Gongola, Kaduna, Kano, Kwara, Niger, Plateau and Sokoto States.

[3] The sources of Moslem law are: (a) the Holy Koran; (b) the practice of the Prophet (the *sunna*); (c) the consensus of scholars; and (d) analogical deductions from the Koran and from the practice of the Prophet: A. A. Fyzee, *Outlines of Muhammadan Law* (3rd ed., 1964) pp. 18-21.

[4] The southern States, that is, the States in the southern part of the country, are Anambra, Bendel, Cross River, Imo, Lagos, Ogun, Ondo, Oyo and Rivers States.

of West Africa. The trading coastal areas which later formed part of Nigeria included Lagos, Benin, Bonny, Brass, New Calabar (now Degema) and Old Calabar (now Calabar). Attempts were made by the indigenous courts in those areas to settle trading disputes between the foreigners and the indigenous people. But the customary court system was very strange to the British and other foreign traders. Moreover, although the British traders were aware of the existence, in England, of the common law, a type of unwritten law, that law was, and still is, different in material respects from customary law. It was generally believed by those litigants that they seldom obtained justice in the courts. The British Government, therefore, appointed Consuls essentially for the purpose of regulating the trade between the British merchants and the indigenous merchants. The first British Consul was appointed in 1849.

His territorial jurisdiction extended from Dahomey to the Cameroons thus covering the entire coastal areas which later formed part of Nigeria. The Consuls established courts known as Consular Courts which dealt with trading disputes between indigenous and British traders. In addition to those courts there were courts known as equity courts established jointly by the foreign traders and the indigenous traders in the coastal areas of Benin, Bonny, Brass, New Calabar, Old Calabar and a few other coastal areas outside Lagos for the purpose of settling trading disputes. Equity courts based their decisions on general notions of justice. They were very popular courts. The establishment of equity courts and consular courts was not by the authority of the British Government but in 1872, a British Order in Council provided for the reorganisation of equity courts and the formal establishment of consular courts. Under the Order, both types of courts were to be under the control of the Consul. It should be mentioned, however that in all the trading areas including Lagos, the indigenous courts continued to administer justice in cases involving only the indigenous people. In 1861, Lagos was ceded to the British Crown under a Treaty of Cession.

B. 1862 TO 1899

In 1862, the British Administration made Lagos a British colony or settlement and established a court there. Under Ordinance No. 3 of 1863, the British Administration introduced English law into the Colony with effect from March 4, 1863. The first Supreme Court of the colony was established in 1863 by the Supreme Court Ordinance 1863.[5] The court had civil and criminal jurisdiction. In 1866, the British settlements of Lagos, the Gold Coast, Sierra Leone and Gambia

---

[5] No. 11 of 1863.

were placed under one government known as the Government of the West African Settlements. Among the courts established for Lagos by the new government were the Court of Civil and Criminal Justice which replaced the Supreme Court, and the West Africa Court of Appeal whose judges were the judges of the Supreme Court of Sierra Leone. Appeals from the highest court sitting in each of the British settlements (the Court of Civil and Criminal Justice in the case of Lagos) lay to the West Africa Court of Appeal. Further appeal lay to the Judicial Committee of the Privy Council. A number of other courts were established in Lagos before 1874. Trial by jury (a panel of lay people which determines questions of fact before courts) in criminal cases was introduced during this period.

In 1874, a separate single government was established for the British settlements of Lagos and the Gold Coast both of which were together called the Gold Coast Colony. Accordingly, the West Africa Court of Appeal did not function as a court for the new Colony. The Supreme Court Ordinance 1876[6] established a Supreme Court for the Colony of Lagos and the territories in the neighbouring adjacent territories over which the British Government had jurisdiction. The common law of England, the doctrines of equity and statutes of general application in force in England on July 24, 1874 were applied by the court. Whenever there was a conflict between a common law rule and a doctrine of equity on the same matter, the doctrine of equity was to prevail. The statutes applied subject to local circumstances. In other words, if circumstances which must be present before any such statute could be applied were absent in Lagos and in the other territories within the jurisdiction of the court, the statute was not applicable. Thus, the Bankruptcy Act 1869[7] of England was not applicable because the machinery for its application was not available.[8] Also applicable were local laws and customs which were neither repugnant to natural justice, equity and good conscience nor incompatible with any local statute. The Supreme Court was divided into three arms, namely, the Full Court (a court of appeal), the Divisional Courts having original and appellate jurisdiction and the District Commissioners' Courts. Appeals from the decisions of the district commissioners' courts lay to the divisional courts. The Full Court heard appeals from the decisions of the divisional courts. It should be pointed out that the indigenous courts which had been established before the introduction of British administration continued to function. Their jurisdiction was questioned in a Gold Coast case, *Oppon* v. *Ackinie*.[9] In that case, the plaintiff, a

[6] No. 4 of 1876.

[7] 32 & 33 Vict. c. 71.

[8] *Halliday* v. *Alapatira* (1881) 1 N.L.R. 1.

[9] (1887) J. M. Sarbah, *Fanti Customary Laws* (3rd ed., 1968), p. 232.

subject of a local chief, brought an action against the chief for damages for unlawful imprisonment on the grounds that the chief's judicial powers had ceased by virtue of the application of the Supreme Court Ordinance 1876. The divisional court sitting as a court of appeal upheld the contention of the plaintiff. The chief then appealed against the decision to the Full Court. The Full Court, reversing the judgment of the divisional court, held that the wording of the Ordinance was not inconsistent with the view that the jurisdiction of the Supreme Court and that of the chiefs' courts were to be co-existent. The Full Court also held that the Ordinance did not in any way impair the pre-existing judicial powers of the local chiefs.

The introduction of English law into the British colony of Lagos marked a turning-point in the history of the legal system of Nigeria. Although the reception of English law was effected by local legislation, it should be noted that the legislation was passed not by a body of indigenous people but by the British Administration. It is worthy of note, however, that the three classes of English law received during this period — the common law, equity and English statutes — are today, more than one century after the first reception, still sources of Nigerian law.

The British Administration averted trouble by not rejecting local laws and customs in their entirety. No doubt, by subjecting local laws and customs to the tests of repugnancy to natural justice, equity and good conscience, and incompatibility with local statutes, the Administration had relegated local laws and customs. It should be quickly pointed out, however, that the subjection had produced salutary effects for there were, at that time, certain customs that were quite objectionable to the civilised world and only slavishly adhered to by the community. In any case, those tests are contained in the current statute books of Nigeria.

By the end of the period, one combined effect of the reception of English law, the establishment of English-type courts and the relegation of local laws and customs was already being felt. It was the emergence of a new society consisting of indigenous people who had embraced the English culture and had therefore tended to prefer the English way of life to the traditional pattern of life. Such people entered into commercial relations governed by English law. The existence of that society side by side with the traditional society marked the beginning of the conflict of cultures now noticeable in many parts of the country.[10]

In 1886, the British Administration established a separate government for the colony of Lagos. Consequently, a new Supreme Court

---

[10] See O. Adewoye, "Prelude to the Legal Profession in Lagos 1861-1880" [1970] J.A.L. 98 at p. 101.

Ordinance similar to that of 1876 was passed for Lagos. Under an Order in Council of 1886 the legislature of the colony of Lagos was empowered to make laws for the territories in the neighbourhood (the protected territories) over which the British Government had acquired jurisdiction. The colony and the protected territories were together known as the Colony and Protectorate of Lagos. The Supreme Court of the Colony of Lagos then had jurisdiction in the Protectorate (the protected territories) which by 1891 had extended to other areas near the colony.

Territories under the Control of the Royal Niger Company

A number of British firms traded along the banks of River Niger. They were later amalgamated and the resulting unit received a Royal Charter under the name "National African Company" in 1886. The company was later renamed "Royal Niger Company." The charter gave the company power to administer justice in the territories where it was operating.[11] The company was enjoined to have careful regard to the "customs and laws of the class or tribe or nation" to which the parties respectively belonged, in dispensing justice. The company established some courts which functioned until 1899 when its charter was revoked.

The Niger Coast Protectorate

In 1885, a protectorate known as the Oil Rivers Protectorate was established by the British Government but the actual inauguration of the Protectorate occurred in 1891. The Protectorate consisted of Benin, Brass, Bonny, Old Calabar, New Calabar and Opobo. In 1893, it was extended and renamed "Niger Coast Protectorate." The Protectorate was divided into two parts by the territories of the Royal Niger Company.[12]

Before the Protectorate was established, consuls had been appointed to the area under an Order in Council of 1872 which empowered them to observe treaties made between the British Government and the local chiefs and to make rules and regulations for the peace, order and good government of "British subjects," a term defined in the Order to include "all persons, natives and others, properly enjoying Her Majesty's [the Queen of England's] protection in

---

[11] See *Remission of Payments to the Exchequer under the Royal Niger Company Act 1800 — Memorandum on the Financial Resolution*, Cmnd. 5488 (1973).

[12] Report on the Administration of the Niger Coast Protectorate August 1891 to August 1894, Cmnd. 7596 (1895).

the specified territories." Under an Order in Council of 1899, a Con-
sul-General was appointed for the area. The Order provided for the
establishment of consular courts having jurisdiction over all British
subjects and over subjects of other European states who consented
to the jurisdiction of the courts. Furthermore, the courts had jurisdiction over a person where the state, king or chief, or government of
which he was a subject or under whose protection he was had agreed
or consented to the exercise of jurisdiction by British courts. Appeals
from the decisions of consular courts lay to the Supreme Court of the
Colony of Lagos.

C. 1900 TO 1913

The Protectorate of Southern Nigeria

The Niger Coast Protectorate and the territories of the Royal Niger
Company south of Idah together with Idah were amalgamated by
the Southern Nigeria Order in Council 1899 to form a new protectorate with effect from January 1, 1900. The new protectorate was
named "Protectorate of Southern Nigeria." The Order provided for
the appointment of a High Commissioner who was to be empowered
to make laws for the Protectorate by Proclamation. The High Commissioner established a Supreme Court by the Supreme Court Proclamation 1900[13] whose provisions were substantially the same as the
provisions of the Supreme Court Ordinance 1876 except that the
proclamation named January 1, 1900 in place of July 24, 1874 as the
date by reference to which applicable English statutes of general
application were to be determined. The Supreme Court had original
and appellate jurisdiction in civil and criminal cases throughout the
Protectorate. By the Commissioners Proclamation 1900[14] Commissioners' Courts which constituted an arm of the Supreme Court were
established. It would be recalled that no statutory native court had
been established in the Colony and Protectorate of Lagos and that it
was held in *Oppon* v. *Ackinie*[15] that the Supreme Court Ordinance
1876 did not in any way impair the judicial powers of the pre-existing
indigenous courts. A different attitude was adopted by the British
Administration with respect to the Protectorate of Southern
Nigeria. Courts were established there by statute essentially for the
administration of customary law, the law hitherto administered by
the indigenous courts. The Native Courts Proclamation 1900[16] esta-

[13] No. 6 of 1900.
[14] No. 8 of 1900.
[15] (1887) J. M. Sarbah, *Fanti Customary Laws* (3rd ed., 1968), p. 232.
[16] No. 9 of 1900.

blished "Native Courts" and the Native Courts Proclamation 1901[17] which replaced it provided that the civil and criminal jurisdiction of a statutory native court in a district was to be exclusive of any jurisdiction by any traditional authority.[18] Therefore, in any district where a statutory native court had been established no indigenous court had any jurisdiction.[19]

That step taken by the British Administration had a tremendous effect on the legal system of the Protectorate. The traditional authority of the indigenous courts which authority was in accordance with the customs of the local community was to disappear. Such courts were to cease to exist lawfully. In their place, courts described as native courts and established not by local custom but by English-type law were to exist. The authority for the existence of the "native" courts was to be derived from Enlgish-type law. Thus, although the courts were to be empowered to administer local laws and customs, traditional authority had to be on the wane.

Two classes of native courts were established by the Native Courts Proclamation 1900. They were Minor Courts and Native Councils.

A minor court was to consist of such number of members as the High Commissioner might appoint. It had original civil jurisdiction generally in personal suits in which the claim did not exceed £25, cases involving succession to movable property not exceeding £50 in value and cases involving ownership or possession of land under customary law. It had original criminal jurisdiction in offences which could be adequately punished by a sentence of imprisonment for six months with or without a fifteen-stroke flogging, a fine of £50 or imprisonment for three months with a fine of £25. The offences included putting a person in fetish, wilfully disobeying a lawful order of the head of a house, taking or seducing another man's wife and being in unlawful possession of property. A native council was to consist of the District Commissioner as President and such other members as the High Commissioner might appoint. In general, its original civil jurisdiction was the same as that of a minor court. With respect to personal suits and succession to movable property, however, the monetary value limit for a Native Council was £200. It had criminal jurisdiction in offences which could be adequately punished by a sentence of imprisonment for two years with or without a fifteen-stroke flogging, a fine of £100 or imprisonment for one year with a fine of £100. A native council heard appeals from the decisions of minor courts. It also had general supervisory powers over all the

[17] No. 25 of 1901.
[18] *Ibid.* s. 12.
[19] *Contra* T. O. Elias *op. cit.* (n. 1, above), p. 102.

minor courts in its district. It was empowered to make rules embodying any customary law in its district, to regulate and protect trade and, generally, to provide for the peace, good order and welfare of the "natives" there. The rules were subject to approval by the High Commissioner.

Minor courts and native councils also had power to make bye-laws for several purposes including the construction and protection of roads, the care of unoccupied land and the conservation of forests.

The composition and functions of the statutory courts deserve comments at this juncture. A native council which purported to be a court for the indigenous people was presided over by a white man, the District Commissioner, and the other members of the court were people appointed at the will of the High Commissioner. Thus, there was ample opportunity for the appointment of indigenous people who would always bend to the will of the District Commissioner. In the circumstances, the court was much different from the traditional courts of the indigenous people.

Native councils and minor courts performed not only judicial functions but also legislative and executive functions. Such multiplicity of functions was certainly not in the interest of the administration of justice. Under the Native Courts Proclamation 1901 which effected a reform of the court system and repealed the Native Courts Proclamation 1900, the two classes of statutory courts continued to exist. It should be emphasised that with effect from January 1, 1902 when the Native Courts Proclamation 1901 came into force, indigenous courts functioning within the territorial jurisdiction of a statutory native court became illegal courts.

It would be recalled that the Supreme Court of the Colony of Lagos exercised jurisdiction in the Colony and Protectorate of Lagos. The court's jurisdiction extended to other territories under treaties entered into between the Governor of the Colony of Lagos and the authorities of the respective territories in 1904 but the territories did not then become part of the Protectorate of Lagos. Indeed, an agreement with one of the territories, Egbaland, contained a promise on the part of the British Government not to annex Egbaland. It seems clear, however, that before 1906, Egbaland and the other territories including Ibadan, Oyo and Ife had become part of the Protectorate of Lagos.[20]

The Colony and Protectorate of Southern Nigeria

In 1906, the Colony and Protectorate of Lagos and the Protectorate of Southern Nigeria were amalgamated to form the Colony and Pro-

[20] See Blue Book 1905.

tectorate of Southern Nigeria. A new native courts enactment, the Native Courts Proclamation 1906[21] was made for the new territory. Many of its provisions were the same as the provisions of the Native Courts Proclamation 1901. But there were some important differences. For instance, the new proclamation provided that:

(a) the members of every native court were to include the Divisional Commissioner, the Travelling Commissioner, the District Commissioner and the Assistant District Commissioner;

(b) all the officers of a native court in any Division were to be under the authority of the Divisional Commissioner;

(c) all the native courts were to exercise their judicial functions under the instruction of the Chief Justice or any other judge of the Supreme Court;

(d) whenever a minor court was presided over by a Divisional Commissioner or Assistant District Commissioner, the jurisdiction and powers of the court were to be the same as those of a Native Council.

The native court system of the Colony and Protectorate of Southern Nigeria, like that of the Protectorate of Southern Nigeria, was defective in many respects. More white people were *ex-officio* members of the native courts. It is reported that local chiefs who served as members of the native councils abused their powers. It is also said that native court clerks often received bribes and that they even tried cases.[22] Such abuse was no doubt facilitated by the widespread illiteracy among the members of the indigenous community. It is worthy of note that under the Native Courts Proclamation 1906, the native courts were to exercise their judicial functions under the instruction of the Chief Justice or any other judge of the Supreme Court. But notwithstanding this provision, the native court system was a failure.

The Protectorate of Northern Nigeria

The Northern Nigeria Order in Council 1899 which came into operation on January 1, 1900 established a protectorate, named "Protectorate of Northern Nigeria," comprising territories of the Royal Niger Company north of Ida. A High Commissioner was appointed to make laws for the Protectorate. He made the Protectorate Courts Proclamation 1900[23] which established a Supreme Court, provincial courts and cantonment courts. "Native" courts were established by a

---

[21] No. 7 of 1906.
[22] See T. O. Elias, *op. cit.* (n. 1 above), p. 111.
[23] No. 4 of 1900.

separate Proclamation, the Native Courts Proclamation 1900.[24]

The Supreme Court could hear civil and criminal cases not only as a court of appeal but also as a court of first instance. It had original jurisdiction in cantonment areas (areas under the direct control of Government) and other areas that might be specified for the purpose by the High Commissioner. Such jurisdiction was exercised in cases transferred to it from the provincial, cantonment and native Courts and also cases which the High Commissioner might direct it to hear. The court administered the common law of England, doctrines of equity and statutes of general application which were in force in England on January 1, 1900. It also applied customary law.

A provincial court was established in each province. It was presided over by a Resident, an Assistant Resident or a Justice of the Peace. The court had jurisdiction in civil and criminal cases. In criminal cases, the Resident in charge of a province had unlimited powers but when any other administrative officer constituted the court his powers were limited, the limit depending on his status. Sentences of death, deportation, imprisonment for a term exceeding six months, corporal punishment exceeding twelve-stroke flogging and a fine exceeding £50 were not to be executed except in cases of emergency unless they had been confirmed by the High Commissioner. The Further Amendment Proclamation 1907[25] provided that the High Commissioner could delegate the power of confirmation to the Chief Justice. The law administered by the court consisted of the common law of England, the doctrines of equity, statutes of general application that were in force in England on January 1, 1900 and customary law.

Every area under the direct control of the Government constituted a cantonment and had a court known as a cantonment court presided over by a magistrate styled "Cantonment Magistrate." A cantonment magistrate was appointed by the High Commissioner. Every cantonment magistrate was a Commissioner of the Supreme Court. A cantonment court could hear civil and criminal cases. The Supreme Court exercised supervisory jurisdiction over it by means of monthly lists of cases heard and determined by it. The lists were sent to the Chief Justice.

In general, a native court was to consist of one or more persons appointed by a head chief or emir, with the approval of the Resident. Where there was no head chief or emir, the Resident was to appoint members. The Resident was empowered to determine with the consent of the head chief or head emir of the province in what places native courts were to be established and then he was to establish

---

[24] No. 5 of 1900.
[25] No. 11 of 1907.

native courts there by warrant, the warrants stating the limits of the jurisdiction of the courts. A native court administered customary law not repugnant to natural justice and humanity. Legal representation was not permitted unless the Resident gave a written permission with respect to such representation. The Native Courts Proclamation 1906[26] reformed the court system. It provided for the establishment of two kinds of native courts, namely, Alkali's Court and Judicial Council. An alkali's court was to consist of an alkali as president with whom other persons might sit as co-judges or as assessors. A judicial council was to consist of an emir, a chief or a district headman as president with whom other persons might sit as co-judges or as assessors. Court members were to be appointed by the Resident after consultation with the emir, if there was any, subject to the approval of the High Commissioner. The Native Courts Proclamation 1906 permitted the spouse, guardian, servant, master or any inmate of the household of a plaintiff or defendant to appear for him. The Alkali's Court at the capital city of a province or the Judicial Council in the same city if presided over by an emir could be designated a Native Court of Appeal by the Resident. Appeals lay to any such court from the decisions of native courts specified by the Resident for the purpose. The Proclamation also provided that a native court could with the concurrence of the head emir or of the head chiefs of a district and subject to the approval of the High Commissioner makes rules embodying the customary law of its district. Under the Proclamation, it was an offence to adjudicate in disputes without authority.

It would have been noted that the legal system in the Protectorate of Northern Nigeria was slightly better than that in the Colony and Protectorate of Southern Nigeria. In particular, with respect to the native court system, it should be noted that head chiefs in the northern Protectorate were empowered to appoint members of native courts with the approval of the Resident. In the Colony and Protectorate of Southern Nigeria, no chief had such powers.

A brief mention should however be made here of the provincial courts which were manned by administrative officers. The British Administration felt that the establishment of such courts was necessary in view of the shortage of qualified personnel and of the need to ensure that litigants obtained justice cheaply. The administration considered the introduction of the provincial court system a success nothwithstanding the fact that the administrative officers combined their heavy administrative duties with their judicial functions and the fact that they had little knowledge of the law.

[26] No. 1 of 1906.

D. JANUARY 1914 TO SEPTEMBER 1960

The Colony and Protectorate of Southern Nigeria and the Protectorate of Northern Nigeria were amalgamated on January 1, 1914 to form the Colony and Protectorate of Nigeria. Thus, Nigeria as a political unit came into existence on that date. Three types of court were established for the country, namely, the Supreme Court, the provincial courts and the native courts.

The Supreme Court was established by the Supreme Court Ordinance 1914.[27] Its provisions were similar to the provisions of the Supreme Court enactments of the two amalgamated units. Thus, the law administered by the court included the common law of England, doctrines of equity and statutes of general application which were in force in England on January 1, 1900. The court had original and appellate jurisdiction in civil and criminal cases.

The Provincial Courts Ordinance 1914[28] established in the country a provincial court system similar to that established in the Protectorate of Northern Nigeria. Appeals lay from the decisions of the provincial courts in civil cases to the Supreme Court. There was no provision for appeal in criminal cases. The system was criticised adversely by several people, notably lawyers. It was argued that the non-judicial functions of the administrative officers who manned the courts were so onerous that it would be difficult for them to administer justice in the cases before them. The lawyers spoke against the power of confirmation of sentences exercisable by the Governor-in-Council as the executive arm of the Government and the absence of legal representation in the courts. The Government explained that the structure of the courts was in the interest of achieving justice cheaply throughout the country.[29] Obviously, the existence of courts easily accessible to the people does not necessarily serve the needs of justice. Inadequacy of qualified judicial personnel is certainly no good excuse for placing in the hands of very busy administrative officers judicial functions in addition to their administrative duties. Judicial functions are normally not properly performed by tired brains, however zealous such brains may be. Moreover, an essential feature of dispensing justice is the possession, by the court, of a sound knowledge of the law being administered. With little or no knowledge of the English law and hardly a smattering of knowledge of the local customs, the administrative officers had little chance of administering justice in accordance with the received English law or the local customs.

[27] No. 6 of 1914.
[28] No. 7 of 1914.
[29] See T. O. Elias, *op. cit.* (n. 1, above), pp. 129-134.

The Native Courts Ordinance 1918[30] provided for the establishment of native courts in the country. They were established by warrant. There were four classes of native courts, namely, Grades A, B, C, and D courts. The jurisdiction and powers of the courts depended on their grades, Grade A courts having the highest jurisdiction and powers and Grade D courts having the lowest. All the courts had civil and criminal jurisdiction. Only Grade A courts had powers to impose a death sentence but such sentence could not be executed unless it had been confirmed by the Governor. In the northern Provinces a native court could consist of an alkali with or without "native" assistants. In the southern Provinces, a native court could consist of a "native" judge. In any Province, northern or southern, a native court might consist of: (a) a head chief with or without minor chiefs or other persons sitting as co-judges or as assessors; or (b) chiefs or other persons representing indigenous people in the area of jurisdiction of the court. The District Officer had supervisory powers over a native court. Every member of a provincial court could transfer any case from a native court to his own court. He could order a retrial of a case already tried by a native court and he could suspend or modify the sentence imposed by a native court. Every Commissioner of the Supreme Court could, through the District Officer, call for the records of a native court in its District. The chief alkali's court, the head chief's court or a native court comprising at least three of the chiefs of a Division could sit as a native court of appeal for the Division. Legal practitioners were not permitted to appear in the courts. Each native court administered the customary law prevailing in its area of jurisdiction together with any statutory provision that it might be empowered by the Governor to administer. In general, a native court had jurisdiction over all "natives" but natives who were either Government servants or those who were not ordinarily subject to the jurisdiction of native courts and did not live permanently in the area of the court's jurisdiction were subject to the jurisdiction of the court only if they consented or the Resident consented on their behalf, in civil cases, and only if they or the lieutenant-Governor consented in criminal cases. Moreover, the Governor could exempt any person or class of persons from the jurisdiction of a native court.

The 1933 Reform

The court systems of Nigeria had attracted such serious adverse criticisms that reform was effected by legislation in 1933.

[30] No. 5 of 1918.

The Protectorate Courts Ordinance 1933[31] established a High Court and magistrates' courts for the Protectorate. In the Protectorate, the jurisdiction of the High Court and the Supreme Court was generally the same. But, of the two, only the Supreme Court had jurisdiction in probate, divorce and matrimonial cases, admiralty cases and proceedings under specified Ordinances.

The Protectorate Courts Ordinance 1933 provided that the British-type courts established by it (the High Court and the magistrates' courts) had no original jurisdiction in cases raising any issue as to title to, or interest in, land and which were subject to the jurisdiction of a native court, except where the Governor-in-Council directed otherwise or where the case in question was transferred from a native court under the Native Courts Ordinance 1933.[32] It was the intention of the British Administration to reserve for native courts original jurisdiction in those matters. The Administration was of opinion that the matters were within the peculiar knowledge of native courts and that it was in the interest of justice that such courts should normally exercise exclusive jurisdiction in those matters.[33] The opinion was based on the fact that in general, the native courts were constituted by indigenous people who were versed in local customs governing those matters.

Appeals from the decisions of the magistrates' courts lay to the High Court. In some cases, appeals lay from a native court direct to the High Court.

Appeals from the decisions of the Supreme Court and the High Court lay to the West African Court of Appeal, a court which had been established by the West African Court of Appeal Order in Council 1928. The Order was extended to Nigeria by the West African Court of Appeal Ordinance 1933.[34] This anomalous duality of channels of appeal to the West African Court of Appeal was created apparently because in terms of quality of personnel, the Supreme Court was hardly superior to the High Court. Indeed, the Chief Justice (the head of the Supreme Court) was the Chief Judge of the High Court and the Puisne Judges of the Supreme Court were normally Judges of the High Court.[35]

Appeals from the decisions of the West African Court of Appeal lay to the Judicial Committee of the Privy Council.[36]

The magistrates' courts had jurisdiction to hear summarily civil and criminal cases. They exercised civil jurisdiction in personal suits

[31] No. 45 of 1933.
[32] No. 44 of 1933.
[33] See *Nthah* v. *Bennieh* (1930) 2 W.A.C.A. 1, at p. 3 (a Gold Coast case).
[34] No. 47 of 1933.
[35] See T. O. Elias, *op. cit.* (n. 1, above), p. 145.
[36] West African (Appeal to Privy Council) Order in Council 1930.

involving not more than £100 and suits involving landlord and tenant where the claim did not exceed £100. They were empowered to try summary offences. Appeals from the decisions of native courts normally lay to the magistrates' courts. A magistrate could transfer cases from a native court to another or to his own court.

Legal practitioners could appear in the High Court and magistrates' courts. It is significant to note that the Protectorate Courts Ordinance 1933 abolished the provincial court system by repealing the Provincial Courts Ordinance 1914.

The Native Courts Ordinance 1933[37] increased the civil jurisdiction of the native courts. The Ordinance also provided for complicated systems of appeal. The Resident was empowered to make a Chief Alkali's Court, or a native court presided over by a head chief or a court comprising at least three chiefs or headmen in a Division, a court of appeal for native courts in the province. Any such court of appeal was called a Final Court of Appeal when presided over by a head chief. Appeals lay from the decisions of a native court sitting as a court of first instance to a court designated "Native Court of Appeal" or to a native court designated "Final Native Court of Appeal," or to a magistrate's court or to the High Court. If there was no right of appeal to any of those courts, appeals lay, in general, to the district officer. No appeal lay to a magistrate's court, the High Court or a District Officer in any matter relating to marriage, family status, guardianship of children, inheritance, testamentary disposition or administration of estate. In 1943, all these matters were considered to be within the peculiar knowledge of the native courts. Accordingly, as a general rule, the British-type courts ceased to have original jurisdiction in the matters.[38] In general, an appeal could lie from a decision of a native court to a District Officer, from a decision of the District Officer to the Resident, and from a decision of the Resident to the Governor. But no appeal lay to the District Officer, the Resident or the Governor in matters relating to marriage, family status, guardianship of children, inheritance, testamentary disposition or administration of estate.

It should be noted that a District Officer must sit as the president of any native court whenever the court was hearing a suit or appeal relating to land.

The Resident and the District Officer had powers to transfer cases and to review judgments. A case could be transferred by any of them from one native court to another or to a magistrate's court or to the High Court. The Resident or the District Officer could order retrial of a case before the trial native court or before another native court,

[37] No. 44 of 1933.
[38] See *e.g.* Supreme Court Ordinance 1943 (No. 23 of 1943).

a magistrate's court or the High Court. An order made by a District Officer in the exercise of his power of transfer or review could be annulled by the Resident.

The Establishment of Statutory
"Native" Courts in the Colony

Indigenous courts in the Colony exercised jurisdiction in civil and criminal cases until 1938 when native courts were established there under the Native Courts (Colony) Ordinance 1937.[39] The Ordinance provided for the establishment of native courts by warrant in the Colony outside the township of Lagos. The courts had civil and criminal jurisdiction. Appeals from their decisions lay to magistrates' courts.

The 1943 Legislation

In 1943, a number of statutes were passed to reform the legal system. They included the Native Courts (Colony) Ordinance 1943[40] which slightly amended the Native Courts (Colony) Ordinance 1933; the Magistrates' Courts Ordinance 1943[41]; the Supreme Court Ordinance 1943[42]; the West African Court of Appeal Ordinance 1943[43] which amended the West African Court Ordinance 1933 slightly and the Children and Young Persons Ordinance 1943.[44]

The Magistrates' Courts Ordinance 1943 established new magistrates' courts throughout the country to replace the courts of the Commissioners of the Supreme Court in the Colony and the magistrates' courts in the Protectorate. The Supreme Court Ordinance 1943 established a Supreme Court of Justice for the whole country in place of the Supreme Court of Nigeria and the High Court of the Protectorate.

The same Ordinance extended the list of matters with respect to which native courts had exclusive original jurisdiction. It provided that the Supreme Court was not to exercise original jurisdiction in any matter subject to the jurisdiction of a native court and relating to marriage, family status, guardianship of children, inheritance or disposition of property on death, except where the Governor-in-Council directed otherwise or where the case was transferred from a native court under the native courts legislation. The Children and Young

[39] No. 7 of 1937.
[40] No. 7 of 1943.
[41] No. 43 of 1943.
[42] No. 33 of 1943.
[43] No. 30 of 1943.
[44] No. 41 of 1943.

Persons Ordinance 1943 provided for the establishment of juvenile courts for the purpose of dealing with children (persons under the age of 14 years) and young persons (persons who had attained the age of 14 years but were under the age of 17 years).

The Legal System Under the 1954 Constitution

Under the Nigeria (Constitution) Order in Council 1954,[45] Nigeria had a truly federal constitution with effect from October 1, 1954. On that date, Nigeria became a Federation comprising three regions — the Northern, Western and Eastern Regions — and a federal territory (Lagos). The Constitution established for the whole country a court known as the Federal Supreme Court. A High Court was established for Lagos and each Region, too, had a High Court.[46] In addition, there were magistrates' courts in each jurisdiction.[47] Appeals from the magistrates' courts of each jurisdiction lay to the High Court of that jurisdiction. The Western and Eastern Regions had statutory courts called "Customary Courts" and the Northern Region had statutory courts named "Native Courts." In 1956, the Northern Region established a customary court of appeal known as the Moslem Court of Appeal for the purpose of hearing appeals from the decisions of native courts in civil and criminal cases governed by Moslem law. A new customary court of appeal, the Sharia Court of Appeal was established on September 30, 1960 to replace the Moslem Court of Appeal. On the same day, a court known as the Court of Resolution was established for the purpose of adjudicating in jurisdictional disputes between the High Court of the Region and the Sharia Court of Appeal. The District Courts Law established District Courts as courts of civil jurisdiction on that day. Their jurisdiction was the same as that hitherto exercisable by magistrates' courts with respect to civil cases. The Criminal Procedure Code Law 1960 which came into operation on the same day provided for the establishment of magistrates' courts to replace the pre-existing magistrates' courts and to exercise criminal jurisdiction. Another Northern Region statute which came into operation on that day was the Penal Code Law 1959. Some of the aspects of the legal system will now be examined in some detail.

[45] S.I. 1954 No. 1146.

[46] High Court of Lagos Ordinance (Fed. and Lagos Laws 1958, Cap. 80), Northern Region High Court Law 1955 (No. 5 of 1955); High Court Law (W.R.N. Laws 1959, Cap. 44); Eastern Region High Court Law 1955 (No. 27 of 1955).

[47] See Magistrates' Courts (Lagos) Ordinance (Fed. and Lagos Laws 1958, Cap. 113); Magistrates' Courts (Northern Region) Law 1955 (No. 7 of 1955); Magistrates' Courts Law (W.R.N. Laws 1959, Cap. 74); Magistrates' Courts Law 1955 (No. 10 of 1955) (E.R.N.)

1. The Federal Supreme Court

The Federal Supreme Court had original jurisdiction in (a) disputes between the Regions, (b) disputes between a Region and the Federal Government, (c) cases arising from treaties involving foreign representatives in Nigeria and (d) cases relating to the validity of a law made by the Federal Government. Appeals lay to the court from the High Courts of the Regions and from the High Court of Lagos. Appeals from the decisions of the Federal Supreme Court lay to the Judicial Committee of the Privy Council, the West African Court of Appeal having ceased to be in the hierarchy of the courts under the Constitution.

2. The court systems in the Northern Region

The Native Courts Law 1956[48] established in the Northern Region Native Courts first of four grades but later of five grades, namely, A, A Limited, B, C and D. Of the courts presided over by emirs or chiefs, some were classified as A Courts and others as A Limited Courts. Native courts had civil and criminal jurisdiction. Grade A courts had unlimited jurisdiction and powers but any death sentence imposed by them was subject to confirmation by the executive arm of the Government. Appeals from some Grade B courts and from Grades C and D courts lay to a court designated a native court of appeal by the Resident. Appeals from Grades A and A Limited courts and from other Grade B courts lay to the Moslem Court of Appeal in cases governed by Moslem law, and to the High Court in other cases. Appeals from the decisions of the Moslem Court of Appeal lay to the High Court constituted by at least two judges sitting with at least two assessors. It is significant to note, however, that in general the High Court had no supervisory powers over the Moslem Court of Appeal. Notwithstanding, there was some discontent among the Moslems over the status of the Moslem Court of Appeal in relation to the High Court.

In 1958, the Government of the Northern Region appointed a panel of jurists to advise it on the reform of the legal system in relation to the application of Moslem law on the one hand and non-Moslem law on the other. The panel recommended the enactment of a Penal Code Law and a Criminal Procedure Code Law for application throughout the Region in place of the Criminal Code Ordinance[49] and the Criminal Procedure Ordinance[50] which had been applicable together with customary criminal law in all the Regions.[51] It was also recommended that the Moslem Court of Appeal be

[48] No. 6 of 1956.
[49] Nigeria Laws 1948, Cap. 42.
[50] Nigeria Laws 1948, Cap. 43.
[51] See also Fed. and Lagos Laws 1958, Cap. 42 and 43.

replaced by a new court which should hear appeals only in cases involving Moslem personal law. In accordance with the recommendations, the Sharia Court of Appeal Law 1960[52] established the Sharia Court of Appeal as a customary appeal court to hear appeals from the native courts in cases involving Moslem personal law. The principal law to be applied by the court was Moslem law of the Maliki School as customarily interpreted at the place where the court at first instance heard the case. Appeals from the native courts in cases not involving Moslem personal law lay to the High Court. The Native Courts (Amendment) Law 1960[53] provided for the establishment of provincial courts in the Region. Provincial courts were native courts having original and appellate jurisdiction and equivalent in status to Grade A Limited courts. There was one in each province. The judges of the court were public officers in the public service of the Region. By virtue of the amending law, appeals from the decisions of Grades B, C and D courts in a province lay to the provincial court. Appeals from the decisions of Grades A and A Limited courts and from provincial courts lay to the Sharia Court of Appeal in cases governed by Moslem personal law, and to the Native Courts Appellate Division of the High Court established by the Northern Region High Court (Amendment) Law 1960[54] in all other cases. The Division was to be constituted by two judges of the High Court and a judge of the Sharia Court of Appeal.[55] The Court of Resolution was established by the Court of Resolution Law 1960[56] for the purpose of resolving disputes on jurisdiction between the High Court and the Sharia Court of Appeal. The Penal Code Law 1959[57] and the Criminal Procedure Code Law 1960[58] both of which came into operation on September 30, 1960 replaced, respectively, the Criminal Code

---

[52] No. 16 of 1960.

[53] No. 10 of 1960.

[54] No. 14 of 1960. S. 27 of the Northern Region High Court Law 1955 as amended by this law in general, prohibited the High Court from making any of the prerogative orders of mandamus, prohibition and certiorari and from granting an injunction in lieu of *quo warranto* in respect of any proceedings in a native court or in the Sharia Court of Appeal. The amendment came into operation on August 15, 1960.

[55] For a long time, no Sharia Court judge could sit in the Division because it was held by the Federal Supreme Court in *Olawoyin* v. *Commissioner of Police* [1961] 1 All N.L.R. 203 that s. 59c of the Northern Region High Court Law 1955 (inserted by the Northern Region High Court (Amendment) Law 1960) which provided that a Sharia Court judge was to sit in the High Court Division was unconstitutional. Accordingly, the Constitution had to be amended to permit a Sharia Court judge to sit in the Division.

[56] No. 17 of 1960.

[57] No. 18 of 1959. The Penal Code (Northern Region) Federal Provisions Ordinance 1960 (No. 25 of 1960) re-enacted provisions of the Penal Code dealing with Federal offences.

[58] No. 11 of 1960.

Ordinance and the Criminal Procedure Ordinance in the North. The penal code was considered quite satisfactory by the Moslem community because it contained provisions embodying the Moslem law of crime.

3. Customary Courts in the Western Region

The Customary Courts Law[59] made in 1957 provided for the establishment of four grades of customary courts — A, B, C and D in the Western Region. A board known as the Local Government Service Board was established in the same year under the Local Government Law[60] and empowered to appoint and dismiss Customary Court members. All Grade A courts were to be presided over by legal practitioners. Such Grade B courts as might be specified were also to be presided over by legal practititioners. Customary courts had civil and criminal jurisdiction. In any customary court presided over by a legal practitioner, legal practitioners had the right to appear. Appeals lay from the decisions of any customary court not presided over by a legal practitioner to a higher-grade customary court designated a customary court of appeal in relation to the lower-grade customary court, if any. Where there was no such court of appeal, appeals lay to magistrates' courts. Appeals from the decisions of all Grade A courts and Grade B courts presided over by legal practitioners lay to the High Court.

4. Customary Courts in the Eastern Region

The Customary Courts Law 1956[61] provided for the establishment of customary courts in the Eastern Region. There were to be two divisions of the courts namely district courts (subdivided into Grades A and B), and county courts which were to be customary courts of appeal. Under the law, as amended by the Customary Courts (Amendment) Law 1957,[62] appeals were to lie from a district court to a county court designated for the purpose. If there was no such county court appeals lay to a magistrate's court. The Native Courts Ordinance[63] continued to apply as a transitional provision. Under the Ordinance, there were two channels of appeal. By the first channel, appeals from the decisions of native courts lay to magistrates' courts and further appeals lay to the High Court and finally to the Federal Supreme Court. Cases through the second channel went from native courts to the district officer from whom the case went to the Resident whose decisions could go on appeal to the Governor.

[59] W.R.N. Laws 1959, Cap. 31.
[60] W.R.N. Laws 1959, Cap. 68.
[61] No. 21 of 1956.
[62] No. 12 of 1957.
[63] Nigeria Laws 1948, Cap. 142.

The Chief Justice of the Region later replaced the Governor as an appellate authority for the native courts.[64]

5. Revised editions of legislation

In 1958, a revised edition of the laws of the Federation of Nigeria and Lagos containing Ordinances in force on June 1, 1958 was prepared. The edition which consisted of 12 volumes also contained subsidiary legislation and English statutes extending to Nigeria. Ordinances in force throughout the Federation as Federal laws were not separated from Ordinances in force in Lagos only.

A revised edition of the laws of the Western Region was prepared in 1959. The laws contained in the edition included Ordinances in force in the country before October 1, 1954 which were considered by the Law Revision Commissioner to be dealing with subjects within the legislative competence of the Region and accordingly deemed to be enacted by the legislature of the Region by virtue of the Nigeria (Constitution) Order in Council 1954. The edition also contained laws enacted by the Legislature of the Region and subsidiary legislation. It consisted of six volumes.

E. OCTOBER 1, 1960 TO JANUARY 16, 1966

Nigeria became an independent country within the Commonwealth on October 1, 1960.[65] The country was then a federation consisting of the federal territory of Lagos and three Regions, namely Northern Nigeria, Western Nigeria and Eastern Nigeria. The constitution of the Federation and the constitutions of the Regions were scheduled to the Nigeria (Constitution) Order in Council 1960.[66] Under the Constitution of the Federation, from October 1, 1960 to September 30, 1963, Parliament (the Federal Legislature) was, in general, exclusively empowered to make laws for the country on matters within the Exclusive Legislative List. Parliament also had exclusive powers to legislate for Lagos on all matters. With respect to matters within the Concurrent Legislative List, Parliament was empowered to legislate for the Federation and each Regional Legislature was empowered to legislate for the Region. Each Regional Legislature had, in general, exclusive legislative powers with respect to matters outside the Lists. Whenever a conflict arose between a law made by a Regional Legislature and a law validly made by Parliament the law made by Parliament prevailed. Enactments made by the Federal Legislature were called "Acts" and those made by Regional Legislatures were called

---

[64] Native Courts (Interim Provisions) Law 1960 (No. 12 of 1960).
[65] Nigeria Independence Act 1960 (8 & 9 Eliz. 2, c. 55).
[66] S.I. 1960 No. 1652; L.N. 159 of 1960.

"Laws." By virtue of the Designation of Ordinances Act 1961[67] Ordinances which were enacted before October 1, 1960 and which were still in force as federal statutes were to be called "Acts."[68]

The court systems remained basically the same. The Judicial Committee of the Privy Council was still the highest court for Nigeria. There was a Federal Supreme Court consisting of the Chief Justice of the Federation and federal justices. Lagos still had a High Court and magistrates' courts. Each Region, too, had a High Court, magistrates' courts and customary courts. The Court of Resolution of Northern Nigeria continued to exist. The Constitution of the Federation provided that appeals lay to the Federal Supreme Court from the decisions of the Sharia Court of Appeal on questions relating to the interpretation of the Constitution of the Federation or that of a Region and on questions involving the contravention of the Constitution of the Federation with respect to fundamental rights. A Judicial Service Commission was established for each Region. The Chief Justice of the Federation and the Chief Justice of Lagos were appointed by the Governor-General in accordance with the advice of the Prime Minister. All the other judges of the Federal Supreme Court and the High Court of Lagos were appointed by the Governor-General on the advice of the Judicial Service Commission for the Federation. The Chief Justice of each Region was appointed by the Governor of the Region on the advice of the Premier and all the other Judges of the High Court of the Region were appointed by the Governor on the advice of the Judicial Service Commission for the Region.

The Constitution of the Federation provided that with the exception of contempt of court at common law, no person was to be convicted of an offence unless the offence was defined by a written law and the penalty for it prescribed by a written law.[69] Thus, customary criminal law was abolished.[70]

A fourth Region of Nigeria known as Midwestern Nigeria was created out of Western Nigeria on August 9, 1963. In general, the laws in force in Western Nigeria immediately before the creation of the new Region were to continue to apply in the territory constituting the new Region until they were repealed or modified.[71]

A new Constitution of the Federation[72] came into operation on

---

[67] No. 57 of 1961. The Act came into operation on December 28, 1961.

[68] See Nigeria (Constitution) Order in Council 1954 (S.I. 1954 No. 1146); Nigeria (Constitution) Order in Council 1960 (S.I. 1960 No. 1652).

[69] Nigeria (Constitution) Order in Council 1960 (S.I. 1960 No. 1652), Second Sched., s. 21 (10).

[70] See *Aoko* v. *Fagbemi* [1961] 1 All N.L.R. 400.

[71] Mid-Western Region (Transitional Provisions) Act 1963 (No. 19 of 1963), Constitution (Transitional Provisions) Act 1963 (No. 21 of 1963).

[72] Act No. 20 of 1963.

October 1, 1963. The Constitution abolished the monarchy[73] and the country became a republic within the Commonwealth. New Constitutions of Northern, Western and Eastern Nigeria came into force on the same day. Midwestern Nigeria was then being governed under a transitional enactment[74] and a Constitution made for it in 1964 came into force fully at the end of the transitional period.[75] The Judicial Committee of the Privy Council ceased to be a court for Nigeria. The Federal Supreme Court was abolished and a new court known as the Supreme Court of Nigeria was established as the highest court for Nigeria. There was provision in the Constitution of each Region for the establishment of a Court of Appeal as a court whose position in the hierarchy of courts for the Region was to be between the High Court of the Region and the Supreme Court of Nigeria. No such court of appeal was established during this period. It is significant to note that the Judicial Service Commissions ceased to exist. The Chief Justice of Nigeria was to be appointed by the President in accordance with the advice of the Prime Minister. The other judges of the Supreme Court (Justices of the Supreme Court) too were to be appointed by the President on the advice of the Prime Minister except that with respect to each of the four Regions, one Justice of the Supreme Court was to be appointed by the President on the advice of the Premier of the Region.[76] Similarly, the Judges of the High Court of each Region were to be appointed by the Governor on the advice of the Premier. The Supreme Court had original jurisdiction in disputes between the Federation and a Region or between Regions. Parliament was empowered to confer upon the court jurisdiction to advise the President, or the Governor of a Region with respect to the exercise of the prerogative of mercy.

The customary court systems were reformed notably with respect to the control and supervision of the courts. In Northern Nigeria, native courts styled "Area Courts" were established.[77] The judges of the courts were public officers in the public service of the Region and were therefore appointed by the Public Service Commission of the Region. The area courts thus constituted the second class of native courts whose judges were public officers in the Regional Public Service, the first being the provincial courts established in 1960. All the other native courts were under the control of native authorities. In Western Nigeria, Grade D customary courts were abolished by the

---

[73] Her Majesty Queen Elizabeth II ceased to be Nigeria's Head of State.
[74] Constitution (Transitional Provisions) Act 1963 (No. 21 of 1963).
[75] Mid-Western Nigeria Act 1964 (No. 3 of 1964).
[76] Constitution of the Federation (Act No. 20 of 1963).
[77] Native Courts (Amendment) Law 1963 (No. 11 of 1963), Native Court (Amendment No. 2) Law 1963 (No. 40 of 1963).

Administrator of the Region in 1962 during an emergency administration which followed the declaration by Parliament of a state of emergency with respect to the Region.[78] In order to avoid any doubt as to the continued operation of the abolition order, the Legislature of the Region abolished the courts after the period of emergency by the Customary Courts (Amendment) Law 1964.[79]

In 1965, a revised edition of the laws of Northern Nigeria that were in force on October 1, 1963 was published. It consisted of six volumes. A ten-volume revised edition of the laws of Eastern Nigeria in force on October 1, 1963 was also published.

That was the position of the legal system until January 15, 1966 when a military revolution occurred in the country. On January 16, 1966, the revolutionaries were in the process of reaching full effective control of government.

F. January 17, 1966 to the Present Time

On January 17, 1966, the military government had assumed full effective control of the machinery of government.[80] The Constitution (Suspension and Modification) Decree 1966[81] was the first law made by the new government known as the Federal Military Government. The Decree was made on March 4, 1966 and deemed to have come into operation on January 17, 1966. It suspended certain provisions of the Constitutions of the Federation and the Regions, and modified some other provisions of the constitutions. The Decree provided that the Federal Military Government had power to make laws for the whole country or any part of it on any matter.[82] There was also provision in the Decree for the appointment of a Military Governor for each Region. A Military Governor was empowered to make laws for the Region on any matter which was not within the Legislative Lists contained in the Constitution of the Federation. He could legislate for the Region on a matter within the Concurrent List with the prior consent of the Head of the Federal Military Government.[83] Laws made by the Federal Military Government were called "Decrees" and those made by a Military Governor were called "Edicts."

---

[78] Customary Courts (Amendment) Order 1962 (W.N.L.N. 300 of 1962), para. 10.
[79] No. 11 of 1964, ss. 8 and 29.
[80] The General Officer Commanding the Nigerian Army announced on January 17, 1966 that he had been formally invested with authority as Head of the Federal Military Government and Supreme Commander of the Armed Forces. See Government Notice No. 148, *Federal Republic of Nigeria Official Gazette* No. 6, Vol. 53 of January 26, 1966.
[81] No. 1 of 1966.
[82] *Ibid.* s. 3.
[83] *Ibid.* s. 4.

Decrees prevailed over the Constitutions of the Federation and the Regions and over all other laws. Where an Edict made by the Military Governor of a Region was inconsistent with a Decree or with an Act of Parliament or with the Constitution of the Region the Edict was void to the extent of its inconsistency.

By virtue of the Constitution (Suspension and Modification) (No. 5) Decree 1966[84] which came into force on May 24, 1966, the Government of Nigeria became known as the National Military Government. The Legislative Lists scheduled to the Constitution of the Federation[85] were abolished by the Decree. The Decree also abolished all Regions and provided that the territory hitherto constituting each Region had become a Group of Provinces. Thus, the government became a unitary government.

On July 29, 1966, another military revolution occurred in Nigeria. By the Constitution (Suspension and Modification) (No. 9) Decree 1966[86] Nigeria again became a federation comprising four Regions and a federal territory with effect from September 1, 1966. The Constitution (Suspension and Modification) Decree 1967[87] was made to implement the agreement reached by the military leaders at a meeting held at Aburi, Ghana, to settle disputes arising from the second military revolution. The Decree which was deemed to have come into operation on January 17, 1966, repealed the Constitution (Suspension and Modification) Decree (Nos. 1-10) of 1966[88] and reduced considerably the legislative powers of the Federal government. The Constitution (Repeal and Restoration) Decree 1967[89] repealed the Constitution (Suspension and Modification) Decree 1967 and thus revived a number of Decrees including the first Decree made by the Federal Military Government, the Constitution (Suspension and Modification) Decree 1966.[90] The legislative powers of the Federal Military Government and those of the Military Governors were fully restored.

As a civil war was imminent, the Federal Military Government made the States (Creation and Transitional Provisions) Decree 1967[91] which came into force on May 27, 1967. The Decree divided the country into 12 States, namely the North-Western, North-Central, Kano, North-Eastern, Benue-Plateau, Central-West (later

---

[84] No. 34 of 1966.

[85] Act. No. 20 of 1963.

[86] No. 59 of 1966.

[87] No. 8 of 1967.

[88] s. 15. See Constitution (Suspension and Modification) (No. 10) Decree 1966 (No. 69 of 1966), s. 2(2).

[89] No. 13 of 1967.

[90] No. 1 of 1966.

[91] No. 14 of 1967.

Kwara[92]) Lagos, Western, Mid-Western, Central-Eastern (later East-Central[93]) South-Eastern and Rivers States. There was no longer a federal territory.

In general, by virtue of the States (Creation and Transitional Provisions) Decree 1967, the laws in force in any part of the country immediately before the creation of States were to continue to apply in that part until they were repealed or modified by the appropriate authority. For instance, the 1963 revised edition of the laws of Northern Nigeria continued to apply in general in each of the then six northern States.[94] The Advisory Judicial Committee established by the Constitution (Suspension and Modification) Decree 1966[95] continued to function. The Committee consisted of the Chief Justice of Nigeria as Chairman, the Chief Justice of each of the States, the Grand Kadi of the Sharia Court of Appeal of the northern States and the Attorney-General of the Federation. The Solicitor-General of the Federation was Secretary to the Committee. The following judges were appointed by the Supreme Military Council after consultation with the Advisory Judicial Committee: Justices of the Supreme Court, the President and Judges of the Federal Revenue Court (a newly established Federal High Court), the Grand Kadi and other judges of the Sharia Court of Appeal, the President and Justices of Appeal of the Court of Appeal of the Western State (a court to which appeals from the High Court of the Western State lay), the Chief Justices of the States and other judges of the High Courts of the States. The committee had no role to play in the appointment of the Chief Justice of Nigeria. The power to appoint a person to the office of Chief Justice of Nigeria was vested in the Head of the Federal Military Government.[96]

On July 29, 1975, a third military revolution occurred in Nigeria. The new government in stating its programme of activities announced that civilian democratic rule would be restored on October 1, 1979.[97] Accordingly, a Constitution Drafting Committee whose members included lawyers, social scientists and some former active politicians, was appointed in October 1975 to draft a new constitution for Nigeria. The Committee submitted a draft constitution to the government in September 1976.[98] In accordance with the gov-

[92] Central-West (Change of Name, etc.) Decree 1968 (No. 7 of 1968).
[93] Central-Eastern (Change of Name) Decree 1970 (No. 25 of 1970).
[94] The North-Western, North-Central, Kano, North-Eastern, Benue-Plateau and Kwara States.
[95] No. 1 of 1966, s. 11.
[96] Constitution of the Federation (Act No. 20 of 1963) s. 112(1) as amended by the Constitution (Amendment) Decree 1972 (No. 5 of 1972).
[97] *Evening Times*, October 1, 1975, p. 1.
[98] *Daily Times*, September 15, 1976, p. 1.

ernment programme, new States have been created in Nigeria.[99] The country is experiencing sweeping social reforms under the present regime. Many public officers have been compulsorily retired on such grounds as corruption, inefficiency and divided interest.[1] The Constitution (Basic Provisions) Decree 1975[2] made on October 15, 1975 and deemed to have come into operation on July 29, 1975 re-enacted many of the constitutional provisions in force in the country immediately before the 1975 military revolution. In particular, many of the provisions of the first Decree made by the first military government, the Constitution (Suspension and Modification) Decree 1966[3] were re-enacted by the 1975 Decree. In some cases, the re-enactment took the form of incorporating by reference the provisions of the 1966 Decree.[4] Therefore the 1966 Decree was not expressly repealed. But the 1966 Decree is to cease to have effect except as provided in the 1975 Decree.[5] There are, however, some significant changes effected by the 1975 Decree. The Decree established a Supreme Military Council different in composition from the former Supreme Military Council. Unlike the position under the Constitution (Suspension and Modification) Decree 1966, the Military Governors of the States are not members of the Supreme Military Council.[6] Moreover, the Attorney-General of the Federation is to attend the meetings of the Supreme Military Council only in an advisory capacity.[7] Section 8 of the Constitution (Basic Provisions) Decree 1975 states that the functions of the Council include:

(a) the determination from time to time of national policy on major issues affecting the country;

[99] States (Creation and Transitional Provisions) Decree 1976 (No. 12 of 1976).
[1] See Public Service Commission (Disciplinary Proceedings) (Special Provisions) Decree 1976 (No. 3 of 1976).
[2] No. 32 of 1975.
[3] No. 1 of 1966.
[4] See Constitution (Basic Provisions) Decree 1975, s. 14.
[5] See Constitution (Basic Provisions) Decree 1975, s. 21(3).
[6] See Constitution (Basic Provisions) Decree 1975, s. 6(2). The subsection provides that the Supreme Military Council is to consist of: (a) the Head of the Federal Military Government who is to be the President of the Council; (b) the Chief of Staff, Supreme Headquarters; (c) the Chief of Army Staff; (d) the Chief of Naval Staff; (e) the Chief of Air Staff; (f) the Inspector-General of the Nigeria Police; (g) the General Officer Commanding 1st Division, Nigerian Army; (h) the General Officer Commanding 2nd Division, Nigerian Army; (i) the General Officer Commanding 3rd Division, Nigerian Army; (j) the General Officer Commanding 4th Division, Nigerian Army; (k) 12 designated members, being senior officers of the Nigerian Armed Forces and the Nigeria Police Force of whom six are to be from the Nigerian Army, three from the Nigerian Navy, two from the Nigerian Air Force and one from the Nigeria Police Force; and (l) such other members as the Council may from time to time appoint.
[7] See Constitution (Basic Provisions) Decree 1975, s. 6(5).

   (b) dealing with constitutional matters, including amendments of the Constitution of the Federation[8];

   (c) dealing with all national security matters, such function including the authority to declare war or proclaim a state of emergency or martial law;

   (d) exclusive responsibility for the appointment of the Head of the Federal Military Government, the Chief of Staff (Supreme Headquarters), the Chief of Army Staff, the Chief of Naval Staff, the Chief of Air Staff, the General Officers Commanding, the Inspector-General of the Nigeria Police, Military Governors, members of the National Council of States and of the Federal Executive Council;

   (e) the ratification of the appointment of such senior public officers as the Council may from time to time specify; and

   (f) the general supervision of the National Council of States and the Federal Executive Council both of which were established by the Decree.

The members of the National Council of States include the Military Governors of the States.[9]

The Federal Executive Council is established by section 6(6) of the Constitution (Basic Provisions) Decree 1975. There is an Executive Council for each State.[10]

According to the 1975 Decree, the Advisory Judicial Committee consists of:

   (a) the Chief Justice of Nigeria who is the Chairman;

   (b) the Attorney-General of the Federation;

   (c) the President of the Federal Court of Appeal (a newly-established court)[11];

   (d) the President of the Federal Revenue Court;

   (e) the Chief Justice of each of the States; and

   (f) one Grand Kadi of the Sharia Court of Appeal appointed annually in rotation by the Supreme Military Council from the States having a Sharia Court of Appeal.[12]

---

[8] Act No. 20 of 1963.

[9] See Constitution (Basic Provisions) Decree 1975, s. 6(4). The other members of the Council are (a) The Head of the Federal Military Government who is the President of the Council; (b) the Chief of Staff, Supreme Headquarters; (c) the Chief of Army Staff; (d) the Chief of Naval Staff; (e) the Chief of Air Staff; (f) the Inspector-General of the Nigeria Police; and (g) such other members as the Supreme Military Council may from time to time appoint. The Attorney-General of the Federation attends meetings of the Council in an advisory capacity. See s. 6(5) of the Decree (No. 32 of 1975).

[10] See Constitution (Basic Provisions) Decree 1975, s. 7(1).

[11] See Federal Court of Appeal Decree 1976 (No. 43 of 1976). The Decree came into force on October 1, 1976.

[12] Constitution (Basic Provisions) Decree 1975, s. 13(1).

The Federal Court of Appeal mentioned in the 1975 Decree was established in October 1976. Appeals lie from all the High Courts including the Federal Revenue Court to the Federal Court of Appeal, the Court of Appeal of each of the States of Ogun, Ondo and Oyo having been abolished by section 3(1) of the Constitution (Amendment) (No. 2) Decree 1976[13] with effect from March 31, 1976. Appeals from the Federal Court of Appeal lie to the Supreme Court of Nigeria.

The Advisory Judicial Committee is to advise the Supreme Military Council on:

(a) the appointment of the President and the Justices of the Federal Court of Appeal;

(b) the appointment of the President and other judges of the Federal Revenue Court, the President of the National Industrial Court (a newly established court[14]), the Chief Judges[15] and other Judges of the High Courts of the States, and the Grand Kadi and other judges of the Sharia Courts of Appeal of the States; and

(c) any matter pertaining to the judiciary that may be referred to the Committee by the Supreme Military Council.[16]

Section 13(3) of the Constitution (Basic Provisions) Decree 1975 in stating the duty of the Advisory Judicial Committee omits any express reference to advising the Supreme Military Council on the appointment of Justices of the Supreme Court. Under section 112 of the Constitution of the Federation as amended by the Constitution (Suspension and Modification) Decree 1966, Justices of the Supreme Court were to be appointed by the Supreme Military Council acting after consultation with the Advisory Judicial Committee. But section 14(2) of the 1975 Decree provides that the provisions of the Constitution of the Federation as amended by the 1966 Decree are to continue in force subject to the 1976 Decree. Accordingly, the Advisory Judicial Committee no longer has the duty of advising the Supreme Military Council on the appointment of Justices of the Supreme Court unless the Council refers such issues of appointment to the Committee as "any matter pertaining to the judiciary" within the meaning of section 13(3)(c) of the 1975 Decree. Such reference is unlikely in practice for all the members of the Committee (excluding the Chief Justice of Nigeria) are persons who are most likely to be considered for appointment to the office of Justice of the Supreme

---

[13] No. 42 of 1976.
[14] See Trade Disputes Decree 1976 (No. 7 of 1976).
[15] See Chief Justice of a State (Change of Title) Decree 1976 (No. 41 of 1976).
[16] See Constitution (Basic Provisions) Decree 1975, s. 13(3).

Court and it seems that it is for that reason that the Committee is not expressly entrusted by the 1975 Decree with the task of giving advice on the appointment of Justices of the Supreme Court.

The States (Creation and Transitional Provisions) Decree 1976[17] divided the country into the following 19 States with effect from February 3, 1976: Anambra, Bauchi, Bendel, Benue, Borno, Cross River, Gongola, Imo, Kaduna, Kano, Kwara, Lagos, Niger, Ogun, Ondo, Oyo, Plateau, Rivers and Sokoto.[18] With effect from the following day, the Federal Capital Territory Decree 1976[19] established a federal capital territory a large part of which was carved out of Niger and Plateau States. Thus, Nigeria now consists of a federal capital territory and 19 States.[20] The former East-Central State was divided into two States, namely, Anambra and Imo. The former North-Eastern State was divided into three States, namely, Bauchi, Borno and Gongola. The former North-Western State was divided into two States, namely, Niger and Sokoto. The former Benue-Plateau State was divided into two States, namely, Benue and Plateau. The former Western State was divided into three States, namely, Ogun, Ondo and Oyo. In general, Kano, Kwara, Lagos and Rivers are, respectively, the same as States by those names under the 1967 State-Creation Decree.[21] In general, the former North-Central State was simply renamed Kaduna, the former South-Eastern State merely renamed Cross River and the former Midwestern State simply renamed Bendel. But there are some boundary adjustments, notably in the case of Kwara — a portion of the former Kwara State forms part of Benue.

In general, the laws in force immediately before February 3, 1976 (the date of creation of the new States) in any area of the country now forming part of a State under the 1976 Decree continue to apply in that area until they are repealed or modified by the appropriate authority. The application of the laws is subject to modifications necessary to bring the laws into conformity with the Decree, for example, changing the name East-Central State to Anambra State in the application of a statute of the former East-Central State to Anambra.[22]

Decrees now constitute the supreme law in Nigeria. Each of the military revolutions of January 15, 1966, July 29, 1966 and July 29, 1975 removed the pre-existing legal order. Any part of the Constitution of the Federation or of the Constitutions of the former Regions

[17] No. 12 of 1976.
[18] *Ibid.* s. 1 and Schedule.
[19] No. 6 of 1976.
[20] See Federal Capital Territory Decree 1976, s. 1 and Schedule.
[21] States (Creation and Transitional Provisions) Decree 1967 (No. 14 of 1967).
[22] See States (Creation and Transitional Provisions) Decree 1976 (No. 12 of 1976).

that is in force applies only by virtue of a Decree. But in *Lakanmi* v. *Attorney-General (West)*,[23] the Supreme Court held that a Decree was void notwithstanding the provisions of section 6 of the Constitution (Suspension and Modification) Decree 1966 which provided that no question as to the validity of a Decree was to be entertained by a court of law.[24] Subsequently, a new Decree, the Federal Military Government (Supremacy and Enforcement of Powers) Decree 1970[25] was made. The preamble to the Decree states correctly the legal position. It reads:

"Whereas the military revolution which took place on January 15 1966 and which was followed by another on July 29 1966, effectively abrogated the whole pre-existing legal order in Nigeria except what has been preserved under the Constitution (Suspension and Modification) Decree, 1966 (1966 No. 1):"

Section 1 of the Decree provides that the preamble forms part of the enactment.

The Supreme Court of Nigeria is still the highest court for Nigeria. The only provisions of the Constitution of the Federation[26] relating to the jurisdiction of the court expressly declared as original jurisdiction by the Constitution were suspended in 1966. The provisions had given the court original jurisdiction in disputes between the Federation and a Region or between Regions. Now, under section 121F of the Constitution of the Federation, a section inserted by section 1 of the Constitution (Amendment) (No. 2) Decree 1976, the Federal Court of Appeal is the only court which has original jurisdiction in any dispute between the Federation and a State or between States. The Supreme Court hears appeals from the decisions of the Sharia Courts of Appeal of the northern States, the National Industrial Court (a newly-established court[27]) and the Federal Court of Appeal. Appeals lie to the Federal Court of Appeal from the decisions of the Federal Revenue Court, the High Courts of the States and such other courts or tribunals as may be specified by law.

The Federal Revenue Court is a Federal High Court established by the Federal Revenue Court Decree 1973.[28] The court has civil and

[23] (1971) 1 U.I.L.R. 210.
[24] See A. Ojo, "The Search for a Grundnorm in Nigeria — The Lakanmi Case," *International and Comparative Law Quarterly*, Vol. 20, No. 1 (1971) p. 117; T.O. Elias, "The Nigerian Crisis in International Law," *Proceedings of the Second Annual Conference and Dinner of the Nigerian Society of International Law, 1970*, p. 137; "Note, Challenging the Validity of Decrees and Edicts," *Nigerian Bar Journal*, Vol. VIII (1967), p. 55.
[25] No. 28 of 1970.
[26] Act. No. 20 of 1963.
[27] See Trade Disputes Decree 1976 (No. 7 of 1976), s. 14(1).
[28] No. 13 of 1973.

criminal jurisdiction with respect to certain federal matters. Such jurisdiction had hitherto been exercised by State courts acting as Federal courts by virtue of enabling legislation.[29] Cases which the court could hear include federal revenue cases and cases involving copyright, trade marks or admiralty. State courts are no longer empowered to exercise jurisdiction in cases within the jurisdiction of the court but the Head of the Federal Military Government may vest jurisdiction in respect of any such case in a State court.

The Robbery and Firearms (Special Provisions) Decree 1970[30] provides for the establishment of special tribunals for the purpose of trying robbery and related offences, and firearms offences. The Offences Against the Person (Special Provisions) Decree 1974[31] provides for the establishment of tribunals for the trial of kidnapping and lynching offences and related offences. Currency offences tribunals may be established under the Counterfeit Currency (Special Provisions) Decree 1974[32] for the trial of currency offences. Any of the special tribunals must, in certain cases, impose a death sentence in respect of an offence. The tribunal may order that a death sentence be executed by causing the offender to be killed by a firing squad. A conviction or sentence imposed by any of the tribunals is subject to confirmation by an appropriate authority who is the Head of the Federal Military Government in the case of currency offences, the Military Governor in the case of tribunals established to try firearms, robbery and related offences; and the establishing authority (the Head of the Federal Military Government or the Military Governor) in respect of tribunals established by the particular establishing authority to try kidnapping, lynching and related offences.

The Treason and Other Offences (Special Military Tribunal) Decree 1976[33] provided for the establishment of a special military tribunal for the purpose of the trial of any person whether or not a member of the armed forces who before February 23, 1976 committed treason, murder or any other offence in connection with any act of rebellion against the Federal Military Government.[34] A tribunal was constituted under the Decree to try persons charged with offences in connection with an attempted coup of February 13, 1976.

A new court known as the National Industrial Court was esta-

---

[29] See *e.g.* State Courts (Federal Jurisdiction) Act (Fed. and Lagos Laws 1958, Cap. 177).

[30] No. 47 of 1970. See also Robbery and Firearms (Special Provisions) (Amendment) Decree 1974 and Robbery and Firearms (Special Provisions) (Amendment)(No. 2) Decree 1974.

[31] No. 20 of 1974.

[32] No. 22 of 1974.

[33] No. 8 of 1976.

[34] *Ibid.* s. 1.

blished by the Trade Disputes Decree 1976[35] for the purpose of settling trade disputes.[36] The Decree also provided for the establishment
of an Industrial Arbitration Panel and arbitration tribunals for the
purpose of dealing with trade disputes.[37]

Some aspects of the legal systems of the States under the military
government will now be examined.

A revised edition of the laws of Lagos State has been published.
The edition consists of eight volumes which contain, in general, the
laws of the State in force on April 1, 1973 together with some federal
laws.

The Customary Courts Edict 1973[38] repealed the Customary
Courts Law[39] and provided for the establishment of a single grade of
customary courts outside the city of Lagos.

With effect from April 1, 1968 all the native courts in the then
northern States were abolished. New courts known as area courts
were established by the respective Chief Justices of the States under
the respective Area Courts Edicts to replace the native courts.[40]
Judges of the new courts are public officers in the public service of
the appropriate State. Area courts are under the control of the High
Court. The supervisory powers of the High Court over them are,
however, as limited as its supervisory powers over the native courts.
Thus, in general, the High Court is not empowered to issue an order
of *mandamus, certiorari* or prohibition, or an injunction in lieu of
quo warranto in respect of an area court.

The Area Courts Edicts apply in the present 10 northern States[41]
by virtue of the States (Creation and Transitional) Provisions
Decree 1976.[42]

A Court of Appeal established in Western Nigeria shortly before
the creation of States in 1967 functioned as a court of the Western
State by virtue of the States (Creation and Transitional Provisions)
Decree 1967. With respect to the Western State, the Court was
between the High Court of the State and the Supreme Court in the
hierarchy of courts for the State.[43] By virtue of the 1976 State-creation Decree, there was a Court of Appeal for each of the States of
Ogun, Ondo and Oyo on the creation of those States. The Courts of

[35] No. 7 of 1976.
[36] *Ibid.* s. 14(1).
[37] *Ibid*, s. 7.
[38] No. 10 of 1973.
[39] W.R.N. Laws 1959, Cap. 31.
[40] *See e.g.* Area Courts Edict 1968 (No. 1 of 1968) (N.E.S.).
[41] Bauchi, Benue, Borno, Gongola, Kaduna, Kano, Kwara, Niger, Plateau and
Sokoto.
[42] No. 12 of 1976.
[43] See Court of Appeal Edict 1967 (No. 15 of 1967)(W.N.); Constitution (Miscellaneous Provisions) (No. 2) Decree 1967 (No. 27 of 1967), s. 3.

Appeal were abolished by the Constitution (Amendment) (No. 2) Decree 1976 with effect from March 31, 1976.

The Western State established in 1975 a Law Commission for the purpose of promoting the revision of the law including customary law.[44]

Before the creation of States in 1967, the Customary Courts Edict 1966[45] had been made by the Military Governor of Midwestern Nigeria to replace the Customary Courts Law[46] with respect to Mid-western Nigeria. The Edict was in force in the Midwestern State on the creation of States in Nigeria. It established a single grade of customary courts with very little jurisdiction and powers. It is significant to note that the Edict provided that no person was qualified to be president or member of a customary court unless he was a native of the area of jurisdiction of the court. The reason for this provision could be found in the Customary Courts Rules 1966[47] made under the Edict. Under the Rules, it was provided that any party relying on a rule of customary law was not required to prove the rule where the customary law was that of the court's area of jurisdiction.[48] An indigenous member of a court's jurisdiction would likely be familiar with the customary law of the area. In any case, it would be easier to find a person familiar with the customary law from among the indigenous members of the community than from among other persons. It appears that the Government policy was to appoint only indigenous persons who were versed in the customary law of the local community. Thus it was unnecessary to prove such customary law before them. Another significant aspect of the Rules is the provision which stated that whenever a customary court stated in a judgment that any particular customary law was the appropriate customary law there was a presumption that the customary law was correct, subject to section 22(*a*) of the Customary Courts Edict 1966, which dealt with the choice of the appropriate customary law, until the contrary was proved unless the customary law stated was at variance with any previous subsisting judgment of the High Court of the State or of the Supreme Court.[49] That provision was a useful step towards achieving certainty of customary law.[50] In spite of the advance of these statutory provisions, customary courts were abolished in the State with

---

[44] Law Commission Edict 1975 (No. 8 of 1975).

[45] No. 38 of 1966.

[46] W.R.N. Laws 1959, Cap. 31.

[47] M.N.L.N. 37 of 1967.

[48] *Ibid.* Ord. X, r. 6(3).

[49] *Ibid.* Ord. X, r. 6(5).

[50] See A. O. Obilade, "Reform of Customary Court Systems in Nigeria under the Military Government" [1969] J.A.L. 28 at pp. 40-43.

effect from March 31, 1973.[51] The abolition is effective in Bendel by virtue of the States (Creation and Transitional Provisions) Decree 1976. But there is a proposal to re-establish customary courts in the State.

The Military Governor of Eastern Nigeria made the Customary Courts (No. 2) Edict 1966[52] which repealed the Customary Courts Law.[53] That Edict was in force in the Central-Eastern (later East-Central), South-Eastern and Rivers States on the creation of States in 1967, by virtue of the States (Creation and Transitional Provisions) Decree 1967. The Edict provided for the establishment of two types of customary courts, namely, district courts and customary courts of appeal. A customary court of appeal was presided over by a legal practitioner and legal practitioners could appear before the court. Appeals from the decisions of a district court lay to a customary court of appeal. The High Court of each of the three States heard appeals from the decisions of a customary court of appeal in the State. The Chief Justice of the State had general supervisory powers over customary courts of appeal in the State. The Customary Courts (No. 2) Edict 1966 is now in force only in the Rivers State. But since 1970, when the civil war in Nigeria ended, customary courts have not functioned in the State. The South Eastern State Customary Courts Edict 1969[54] which repealed the Customary Courts (No. 2) Edict 1966 in its application to the State provided for two classes of customary courts, namely, district courts and customary courts of appeal. Many of the provisions of the 1969 Edict relating to customary courts of appeal have been suspended and other provisions relating to such courts have been modified to replace the courts of appeal with magistrates' courts.[55] Accordingly, appeals lay from district courts to magistrates' courts. Preliminary inquiries into indictable offences were abolished in the State by the Criminal Justice (Miscellaneous Provisions) Edict 1973.[56] By virtue of the States (Creation and Transitional Provisions) Decree 1976, the 1969 Edict as amended by the 1973 Edict applies in Cross River State.

In the East-Central State Customary Courts were abolished by the Magistrates' Courts Law (Amendment) Edict 1971.[57] Preliminary inquiries into indictable offences were abolished in the State by the

[51] Customary Courts (Abolition) Edict 1973 (No. 18 of 1973).
[52] No. 29 of 1966.
[53] E.N. Laws 1963. Cap. 32.
[54] No. 9 of 1969 (S.E.S.). The Edict is now cited as the Customary Courts Edict 1969. See Customary Courts (Miscellaneous Provisions) Edict 1976 (No. 4 of 1976) (C.R.S.).
[55] Customary Courts (Miscellaneous Provisions) Edict 1971 (No. 6 of 1971).
[56] No. 4 of 1973. (S.E.S.).
[57] No. 23 of 1971.

Criminal Procedure (Miscellaneous Provisions) Edict 1974.[58] Both
Edicts apply in Anambra and Imo by virtue of the States (Creation
and Transitional Provisions) Decree 1976.

Bendel State now has a revised edition of its laws. The edition
came into operation in January 1978. The wording of the laws published in the edition is, in general, identical with that of the pre-existing laws for the Law Revision Commissioner had no power to make
any alteration or amendment in the substance of the pre-existing
laws.

Mention should also be made of the Chief Justice of a State
(Change of Title) Decree 1976[59] which changed the title of Chief Justice of a State to "Chief Judge of a State" with effect from August 5,
1976.

[58] No. 18 of 1974.
[59] No. 41 of 1976.

Part 3

THE SOURCES OF NIGERIAN LAW

CHAPTER 3

PRELIMINARY CONSIDERATIONS AND INTERPRETATION OF STATUTES

A. PRELIMINARY CONSIDERATIONS

THE term "source of law" is used in various senses. First it means the ultimate origin of the whole body of a legal system — the origin from which the system derives its validity, be it the electorate, a special body, the general will or the will of a dictator. In this sense, a source of law is a formal source of law.[1] Secondly, the term is used to name the historical origin of a rule of law. Thus, the common law is a historical source of English law for the origin of many rules of English law may be traced back to the common law. Thirdly, the term means a material containing the rules of law. Statute books, law reports and textbooks are sources of law in this sense. A source in this sense is said to be a literary source. Fourthly, "source of law" means the fountain of authority of a rule of law, that is, the origin from which a legal rule derives its authority. It is the means through which a rule forms part of the body of law.[2] In this sense, a source of law is a legal source. Examples of legal sources are legislation and judicial precedents. Thus, the legal source of the general proposition that it is unlawful to kill another person is, with respect to Lagos State, the Criminal Code of the State.[3] It is in this fourth sense that the term is used henceforth in this Part.

The sources of Nigerian law are:
(1) Nigerian legislation.
(2) English law[4] which consists of:
    (a) the received English law comprising:
        (i) the common law;
        (ii) the doctrines of equity;
        (iii) statutes of general application in force in England on January 1, 1900[5];

---

[1] See R. J. Walker and M. G. Walker, *The English Legal System* (3rd ed., 1972), p. 92.
[2] *Ibid.*
[3] Lagos Laws 1973, Cap. 31.
[4] See Law (Miscellaneous Provisions) Law (Lagos Laws 1973, Cap. 65), s. 2; High Court Law (N.N. Laws 1963, Cap. 49), s. 28; Law of England (Application) Law (W.R.N. Laws 1959, Cap. 60), s. 3; High Court Law (E.N. Laws 1963, Cap. 61), s. 15; Law (Miscellaneous Provisions) Act (named by s. 28 of the Interpretation Act 1964, No. 1 of 1964), s. 45.
[5] By virtue of s. 4 of the Law of England (Application) Law and the States (Creation and Transitional Provisions) Decree 1976 (No. 12 of 1976), English statutes on matters within the legislative competence of Bendel, Ogun, Ondo and Oyo are not in force in those States.

  (iv) statutes and subsidiary legislation on specified matters.
  (b) English law made before October 1, 1960 and extending to
    Nigeria.
  (3) Customary law.
  (4) Judicial precedents.

The application of the sources involves, in varying degrees, interpretation of statutes. Therefore, in order to understand the sources clearly it is necessary at the outset to study the principles and rules applied by the courts in interpreting statutes.

B. INTERPRETATION OF STATUTES

The primary duty of the courts in interpreting statutes, that is, laws enacted by the legislature, is to find the intention of the legislature.[6] But the intention is to be discovered from the wording of the statute. It must be an intention manifested by the words used. If every word had only one meaning this task would have been very easy. Words, however, have no particular meaning except in a context. Moreover, owing to human failings, it is impossible to foresee all the kinds of events that may occur in future in relation to any particular matter being legislated upon and provide adequate unambiguous expressions in the legislation to deal with the matter in all circumstances. Some words used in statutes represent such vague standards that the task of interpreting them may be likened to that of making subsidiary legislation.[7] Examples of such words are "reasonable time" and "inordinate delay." Generally, when the wording of a statute is clear there is little problem of interpretation. But sometimes, although the wording is clear, giving effect to the clear meaning would lead to absurd results. It is the duty of the court to grapple with this problem, bearing in mind the primary object — finding the intention of the legislature. A statute which is ambiguous or not clear may be difficult to interpret. Yet, it is the duty of the court to discover the intention of the legislature from the wording. In some cases, it is obvious from the statute that the legislature has used a wrong word and that the intention of the legislature as discovered from the statute cannot be given effect unless the mistake is corrected. Cases of obvious gaps in statutes also arise. The courts are not entitled to fill gaps in statutes. Where there is a gap in a statute, it is only the legislature that can fill it — by a subsequent enactment.[8] The courts are not to guess

---

[6] *Onasile* v. *Sami* [1962] 1 All N.L.R. 272.

[7] Douglas Payne, "*The Intention of the Legislature in the Interpretation of Statutes*" (1956) 9 C.L.P. 96 at p. 105.

[8] *Okumagba* v. *Egbe* [1965] 1 All N.L.R. 62 at p. 65; *Magor and St. Mellons Rural District Council* v. *Newport Corporation* [1952] A.C. 189 at pp. 190-191; *London Transport Executive* v. *Betts* [1958] 2 All E.R. 636 at p. 655.

the intention of the legislature; they have to discover that intention. But it does appear that in interpreting statutes the courts sometimes pay only lip-service to the view that the duty of a court is to state the law and not to make it.[9]

The general common law[10] principles and the statutory rules applied by the courts in interpreting statutes will now be examined. There are three main general principles of interpretation, namely, the Literal Rule, the Golden Rule and the Mischief Rule. They are not in fact rules; they are mere guiding principles.

The Literal Rule

According to the Literal Rule, statutes are to be interpreted literally. Words used in statutes are, thus, to be construed in their usual grammatical sense. If the words are used in relation to a trade or business they are to be given their usual meaning in the trade or business. It is immaterial that hardship would result from literal interpretation. For example, in *R.* v. *Bangaza*,[11] the Federal Supreme Court had to interpret section 319(2) of the Criminal Code[12] which provided that "Where an offender who in the opinion of the court has not attained the age of seventeen years has been found guilty of murder, such offender shall not be sentenced to death but shall be ordered to be detained ... " The court found that it was clear from the wording that the relevant age was the age at the time of the conviction and not the age at the time of the commission of the offence. The court, therefore, rejected the view that the relevant age was the age at the time of the commission of the offence. Accordingly, where an offender under that provision was under the age of 17 years when he committed the offence, he must be sentenced to death unless the verdict was given before he attained the age of 17 years.[13] Similarly, in *Adegbenro* v. *Akintola*,[14] the Judicial Committee of the Privy Council in interpreting section 33(10) of the Constitution of Western Nigeria which empowered the Governor to remove the Premier if "it appears to him that the Premier no longer commands the support of a majority of the House of Assembly" explained that by the words "it appears to him" the legislature intended that the judgment as to

---

[9] Douglas Payne, *op. cit.* (n. 7, above). Compare *Okumagba* v. *Egbe* [1965] 1 All N.L.R. 62 at p. 65.

[10] The common law of England applies in all jurisdictions in Nigeria subject to Nigerian legislation.

[11] (1960) 5 F.S.C. 1.

[12] Fed. and Lagos Laws 1958, Cap. 42.

[13] The provision was later amended by the Criminal Justice (Miscellaneous Provisions) Decree 1966 (No. 84 of 1966).

[14] [1962] 1 All N.L.R. 465.

whether the Premier no longer commanded the support of a majority of the House was to be left to the Governor's assessment without any limitation as to the material on which he was to base his judgment or the contacts to which he might resort for the purpose.[15] Accordingly, the Privy Council held that the Governor could remove the Premier from office under the provision without a prior decision or resolution on the floor of the House showing that the Premier no longer commanded the support of a majority of the House.

The principle that the wording of a statute is to be construed literally is only a general principle which must be applied only where the wording is clear and unambiguous.[16]

The Golden Rule

The Golden Rule was formulated in *Beck* v. *Smith*.[17] It states, "It is a very useful rule in the construction of a statute to adhere to the ordinary meaning of the words used, and to the grammatical construction unless that is at variance with the intention of the legislature to be collected from the statute itself, or leads to any manifest absurdity or repugnance, in which case the language may be varied or modified so as to avoid such inconvenience but no further."

Accordingly, where the words to be interpreted are ambiguous, it is the court's duty to interpret the words in such a manner as to avoid absurdity. Thus, in *R* v. *Princewell*,[18] the court held that the word "marries" in section 370 of the Criminal Code was not to be construed as contracting a valid marriage but as going through a form of marriage known to or recognised by the law. To hold otherwise would have negatived the intention of the legislature.[19] Similarly, where it is impossible to comply with the provisions of a statute when they are construed literally, the general rule is that the court would not adopt the literal interpretation.[20] The court would interpret the provisions in such a way as to avoid the absurdity and at the same time reflect the intention of the legislature.[21]

Another example of the application of the Golden Rule is *Council of the University of Ibadan* v. *Adamolekun*.[22] In that case, the Supreme Court had to determine whether an Edict made by the Mili-

---

[15] *Ibid.* at pp. 476-477.
[16] *Nabhan* v. *Nabhan* [1967] 1 All N.L.R. 47 at p. 54. On the interpretation of Criminal Codes based on the common law, se *Obaji* v. *State* [1965] 1 All N.L.R. 269.
[17] (1836) 2 M. & W. 191 at p. 195; 150 E.R. 724 at p. 726.
[18] [1963] 2 All N.L.R. 31.
[19] See also *Akinosho* v. *Enigbokan* (1955) 21 N.L.R. 88.
[20] *Commissioner of Police* v. *Okoli*, 1966 N.N.L.R. 1 at p. 4.
[21] *Ibid.* See also *Awe* v. *Alabi* [1970] 2 All N.L.R. 16.
[22] [1967] 1 All N.L.R. 213.

tary Governor of Western Nigeria could be declared void by the court. By virtue of section 3(4) of the Constitution (Suspension and Modification) Decree 1966[23] where an Edict was inconsistent with a Decree, the Edict was void to the extent of the inconsistency. But section 6 of the same Decree provided: "No question as to the validity of this or any other Decree or of any Edict shall be entertained by any court of law in Nigeria." It was therefore argued by counsel that even if the Edict in question was void, the court could not declare it void. This interpretation of section 6 of the Decree is consistent with the Literal Rule. But literal interpretation of the section would lead to absurdity. If the court could not declare an Edict void even though the Edict is void by reason of its inconsistency with a Decree, the court would face the problem of applying two inconsistent laws to the same facts until a declaratory Decree is made.[24] The court read the Decree as a whole and held that an Edict could be declared void by the court by reason of its inconsistency with a Decree.[25] Similarly, in *Awolowo* v. *Federal Minister of Internal Affairs*,[26] the court had to interpret section 21(5)(*c*) of the Constitution of the Federation[27] which provided that an accused person was "entitled to defend himself in person or by legal representatives of his own choice." The court held that under the provision the legal representative chosen if outside Nigeria must be a person who could enter Nigeria as of right. It also stated that such a representative must be someone who was not under any disability. The Supreme Court affirmed the judgment.[28]

In applying the Golden Rule, the courts sometimes construe the word "or" as "and" in such a way as to avoid absurdity.[29] It must be emphasised, however, that the primary object of the court in adopting such construction is to give effect to the intention of the legislature. Although the interpretation enactments contain a presumption that the word "or" is to be construed as a disjunctive word, that presumption is subject to any contrary intention in the statute being interpreted.[30]

---

[23] No. 1 of 1966.
[24] "Note: Challenging the Validity of Decrees and Edicts," *Nigerian Bar Journal*, Vol. VIII (1967), 55 at p. 56.
[25] *Council of the University of Ibadan* v. *Adamolekun* [1967] 1 All N.L.R. 213 at p. 224.
[26] 1962 L.L.R. 177.
[27] Nigeria (Constitution) Order in Council 1960 (S.I. 1960 No. 1652).
[28] *Awolowo* v. *Sarki* [1966] 1 N.L.R. 178.
[29] *Ejoh* v. *I.G.P.* [1963] 1 All N.L.R. 250; *R.* v. *Eze* (1950) 19 N.L.R. 110.
[30] See *e.g.* Interpretation Act 1964 (No. 1 of 1964), ss. 1 and 18(3); *Jammal Steel Structures Ltd.* v. *African Continental Bank Ltd.* [1973] 1 All N.L.R. 208; (1973) 11 S.C. 77.

The Mischief Rule

According to the Mischief Rule, in order to interpret a statute properly, it is necessary "to consider how the law stood when the statute to be construed was passed, what the mischief was for which the old law did not provide and the remedy provided by the statute to cure the mischief."[31] The court is then to construe the statute in such a manner as to "suppress the mischief and advance the remedy . . ."[32]

The principle is applicable only where the meaning of the statutory provision is ambiguous. Thus, in *Balogun* v. *Salami*,[33] the court considered the history of the Registration of Titles Act[34] and said that the ban attending dealings in family land was sale of such land by some members of the family followed by repudiation of the transaction by other members of the family on grounds of absence of the family's consent. The court said that the purpose of the Act was to remove the ban. It then interpreted the provision in the light of this history. Another case in which the principle was applied was *Akerele* v. *I.G.P.*[35] where the court had to interpret the word "accuse" in section 210(*b*) of the Criminal Code.[36] Rejecting the argument that the word meant making a formal accusation by swearing to an information under oath, Ademola J. (as he then was) said "It appears to me that the short history behind this Chapter of the Code is to prohibit indiscriminate accusations of witchcraft and to stop the practice of trial by ordeal and the like by making them punishable."

Other General Principles of Interpretation

It is a general principle that a statute is to be construed in such a manner as not to command doing what is impossible[37] — *Lex non cogit ad impossibilia*.[38] In principle, where a provision is reasonably susceptible of two interpretations and it is found that by one interpretation the provision would be valid and by the other it would be invalid the provision ought to be construed in such a manner as to make it valid. In other words, the statute is to be construed *ut res magis valeat quam pereat*.[39] Provisions being interpreted should not be read in

[31] *Re Mayfair Property Co.* [1898] 2 Ch. 28 at p. 35, cited with approval in *Balogun* v. *Salami* [1963] 1 All N.L.R. 129.

[32] *Heydon's* case (1584) 3 Co. Rep. 7a; 76 E.R.638, the case in which the principle was formulated.

[33] [1963] 1 All N.L.R. 129. See also *Jammal Steel Structures Ltd.* v. *African Continental Bank Ltd.* [1973] 1 All N.L.R. 208; (1973) 11 S.C. 77.

[34] Fed. and Lagos Laws 1958, Cap. 181.

[35] (1955) 21 N.L.R. 37.

[36] Nigeria Laws 1948, Cap. 42.

[37] *C.O.P.* v. *Okoli,* 1966 N.N.L.R. 1.

[38] *i.e.* the law does not compel the doing of impossibilities.

[39] *i.e.* that it may rather have effect than be destroyed. See *Osho* v. *Phillips* [1972] 1 All N.L.R. 276.

isolation.[40] Thus, words are to be construed in their context and any section part of which is being interpreted must be read as a whole.[41] In general, a statute must be read as a whole.[42] Sometimes, it is only by doing so that the court can discover from the statute the intention of the legislature. Where a section being interpreted is not clear, all relevant sections must be considered.[43] Where a provision is ambiguous, earlier statutes *in pari materia*[44] may be referred to in interpreting it.[45]

There are also presumptions of interpretation. One of the presumptive principles is the *Ejusdem Generis* Rule. According to the principle, where particular words of the same class are followed by general words, the general words must be construed to be similar in meaning to the particular words.[46] For instance, in *Nasr* v. *Bouari*[47] the question before the court was whether premises used partly as living accommodation and partly as a night club were premises within the meaning of section 1(1) of the Rent Control (Lagos) Amendment Act 1965.[48] The Act defined "premises" as "a building of any description occupied or used by persons for living or sleeping or other lawful purposes, as the case may be, whether or not at any time it is also occupied or used under any tenancy as a shop or a store . . . " The premises in question were not used as a shop or store. The court had to determine whether "other lawful purposes" meant any lawful purposes other than premises for living or sleeping, or only any lawful purposes of the class of living or sleeping. The court held that "other unlawful purposes" must be confined in meaning to purposes similar to living or sleeping. Accordingly, it was held that premises used partly as a night club were not premises within the meaning of the provision notwithstanding the fact that they were also partly used for living.[49] The courts have stated that the doctrine should be applied with caution.[50] It should be applied only where the application would be consistent with the intention of the legislature.[51] Where the history and structure of the statute strongly indicate that

---

[40] *Council of the University of Ibadan* v. *Adamolekun* [1967] 1 All N.L.R. 213.
[41] See *Nabhan* v. *Nabhan* [1967] 1 All N.L.R. 47 at p. 54.
[42] *Council of the University of Ibadan* v. *Adamolekun* [1967] 1 All N.L.R. 213.
[43] *Akintola* v. *Aderemi* [1962] 1 All N.L.R. 442.
[44] *i.e.* upon the same matter.
[45] *Nasr* v. *Bouari* [1969] 1 All N.L.R. 37 at p. 55,
[46] *Board of Customs and Excise* v. *Viale* [1970] 2 All N.L.R. 53.
[47] [1969] 1 All N.L.R. 35. See also *Jammal Steel Structures Ltd.* v. *African Continental Bank Ltd.* [1973] 1 All N.L.R. 208; (1973) 11 S.C. 77.
[48] No. X of 1965.
[49] See also *Onasile* v. *Sami* [1962] 1 All N.L.R. 272.
[50] *Board of Customs and Excise* v. *Viale* [1970] 2 All N.L.R. 53 at p. 61.
[51] *Ibid.*

the intention of the legislature would be given effect only by applying the doctrine, the doctrine ought to be applied.[52]

Internal Aids

In interpreting a provision of a statute other parts of the statute are referred to by the courts. It must be emphasised, however, that unless otherwise provided by another enactment, for instance, the interpretation enactment — or by the statute whose provisions are being interpreted, only the sections of a statute form part of the enactment. The Interpretation Act 1964[53] applies to every federal enactment in the absence of a contrary intention in the enactment. Similarly, the Interpretation Law[54] of each State applies to every enactment of the State in the absence of a contrary intention in the enactment. The various interpretation laws provide that punctuation forms part of the enactment and that it must be considered in construing a statute.[55] They also provide that a heading or marginal note to a statute does not form part of the enactment and is intended for convenience or reference only.[56] It is proper to refer to the long title and the preamble where the words being interpreted are ambiguous. Where the preamble is declared by the statute to be part of the enactment, it ought to be examined in case of ambiguity.[57] Schedules form part of the enactment if they are incorporated by the enacting sections[58] and they may be referred to when any enacting section being interpreted is ambiguous. Of course a proviso to a section forms part of the section. A section is, therefore, not read as a whole unless the proviso to it is read together with it. It is established that where the main part of the section is plain, a proviso cannot alter the plain meaning[59]; but where the words used in the main part are reasonably susceptible of more than one meaning a proviso ought to be examined for it may show the meaning which the words are intended to bear.[60]

A statute usually contains an interpretation section which normally applies unless the context otherwise requires. The courts some-

---

[52] *Onasile* v. *Sami* [1962] 1 All N.L.R. 272 at p. 276, citing with approval *Attorney-General* v. *Brown* [1920] 1 K.B. 773 at p. 798.

[53] No. 1 of 1964.

[54] See *e.g.* Interpretation Law (Lagos Laws 1973, Cap. 57), s. 1.

[55] See *e.g.* Interpretation Act 1964, s. 3(1).

[56] See *e.g.* Interpretation Act 1964, s. 3(1).

[57] See *e.g. Adejumo* v. *Military Governor, Lagos State* [1972] 1 All N.L.R. 159; Federal Military Government (Supremacy and Enforcement of Powers) Decree 1970 (No. 28 of 1970).

[58] See *e.g.* Criminal Code Law (Lagos Laws 1973, Cap. 31), s. 2 and Schedule.

[59] *Anya* v. *State*, 1966 N.M.L.R. 62; *Nabhan* v. *Nabhan* [1967] 1 All N.L.R. 47 at p. 54.

[60] *Nabhan* v. *Nabhan* [1967] 1 All N.L.R. 47 at p. 54.

times find definitions in interpretation sections misleading.[61]

External Aids

The application of any of the three main principles of interpretation of statutes involves the use of external aids. Dictionaries are generally referred to in ascertaining the usual meanings of words and in determining whether a word is reasonably susceptible of two different meanings. The history of a statute is considered in applying the Mischief Rule.

External statutory aids are contained in the interpretation laws which apply subject to the provisions of the enactments being interpreted. For instance, section 6(1) of the Interpretation Act 1964 states the effect of the repeal of an enactment. It provides, in part, that the repeal of an enactment does not "affect any investigation, legal proceeding or remedy in respect of such right, privilege, obligation, liability, penalty, forfeiture or punishment;" and that "any such investigation, legal proceeding or remedy may be instituted, continued or enforced, and any such penalty, forfeiture or punishment may be imposed, as if the enactment had not been repealed."[62] The interpretation laws also provide that, in general, a statute does not bind the State.[63] Furthermore they provide that words importing the masculine gender are to be construed to include females,[64] that words in the singular include the plural and those in the plural include the singular.[65] By virtue of the Interpretation legislation, where a punishment is prescribed with respect to an offence that punishment is the maximum punishment for the offence, in the absence of a contrary intention in the statute creating the offence.[66] The legislation also defines a number of expressions. Section 18(3) of the Interpretation Act 1964 provides, for instance, that the word "or" and the word "other" are to be construed disjunctively and not as implying similarity.

---

[61] *Aluko* v. *D.P.P., Western Nigeria* [1963] 1 All N.L.R. 398.

[62] Interpretation Act, s. 6(1) (*e*). See also Interpretation Law (Lagos Laws 1973, Cap. 57), s. 6(1)(*e*); Interpretation Law (W.R.N. Laws 1959, Cap. 51), s. 12; Interpretation Law (N.N. Laws 1963, Cap. 52), s. 12; Interpretation Law (E.N. Laws 1963, Cap. 66.), s. 13; *In re Edewor*, 1969 N.M.L.R. 273.

[63] See. *e.g.* Interpretation Law (N.N. Laws 1963, Cap. 52), s. 65.

[64] See *e.g.* Interpretation Act 1964, s. 14(*a*).

[65] See *e.g.* Interpretation Act 1964, s. 14(*b*).

[66] See *e.g.* Interpretation Act 1964, ss. 1 and 14 (*b*).

CHAPTER 4

NIGERIAN LEGISLATION

NIGERIAN legislation consists of statutes and subsidiary legislation. Statutes are laws enacted by the Legislature — the legislative arm of government. Subsidiary legislation is law enacted in the exercise of powers given by a statute. It is also known as subsidiary instrument or delegated legislation. It consists of rules, orders, regulations, bye-laws and other instruments made under the authority of statutes. Examples of subsidiary legislation are rules, orders and regulations made by Ministers, Commissioners under the military government, and Chief Justices.[1] A statute is usually referred to as the principal law in a later statute amending it. A statute under which subsidiary legislation is made is referred to as an enabling statute.

Nigerian statutes consist of:

(a) Ordinances;
(b) Acts;
(c) Laws;
(d) Decrees;
(e) Edicts.

Ordinances are laws passed by the Nigerian Central Legislature before October 1, 1954. The Nigeria (Constitution) Order in Council 1954[2] introduced a federal constitution into Nigeria. By virtue of section 57 of the Constitution of the Federation scheduled to the Order, any Ordinance in force on October 1, 1954 was to be deemed to be a law made by the Federal Legislature or a law made by a Regional Legislature or a law made separately by the Federal and Regional Legislatures, roughly in accordance with the distribution of legislative powers under the Constitution. Under the Nigeria (Constitution) Order in Council 1960[3] all Ordinances dealing with matters within the exclusive legislative competence of the Federal Legislature (Parliament) were deemed to be enactments of the Federal Legislature and, in general, all Ordinances within the legislative competence of the Regional Legislature were deemed Regional laws.[4] Each of the Legislatures of Western, Northern and Eastern Nigeria had to determine whether any particular Ordinance made before 1954 was within its legislative competence before publishing it as a Regional law in the revised edition of the Laws in force in the

---

[1] See *e.g.* the Right-Hand Traffic Regulations 1972 (L.N. 12 of 1972).
[2] S.I. 1954 No. 1146.
[3] S.I. 1960 No. 1652.
[4] *Ibid.* s. 3(1) and (6). See also Constitution of the Federation (Act No. 20 of 1963), ss. 154 and 156.

Region.[5] The courts may hold that an Ordinance so published was not within the competence of the Regional Legislature.[6] Some Ordinances within the legislative competence of the legislatures were not included in the revised editions. Such Ordinances were in force as Regional laws and they are now in force as State laws in so far as they have not been repealed. Thus, the Criminal Procedure Ordinance[7] is in force in Ogun State. By virtue of the Designation of Ordinances Act 1961[8] where an Ordinance made before October 1, 1954 was deemed to be an enactment of the Federal Legislature and was still in force on October 1, 1960 it was to be known as an Act. The Act did not affect such Ordinances in their application as Regional laws where the Ordinances were also deemed to be Regional laws. Such laws were still known as Ordinances in their application as Regional laws where they were not included in the revised editions of the laws. Thus, with respect to State offences, the Criminal Procedure Ordinance, and not the Criminal Procedure Act[9] was in force in Western Nigeria and is now in force in Ogun, Ondo and Oyo States. But a State law may provide for the application of such Acts in place of the Ordinances. Thus, the Criminal Procedure Act applied in Bendel State with respect to State offences.[10]

An Act, as Nigerian legislation, is an enactment made, or deemed to be made, by the Federal Legislature before January 16, 1966.[11] In general, a law is simply any enactment made by the Legislature of a Region or having effect as if made by that legislature, or any subordinate legislation made under such an enactment. But the term "Law" is defined in the Interpretation Law of Lagos State to include any Edict and any subordinate legislation made under the Edict.[12] A Decree is an enactment made by the Federal Military Government. An Edict is an enactment made a Military Governor or by the Administrator of the former East-Central State.

Decrees now constitute the supreme law of the land. Such parts of the Constitution of the Federation and the Constitutions of the former Regions that are in operation apply only by virtue of Decrees.[13]

No court is entitled to inquire into the validity of a Decree or of

---

[5] See *e.g.* W.R.N. Laws 1959, Vol. I, Preface.

[6] W.R.N. Laws 1959, p. 11.

[7] Nigeria Laws 1948, Cap. 43.

[8] No. 57 of 1961.

[9] Fed. and Lagos Laws 1958, Cap. 43.

[10] High Court Law 1964 (No. 9 of 1964) (M.W.N.), s. 12.

[11] A military revolution occurred in Nigeria on January 15, 1966. See Federal Military Government (Supremacy and Enforcement of Powers) Decree 1970 (No. 28 of 1970), Preamble.

[12] See Interpretation Law (Lagos Laws 1973, Cap. 57), s. 18(1).

[13] Constitution (Basic Provisions) Decree 1975 (No. 32 of 1975), s. 14(2); Constitution (Suspension and Modification) Decree 1966 (No. 1 of 1966), s. 1.

any subsidiary legislation made under a Decree.[14] But the court may determine whether a Decree is inconsistent with a later Decree with a view to deciding whether the earlier Decree has been repealed impliedly. No court is entitled to inquire into the validity of an Edict or of any subsidiary legislation made under it except on the ground that the Edict is inconsistent with the provisions of a Decree.[15] Where a law made before January 16, 1966 by a Regional Legislature (or having effect as if so enacted) or made after that date by a Military Governor (or the Administrator of the former East-Central State) is inconsistent with any law validly made by Parliament[16] before that date (or having effect as if so enacted) or with any law made by the Federal Military Government after that date, the law made by Parliament or the law made by the Federal Military Government prevails and the Regional enactment or the Edict made by the Military Governor (or Administrator) is void to the extent of its inconsistency.[17]

A statute consists of several parts. The part known as the long title usually states the general purposes of the statute. An example is "An Act to provide for the establishment of a Teaching Hospital for Lagos and of a Management Board for the Hospital; and for purposes connected therewith."[18] The preamble usually indicates, in some detail, the purpose of the statute and the reason for passing it. For instance, the preamble to the Criminal Procedure (Northern Region) Act 1960[19] reads:

"Whereas the Legislature of the Northern Region has repealed or proposes to repeal the provisions of the Criminal Procedure Ordinance to the extent that they take effect as the law of that Region, and to replace the same with a new Code of Criminal Procedure; And whereas in respect of Federal offences it is expedient to assimilate the practice and procedure of the courts of the Northern Region with the practice and procedure of those courts in respect of Regional offences; And whereas it is expedient to make new provision in relation to the jurisdiction and powers of the courts of the Northern Region in respect of Federal offences ... "

The inclusion of preambles in statutes is no longer common. The enacting sections constitute the most important part of the statute.

---

[14] Constitution (Basic Provisions) Decree 1975, s. 4.
[15] See Constitution (Basic Provisions) Decree 1975, s. 4; *Adejumo* v. *Military Governor, Lagos State* [1972] 1 All N.L.R. 159.
[16] *i.e.* the Federal Legislature.
[17] Constitution (Basic Provisions) Decree 1975, s. 1(4).
[18] Lagos University Teaching Hospital Act 1961 (No. 70 of 1961).
[19] No. 20 of 1960.

They are the actual text of the statute. They make new law, modify existing law, declare law or repeal existing law. They include interpretation sections, sections stating the extent of operation of the statute and commencement sections which state when the statute comes into operation or when it was deemed to have come into operation, if retroactive. Sometimes a date appears in square brackets immediately below the long title. It is the date of commencement of the statute. Side notes, otherwise known as marginal notes, appear beside sections. They are used for the purpose of facilitating reference. Sometimes, headings are used to separate one group of closely-related sections from other groups of sections. The short title is a short form of the title. It is stated for the purpose of citation. Schedules contain details of matters dealt with by the enacting sections. They are usually used when the inclusion of details in the enacting sections would make the statute clumsy or unwieldy.

Law-making under the military government is a comparatively easy exercise. It does not involve publication of bills or heated debates (involving amendment to bills) in legislative Houses. A Decree is made when it is signed by the Head of the Federal Military Government and an Edict is made when it is signed by the Military Governor of the State.[20] This comparative ease accounts for several faults found in legislation today. Decrees are amended so often that one sometimes wonders whether the drafting was done without examining in detail what the legislature intended to achieve by the legislation.[21]

Legislation is the most important instrument of legal development. It has a tremendous effect on all the other sources of law. It can readily alter their content. It is also a useful tool for the social, economic and technological development of the country.[22]

There is need for a detailed study of existing Nigerian legislation with a view to determining whether it serves the purpose of the country's developmental goals. As a step in this direction the Law Commission Edict 1975[23] was made by the Military Governor of the

---

[20] Constitution (Basic Provisions) Decree 1975, s. 3.
[21] See *e.g.* States (Creation and Transitional Provisions) Decree, 1967 (No. 14 of 1967) made on May 27, 1967 and amended by the following enactments: (a) the States (Creation and Transitional Provisions) (Amendment) Decree 1967 (No. 19 of 1967) made on May 31, 1967, (b) the Constitution (Miscellaneous Provisions) Decree 1967 (No. 20 of 1967) made on June 8, 1967, (c) the States (Creation and Transitional Provisions) (Amendment) (No. 2) Decree 1967 (No. 25 of 1967) made on June 29, 1967 and (d) the States (Creation and Transitional Provisions) (Amendment) Decree 1974 (No. 16 of 1974).
[22] See *e.g.* National Science and Technology Development Agency Decree 1977 (No. 5 of 1977); Nigerian Enterprises Promotion Decree 1977 (No. 3 of 1977); Nigeria Atomic Energy Commission Decree 1976 (No. 46 of 1976).
[23] No. 8 of 1975.

Western State in April 1975. By virtue of the States (Creation and Transitional Provisions) Decree 1976[24] the Edict now applies in Ogun, Ondo and Oyo States. A law commission established under the Edict is required to keep the law under review with a view to its systematic development and reform. Before the creation of States in 1976, the Law Commission of the former Western State had started functioning. It is worthy of note that some States which had no collected laws consisting of a revised edition of the legislation in force in the States have taken steps to ensure that volumes of such collected laws are prepared. A revised edition of the laws of Lagos State was published in 1974.[25] A revised edition of the laws of Bendel State has been prepared under the Revised Edition (Laws of the Bendel State of Nigeria) Edict 1976.[26] A revised edition of the laws of the former South-Eastern State (now Cross River State) is being prepared.[27] A committee has been appointed to prepare a new revised edition of the laws of the Federation.[28] The committee was appointed by section 1(1) of the Revised Edition (Laws of the Federation) Decree 1971.[29]

[24] No. 12 of 1976.
[25] The edition was prepared by Sir Lionel Brett, a retired judge of the Supreme Court who was appointed Commissioner for that purpose. See Revised Edition (Laws of Lagos State of Nigeria) Edict 1970 (No. 15 of 1970), s. 1(1).
[26] See Revised Edition (Laws of the Bendel State of Nigeria) Edict 1976 (No. 2 of 1976), s. 3(1) which appointed Sir Lionel Brett Commissioner for the purpose of the preparation of the edition.
[27] See Revised Edition (Laws of South-Eastern State of Nigeria) Edict 1975 (No. 15 of 1975), s. 1(1) which appointed Sir Lionel Brett Special Commissioner for the preparation of the edition.
[28] The committee was appointed in 1971.
[29] No. 52 of 1971.

CHAPTER 5

ENGLISH LAW

A. THE RECEIVED ENGLISH LAW

THE received English Law as a source of Nigerian law[1] consists of the common law, doctrines of equity, statutes and subsidiary legislation. It has been introduced into Nigerian law by Nigerian legislation. The history of the reception dates back to 1863 when Ordinance No. 3 of that year introduced English law into the Colony of Lagos. Usually, where a court is empowered to administer the received law, provisions relating to its application by the court are contained in the enactment which created the court and subsidiary legislation made under the enactment. For instance, various High Court enactments, the magistrates' courts Laws of the southern States and the District Courts legislation of the northern States contain such provisions. The current Nigerian enactments that have received English law include the Law (Miscellaneous Provisions) Act[2] in force as federal law throughout the country; the Law (Miscellaneous Provisions) Law[3] and the High Court Law[4] both of Lagos State; the Law of England (Application) Law[5] in force in Bendel, Ogun, Ondo and Oyo States; the High Court Law[6] of the northern States; and the High Court Law[7] in force in Anambra, Cross River, Imo and Rivers States. The reception provisions applicable in each jurisdiction are substantially the same in wording as the reception provisions in force in the other jurisdictions except that the Law of England (Application) Law does not receive English statutes. The various reception enactments will now be examined in some detail. First, it is intended to deal with those enactments which have received in general terms the common law, the doctrines of equity and the statutes of general application that were in force in England on January 1, 1900.

---

[1] The received English law as a source of Nigerian law excludes English law received by being enacted or re-enacted as Nigerian legislation. The latter type of received English law is not a source of Nigerian law. It is the resulting Nigerian legislation that is a source of the law. See e.g. the Defamation Act 1952 (15 & 16 Geo. 6 & 1 Eliz. 2, c. 66) whose provisions were re-enacted as part of the Defamation Law (W.R.N. Laws 1959, Cap. 33).

[2] See Interpretation Act 1964 (No. 1 of 1964), s. 28.

[3] Lagos Laws 1973, Cap. 65.

[4] Lagos Laws 1973, Cap. 52.

[5] W.R.N. Laws 1959, Cap. 60, s. 3. See also High Court (Civil Procedure) Rules (W.R.N. Laws 1959, Cap. 44), Ord. 35, r. 10.

[6] N.N. Laws 1963, Cap. 49, ss. 28, 29 and 35.

[7] E.N. Laws 1963, Cap. 61, s. 15.

Section 2 of the Law (Miscellaneous Provisions) Law[8] provides as follows:

> "2(1) Subject to the provisions of this section and except in so far as other provision is made by any Federal or State enactment, the common law of England and the doctrines of equity, together with the statutes of general application that were in force in England on the first day of January, 1900, shall be in force in the Lagos State.
>
> (2) The statutes of general application referred to in subsection (1) together with any other Act of Parliament with respect to a matter within the legislative competence of the Lagos State which has been extended or applied to the Lagos State shall be in force so far only as the limits of local jurisdiction and local circumstances shall permit and subject to any Federal or State law.
>
> (3) For the purpose of facilitating the application of the said Imperial laws they shall be read with such formal verbal alterations not affecting the substance as to names, localities, courts, officers, persons, moneys, penalties and otherwise as may be necessary to render the same applicable to the circumstances."

Unlike the above provision, section 28 of the High Court Law of the northern States mentions the received common law simply as "the common law" and not as "the common law of England." That is the only reception law which omits the words "of England" in relation to the common law but the term "common law" is interpreted by the courts as the common law of England. Having regard to Nigeria's historical link with England,[9] the term could not, without more, have been intended to mean anything other than the common law of England. Similarly, although of all the general reception provisions mentioned above,[10] it is only section 3 of the Law of England (Application) Law[11] that refers expressly to England in relation to the doctrines of equity, it is clear that doctrines received are the English doctrines of equity.

With respect to the date January 1, 1900, it is clear from section 2 of the Law (Miscellaneous Provisions) Law that the date applies to the statutes only and not to the "common law" or "equity" both of which are separated from "the statutes" by the use of the words "together with." But it is the word "and" that is used in the equivalent part of this provision in section 15 of the High Court Law[12] of the

---

[8] Lagos Laws 1973, Cap. 65.
[9] See Chap. 2, above.
[10] See p. 69, above.
[11] W.R.N. Laws 1959, Cap. 60.
[12] E.N. Laws 1963, Cap. 61.

eastern States.[13] This provision of the High Court Law is capable of two interpretations in respect of the date. The first is that the date applies to all the three types of English law mentioned and the second is that the date applies to the statutes only. But an examination of the reception enactments in force in the other jurisdictions suggests that the ambiguity should be resolved in favour of the view that the date applies to the statutes only, particularly because the wording of the High Court Law of the eastern States does not clearly suggest an intention, in relation to date, on the part of the Legislature that passed it, different from that of the respective Legislatures which passed the reception enactments in force in the other jurisdictions. For instance, under section 28 of the High Court Law[14] of the northern States, each of the three types of English law is listed in a separate paragraph and the date is mentioned only in the paragraph listing the statutes.[15] Section 3 of the Law of England (Application) Law of Bendel, Ogun, Ondo and Oyo States which receives only the common law and equity does not contain any date. It seems obvious, therefore, that the date is omitted because it applied to the statutes only, under the pre-existing law.[16]

Another point which should be mentioned in relation to the application of the common law and equity in Nigeria is that where there is a conflict between a rule of the common law and a doctrine of equity on the same matter the doctrine of equity prevails, generally.[17]

It should also be stated that in determining any applicable rule of the common law of England or any applicable English doctrine of equity, the decisions of the courts of England are a mere guide to the Nigerian courts.[18] The Nigerian courts are free to hold that what is accepted by the English courts including the highest court of Eng-

---

[13] The eastern States, that is, the States in the eastern part of the country are Anambra, Cross River, Imo and Rivers.

[14] N.N. Laws 1963, Cap. 49.

[15] The section provides in its application to Kano State, for instance, as follows:
"28. Subject to the provisions of any written law and in particular of this section and of sections 26, 33 and 35 of this Law —
  (a) the common law;
  (b) the doctrines of equity; and
  (c) the statutes of general application which were in force in England on the 1st day of January, 1900,
shall, in so far as they relate to any matter with respect to which the Military Governor of Kano State is for the time being competent to make laws, be in force within the jurisdiction of the court."

[16] *i.e.* Western Region High Court Law 1955 (No. 3 of 1955), s. 14. *Contra* Robert B. Seidman, "A Note on the Construction of the Gold Coast Reception Statute," [1969] J.A.L. 45 at p. 49. See A. N. Allott, *New Essays in African Law* (1970), pp. 60-69.

[17] See, *e.g.* the High Court Law (N.N. Laws 1963, Cap. 49), s. 31.

[18] See *Alli* v. *Okulaja* [1970] 2 All N.L.R. 35; Jill Cottrell, "An End to Slavishness? A Note on *Alli* v. *Okulaya*" [1973] J.A.L. 247.

land (the House of Lords) as the common law rule or equitable doctrine on a particular matter is not in fact the English rule or doctrine on the matter.[19]

In all the jurisdictions "statutes of general application that[20] were in force in England on the first day of January, 1900" have been received, except that such statutes are not received in Bendel, Ogun, Ondo and Oyo States in so far as they deal with matters within the legislative competence of those States.[21] In order to fall within this class of statutes, a statute must have been in force in England on January 1, 1900. A statute in force on that date does not fall outside the class merely because it is not applicable in other parts of the United Kingdom. In spite of the position of the words "in England," the test of general application in terms of territory is England.[22] The courts have, however, not found it easy to determine the full ambit of the words "of general application." The question is, what further test must be satisfied by a statute applicable throughout England before it could be a statute of general application within the meaning of the reception enactments? Cases in which attempts have been made to interpret the words will now be examined. In *Attorney-General* v. *John Holt & Co.*,[23] Osborne C.J. approved of a "rough but not infallible test" suggested in a previous decision. The test was couched in the following words:

> "Two preliminary questions can, however, be put by way of a rough, but not infallible test, viz.: (1) by what Courts is the Statute applied in England? and (2) to what classes of the community in England does it apply? If on the 1st January, 1900, an Act of Parliament were applied by all civil or criminal Courts, as the case may be, to all classes of the community, there is a strong likelihood that it is in force within the jurisdiction. If on the other hand, it were applied only by certain Courts (*e.g.*, a Statute regulating procedure), or only to certain classes of the community (*e.g.*, an Act regulating a particular trade), the probability is that it would not be held to be locally applicable."

This suggested test is faulty in many respects. Presumably for this reason many of its aspects have never been relied upon. For instance, it has never been held by any court in any reported case — not even in *Attorney-General* v. *John Holt & Co.* itself — that an enactment is

---

[19] *Ibid.* Compare A. E. W. Park, *The Sources of Nigerian Law* (1963), pp. 62-64.
[20] The word "that" is used in substitution for the word "which" contained in other Nigerian enactments that receive English statutes of general application.
[21] See *e.g.* Law of England (Application) Law (W.R.N. Laws 1959, Cap. 60), s. 4.
[22] *Young* v. *Abina* (1940) 6 W.A.C.A. 180. *Contra Okpaku* v. *Okpaku*, 12 W.A.C.A. 137, a case decided *per incuriam*. See *Lawal* v. *Younan* [1961] 1 All N.R. 245.
[23] (1910) 2 N.L.R. 1 at p. 21.

not a statute of general application merely because it was not applied by all civil or criminal courts in England. Contrary to the requirement of the rough test, English statutes applied by only a limited class of courts in England, particularly statutes regulating procedure, have been held to be statutes of general application in England. For instance, in *Inspector-General of Police* v. *Kamara*,[24] the West African Court of Appeal held that the Summary Jurisdiction Act 1948,[25] a statute which applied in England to only magistrates' courts, was a statute of general application. Similarly, in *Ribeiro* v. *Chahin*,[26] the West African Court of Appeal held that the Common Law Procedure Act 1852 was a statute of general application that was in force in England on July 24, 1874.[27] The statement, in the test, that a statute "applied only by certain Courts (*e.g.* a Statute regulating procedure)," would probably not be held to be "locally applicable" was, of course an *obiter dictum* for the statute in question, the Crown Suits Act 1769[28] was applied by all courts in England. Similarly, there is no binding authority for the view, expressed in the rough test, that if a statute applied "only to certain classes of the community (*e.g.* an Act regulating a particular trade)" it would probably not be held to be a statute of general application.

The case law on this subject, however, appears to support the view expressed in the test in *Attorney-General* v. *John Holt & Co.*[29] that an English statute which applied to all classes of the community in England on January 1, 1900 would very likely be held to be a statute of general application. For instance, in *Lawal* v. *Younan*,[30] the Federal Supreme Court held that the Fatal Accidents Act 1846[31] and the Fatal Accidents Act 1864[32] both of which applied to all classes of the community in England were statutes of general application in England. Similarly, in *Braithwaite* v. *Folarin*[33] the West African Court of Appeal in holding that the Fraudulent Conveyances Act 1571[34] was a statute of general application said, "The Statute in question is in our view a Statute of general application, applying as it does quite generally to ordinary affairs and dealings of men without any qualification or speciality restricting its application." Furthermore, in

[24] (1943) 2 W.A.C.A. 185.
[25] 11 & 12 Vict. c. 43.
[26] (1954) 14 W.A.C.A. 476.
[27] That was the date fixed in relation to the reception, in the Gold Coast, of English statutes of general application.
[28] 9 Geo. 3, c. 16 (Nullum Tempus Act).
[29] (1910) 2 N.L.R. 1 at p. 21.
[30] [1961] 1 All N.L.R. 245.
[31] 9 and 10 Vict. c. 93.
[32] 27 and 28 Vict. c. 95.
[33] (1938) 4 W.A.C.A. 76.
[34] 13 Eliz. 1, c. 5.

Young v. *Abina*,[35] the West African Court of Appeal said of the Land Transfer Act 1897[36]: "The Land Transfer Act of 1897 applied quite generally to all estates in England of persons dying after 1st January 1898. It is difficult to see how a statute could be of more 'general application' in England than that, and it was in force in England on 1st January, 1900."[37] In fact, the statute applied to the estates of persons who died after 1897 holding legal interests in land. It has, however, been argued that because persons dying after a particular date holding legal interests in land were not "all classes of the community" the court was wrong in stating that it was difficult to see how a statute could be of more general application.[38] It is submitted that this ingenious argument takes a narrow view of the extent of application of statutes. Every statute deals with a particular subject-matter. With respect to its subject-matter — holding legal interests in land at the time of death — the Act applied to all classes of persons without any distinction with effect from its date of commencement. Every person was a potential owner of a legal interest in land to whom the Act could apply. But if at the time of his death a person did not hold a legal interest in land the Act would not in fact apply to him. It is submitted that a statute applies to all classes of the community if, with respect to its subject-matter, all classes of persons are potentially within the ambit of the statute even if it is unlikely that the statute will ever be applied to a particular person or a particular class of persons. It is only on this broad view of the extent of application of statutes that any statute can be said to apply to all classes of the community.[39]

In the light of the decisions of the courts, therefore, a statute would probably be held to be a statute of general application that was in force in England on January 1, 1900, if the following conditions are satisfied:

(a) That the statute was in force in England on January 1, 1900;

and (b) That in respect of its subject-matter, it applied to all classes of the community in England on that date.

But the case law on this subject does not support the converse of the second condition. It is not the law that a statute would be held to be outside the class of statutes of general application by reason only that it applied to only limited classes of the community. Indeed, it has been suggested that a statute which satisfies the first condition

---

[35] (1940) 6 W.A.C.A. 180 at pp. 183-184.

[36] 60 and 61 Vict. c. 65.

[37] See also *Olanguno* v. *Ogunsanya* [1970] 1 All N.L.R. 223 at pp. 226-227; *Ajao* v. *Sonola* (1973) 5 S.C. 119 at pp. 122-124.

[38] A. E. W. Park, *op. cit.* (n. 19, above), p. 28.

[39] See *e.g.* the Infants Relief Act 1874 (37 & 38 Vict, c. 62).

should be held to be a statute of general application if it applied to all members of any class of the community in England on January 1, 1900.[40]

There is no binding authority in the case law mentioning any complete specific criteria for the determination of statutes of general application in force in England on January 1, 1900. Having regard to the apparent reluctance of the courts to explain in detail the principles on which their decisions on this matter are based,[41] it is unlikely that there would be any such binding authority in the near future.[42]

It would have been observed that statutes of general application are received in general terms, without reference to their subject-matter. Another class of received English statutes consists of statutes received by reference to their subject-matter. For instance, in all the States except Bendel, Ogun, Ondo and Oyo, the received English law of probate consists of the common law, equity, statutes and subsidiary legislation.[43] Thus, section 33 of the High Court Law[44] of the northern States provides:

> "The jurisdiction of the High Court in probate cases and proceedings may subject to the provisions of the Law and especially section 34[45] and to rules of court be exercised by the court in conformity with the law and practice[46] for the time being in force in England."

Similarly, the law of probate (including statutes) for the time being in force in England is applicable in Lagos State.[47]

The courts have construed the words "for the time being in force in England" as "in force in England at any particular time when the

---

[40] A. E. W. Park, *op. cit.* (n. 19, above), p. 28.

[41] *Lawal* v. *Younan* [1961] 1 All N.L.R. 245 at p. 255.

[42] A number of cases in which the question whether a statute was one of general application in England or not was considered were listed, together with the statutes involved, by Brett F.J. in *Lawal* v. *Younan* [1961] 1 All N.L.R. 245 at pp. 254-255.

[43] By virtue of s. 4 of the Law of England (Application) Law, English statutes dealing with matters within the legislative competence of Bendel, Ogun, Ondo and Oyo States are not in force in those States. Probate matters are within the legislative competence of the States.

[44] N.N. Laws 1963, Cap. 49.

[45] s. 34 deals with the application of customary law.

[46] Provisions of Nigerian legislation introducing the common law and equity into Nigeria in general terms are subject to reception provisions introducing the rules of the common law and equity on specified matters into Nigeria. See *e.g.* High Court Law (N.N. Laws 1963, Cap. 49), s. 28. Where the rules of the common law and equity on a specified matter are received together with the English statutory law on the matter, the statutory law prevails in case of conflict between it and a rule of the common law or equity. Of course, where there is a conflict between the received common law and the received equity on the same matter equity prevails generally.

[47] High Court Law (Lagos Laws 1973, Cap. 52), s. 16.

received law is to be applied" and not as "in force in England at the date of comencement of the reception statute."[48] The English law of probate in force in Lagos State and in each of the northern States is, therefore, the one currently in force in England. Any change in the English law automatically applies in those States.[49]

With respect to the eastern States, the reception statute relating to probate contains a limiting date. It provides as follows:

"The jurisdiction of the Court in probate causes and matters shall, subject to the law and to any rules of Court, be exercised in conformity with the law and practice in force in England on the thirtieth day of September, 1960."[50]

It is, thus, clear that changes in the English law of probate after that date have no effect in any of the eastern States.

In addition to the common law, the doctrines of equity, statutes of general application and statutes on specified matters, Nigerian reception statutes have introduced English subsidiary legislation. Such legislation applies throughout the country by virtue of Federal and State enactments. For instance, Rule 36 of Order VII of the Supreme Court Rules 1961[51] provides with respect to civil appeals that where no other provision is made by the Rules the rules of procedure and practice "for the time being"[52] in force in the Court of Appeal in England are to apply in so far as they are "not inconsistent with these Rules . . . " Similarly, the rules of procedure and practice for the time being in force in the High Court of Justice in England apply to the High Courts of Bendel, Lagos, Ogun, Ondo and Oyo States and also to the High Courts of the northern States, subject to local enactment. For example, Rule 10 of Order 35 of the High Court (Civil Procedure) Rules[53] of Bendel,[54] Ogun, Ondo and Oyo States provides as follows:

---

[48] *Taylor* v. *Taylor* (1935) 2 W.A.C.A. 348 at p. 349. See also *Whyte* v. *Commissioner of Police*, 1966 N.M.L.R.215 at p. 218 where the court in interpreting Ord. 35 r. 10, of the High Court (Civil Procedure) Rules (W.R.N. Laws 1959, Cap. 44) which provides for the application of the "procedure and practice for the time being in force in England" said that "for the time being" meant "current at the time the rule is to be applied."

[49] The position was similar throughout Nigeria with respect to matrimonial causes other than those governed by customary law until the commencement of the Matrimonial Causes Decree 1970 (No. 18 of 1970). Such causes are within the Exclusive Legislative List under the Constitution of the Federation (Act No. 20 of 1963).

[50] High Court Law (E.N. Laws 1963, Cap. 61), s. 17.

[51] L.N. 96 of 1961.

[52] See n. 48, above.

[53] W.R.N. Laws 1959, Cap. 44.

[54] By virtue of s. 53(3) of the High Court Law 1964 (No. 9 of 1964) of Bendel State, the rules are to apply in that State as they were on February 12, 1964 until rules are made under the law.

"Where no provision is made by these rules or by any other written laws[55] the procedure and practice in force for the time being in the High Court of Justice in England shall so far as they can be conveniently applied, be in force in the Court: provided that no practice which is inconsistent with these rules shall be applied.[56]

But in the eastern States, the applicable English rules of practice and procedure with respect to the High Courts are not the rules "for the time being in force" in England but the rules observed in the High Court of Justice in England on September 30, 1960.[57]

The received English law applies subject to Nigerian legislation. Thus section 2 of the Law (Miscellaneous Provisions) Law[58] states that the common law, the doctrines of equity and the statutes of general application are applicable subject to the provisions of the section "and except in so far as other provision is made by any Federal or State enactment."[59] Accordingly, to the extent that the subject-matter of a rule of the received law is dealt with by a local enactment, the local enactment and not the received law is the applicable law. Moreover, where there is a conflict between the received law and a local enactment, the local enactment prevails. By virtue of the reception statutes, therefore, the received English law applies subject to the application of customary law in appropriate cases.[60] Nigerian legislation is gradually reducing the content of the received English law as a source of Nigerian law. For instance, the common law doctrine of *interesse termini*[61] was abolished by section 163 of the Property and Conveyancing Law[62] and the Defamation Act 1961[63] modified the common law.[64] Similarly, some statutes of general application were repealed impliedly or expressly. Thus, section 7(1)

---

[55] "Written law" includes State or Federal legislation but excludes any Act of Parliament of the U.K. extending to Nigeria, any Order of the Queen in Council, Royal Charter or Royal Letters Patent. See Interpretation Law (W.R.N. Laws 1959, Cap. 51), s. 3.

[56] See also High Court Law (N.N. Laws 1963, Cap. 49), s. 35; High Court Law (Lagos Laws 1973, Cap. 52), s. 16.

[57] High Court Law (E.N. Laws 1963, Cap. 61), s. 16.

[58] Lagos Laws 1973, Cap. 65.

[59] See also High Court Law (Lagos Laws 1973, Cap. 52), s. 16.

[60] See *e.g.* High Court Law (N.N. Laws 1963, Cap. 49), ss. 28, 29 and 33, *Contra Adesubokan* v. *Yunusa*, 1971 N.N.L.R. 71.

[61] An *interesse termini* was an interest — a right of entry — which a lessee of land acquired in the land by virtue of the lease before he was actually in possession of the land.

[62] W.R.N. Laws 1959, Cap. 100. See *Adeponle* v. *Saidi* (1956) 1 F.S.C. 79.

[63] No. 66 of 1961.

[64] The Act was based on the Defamation Act 1952 (15 & 16 Geo. 6 and 1 Eliz. 2, c. 66). See also Law Reform (Contracts) Act 1961 (No. 64 of 1961) which modified the common law by re-enacting provisions of the Law Reform (Frustrated Contracts) Act 1943 (6 & 7 Geo. 6, c. 40).

of the Obscene Publications Act 1961[65] as affected by section 4(1) of the Lagos State (Applicable Laws) Edict 1968[66] provided as follows:

"To the extent that the Obscene Publications Act, 1857[67] is in force in the Lagos State as a statute of general application that Act shall cease to have effect and is hereby repealed."[68]

An example of implied repeal is found in section 2 of the Criminal Justice (Miscellaneous Provisions) Decree 1966.[69] By creating the offence of obtaining credit by fraud, the Decree impliedly repealed section 13(1) of the Debtors Act 1869[70] in its application to Lagos.

Local circumstances constitute another limitation to the application of the received English statutes. Thus, with respect to Lagos State, section 2(2) of the Law (Miscellaneous Provisions) Law[71] provides that the "statutes of general application . . . shall be in force so far only as the limits of local jurisdiction and local circumstances shall permit and subject to any Federal or State law." No doubt, some English statutes are unsuitable for application in Nigeria by reason of the difference between the circumstances prevailing in England and those prevailing in Nigeria. Where a particular factor essential to the application of an English statute is not present in Nigeria, the courts would hold that local circumstances have not permitted its application. For example, the Bankruptcy Act 1883[72] is not in force in Nigeria because the machinery for its application is not available in the country. Brett F.J. in *Lawal* v. *Younan*[73] expressed the view that the "Court would be free to hold that local circumstances did not permit a statute to be in force if it produced results which were manifestly unreasonable or contrary to the intention of the statute."[74] It should be stressed, however, that the fact that some difficulties are encountered in applying an English statute

---

[65] No. 51 of 1961. See now Criminal Code (Lagos Laws 1973, Cap. 31), ss. 233B-233F.

[66] No. 2 of 1968.

[67] 20 & 21 Vict, c. 83.

[68] See also s. 5(6) of the Law Reform Contracts Act 1961 (No. 64 of 1961) which expressly repealed s. 4 of the Statute of Frauds 1677 (29 Car. 2, c. 3).

[69] No. 84 of 1966.

[70] 32 and 33 Vict, c. 62. See P.E.O. Bassey, "Obtaining Credit by Fraud in Nigerian Law," *Nigerian Bar Journal*, Vol. IV, No. 2 (1963), p. 21.

[71] Lagos Laws 1973, Cap. 65.

[72] 46 & 47 Vict. c. 52.

[73] [1961] 1 All N.L.R. 245 at p. 257.

[74] See *Jex* v. *McKinney* (1889) 14 App.Cas. 77 where the Judicial Committee of the Privy Council in holding that the Mortmain Act 1735 (9 Geo. 2, c. 36), a statute of general application, was not in force in British Honduras said that it "was framed for reasons affecting the land and society of England, and not for reasons applying to a new colony." The application of the statute would have resulted in a declaration that the gift of land to certain churches was invalid.

in Nigeria does not mean that local circumstances do not permit its application.[75] Obviously, difficulties do arise in some cases because the statutes were made for England in the light of circumstances which are in some cases much different from circumstances prevailing in Nigeria. If a statute of general application is otherwise applicable, it is the court's duty to solve problems concerning its application in Nigeria in so far as the application would not defeat the purpose of the statute.[76]

The received English statutes apply "so far only as the limits of the local jurisdiction... permit." That the words "limits of the local jurisdiction" do not refer to legislative competence appears clear from section 29 of the High Court Law[77] of each of the northern States which expressly provides that the application of the "Imperial laws" within the legislative competence of the State is subject to the limits of the local jurisdiction. Thus, the words "limits of the local jurisdiction" are not to be construed to mean legislative competence. The words appear superfluous. They may be construed as reference to the rule against extra-territorial legislation applicable to dependent territories but retained in error after the attainment of independence by the country.[78]

The issue now arises whether the provisions relating to local circumstances and local jurisdiction apply to the common law and equity. Section 2(2) of the Law (Miscellaneous Provisions) Law which re-enacted substantially section 45(2) of the Law (Miscellaneous Provisions) Act contains the words "statutes of general application referred to in subsection (1) together with any other Act of Parliament" in substitution for the words "Imperial laws." Presumably, the purpose of this substitution effected in 1972[79] was to resolve doubts that had arisen as to the meaning of "Imperial laws." Similarly, section 15(2)(*a*) of the High Court Law[80] of the eastern States contains the words "Statutes of general application or other Acts of Parliament" in place of the words "Imperial laws." Section 3 of the Law of England (Application) Law[81] which receives only the common law and equity does not mention "Imperial laws." Although section 45(2) of the Law (Miscellaneous Provisions) Act, a Federal law

[75] *Lawal* v. *Younan* [1961] 1 All N.L.R. 245 at p. 250.
[76] Compare *Chief Young Dede* v. *African Association* (1910) 1 N.L.R. 130; *Adeoye* v. *Adeoye* 1962 N.R.N.L.R. 63.
[77] N.N. Laws 1963, Cap. 49.
[78] A. E. W. Park, *op. cit.* (n. 19, above), p. 30.
[79] Lagos State (Adaptation of Laws) (Miscellaneous Provisions) Order 1972 (L.S.L.N. No. 16 of 1972). By an oversight, presumably, the words "Imperial laws" in s. 45(3) of the Law (Miscellaneous Provisions) Act in-its application to Lagos State were not altered by the 1972 Order.
[80] E.N. Laws 1963, Cap. 61.
[81] W.R.N. Laws 1959, Cap. 60.

and section 29(1) of the High Court Law[82] of the northern States mention "Imperial laws" as laws which are to apply subject to the limits of the local jurisdiction and to local circumstances, section 45(3) of the Act and section 29(2) of the Law provide that the "Imperial laws" are to be read with verbal alterations. The idea of reading a law normally suggests reading an enactment and in the absence of unambiguous words expressly stating that unenacted law consisting of the common law and equity is to be read, it is suggested that the intention of the legislatures was that "Imperial laws" should be construed as enacted law. Reading section 45 of the Act or section 29 of the Law as a whole would suggest that the words "Imperial laws" mean, throughout the section, statutes of the Parliament of the United Kingdom.[83] It is submitted, therefore, that the provisions relating to local circumstances do not apply to the common law or to equity.[84]

The received statutes are to be read subject to necessary formal verbal alterations not affecting the substance. Thus, "London" in an English statute received as Federal law is to be read as the Federal capital of Nigeria; and it is to be read as Enugu in an English statute received as State law in Anambra State. The various Interpretation enactments[85] provide that any Act of Parliament of the United Kingdom in force must be read with such alterations. Section 15(2)(*b*) of the High Court Law[86] of the eastern States provides that it "shall be lawful for the Court to construe such statutes or Acts with such verbal alterations . . . " But section 45(3) of the Law (Miscellaneous Provisions) Act[87] and section 29(2) of the High Court Law[88] of the northern States provide that the "Imperial laws . . . shall be read with such formal verbal alterations . . . " The argument adduced in interpreting "Imperial laws" in relation to "local circumstances" and to "the limits of the local jurisdiction" apply to verbal alteration of Imperial laws. The words "Imperial laws" in relation to verbal alterations mean statutes of the Parliament of the United Kingdom.

---

[82] N.N. Laws 1963, Cap. 49.
[83] See also Interpretation Law (N.N. Laws 1963, Cap. 52), s. 13; Interpretation Law (W.R.N. Laws 1959, Cap. 51), s. 13; Interpretation Law (E.N. Laws 1963, Cap. 66), s. 15.
[84] *Contra* Robert B. Seidman "A Note on the Construction of the Gold Coast Reception Statute" [1969] J.A.L. 45 at p. 50.
[85] See n. 83, above.
[86] E.N. Laws 1963, Cap. 61.
[87] See Interpretation Act 1964 (No. 1 of 1964), s. 28.
[88] N.N. Laws 1963, Cap. 49.

B. ENGLISH LAW EXTENDING TO NIGERIA

English law extending to Nigeria is the law introduced into Nigeria directly by English legislation. This class of English law should be clearly distinguished from the received English law. The latter is introduced into Nigeria directly by Nigerian legislation. English law extending to Nigeria consists of statutes[89] and subsidiary legislation[90] made on or before October 1, 1960 and not yet repealed by an appropriate authority in Nigeria.[91] English enactments, extending to Nigeria, that have been repealed since independence include the Copyright Act 1911,[92] the Nigeria Independence Act 1960[93] and the Nigeria (Constitution) Order in Council 1960.[94] Like the received English statutes, English law extending to Nigeria is subject to Nigerian legislation, limits of local jurisdiction, local circumstances and formal verbal alterations.[95] Moreover, because no English law enacted in England after October 1, 1960 applies by its own force in Nigeria, any English law extending to Nigeria continues to apply in Nigeria, notwithstanding its repeal in England after that date, until it is repealed by an appropriate authority in Nigeria.[96]

---

[89] The statutes consisted of Acts of the U.K. Parliament and prerogative Orders in Council. Prerogative Orders in Council are not subsidiary legislation. They are original laws made by the Crown as a legislature and are, therefore, statutes. Such Orders were made for the Colony of Lagos. See S.G.G. Edgar (ed.), *Craies on Statute Law* (17th ed., 1971), p. 289.

[90] The subsidiary legislation includes Orders in Council made under Acts of the U.K. Parliament.

[91] Nigeria Independence Act 1960 (8 and 9 Eliz. 2, c. 55); Nigeria (Constitution) Order in Council, 1960 (S.I. 1960 No. 1652), s. 1.

[92] 1 & 2 Geo. 5, c. 46. The Act was applied to Nigeria by Order in Council No. 912 of 1912 (Fed. and Lagos Laws 1958, Vol. XI, p. 222). It was repealed by s. 18 of the Copyright Decree 1970 (No. 61 of 1970).

[93] 8 and 9 Eliz. 2, c. 55.

[94] S.I. 1960 No. 1652 (L.N. 159 of 1960). See also s. 21(3) of the Extradition Decree 1966 (No. 87 of 1966) which repealed, *inter alia*: (a) the West African (Fugitive Offenders) Order in Council 1923 (No. 596 of 1924); (b) the Extradition Act 1870 (33 & 34 Vict. c. 52); (c) the Extradition Act 1873 (36-37 Vict. c. 60); (d) the Extradition Act 1895 (58 & 59 Vict. c. 33); (e) the Extradition Act 1906 (6 Edw. 7, c. 15); and (f) the Fugitive Offenders Act 1881 (44 & 45 Vict. c. 69).

[95] See *e.g.* Law (Miscellaneous Provisions) Law (Lagos Laws 1973, Cap. 65), ss. 2(2) and 3; Interpretation Law (E.N. Laws 1963, Cap. 66), s. 15; Interpretation Law (N.N. Laws 1963, Cap. 52), s. 13; Interpretation Law (W.R.N. Laws 1959, Cap. 51), s. 13; Law (Miscellaneous Provisions) Act, s. 15 (see Interpretation Act 1964, s. 28).

[96] See *e.g.* s. 6 of the Civil Liability (Miscellaneous Provisions) Act 1961 (No. 33 of 1961) in relation to the continued application in the City of Lagos of the Carriage by Air Act 1932 (22 & 23 Geo. 5, c. 36) after the repeal, in England, of the 1932 Act by the Carriage by Air Act 1961 (9 & 10 Eliz. 2, c. 27). The provisions of the 1961 Act have now been incorporated in section 21 of the Law Reform (Torts) Law (Lagos Laws 1973, Cap. 67).

C. A CRITICAL EXAMINATION OF THE CONTENT OF ENGLISH LAW AS A SOURCE OF NIGERIAN LAW

One noticeable feature of the content of English law as a source of Nigerian law is that many English rules which, long ago, have been considered unsuitable in England and have been repealed or replaced there by new rules remain in force in Nigeria. For instance, English law repealed in England in 1925 forms a large part of the land law applicable in Anambra, Cross River, Imo, Lagos and Rivers States. It should also be mentioned that as a result of the reception of English statutes by reference the exact content of the statutory law in force in Nigeria cannot be readily ascertained. In 1959, the Legislature of the Western Region of Nigeria re-enacted as local legislation selected provisions of English statutes and made the Law of England (Application) Law[97] by virtue of which no statute of the United Kingdom Parliament within the limits of the Region's legislative competence was to be in force in the Region. Such a step, rather than the piecemeal method of replacing English statutes with Nigerian enactments is recommended to all the jurisdictions in the country except Bendel, Ogun, Ondo and Oyo States where the Law of England (Application) Law applies. But in receiving English or other foreign ideas in law-making the social values of the local community should be carefully considered. Suitability in th locality should be one of the conditions to be satisfied before an English statute, repealed or current in England, is re-enacted as Nigerian legislation. The question of suitability constitutes a major adverse criticism of the property legislation of Bendel, Ogun, Ondo and Oyo States, and the Matrimonial Causes Decree 1970.[98]

---

[97] W.R.N. Laws 1959, Cap. 60.
[98] No. 18 of 1970. See O. R. Marshall, "A Critique of the Property Legislation of Western Nigeria" [1965] Nig.L.J., p. 151; A. B. Kasunmu, "The Matrimonial Causes Decree, 1970: A Critical Analysis," Nig.J. Contemp. Law (1971), p. 88.

CHAPTER 6

CUSTOMARY LAW

A. INTRODUCTION

CUSTOMARY law consists of customs accepted by members of a community as binding among them. In Nigeria, customary law may be divided in terms of nature into two classes, namely, ethnic or non-Moslem customary law and Moslem law. Ethnic customary law in Nigeria is indigenous. Each system of such customary law applies to members of a particular ethnic group. Moslem law is religious law based on the Moslem faith and applicable to members of the faith. In Nigeria, it is not indigenous law; it is received customary law introduced into the country as part of Islam.

Ethnic customary law is unwritten. There are several such customary law systems in the country, each ethnic group having its own separate system. For instance, the customary law system of a town in Ogun State may be different from the customary law system of a neighbouring town in the State even though the indigenous people of both towns are Yorubas, for the Yorubas consist of several ethnic groups. Similarly, the customary law of an Ibo town in Anambra State may be different from that of a neighbouring Ibo town in the State. This diversity of customary law systems is a major obstacle to uniformity of customary law systems in each State. It should be noted, however, that in many respects the ethnic customary law of an area is similar to that of another area where the indigenous people in both areas belong to the same tribe. Thus, there are certain rules of customary law common to all Yoruba areas in the country.

Unlike ethnic customary law Moslem law is principally in written form. The sources of Moslem law are the Holy Koran, the practice of the Prophet (the *sunna*), the consensus of scholars, and analogical deductions from the Holy Koran and from the practice of the Prophet.[1] Moslem law is alternatively called "Islamic Law" or "the Shari'a" (the sacred law of Islam). The version of Moslem law in force in Nigeria is Moslem law of the Maliki School.[2]

---

[1] See A. A. Fyzee, *Outline of Muhammadan Law* (3rd ed., 1964), pp. 18-21; J. Schacht, *The Origins of Muhammadan Jurisprudence*, p. 1.

[2] See *e.g.* s. 14 of the Sharia Court of Appeal Law (N.N. Laws 1963, Cap. 122) which empowers the Sharia Court of Appeal of each of the northern States to administer Moslem law of the Maliki School as customarily interpreted at the place where the trial at first instance took place.

B. The Characteristics of Customary Law

It would have been clear from the description, just given, of ethnic-group customary law that one of the features of this type of customary law is its acceptance as an obligation by the community. It is recognised as law by the members of the ethnic group.[3] It is "a mirror of accepted usage."[4] Another feature of this type of law is its flexibility. Its rules change from time to time; in particular they reflect the changing social and economic conditions.[5] As Osborne C.J. said in *Lewis* v. *Bankole*,[6]

> "One of the most striking features of West African native custom . . . is its flexibility; it appears to have been always subject to motives of expediency, and it shows unquestionable adaptability to altered circumstances without entirely losing its character."

An illustration of this feature of flexibility is found in customary land law. For instance, under the customary law system of the city of Lagos, absolute alienability of land was not permitted.[7] Land belonged to the family and no individual could own any piece of land absolutely.[8] But, later, the custom began to change in response to the social needs of the community. Consequently, today, the customary law now recognises absolute transfer of title to land to individuals.[9] Furthermore, formerly, any transaction involving the use of writing was considered to be outside the province of ethnic-group customary law. But that position has changed. Thus, a written agreement may be governed by such customary law.[10]

Moslem law, on the other hand, is principally in written form[11] and is comparably rigid. Its content is not readily affected by social change.

C. Establishing Customary Law

There are two methods of establishing customary law before the courts, namely, by proof and by judicial notice.

[3] See *Eshugbayi Eleko* v. *Government of Nigeria* [1931] A.C. 662 at p. 673.
[4] *Owonyin* v. *Omotosho* [1961] 1 All N.L.R. 304 at p. 309.
[5] *Alfa* v. *Arepo* [1963] W.N.L.R. 95.
[6] (1908) 1 N.L.R. 81 at pp. 100-101.
[7] (1908) 1 N.L.R. 81 at p. 83.
[8] *Ibid.* See *Amodu Tijani* v. *Secretary, Southern Nigeria* [1921] 2 A.C. 399.
[9] See *e.g. Alade* v. *Aborishade* (1960) 5 F.S.C. 167, *Oshodi* v. *Balogun* [1936] 2 All E.R. 1632.
[10] See *Alfa* v. *Arepo* [1963] W.N.L.R. 95, *Rotibi* v. *Savage* (1944) 17 N.L.R. 77.
[11] See n. 1 above.

1. *Proof of Customary Law*

(a) Proof before courts other than customary and area courts

The two methods of establishing customary law are provided for, with respect to courts other than customary and area courts, by identically-worded provisions of the Evidence enactments.[12]

Section 14(1) of each of the enactments[13] provides:

"14(1) A custom may be adopted as part of the law governing a particular set of circumstances if it can be noticed judicially or can be proved to exist by evidence. The burden of proving a custom shall lie upon the person alleging its existence."

Section 14(2) of the enactment states the circumstances in which judicial notice of a custom may be taken by the court and section 14(3) provides that where a custom cannot be established by judicial notice it may be established by proof.

Therefore, unless a custom is judically noticed, the party contending that it exists has to prove it as a fact. In other words, he has to prove its existence by evidence.[14] By virtue of the Evidence enactments, "native chiefs or other persons having special knowledge" of customary law may be called to express their opinion as evidence on a point of customary law[15] for such opinion is declared to be relevant by the enactments.[16] A party is required to call his own witnesses to prove a custom in question. But the courts sometimes call chiefs to give evidence. The rules of evidence permit the use of books in evidence. For example, section 58 of the Evidence Law of Lagos State provides that "any book or manuscript recognised by natives as a legal authority" is relevant in determining questions of customary law. It seems obvious that under this provision and equivalent provisions of all the other Evidence enactments, a book or manuscript may be relied upon by the court in determining a question of customary law only if the book or manuscript is recognised by the indigenous people concerned as an authoritative document stating one or more customs accepted by them as binding among them and the book or manuscript had formed part of the evidence before the court.[17] It appears that the provisions do not permit citing books or manuscripts as legal authorities. Accordingly, it has been held in

---

[12] Evidence Law (Lagos Laws, 1973, Cap, 39); Evidence Ordinance (Nigeria Laws 1948, Cap. 63) (in force in Bendel, Ogun, Ondo and Oyo); Evidence Law (N.N. Laws 1963, Cap. 40); Evidence Law (E.N. Laws 1963, Cap. 49).

[13] *Ibid.*

[14] See *e.g.* Evidence Law (Lagos Laws 1973, Cap. 39).

[15] Evidence Law (Lagos Laws 1973, Cap. 39) ss. 56(1) and 58.

[16] *Ibid.*

[17] *Adedibu* v. *Adewoyin* (1951) 13 W.A.C.A. 191.

Adedibu v. *Adewoyin*[18] that where a court in its judgment relies on a book which was not tendered in evidence during the proceedings there is no compliance with section 58 of the Evidence Act,[19] a provision substantially the same in wording as section 58 of the Evidence Law of Lagos State. But there are a number of decisions in which the courts, in determining questions of customary law have relied on books or manuscripts which were not tendered in evidence.[20] They include decisions of the Federal Supreme Court[21] and those of the Judicial Committee of the Privy Council.[22] It should be observed, however, that section 58 of the Evidence Act declares as "relevant" not only "any book or manuscript recognised by natives as a legal authority" but also "the opinions of native chiefs or other persons having special knowledge" of customary law. If a book not tendered in evidence before the courts could be relied upon by the court under section 58 of the Evidence Act, it would follow that the opinion of a chief or other person having special knowledge of customary law may be relied upon under the provision even though the opinion is given outside the court and is therefore not evidence before the court. The courts have not drawn this logical conclusion from their strained interpretation of that part of section 58 of the Evidence Act relating to books or manuscripts. The Supreme Court of Nigeria should be interested in having the opportunity of expressing its opinion on the correct interpretation of section 58 of the Evidence Act. Meanwhile, notwithstanding the application of the provision by the Federal Supreme Court and the Judicial Committee of the Privy Council, the decision in *Adedibu* v. *Adewoyin*,[23] which is in conformity with the wording of the provision, should be regarded as a correct interpretation of the provision.

A party to an action cannot succeed by merely proving the existence of a custom which he relies on. In order to succeed, he must prove its existence in relation to a particular set of circumstances.[24] In other words, he must prove that the existing custom governs the situation. On a general subject, there may be two existing customs one of which may be the general custom and the other the exception. For example, in respect of intestate succession among the Yorubas of Egbaland,[25] there are two existing customs governing the devolu-

---

[18] (1951) 13 W.A.C.A. 191.
[19] Fed. and Lagos Laws 1958, Cap. 62.
[20] See *e.g. Adeseye* v. *Taiwo* (1956) 1 F.S.C. 84; *Suberu* v. *Sunmonu* (1957) 2 F.S.C. 33; *Oyekan* v. *Adele* [1957] 1 W.L.R. 876 at p. 882; *Balogun* v. *Oshodi* (1929) 10 N.L.R. at p. 50.
[21] *Adeseye* v. *Taiwo* (1956) 1 F.S.C. 84.
[22] *Oyekan* v. *Adele* [1957] 1 W.L.R. 876.
[23] (1951) 13 W.A.C.A. 191.
[24] See *e.g.* Evidence Law (Lagos Laws 1973, Cap. 39); s. 14(1).
[25] Abeokuta area in Ogun State.

tion of the property of a deceased person who had more than one wife. They are *Idi-Igi* (the general custom), a custom whereby the property of the deceased is divided among his children *per stirpes* (the property being divided first equally into the number of wives, the share attributable to each wife being then divided equally among her own children), and *Ori-Ojori* (the exception to the general custom), a custom whereby the property is divided among the children *per capita* (the property being divided equally among the children). If a party proves the existence of one of two relevant customs the other party may prove the existence of the other custom. Where both customs are valid,[26] the court has to decide which of the two applies to the particular set of circumstances, that is, which of the two governs the situation. Thus, in *Adeniji* v. *Adeniji*,[27] the Supreme Court in interpreting the decision in *Dawodu* v. *Danmole*,[28] said,

"(1) that the Idi-Igi method of distribution of the estate of a deceased person is an integral part of the Yoruba native law and custom;

(2) that since it is a universal method it should be adopted except where there is a dispute among the decendants [*sic*] of the intestate as to the proportions into which the estate should be divided;

(3) that where there is such a dispute the head of the family is empowered to and should decide whether Ori-Ojori ought in the particular case to be adopted instead of Idi-Igi; and

(4) that any such decision must prevail."[29]

In that case, there was a dispute among the descendants as to the proportions into which the estate should be divided. The court therefore held that in the absence of evidence of a decision of the head of the family as to which of the two customs should be adopted the trial judge was wrong in holding that the *Ori-Ojori* custom applied.

(b) Proof before customary and area courts

It would have been observed that it is by virtue of the Evidence enactments that customary law is initially a question of fact. The Evidence Law in force in Anambra, Cross River, Imo and Rivers States

---

[26] A custom is valid if: (a) it is not repugnant to natural justice, equity and good conscience; (b) it is not incompatible with any law for the time being in force; and (c) it is not contrary to public policy. See *e.g.* s. 26(1) of the High Court Law (Lagos Laws 1973, Cap. 52) and s. 14(3) of the Evidence Law (Lagos Laws 1973, Cap. 39).
[27] [1972] 1 All N.L.R. 298.
[28] (1958) 3 F.S.C. 46.
[29] *Adeniji* v. *Adeniji* [1972] 1 All N.L.R. 298 at pp. 305-306. See also *Akinyede* v. *Opere* [1968] 1 All N.L.R.65 at pp. 67 and 71; *Danmole* v. *Dawodu* [1962] 1 W.L.R. 1053.

provides that the Law does not apply to judicial proceedings in customary courts.[30] The Evidence Ordinance which applies in Bendel, Ogun, Ondo and Oyo States provides that the Ordinance does not apply to judicial proceedings in customary courts unless an order made under the Ordinance provides otherwise.[31] No such order exists. With respect to Lagos State, the relevant prohibitory law in force immediately before the 1973 revised edition of the laws of Lagos State came into operation was section 1(4)(*c*) of the Evidence Act. But surprisingly, that provision is not contained in the Evidence Law in the revised edition. In its place there is section 1(2) of the Evidence Law which provides:

"This Law shall apply to all judicial proceedings in or before any court established in the Lagos State but it shall not apply to proceedings before an arbitrator."

Section 2(1) of the Law provides that "court" includes all judges and magistrates and, except arbitrators, all persons legally authorised to take evidence. Customary courts are authorised to take evidence.[32] It seems therefore that a customary court is a court within the meaning of the Evidence Law and that accordingly the Law applies to all judicial proceedings in customary courts in the State. This would mean a change in the substance of the law. But section 4(2) of the Revised Edition of the Laws of Lagos State Edict 1970[33] makes it quite clear that the Commissioner appointed to prepare the revised edition of the laws had no power to make any alteration or amendment in the matter or substance of any Lagos State Law. It is suggested, therefore, that the Commissioner could not have intended to alter the substance of the law. Moreover, in view of the fact that section 4(2) of the Customary Courts Law[34] provides that no person is qualified to be the president or a member of a customary court unless he is a native of the area of jurisdiction of the court, it is arguable that it is intended that a customary court is to be presumed to be versed in the customary law of its area of jurisdiction and, therefore, that such customary law is a question of law before the court and not a question of fact. It is well settled that the customary law of an area is a question of law before a customary court having jurisdiction in that area

---

[30] E.N. Laws 1963, Cap. 49, s. 1(2)(*c*). It should be noted that there are no customary courts in Imo State. See Magistrates' Courts Law (Amendment) Edict 1971 (No. 23 of 1971) (E.C.S.), 16(1).

[31] Nigeria Laws 1948, Cap. 63, s. 1(4)(*c*). There are no customary courts in Bendel. See Customary Courts (Abolition) Edict 1973 (No. 18 of 1973) (M.W.S.), s. 2.

[32] See Customary Courts Rules (Lagos Laws 1973, Cap. 33), Ord. X.

[33] No. 15 of 1970.

[34] Lagos Laws 1973, Cap. 33.

and versed in the customary law.[35] It is therefore submitted that in the absence of any clear provision of law stating otherwise, section 1(2) of the Evidence Law of Lagos State should not be construed to mean that the Law is intended to apply to judicial proceedings in customary courts.

Section 1(4)(*c*) of the Evidence Law of the northern States[36] provides that the Law does not apply to civil proceedings in area courts unless an order made under the Law provides otherwise. No such order is in force. In criminal proceedings, area courts are to be guided by the provisions of the Evidence Law, in general, but they are bound by sections 137 to 142 of the Law and not by section 14 which provides for proof of customary law.[37] It follows, therefore, that the Evidence enactments do not govern proof of customary law before customary or area courts.[38] Indeed, no legislation governs proof of customary law before such courts.[39] Moreover, customary courts in the southern States[40] are not empowered to administer the common law[41] and although those in the northern States may administer any principle of substantive English law including substantive common law as the law binding between the parties to a transaction,[42] they are not empowered to administer adjective (procedural) common law of which rules relating to proof at common law form

---

[35] See *Ababio II* v. *Nsemfoo* (1947) 12 W.A.C.A. 127, *Ehioghae* v. *Ehioghae* (1964) M.N.L.R. 30.

[36] The northern States, that is the States in the northern part of the country are Bauchi, Benue, Borno, Gongola, Kaduna, Kano, Kwara, Niger, Plateau and Sokoto. See States (Creation and Transitional Provisions) Decree 1976 (No. 12 of 1976), s. 1 and Schedule.

[37] In any case, by virtue of the abolition of customary criminal law proof of customary law in criminal proceedings is no longer important except in cases where statutes define offences by reference to customary law. See *e.g.* Penal Code (N.N. Laws 1963, Cap. 89), s. 387 which punishes adultery when committed by a man "subject to any native law or custom in which extra-marital sexual intercourse is recognised as a criminal offence," s. 388 (adultery by a woman) and s. 403 (drinking of alcohol by a person "of the Moslem faith").

[38] Before the Evidence legislation was passed the rule on proof of customary law now contained in the legislation was part of case law and it had been held that the rule did not apply to customary courts. See *Angu* v. *Attah* (1921) P.C. 1874-1928, p. 43; *Ababio II* v. *Nsemfoo* (1947) 12 W.A.C.A. 127; A. E.W. Park. *The Sources of Nigerian Law* (1963), p. 83.

[39] See, however, Ord. X, r. 6(3) of the repealed Customary Courts Rules 1966 (M.N.L.R. 37 of 1967) made under the repealed Customary Courts Edict 1966 (No. 38 of 1966) (M.W.N.).

[40] The southern States, that is, the States in the southern part of the country are Anambra, Bendel, Cross River, Imo, Lagos, Ogun, Ondo, Oyo and Rivers. See States (Creation and Transitional Provisions) Decree 1976 (No. 12 of 1976), s. 1 and Schedule.

[41] See *e.g. Olalekan* v. *Police* [1962] W.N.L.R. 140 at p. 143; *Amadasun* v. *Ohenso* 1966 N.M.L.R.179; *Akintayo* v. *Atanda* [1963] 2 All N.L.R. 164.

[42] See *e.g.* Area Courts Edict 1968 (No. 4 of 1968) (B.P.S.), s. 20(3).

part. Proof of customary law is, therefore, governed by customary law. This view is supported by the decision of the West African Court of Appeal in *Ababio II* v. *Nsemfoo*,[43] a Gold Coast case[44] where the court said that the law governing proof of customary law before courts as stated by it "has been recognised by this Court in cases where questions of native customary law have been referred to a Native Court for its opinion thereon."[45] It appears that the statement implies that the law on the matter was found in the opinion of the customary courts on the rules of customary law. The rules of customary law on the matter will now be examined.

(i) *Proof of the customary law of the area of jurisdiction of the court*
With respect to the customary law of the area of jurisdiction of the court, the West African Court of Appeal in *Ababio II* v. *Nsemfoo*,[46] said that there was no ground for extending the application of the general rule requiring proof of custom to "Native Courts of which the members are versed in their own customary law, although there is nothing to prevent a party from calling witnesses to prove an alleged custom." The court further said, "If the members of a Native Court are familiar with a custom it is certainly not obligatory upon it to require the custom to be proved through witnesses."[47] In *Ababio II* v. *Nsemfoo*, the customary court in question was the Asantehene's "A" Court, the court of one of the paramount rulers of the Gold Coast. The relevant customary law was that of the area of jurisdiction of the court and the members of the court were versed in that customary law. Therefore, it was not necessary to prove the custom before the court. The case is no authority for the view that proof of customary law before a customary court is not in any circumstances necessary.[48] Rather, it is authority for the view that where the applicable customary law is that of the area of jurisdiction of a customary court and the members of the court are versed in that law proof of the

---

[43] (1947) 12 W.A.C.A. 127.
[44] Subject to statute, the law on this matter is the same throughout West Africa. See N. A. Ollennu, "The Case for Traditional Courts under the Constitution" (1970) 7 U.G.L.J. 82, *Ehigie* v. *Ehigie* [1961] 1 All N.L.R. 842; *Egioghae* v. *Ehioghae* (1964) M.N.L.R. 30. Compare *Fijabi* v. *Odumola* [1955-56] W.R.N.L.R. 133.
[45] *Ababio II* v. *Nsemfoo* (1947) 12 W.A.C.A. 127 at p. 128.
[46] *Ibid.*
[47] *Ibid.*
[48] Indeed, by virtue of the nature of customary law, a decision of a court as to the existence of a rule of customary law does not constitute a binding authority in any subsequent case. In every subsequent case, the rule, in order to be relied upon by a court other than a customary court, must be established by evidence or be judicially noticed. See *e.g.* Evidence Law (Lagos Laws 1973, Cap. 39), s. 14. The question of binding authority does not arise in relation to customary courts unless legislation otherwise provides. See *e.g.* s. 22(*a*) of the repealed Customary Courts Edict 1966 (No. 38 of 1966) (M.W.N.).

law is not necessary.[49] Although it was not in dispute that all the members of the customary court in *Ababio II* v. *Nsemfoo* were versed in the customary law, the reasoning in the case is consistent with the view that the position would have been the same had only one member of the court been versed in the customary law. What was material was whether there was any member of the court who was versed in that law. This view is strengthened by dicta in *Ehioghae* v. *Ehioghae*[50] and *Ehigie* v. *Ehigie*[51] in each of which cases a single person constituted the customary court. But in *Fijabi* v. *Odumola*,[52] the High Court of the Western Region of Nigeria set aside the judgment of a customary court on the ground that a rule of customary law was applied by the court without proof before the court. The court appeared to hold the view that in every case, a rule of customary law must be proved before a customary court before that court could apply it. It is submitted that the case was wrongly decided. It is certainly inconsistent with the rules of customary law and dicta in other decisions on the matter.

Thus, where the customary law in question is that of the area of jurisdiction of a customary court and the court or at least one member of the court is versed in that law, it is unnecessary to prove the customary law.

Under the repealed Customary Court Edict 1966[53] of the former Midwestern State a person was not qualified for appointment as president or member of a customary court unless he was a native of the area of jurisdiction of the court. Presumably, only those natives versed in the customary law of the area were to be appointed presidents or members of the local customary courts. It appears that the requirement was based on the assumption that a native would usually be versed in the local customary law. Accordingly, the Customary Court Rules 1966[54] of the former Midwestern State, now repealed, reduced the principle in *Ababio II* v. *Nsemfoo* into legislative form as follows:

> "Where in any cause or matter before a customary court any party wishes to rely on the customary law of the area of jurisdiction of the court there shall be no need to prove the customary law before the court."[55]

---

[49] A. O. Obilade, "Reform of Customary Court Systems in Nigeria under the Military Government" [1969] 13 J.A.L. at p. 41.
[50] (1964) M.N.L.R. 30.
[51] [1961] 1 All N.L.R. 842.
[52] [1955-56] W.R.N.L.R. 133.
[53] No. 38 of 1966.
[54] M.N.L.N. 37 of 1967.
[55] *Ibid.* Ord. X, r. 6(3).

Where the customary law in question is that of the area of jurisdiction of the court and none of the judges or members of the court is versed in that law, proof of the customary law is necessary. This is clear from the decision of the High Court of Western Nigeria in *Ehigie* v. *Ehigie*,[56] a case on appeal from the Grade A customary court, Benin-City. The learned judge, Fatayi-Williams J. (as he then was) said,

> "Although he is required to apply the customary law of the area of jurisdiction of the court, the President [of the Customary Court] is not required by statute to be a native of the area of jurisdiction of the Customary Court or to have any special qualifications in the customary law of the area. The only statutory qualification is that he should be a legal practitioner."[57]

The learned judge, therefore, held that proof of customary law before the customary court was necessary. But, as explained in *Ehioghae* v. *Ehioghae*,[58] the material question is not whether a customary court judge is a legal practitioner but whether he is not versed in the local customary law. In *Ehigie* v. *Ehigie*,[59] there was no suggestion that the learned Customary Court President was versed in the local customary law.

In determining whether a customary court is versed in the customary law of the area of jurisdiction of the court certain rebuttable presumptions are used by the courts. One of them is that where it is required by statute that a customary court be presided over by a legal practitioner, the court is not versed in the customary law.[60] This presumption may be rebutted by showing that the legal practitioner is in fact versed in the customary law,[61] or if other persons sit with him as court members, that at least one of those persons is in fact versed in the customary law. Furthermore, where the area of jurisdiction of a customary court is so wide that several customary law systems apply in the area, it would be presumed that the court is not versed in the applicable customary law for it would be unreasonable to expect the court "to be familiar with the several systems" of customary law in its area.[62]

---

56 [1961] 1 All N.L.R. 842.
57 *Ibid.*
58 (1964) M.N.L.R. 30.
59 [1961] 1 All N.L.R. 842.
60 See *Ehigie* v. *Ehigie* [1961] 1 All N.L.R. 842.
61 See *Ehioghae* v. *Ehioghae* (1964) M.N.L.R. 30.
62 *Gyang* v. *Gyang*, 1969 N.N.L.R. 99 at p. 100.

(ii) *Proof of the customary law of an area outside the jurisdiction of the court.*

Where the customary law in question is not that of the area of jurisdiction of the customary court proof of the law is necessary.[63] Before the customary court such customary law may be likened to foreign law. In principle, therefore, the rule, applicable in cases involving the area of jurisdiction of the court, that where the court is versed in the customary law proof of the law is unnecessary cannot apply to this case. Under customary law, the court is not deemed to be versed in foreign law. It is, therefore, submitted that in all circumstances where the applicable customary law is not that of the area of jurisdiction of the customary court proof of the law is necessary.[64]

2. *Judicial Notice*

Certain facts are so obvious that they need not be proved before the courts. For example, it is not necessary to prove that human beings have hands, that water is a liquid or that horses are animals. Such facts are said to be judicially noticed by the courts. Every court applies a rule of judicial notice but the authority for the application of the rule in any particular case falls under any of the following three heads, namely, the common law, statute and customary law. Under the common law doctrine of judicial notice the existence or content of rules of the common law, equity, statutes or subsidiary legislation need not to be proved. The common law rule has now been reduced to statutory form. Thus, section 73(1)(*a*) of the Evidence Law of Lagos State[65] provides that the court must take judicial notice of "all laws[66] or enactments and any subsidiary legislation made thereunder having the force of law now or heretofore in force, or hereafter to be in force in any part of Nigeria . . . " The Evidence Law and other evidence enactments provide in identical terms for the circumstances in which the court may take judicial notice of a custom, that is, a rule of customary law.[67]

The evidence enactments do not apply to customary courts and, in general, the evidence legislation does not apply to area courts. Clearly, the provisions of the evidence enactments relating to judi-

---

[63] A. O. Obilade, *op. cit.* (n. 49, above) at p. 42.
[64] *Ibid.*
[65] Lagos Laws 1973, Cap. 39.
[66] This term excludes customs. See Evidence Law (Lagos Laws 1973, Cap. 39) ss. 14 and 73(1)(l).
[67] See *e.g.* Evidence Law (Lagos Laws 1973, Cap. 39) s. 14(2).

cial notice do not apply at all to customary or area courts.[68] Therefore, in the absence of any other enactments relating to judicial
notice, statutory judicial notice does not apply to customary or area
courts. It is now intended to deal in some detail with judicial notice
of customary law in courts other than customary and area courts and
then judicial notice of customary law in customary and area courts.

(a) Judicial notice in courts other than customary and area courts

Judicial notice of customary law in courts other than customary
and area courts is now governed by section 14(2) of each of the Evidence enactments. The subsection provides as follows:

> "(2) A custom may be judicially noticed by the court if it has been
> acted upon by a court of superior or co-ordinate jurisdiction in the
> same area to an extent which justifies the court asked to apply it in
> assuming that the persons or the class of persons concerned in that
> area look upon the same as binding in relation to circumstances
> similar to those under consideration."

The words "may be judicially noticed by the court" appear to show
that under the provision, a court is not bound to take judicial notice
of a custom.[69] It is open to the court to take judicial notice of a custom if the conditions stated in the provision are satisfied. One of the
conditions is that the custom must have been acted upon by a court
of superior or co-ordinate jurisdiction in the same area. Since the subsection mentions persons or the class of persons looking upon the
custom as binding, the words "in the same area" mean in the ethnic-
group area or Moslem-community area within which it is contended
that the custom applies.[70] Thus, where it is relevantly contended that
a custom is the applicable custom at Abeokuta, a Yoruba town, the
words "in the same area" as applied to the situation mean in Abeokuta area, not in Yorubaland and the persons concerned are "the
Abeokuta people" not "the Yorubas." Similarly, in Kano State, the
words "in the same area" in relation to a rule of Moslem law alleged

---

[68] s. 14 of each of the Evidence enactments deals with judicial notice of custom. The
Evidence enactments of the southern States do not apply to civil proceedings in customary courts. Under the Evidence Ordinance (Nigeria Laws 1948, Cap. 63), provisions of the Ordinance apply to customary courts where an Order to that effect is
made under the Ordinance. But there is no such Order. In the northern States, the
Evidence Law (N.N. Laws 1963, Cap. 40) does not apply to civil proceedings in the
area courts unless an order made under the law states otherwise, but no such order
exists. The area courts are bound in criminal proceedings by ss. 137-142 of the Law,
but not s. 14 of the Law.

[69] Compare *e.g.* s. 73(1)(*a*) of the Evidence Act: "The court shall take judicial notice of
the following facts: . . ."

[70] There are two types of customary law in Nigeria, namely, ethnic customary law and
Moslem law. See p. 83, above.

to be applicable in a part of the State mean "in the Moslem community area of the State." That, in practical terms would mean, virtually, "in the entire State." As the Supreme Court of Nigeria said in *Taiwo* v. *Dosunmu*,[71]

"We are of the view that in applying section 14(2) of the Evidence Act, the Court must treat reference to 'the same area' as meaning an area in which some grounds appear for supposing the customs to be uniform."

Uniformity of customs does not connote mere similarities between particular customs. Rather, it does connote a single system of customs.[72] It follows, therefore, that the subsection is not satisfied where a court in Ogun State relies with respect to an Abeokuta custom on judicial decisions given in respect of a custom on a similar matter in Lagos. Even though the indigenous people of both States are Yorubas, two different systems of similar ethnic-group customary law are involved. The similarities arise by virtue of the fact that the two ethnic groups concerned form part of the same tribe, the Yoruba tribe. *A fortiori*, it is wrong on the part of a court in Nigeria to rely on decisions given by a court in Ghana in taking judicial notice of a custom alleged to be applicable in a part of Nigeria.[73] Section 2(1) of the Evidence Act[74] provides that "court" includes all judges and magistrates and, except arbitrators all persons legally authorised to take evidence. Such judges, magistrates or persons legally authorised to take evidence must be those having jurisdiction in the territory within which the enactment applies. The word "court" in any enactment cannot be extended to include courts outside the jurisdiction within which the enactment applies in the absence of express provisions so extending the meaning. Similarly, in the absence of such express provisions, the words "in the same area" in the context are not to be construed to include an area outside the jurisdiction within which the enactment applies. The court of "superior or co-ordinate jurisdiction" must be one having jurisdiction in the geographical area where it is contended that the custom applies. Thus, in each State, magistrates (or, normally, district judges in the northern States) of the same grade are courts of co-ordinate jurisdiction because each magistrate (or, normally district judge) has jurisdiction throughout the State by reference to his

---

[71] [1965] 1 All N.L.R. 399 at p. 404.
[72] Compare, C. O. Olawoye, "Note: Establishing Customary Law: *Akande* v. *Akorede*" Nig. J. Contemp. Law (1971) 260 at pp. 268-270.
[73] *Taiwo* v. *Dosunmu* [1965] 1 All N.L.R.399. See *Okpowagha* v. *Ewehemoma* [1970] 1 All N.L.R. 203 at p. 209.
[74] Fed. and Lagos Laws 1958, Cap. 62.

grade,[75] a judge of the High Court of a State is a court of superior jurisdiction with respect to a magistrate or district judge in the same area within the meaning of the subsection because the judge (the High Court) has jurisdiction throughout the State and, therefore "in the same area" as the magistrate or district judge. It follows that when the court wishing to take judicial notice of a custom is a magistrate's court (or district court in a northern State), it can rely on the decisions of a magistrate (or district judge) having superior or co-ordinate jurisdiction in the State or on the decisions of any judge of the High Court of the State. Any judge of the High Court of a State can rely for the purpose of judicial notice, on the decisions of any other judge of the High Court for under the evidence enactments all the judges constitute courts of co-ordinate jurisdiction.[76]

Before a court takes judicial notice of a custom, it must be satisfied that the extent to which a court of superior or co-ordinate jurisdiction has applied the custom justifies it in assuming that the persons or the class of persons concerned in the area accept the custom as binding in circumstances similar to those under consideration. It does not follow from this that there must have been several cases in which the custom has been applied by the courts in the area before judicial notice can be taken of it. The common law doctrine of judicial notice, in its application to customary law as a fact (as stated in the Gold Coast case of *Angu* v. *Attah*,[77] a decision of the Judicial Committee of the Privy Council) requires frequent proof in the courts as a pre-requisite of judicial notice.[78] But there is nothing clearly to that effect in the evidence enactments. Some judicial decisions given after the introduction in 1945 of statutory judicial notice have relied on the principle in *Angu* v. *Attah*, rather than on the statutory rule. They have therefore stated that a custom must have been frequently followed by the courts before it could be judicially noticed.[79] On the other hand, there are judicial decisions which in relying on the statutory rule have stated that a single decision could be enough in certain circumstances to make the court take judicial notice of a custom.[80] The face is that in a single case evidence to prove a custom may be so clear and tremendous that in a subsequent case the application of the custom in the single case may be taken to satisfy the requirement of extent of application under section 14(2)

---

[75] See *e.g.* Magistrates' Courts Law (W.R.N. Laws 1959, Cap. 74), s. 8; District Courts Law (N.N. Laws 1963, Cap. 33), s. 8.

[76] See *e.g.* the definition of "court" in s. 2(1) of the Evidence Act.

[77] P.C. 1874-1928, p. 43.

[78] See also *Larinde* v. *Afiko* (1940) 6 W.A.C.A. 108.

[79] See *e.g.* *Giwa* v. *Erinmilokun* [1961] 1 All N.L.R. 294 at p. 296.

[80] See *Cole* v. *Akinyele* (1960) 5 F.S.C. 84 in which *Alake* v. *Pratt* (1955) 15 W.A.C.A. 20 was cited as a case in which the court had acted on the custom in question.

of the Evidence Act. Conversley, where there are several cases in none of which very clear or tremendous evidence was adduced the courts would not hold in a subsequent case that the requirement of extent of application under the subsection has been satisfied.

A court of appeal, no doubt, is entitled to apply the law which the lower court is empowered to apply. The court of appeal puts itself in the position of the lower court in respect of establishing customary law by judicial notice. Therefore, if the lower court was entitled under customary law to take judicial notice of a custom, the court of appeal is also entitled to take judicial notice of the custom under customary law even though if the court of appeal had sat as a court of first instance proof by evidence would have been required in the circumstances. This is probably what the High Court of Western Nigeria in *Salau* v. *Aderibigbe*[81] was attempting to state when it said that "although customary law has to be proved in this court when exercising its original jurisdiction, that law is deemed to be within the judicial knowledge of this court when it is exercising its appellate jurisdiction from Customary Courts."

Establishing a custom by judicial notice is an alternative to establishing it by proof.[82] Where a custom cannot be judicially noticed by the court, it may be established by evidence.[83]

Attempts are sometimes made to distinguish between the nature of judicially-noticed customary law and customary law proved by evidence by stating that judicially-noticed customary law is a matter of law and customary law proved by evidence is a matter of fact. It is not in doubt that before courts other than customary courts customary law is initially a question of fact. It becomes a matter of law when it is proved or judicially noticed in a case. It is certainly law for the purpose of the case but its authority as a precedent is limited by reason of the fact that it is law for other purposes only in so far as the custom in question remains unchanged. Having regard to the characteristics of customary law, the position cannot be otherwise. Customary law whether proved by evidence or judicially noticed consists of customs accepted by the people concerned as binding among them. It changes from time to time in the light of social development.[84] The statutory provisions on judicial notice of customary law make the position clear. Under section 14(2) of each of the Evidence

---

[81] [1963] W.N.L.R. 80 at p. 83.

[82] See *e.g.* Evidence Law (Lagos Laws 1973, Cap. 39) s. 14(1); *Okpowagba* v. *Ewehemoma* [1970] 1 All N.L.R. 203 at p. 209; *Apoesho* v. *Awodiya* [1964] 1 All N.L.R. 48; *Taiwo* v. *Dosunmu* [1965] 1 All N.L.R. 399.

[83] See *e.g.* Evidence Law (Lagos Laws 1973, Cap. 39), s. 14(3); *Odunsi* v. *Ojora* [1961] 1 All N.L.R. 283.

[84] *Lewis* v. *Bankole* (1908) 1 N.L.R. 81 at p. 101.

enactments the court is not entitled to take judicial notice of a custom unless it has been applied "in the same area to an extent which justifies the court asked to apply it in assuming that the persons or the class of persons concerned in that area look upon the same as binding in relation to circumstances similar to those under consideration." Where there is evidence that the persons concerned no longer accept the custom as binding among them, there is no authority under the provision for taking judicial notice of the custom. In the light of the evidence the application of the custom does not justify the court to assume that the custom is accepted as binding among them.

On every occasion when the court has to apply a rule of customary law, the rule has to be proved before the court or judicially noticed by the court.[85] Where it is contended that a custom judicially noticed on a previous occasion has ceased to be the custom accepted by the people concerned, the court should allow evidence to be adduced to prove the change, and once there is proof of the change the court is not entitled to take judicial notice of the custom. In *Salami* v. *Salami*[86] the court allowed evidence to be adduced for the purpose of showing that a custom judicially noticed as a Yoruba custom[87] was not applicable at Abeokuta, a Yoruba town. But the court was of opinion that the evidence was unsatisfactory. Similarly, the Federal Supreme Court in *Danmole* v. *Dawodu*[88] allowed evidence to be adduced for the purpose of showing that in Lagos the judicially-noticed custom on succession, *idi-igi* (distribution of estate *per stirpes*) had ceased to be the prevailing custom and had been replaced by *ori-ojori* (distribution of estate *per capita*). The court held that *idi-igi* was still applicable. It has now been held that *ori-ojori* is an alternative applicable custom on the matter.[89] However desirable it may be to achieve certainty of rules by judicial notice, neither the nature of customary law nor the statutory provision on this matter supports the argument that a judicially-noticed rule of customary law cannot be re-examined.[90] It is obvious that where a custom judicially noticed on a previous occasion is applied on another occasion after proof that the custom had changed, it is not customary law that is being applied but the court's notion of what customary law ought to be. Certainly, the courts in Nigeria cannot

---

[85] See *e.g.* Evidence Law (Lagos Laws 1973, Cap. 39), s. 14(1).
[86] [1957] W.R.N.L.R. 10.
[87] The court should have considered taking judicial notice of an Abeokuta custom rather than a Yoruba custom. See also *Eze* v. *Igiliegbe* (1952) 14 W.A.C.A. 61. Compare *Taiwo* v. *Dosunmu* [1965] 1 All N.L.R. 399.
[88] (1958) 3 F.S.C. 46.
[89] *Adeniji* v. *Adeniji* [1972] 1 All N.L.R. 298.
[90] See A. N. Allott, *New Essays in African Law* (1970), p. 279.

rightly be likened to the English judges who went from place to place in England purporting to enforce the customs of the realm from which the common law of England evolved. Evolution of a uniform system of ethnic-type customary law even within a tribal group with the judiciary as the instrument would be a very slow process, having regard to the multiplicity of customary law systems, the nature of customary law[91] and the statutory provisions governing establishing customary law.

(b) Judicial notice in customary courts

As already explained,[92] customary courts are not empowered to administer adjective common law. The common law doctrine of judicial notice forms part of adjective law. Therefore, the doctrine does not apply to customary courts.[93] It has also been explained that the provisions of the Evidence enactments relating to judicial notice do not apply to customary courts.[94] In the absence of any statute providing for judicial notice in customary courts, statutory judicial notice, too, does not apply in customary courts. But proof of certain facts including, in some circumstances, the existence and content of customary law, need not be proved before customary courts.[95] Such facts are said to be judicially noticed. Judicial notice in customary courts is, thus, governed by customary law only. A customary court which is versed in the customary law of its area of jurisdiction is entitled to take judicial notice of the customary law. In other words, the court is deemed to know the law and proof of it before the court is unnecessary.[96] The customary law of the area of jurisdiction of a customary court is, thus, a question of law before the court where the court is versed in customary law. It is the current custom that should be judicially noticed by the court. In principle, although the court is deemed to know the law, where it wishes to take judicial notice of a custom, it should be open to a party who contends that the custom has ceased to be accepted by the people concerned as binding to adduce evidence to prove his contention.

---

[91] With respect to the nature of customary law, see, for example, *Owonyin* v. *Omotosho* [1961] 1 All N.L.R. 304 at p. 309; *Lewis* v. *Bankole* (1908) 1 N.L.R. 81 at 100-101; *Alfa* v. *Arepo* [1963] W.N.L.R. 95; s. 2(1) of the Evidence Law (E.N. Laws 1963, Cap. 49) which defines a custom as a rule which in a particular district, has from long usage, obtained the force of law.

[92] See p. 89, above.

[93] *Contra Salau* v. *Aderibigbe* [1963] W.N.L.R. 80 at 82-83 where Charles J. sitting as the High Court of Western Nigeria, said that the common law doctrine applied to customary courts.

[94] See pp. 93-94, above.

[95] See p. 91, above.

[96] See pp. 91-92, above.

D. The Validity of Customary Law

Rules of customary law are subject to tests of validity prescribed by statute. An applicable rule of customary law is not to be enforced by the courts unless it passes the tests. There are three such tests. The first is that the customary law is not repugnant to natural justice, equity and good conscience; the second is that it is not "incompatible either directly or by implication with any law[97] for the time being in force," and the third is that it is not contrary to public policy. All the statutory provisions on the first two tests are similar in wording and all the statutory provisions on the test of public policy are identical in wording.

Section 26(1) of the High Court Law of Lagos State[98] provides that the "High Court shall observe and enforce the observance of every customary law which is applicable and is not repugnant to natural justice, equity and good conscience nor incompatible either directly or by implication with any law for the time being in force."[99] In addition the proviso to section 14(3) of each of the Evidence enactments[1] contains the repugnancy and public policy tests expressed in the following terms: "provided that in case of any custom relied upon in any judicial proceeding it shall not be enforced if it is contrary to public policy and is not in accordance with natural justice, equity and good conscience." It is now intended to examine the tests in some detail.

1. *The Repugnancy Test*

The courts have never attempted to explain in detail the meaning of the clause. But the views expressed by them in various decisions shed some light upon its purpose and meaning. Lord Wright in *Laoye* v. *Oyetunde*[2] expressed the view that the clause was intended to invalidate "barbarous" customs and Lord Atkin in *Eshugbayi Eleko* v. *Officer Administering the Government of Nigeria*[3] said that a barbar-

---

[97] In the relevant enactments in force in Bendel, Ogun, Ondo and Oyo States, the words "written law" are used in place of the word "law"; see *e.g.* s. 12(1) of the High Court Law (W.R.N. Laws 1959, Cap. 44). "Written Law" includes local legislation and excludes English statutes extending to Nigeria. See s. 3 of the Interpretation Law (1959 W.R.N. Laws, Cap. 51).

[98] Lagos Laws 1973, Cap. 52.

[99] See also High Court Law (N.N. Laws 1963, Cap. 40), s. 34(1); High Court Law (E.N. Laws 1963, Cap. 61), s. 20(1); High Court Law (W.R.N. Laws 1959, Cap. 44), s. 12(1); High Court Law 1964 (No. 9 of 1964) (M.W.N.), s. 13(1).

[1] See Evidence Act (Fed. and Lagos Laws 1958, Cap. 62); Evidence Law (N.N. Laws 1963, Cap. 40); Evidence Law (E.N. Laws 1963, Cap. 49); Evidence Ordinance (Nigeria Laws 1948, Cap. 63).

[2] [1944] A.C. 170.

[3] [1931] A.C. 662 at p. 673.

ous custom must be rejected on the ground of repugnancy to natural justice, equity and good conscience. Both Lord Wright and Lord Atkin, therefore appear to hold the view that a custom is repugnant to natural justice, equity and good conscience if it is uncivilised. This does not mean that a custom fails the repugnancy test if it does not conform to the standard of behaviour acceptable in communities which have reached an advanced stage in social development, for instance, the English community. This point is clear from the cases. For example, in *Lewis* v. *Bankole*[4] the Full Court of the Supreme Court, in 1909, rejected the view of the trial judge that because a custom did not form part of the English doctrines of equity[5] it was invalid by virtue of the repugnancy test. Similarly, the Federal Supreme Court in *Dawodu* v. *Danmole*[6] and the Judicial Committee of the Privy Council in the same case,[7] on appeal, rejected the view expressed by Jibowu J. that the *idi-igi* custom on succession was repugnant to natural justice, equity and conscience. The learned judge was of opinion that the custom by stating that the property of the deceased was to be distributed among his children *per stirpes* rather than *per capita*[8] was inconsistent with the modern idea of equality among the children. The Privy Council in its opinion on this matter said that "the principles of natural justice, equity and good conscience applicable in a country where polygamy is generally accepted should not be readily equated with those applicable to a community governed by the rule of monogamy."[9] But customs clearly below any civilised standard of behaviour would be held to be repugnant to natural justice, equity and good conscience.[10] Thus, in *Edet* v. *Essien*,[11] the appellant had paid dowry in respect of a woman when she was a child. Later, the respondent paid dowry in respect of the same woman to the woman's parents and took her as his wife. The appellant claimed custody of the children of the union on the grounds that under customary law, he was the husband of the woman, that the woman could not contract "another legal marriage" until the dowry paid by him was refunded to him and that he was entitled to any children borne by the woman until the dowry was refun-

[4] (1908) 1 N.L.R. 81 at pp. 99-102.
[5] The learned trial judge, Osborne C.J. considered the clause as three separate units namely, (a) repugnant to natural justice, (b) repugnant to equity and (c) repugnant to good conscience. But the courts usually consider the clause as a whole. See *e.g.* the judgment of the Full Court in the case, (1908) 1 N.L.R. 81 at p. 99.
[6] (1958) 3 F.S.C. 46.
[7] [1962] 1 W.L.R. 105..
[8] See p. 87, above.
[9] [1962] 1 W.L.R. 1053 at p. 1060. See also *Rufai* v. Igbirra N.A. 1957 N.R.N.L.R. 178.
[10] See A. E. W. Park, *The Sources of Nigerian Law* (1963), p. 72.
[11] (1932) 11 N.L.R. 47.

ded to him. The court held that the alleged rule of customary law had not been established. It then said that even if such rule had been established it was of opinion that the custom was repugnant to natural justice, equity and good conscience. Similarly, customs based on the concept of slavery have been declared repugnant to natural justice, equity and good conscience. For instance in *Re Effiong Okon Ata*[12] the court said that a custom whereby the former owner of a slave was entitled to administer the personal property of the slave after the slave's death failed the repugnancy test.[13]

It is not within the province of the courts to modify an uncivilised custom and apply the modified version of the custom. As Lord Atkin said in *Eshugbayi Eleko* v. *Officer Administering the Government of Nigeria*,[14]

> "The Court cannot itself transform a barbarous custom into a milder one. If it still stands in its barbarous character it must be rejected as repugnant to natural justice, equity and good conscience."[15]

When a rule of customary law is modified by the courts the rule in its modified form is no longer a rule of customary law. Lord Atkin in the same case[16] stated the relevant principle as follows:

> "It is the assent of the native community that gives a custom its validity, and, therefore, barbarous or mild, it must be shown to be recognised by the native community whose conduct it is supposed to regulate."

On reading together the two passages from Lord Atkin's opinion, it would be clear that Lord Atkin was not suggesting that once the members of a "native community" accepted a custom as binding it was valid. He was only explaining that an uncivilised custom must be declared invalid and that it could not be modified by the courts. It is wrong to use the assent of the community as the standard for determining whether a custom is repugnant to natural justice, equity and good conscience. The assent of the community is an essential element of a custom. It is relevant only in relation to establishing the existence of a custom as a rule accepted by the community as binding. Suggesting that the validity of a custom should be determined by the standard of behaviour accepted by the community means stating

---

[12] (1930) 10 N.L.R. 65.
[13] (1930) 1 W.A.C.A. 2.
[14] [1931] A.C. 662 at p. 673.
[15] Compare *Re Whyte* (1946) 18 N.L.R. 70, *Mariyama* v. *Sadiku Ejo* 1961 N.R.N.L.R. 81.
[16] *Eshugbayi Eleko* v. *Officer Administering the Government of Nigeria* [1931] A.C. 662 at p. 673.

that every rule accepted by the community as binding is valid.[17] It would follow that no applicable custom would fail the repugnancy test. Clearly, therefore, the standard used must be external to the community.[18] It is the standard of an ordinary civilised society.

Another wrong notion about the repugnancy test relates to the place of the possible results of the application of a custom in the determination of the issue of repugnancy. Clearly, the possible results of the application of a custom are relevant in determining this issue for it is impossible to determine whether a custom is uncivilised or not without considering the possible consequences of its application. It is submitted that in evaluating the possible results, the particular facts of the case in which it is alleged that the custom is applicable are relevant only as an example of facts to which the custom is applicable. Where the application of a custom in a particular case would result in the adoption of an uncivilised standard the court must hold that the custom has failed the test. But it does not follow that where the application in a particular case would not produce that result the custom has passed the test. The court must, in that case, consider other possible results. If there is a possibility that the application of the custom would result in the adoption of an uncivilised standard of behaviour, it must be held that the custom has failed the test even though having regard to the particular facts of the case before the court, that would not be the result in the particular case. In other words, the possible result in the particular case constitutes just one example of possible results. A case illustrating failure to appreciate the place of possible results of the application of customs is *Mariyama* v. *Sadiku Ejo*[19] involving a custom whereby any child born within 10 months of a divorce was the property of the former husband of the child's mother. It seemed clear in that case that the former husband was not the father of the child. The court, therefore, said that the rule was invalid with respect to the case. The court then stated:

> "We must not be understood to condemn this native law and custom in its general application. We appreciate that it is basically sound and would in almost every case be fair and just in its results."[20]

A custom which is invalid for any particular purpose is invalid for all other purposes.

[17] See A. E. W. Park, *op. cit.* (n. 10, above), p. 70.
[18] *Contra* Abiola Ojo, "Judicial Approach to Customary Law" *Journal of Islamic and Comparative Law*, Vol. 3 (1969) 44 at p. 47.
[19] 1961 N.R.N.L.R. 81.
[20] *Ibid.*

2. *The Test of Incompatibility*

Various enactments direct the courts to enforce applicable customary law which is not incompatible with some "law." Many of the
enactments provide that the customary law to be enforced must not
be incompatible with "any law for the time being in force."[21] Others
provide that it must not be incompatible with "any written law."[22]
For example, section 26(1) of the High Court Law of Lagos State[23]
provides as follows:

> "26(1) The High Court shall observe and enforce the observance
> of every customary law which is applicable and is not repugnant to
> natural justice, equity, and good conscience, nor incompatible
> either directly or by implication with any law for the time being in
> force ..."

and section 13(1) of the High Court Law 1964,[24] a Midwestern
Nigeria statute provides as follows:

> "13(1) The High Court shall observe and enforce the observance
> of every customary law which is applicable and is not repugnant to
> natural justice, equity and good conscience, nor incompatible
> either directly or by implication with any written law for the time
> being in force."

It has been argued that "any law for the time being in force"
includes English law in force. Thus, in *Re Adadevoh*[25] the West African Court of Appeal expressed the view, *obiter*, that "any law in
force" included "the rules of the common law as to the unenforceabil-
ity of claims contrary to public policy." Of course, if "any law"
includes the common law it also includes the other classes of the
received English law, namely, equity and statutes. Similarly, in *Adesubokan* v. *Yinusa*[26] the Supreme Court of Nigeria expressed the view
that the term "any law" in section 34(1) of the High Court Law of the
northern States[27] (the equivalent of section 26(1) of the High Court

---

[21] See *e.g.* High Court Law (Lagos Laws 1973, Cap. 52), s. 26(1), High Court Law
(E.N. Laws 1963, Cap. 61), s. 20(1).
[22] See *e.g.* High Court Law 1964 (No. 9 of 1964) (M.W.N.), s. 13(1).
[23] Lagos Laws 1973, Cap. 52.
[24] No. 9 of 1964.
[25] (1951) 13 W.A.C.A. 304 at p. 310.
[26] *Nigerian Lawyers' Quarterly*, Vol. VI, Nos. 1-4, p. 186; *sub nom. Adesubokan* v.
Yinusa, 1971 N.N.L.R. 77. The case was decided on June 17, 1971.
[27] 1963 N.N. Laws, Cap. 49. The subsection provides as follows: "The High Court
shall observe and enforce the observance of every native law and custom which is
not repugnant to natural justice, equity, and good conscience, nor incompatible
either directly or by implication with any law for the time being in force, and
nothing in this law shall deprive any person of the benefit of any such native law or
custom."

Law of Lagos State) included the received English statutes of general application. The court stated as follows[28]:

> "The provisions of the Maliki Moslem law is undoubtedly incompatible with section 3 of the Wills Act 1837.[29] As we stated earlier, a proper construction of section 34(1) of the High Court Law can only apply such Moslem law which is not incompatible with the Wills Act. It is, therefore, clear that the Moslem law which the learned judge applied in this case is incompatible with the Wills Act."

This view being that of the Supreme Court should not be treated lightly. The issue before the lower court, the High Court of the North-Central State (Bello J. as he then was), in that case[30] was whether a Moslem testator could by a will made in accordance with the Wills Act 1837 (a received English statute of general application) validly dispose of his property in a manner inconsistent with Maliki law (the version of Moslem law applicable in the northern States). Under Maliki law, a Moslem testator could not give more than one-third of his estate to persons other than his heirs, and the dispositions to his male children must be in equal shares. The learned trial judge, assuming that the term "any law" in section 34(1) of the High Court Law of the nothern States included the received English statutes, interpreted the words "and nothing in this law shall deprive any person of the benefit of any such native law or custom" in the subsection[31] by stating as follows:

> "It is clear that this injunction limits the operation of 'any law for the time being in force' to the extent of preserving any of the benefits of every native law and custom which is incompatible with that law in force, to which any person is entitled. In other words, the last sentence of the subsection means, for the purpose of this case, that the Wills Act shall not deprive the plaintiff of the benefit of Moslem law."[32]

By this strained interpretation of the law, the learned judge decided that the dispositions under the will in question were void by reason of inconsistency with Moslem law. The Supreme Court quite rightly stated that the native law or custom the benefit of which no person should be deprived of was that native law or custom which had already passed the prescribed tests of validity including the test of incompatibility. Having dealt with that simple matter, the Supreme

---

[28] 1971 N.N.L.R. 77 at p. 83.
[29] 7 Will. 4 & 1 Vict. c. 26.
[30] *Sub nom. Yinusa* v. *Adesubokan* 1968 N.N.L.R. 97.
[31] See n. 27, above.
[32] 1968 N.N.L.R. 97 at p. 104.

Court held that the term "any law" in section 34(1) of the High Court Law of the northern States included the Wills Act 1837 (a received English statute of general application). It is submitted with utmost respect that the Supreme Court in so holding was wrong. The decision of the Supreme Court may be compared with the decision in *Rotibi* v. *Savage*,[33] where it was held that the words "any law," used in relation to the test of incompatibility in section 16 of the Protectorate Courts Ordinance 1933[34] meant any local enactment. It is submitted that that interpretation is consistent with the intention of the Legislature which made the current enactments on the incompatibility test.

Admittedly, it is arguable that, normally, the words "any law for the time being in force" may be construed to include the received English law[35] and English law applying directly to Nigeria. But it should be noted that customary law is so inconsistent with English law that prescribing an incompatibility test by reference to English law would result in a virtual abolition of customary law. It does not seem that such a destructive effect was intended by the Legislatures. Indeed, section 20 of the Supreme Court Ordinance 1914[36] provided for the incompatibility test by reference to local enactment in the following words: "nor incompatible either directly or by necessary implication with any local enactment existing at the commencement of the Ordinance, or which may afterwards come into operation." But section 17 of the Supreme Court Ordinance 1943[37] in dealing with the incompatibility test substituted the words "any law for the time being in force" for the words "any local enactment existing at the commencement of the Ordinance or which may afterwards come into operation." At best the Supreme Court decision on the interpretation of the term "any law" in section 34(1) of the High Court Law of the northern States is binding authority in relation to that Law only, notwithstanding the fact that the subsection is substantially the same in wording as the equivalent provisions in force in Lagos State and the eastern States. The decision is certainly no binding authority with respect to the interpretation of the relevant provisions in force outside the northern States. It is submitted that the words "any law for the time being in force" in the relevant current enactment on the incompatibility test, properly construed, means any local enactment

[33] (1944) 17 N.L.R. 77.

[34] No. 45 of 1933.

[35] The term "received English law" or "received English statute" is used in relation to the incompatibility test in a restrictive sense to connote the received law or statute as a source of Nigerian law. It does not connote English law re-enacted as Nigerian legislation. See p. 69, above.

[36] No. 6 of 1914.

[37] No. 33 of 1943. The Ordinance came into force on June 1, 1945.

for the time being in force.[38] As already indicated, section 13(1) of the High Court Law 1964[39] which is in force in Bendel State provides for the incompatibility test by reference to "any written law for the time being in force."[40] Section 12(1) of the High Court Law of Ogun, Ondo and Oyo States[41] is couched in identical terms. Other provisions prescribing the incompatibility test by reference to the same criterion include section 12(1) of the Area Courts Edict of each of the northern States.[42] The expression "written law" is defined in section 3 of the Interpretation Law in force in Bendel, Ogun, Ondo and Oyo States[43] as follows[44]:

> "written law includes all Ordinances and Laws and all orders, proclamations and letters patent and all regulations and rules of court made by any person or body having authority under any statutory or other enactment to make the same in and for Nigeria or any part thereof, but shall not include any Act of [the United Kingdom] Parliament extending expressly or by implication to Nigeria nor any Order of the Queen in Council, Royal Charter or Royal Letters Patent."

Obviously, Ordinances, Laws, orders, proclamations, letters patent, regulations and rules of court are, in the context, local enactments, that is, Nigerian legislation. All the words contained in the definition after the words "but shall not include" mean, simply, "any Act of the United Kingdom Parliament extending to Nigeria nor any other English statute applying directly to Nigeria."

It should be noted that no mention is made of the received English law in the definition. Clearly, two classes of the received law — the common law and equity — are, by their nature, not written law at all.[45] The absence of any reference to them in the definition, therefore, poses no problem. But it may be argued that because the definition of "written law" is introduced by the word "includes" and not by the word "means" the *definition* is not exhaustive and, therefore, the failure to mention the received English statutes or the received English subsidiary legislation in the definition does not mean that the sta-

---

[38] See S. E. Mosugu, "Moslem Wills and the Courts in Nigeria," Nig. J. Contemp. Law (1972) 105 at pp. 127-129; A. E. W. Park, *op. cit.* (n. 10, above), p. 79.

[39] No. 9 of 1964.

[40] See p. 104, above.

[41] W.R.N. Laws 1959, Cap. 44.

[42] See *e.g.* Area Courts Edict 1968 (No. 4 of 1968) (B.P.S.); Area Courts Edict 1968 (No. 1 of 1968) (N.E.S.).

[43] W.R.N. Laws 1959, Cap.·51.

[44] The wording of this definition is roughly the same as the wording of the definition of the term in the Interpretation Law of the eastern States (E.N. Laws 1963, Cap. 56) and the Interpretation Law of the northern States (N.N. Laws 1963, Cap. 52).

[45] See p. 10, above.

tutes or subsidiary legislation is not "written law" within the meaning of the relevant enactments. But having regard to the fact that the definition expressly mentions local enactments — enactments which are superior in authority to the received law and which in fact introduce the received law into Nigerian law — the argument is, at best very weak.[46] It seems clear, therefore, that the received English law is not "written law" within the meaning of the relevant High Court enactments and other enactments which prescribe the incompatibility test by reference to "written law."

It is, therefore, submitted that in all the enactments containing the incompatibility test, the test is prescribed by reference to local enactment. The courts must not refuse to enforce an applicable rule of customary law unless the rule is incompatible either directly or by implication with a local enactment.

A rule of customary law on a subject matter is incompatible with a local statute or local subsidiary legislation if the local enactment is manifestly intended to govern that subject matter to the exclusion of customary law.[47] A case of direct incompatibility arises where the manifest intention as indicated by express terms is to abolish or modify the customary law rule.[48] Where the co-existence of a rule of customary law and a local enactment is not inconsistent with the manifest object of the local enactment, there is no question of incompatibility. But where, notwithstanding the fact that a local enactment does not expressly abolish or modify a customary law rule, the co-existence of both is inconsistent with the manifest object of the local enactment, there is implicit incompatibility.

Where a received English statute is re-enacted by the local legislature, the resulting enactment is a local enactment[49] and in the absence of any provision excluding, expressly or by implication, customary law matters from the ambit of the enactment rules of customary law on any matter dealt with by the enactment cease to be in force in so far as they are incompatible with the enactment.[50] The Legislature of the Western Region of Nigeria re-enacted, substantially, a

---

46 Moreover, with respect to Bendel, Ogun, Ondo and Oyo States, by virtue of s. 3 of the Law of England (Application) Law (W.R.N. Laws 1959, Cap. 60), no English statute dealing with a matter within the legislative competence of any of the States is in force in the State.

47 See *Salau* v. *Aderibigbe* [1963] W.N.L.R. 80.

48 See *e.g.* the Abolition of Osu System Law (E.N. Laws 1963, Cap. 1).

49 See p. 69, above.

50 See A. E. W. Park, *op. cit.* (n. 10, above), pp. 51-52. Compare L. C. B. Gower, "Nigerian Statutes and Customary Law" [1964] Nig. L.J. 73: "A [local] statute should be construed as not affecting a transaction governed by customary law unless it expressly or by necessary implication provides to the contrary. The main argument in favour of this conclusion is the manifest absurdity which would otherwise result."

number of English statutes as part of the 1959 revised edition of the laws of the Region. Some of the laws, for example, the Prescription Law,[51] contain provisions exempting matters governed by customary law. But others, for example, the Contracts Law,[52] do not contain such provisions. In every case, it is a question of construction whether a local enactment on a particular matter abolishes or modifies the customary law on the matter or is intended to co-exist with the customary law.[53]

3. *The Test of Public Policy*

The test of public policy is stated in section 14(3) of each of the Evidence enactments[54] in these words:

> ". . . in case of any custom relied upon in any judicial proceedings it shall not be enforced if it is contrary to public policy [and is not in accordance with natural justice, equity and good conscience]."[55]

There are only a few reported cases in which reference has been made to public policy in relation to customary law. In discussing the possible existence of a Yoruba custom of legitimation by acknowledgment of paternity, Verity C.J. said *obiter* in *Re Adadevoh*[56] that if such a custom encouraged promiscuity it would be contrary to public policy. The Evidence Ordinance was not referred to in the case. The test of public policy was considered as a common law rule forming part of the incompatibility test.[57] Similarly, in *Alake* v. *Pratt*[58] where it was held that the same Yoruba custom was incompatible with public policy, the court did not refer to the Evidence Ordinance. The court, thus, rejected the view expressed by the trial judge that it was incompatible with public policy to place children born out of wedlock in the same position as children born in wedlock in distributing the estate of the deceased father of all the children. Another case in which public policy was mentioned in relation to customary

---

[51] W.R.N. Laws 1959, Cap. 95.

[52] W.R.N. Laws 1959, Cap. 25.

[53] See E. A. Keay and S. S. Richardson, *The Native and Customary Courts of Nigeria* (1966), pp. 241-245; L. C. B. Gower, "Nigerian Statutes and Customary Law" [1964] Nig.J.J. 73.

[54] Evidence Act (Fed. and Lagos Laws 1958, Cap. 62); Evidence Law (N.N. Laws 1963, Cap. 40); Evidence Law (E.N. Laws 1963, Cap. 49); Evidence Ordinance (Nigeria Laws 1948, Cap. 63).

[55] This provision does not apply to customary or area courts. See *e.g.* s. 1(4)(*c*) of the Evidence Act. See p. 93, above.

[56] (1951) 13 W.A.C.A. 304.

[57] See p. 104, above.

[58] (1955) 15 W.A.C.A. 20.

law was *Cole* v. *Akinyele*[59] in which the Federal Supreme Court held that the same Yoruba custom of legitimation by acknowledgment of paternity was void on the ground of public policy in its application to a child born outside wedlock during the subsistence of a marriage under the Marriage Ordinance.[60] The court observed that under the Legitimacy Ordinance,[61] the legitimation of a child born outside wedlock during the subsistence of a statutory marriage could be effected only by a subsequent statutory marriage between the parents of the children. In this case, too, no reference was made to the Evidence Ordinance by the court. But there is nothing in the wording of the Evidence enactments to support the view that a rule of customary law could be invalid on the ground of public policy in particular circumstances and valid in other circumstances.[62] Therefore, if the court was applying the test of public policy under the Evidence Ordinance, the court was wrong. Even if the court was applying the common law doctrine of public policy, it is suggested that the court was also wrong because no enactment makes customary law subject to any part of the received English law.[63] It has been suggested that the Yoruba custom could have been rejected on the ground of implicit incompatibility with the Legitimacy Ordinance[64] but although the Ordinance prescribed a method of legitimation its wording does not suggest an intention on the part of the legislature to abolish the customary law of legitimation.[65]

All the enactments stating criteria for determining the validity of customary law contain the repugnancy test but only the Evidence enactments contain as a second test the criterion of public policy. The other enactments contain the criterion of incompatibility with any local enactments as a second test. It is not easy to understand the intention of the legislatures in introducing the test of public policy. It could be that they were of opinion that "contrary to public policy" meant incompatible with any local enactment. But if this suggestion is correct it is surprising that the test of incompatibility has not been abolished. There is no doubt, however, that it is much easier to understand the incompatibility test than to understand the test of public policy.

[59] (1960) 5 F.S.C. 84.
[60] Nigeria Laws 1948, Cap. 128.
[61] Nigeria Laws 1948, Cap. 111.
[62] See p. 103, above in relation to the repugnancy test.
[63] See p. 106, above.
[64] A. E. W. Park, *op.cit.* (n. 10, above), p. 79.
[65] See p. 108, above; E. A. Keay and S. S. Richardson, *The Native and Customary Courts of Nigeria* (1966), p. 247.

CHAPTER 7

JUDICIAL PRECEDENT

JUDICIAL precedent or case law consists of law found in judicial decisions. A judicial precedent is the principle of law on which a judicial decision is based. It is the *ratio decidendi* (literally, the reason for the decision). It follows that it is not everything said by a judge in the course of his judgment that constitutes a precedent Only the pronouncement on law in relation to the material facts before the judge constitutes a precedent. Any other pronouncement on law made in the course of a judgment is an *obiter dictum* (a statement by the way) and it does not form part of the *ratio decidendi.*

At common law, the principle of law on which a court bases its decision in relation to the material facts before it must be followed in similar cases by courts below it in the hierarchy of courts and may be followed in similar cases by courts above it in the hierarchy.[1] A settled hierarchy of courts and an efficient system of law reporting are therefore essential to the proper operation of the doctrine of judicial precedent. Where the legal principle must be followed, it is a binding precedent. Where it may be followed, it is a persuasive precedent. When it is said that a judgment, judicial decision or case is binding, what is meant is that the *ratio decidendi* is a binding precedent. The word "judgment" is usually used in a wide sense to mean all that the court says in disposing of a case before it. In law reports, the judgment usually begins immediately after such words as "The following judgment was delivered by . . . " or "The judgment of the court was delivered by . . . " Judgment in this sense usually consists of a statement of the facts of the case, a statement of the issue or issues to be determined, a discussion of relevant legal principles, a statement of the applicable legal principle and the actual judgment, decision or order of the court. The actual judgment or decision with or without an order is the judgment or decision in the narrow sense. Judgment in this sense is binding on the parties to the case only; it is not binding in subsequent cases between other parties. As between the parties to the earlier case, the subject matter of the case is *res judicata*.[2] The distinction between *ratio decidendi* and *res judicata* was well illustrated in *Re Waring*,[3] a case involving a testator who died in 1940, leaving legacies to H. and L. free "from income tax." In 1942, the Court of Appeal of England held in a case to which H. was a party, but to

---

[1] See pp. 114-121, below.
[2] Finally decided. The issue in the case cannot be raised again before the courts.
[3] [1948] Ch. 221.

which L. was not, that by virtue of a statute the legacy was subject to income tax. Later, in *Berkeley* v. *Berkeley*,[4] a similar case to which neither H. nor L. was a party, the House of Lords overruled the 1942 decision. Subsequently, H. and L. applied to the Chancery Division of the High Court to determine whether in view of the House of Lords decision their legacies were subject to income tax. Jenkins J. held that H.'s claim, but not L.'s claim, was *res judicata*, the 1942 decision of the Court of Appeal being binding upon H.; and that the decision of the House of Lords in *Berkeley* v. *Berkeley* applied to L.'s claim.

An *obiter dictum* is not binding in any circumstances. But, like a persuasive precedent, it is of persuasive authority. Usually, it is made without being fully considered by the court.

A. Determining the Ratio Decidendi of a Case

Determining the *ratio decidendi* of a case is not always an easy exercise. It is the province of a court to determine the *ratio decidendi* of a relevant previous case. Where the court in the previous case clearly stated the legal principle on which it based its decision, the court in a later case would usually regard that principle as the *ratio decidendi*. But where the legal principle as stated is wider than the material facts of the case require, the statement of principle is considered in a later case as an *obiter dictum* to the extent of its deviation from the material facts.[5] Similarly, where the statement of principle is too narrow in relation to the material facts, it is the task of the court in a later similar case to state the *ratio decidendi* in its proper form. For instance, in *Barwick* v. *English Joint Stock Bank*,[6] Willes J. delivering the judgment of the court said:

> "But with respect to the question whether a principal is answerable for the act of his agent in the course of his master's business, and *for his master's benefit*, no sensible distinction can be drawn between the case of fraud and the case of any other wrong. The general rule is that the master is answerable for every such wrong of the servant or agent as is committed in the course of the service and *for the master's benefit* though no express command or privity of the master be proved."[7]

But in *Lloyd* v. *Grace, Smith & Co.*,[8] the House of Lords expressed

[4] [1946] A.C. 55.
[5] See *e.g. R.* v. *St. Edmundsbury and Ipswich Diocese* (*Chancellor*) [1948] 1 K.B. 195 at p. 215 and p. 222.
[6] (1866) L.R. 2 Ex. 259.
[7] *Ibid.* at p. 265 (italics supplied).
[8] [1912] A.C. 714.

the view that the reference to the master's benefit in the judgment in *Barwick's* case was not part of the *ratio decidendi*. Accordingly, the court held that an employer was liable for a fraud committed by a servant in the course of his employment, the fact that the fraud was not committed for the benefit of the master notwithstanding. In some cases, the court does not state the reason for the decision or the principle of law on which the decision is based. Nevertheless, the *ratio decidendi* of the case can usually be determined by the court in a subsequent case. Even where the reason for the decision is stated, it may not correctly represent the principle of law on which the decision is based[9] and where a principle of law is stated it may not be considered in a later case as the principle on which the decision is based. Where a court bases its decision in a case on more than one legal principle, each principle constitutes a *ratio decidendi*.[10] The case therefore has as many *rationes decidendi* as the number of principles 'on which it is based.

In determining the *ratio decidendi* of a case, the courts usually consider any one or more of the following factors: the reason for the decision as stated by the judge, the principle of law stated by the judge as that on which the decision was based and the actual decision in relation to the material facts. In addition, the court may consider the interpretation of the case in any later case determined before the instant case. It is sometimes difficult to find the *ratio decidendi* of a case determined by a court consisting of more than one judge.[11] Where the court is divided and the majority judgments are consistent with one another even though each majority judge relies on a legal principle different from that relied upon by any other majority judge, it seems that all the legal principles relied upon in the majority judgments constitute the *rationes decidendi* of the case.[12] Where the majority judgments are consistent with one another and they are based on the same legal principle, that principle is the *ratio decidendi* of the case. In cases where the majority concur in the result but the majority judgments are inconsistent with one another it is difficult to determine the *ratio decidendi*. Suppose, for example, that the majority of the judges in a case are in support of the order of the court but there is no majority in support of any of the grounds of the decision. In such a case, no principle of law enunciated in the judgments as the basis of the decision has received majority support. It is suggested that a proposition of law which is not supported by the majority and which is actually rejected by the majority should not be considered as

---

9 See A. L. Goodhart, "The Ratio Decidendi of a Case" 22 N.L.R. 117.
10 *Jacobs* v. *L.C.C.* [1950] A.C. 361 at p. 369.
11 See R. Cross, *Precedent in English Law* (2nd ed., 1968), pp. 90-101.
12 See *Jacobs* v. *L.C.C.* [1950] A.C. 361 at p. 369.

the *ratio decidendi*. In the circumstances, therefore, it appears that the case should not be cited as a binding authority for any proposition.

B. DISTINGUISHING

The decision of a court in a case is not a binding precedent for any court in any subsequent case if the cases are different from each other in terms of material facts. Where such difference occurs and the previous case is cited as authority, the court in the subsequent case would mention the difference in order to show that the principle in the previous case is not applicable. When this happens, it is said that the court has distinguished the previous case. By virtue of the fact that it is within the province of the court in the instant case to interpret a previous decision, it is often not difficult for a court to avoid following a previous decision by "finding" that the material facts of the previous decision are different from those of the instant case or by showing that what purports to be the *ratio decidendi* of the previous case is not in fact the *ratio decidendi*. Even where a decision is that of a lower court and is, therefore, not a binding precedent, the court often prefers distinguishing it to overruling it.

C. THE DOCTRINE OF JUDICIAL PRECEDENT
AND THE HIERARCHY OF THE COURTS

The doctrine of judicial precedent as a common law doctrine applies to only those courts which are empowered to administer adjective common law of which the doctrine forms part. Customary courts, Sharia Courts of Appeal and area courts are not empowered to apply adjective common law.[13] Therefore, the common law doctrine does not apply to them; nor does any legislation provide for a precedent system in customary courts. The only attempt to prescribe a precedent system in Nigeria could be found in the repealed Customary Courts Rules 1966[14] of the former Midwestern State. The ques-

---

[13] It appears that the area courts may administer substantive common law in certain circumstances. See *e.g.* s. 20(3) of the Area Courts Edict 1968 (No. 4 of 1968) (B.P.S.) which provides: "Nothing contained in this section shall be deemed to preclude the application by an area court of any principle of English law which the parties to any civil case agreed or intended or may be presumed to have agreed or intended should regulate their obligations in connection with the transactions which are in controversy before the court."

[14] M.N.L.N. 37 of 1967. Ord. X, r. 6(5) of the Rules provided that the customary law which a customary court in its judgment stated as the appropriate customary law must, subject to statutory provisions relating to the choice of the appropriate customary law, be presumed to be correct until the contrary was proved except where the customary law as stated was inconsistent with any previous subsisting judgment of the High Court of the State or the Supreme Court.

tion now arises whether there is a rule of precedent under customary law. Although the idea of treating previous decisions with respect and referring to them in deciding a dispute is not unknown to customary law, it appears that there is nothing in the attitude of customary courts, area courts or Sharia Courts of Appeal to support the view that there exists a system of precedents under customary law. The argument against the existence of a rule of precedent under customary law is strengthened by the fact that there is no organised system of law reporting covering decisions of such courts. The discussion of the doctrine of judicial precedent and the hierarchy of the courts is, therefore, limited to courts other than courts established principally for the administration of customary law.

As a general rule under the doctrine of *stare decisis*[15] or binding precedent, a court is bound to follow decisions of a higher court in the hierarchy. But a lower court is not bound to follow a decision of a higher court which has been overruled. Furthermore, a lower court is not bound by a decision of a higher court where that decision is in conflict with a decision of another court which is above such higher court in the hierarchy. Moreover, in principle, a lower court is entitled to choose which of two conflicting decisions of a higher court or of higher courts of equal standing it would follow.[16]

The highest court for Nigeria is the Supreme Court of Nigeria, a court which forms part of the hierarchy of federal courts with respect to federal matters and part of the hierarchy of courts for each State with respect to State matters.[17] There is no complete separate set of federal courts, the only ordinary court which exercises jurisdiction in federal matters to the exclusion of other matters being the Federal High Court, that is, the Federal Revenue Court.[18] The High Court of each State, the magistrates' courts of each State and the district courts of each of the northern States exercise jurisdiction in federal matters[19] in addition to jurisdiction in State matters, subject to the jurisdiction of the Federal Revenue Court.[20] Thus, throughout the country, federal jurisdiction is exercised side by side with State jurisdiction. The federal courts comprise not only courts established by

---

[15] Following (previous) decisions.
[16] See *Chime* v. *Elikwu* 1965 N.M.L.R.71. It should also be noted that a binding precedent may be abolished by legislation. See *e.g. Lakanmi* v. *Attorney-General (West)* (1971) 1 U.I.L.R. 201; Federal Military Government (Supremacy and Enforcement of Powers) Decree 1970 (No. 28 of 1970).
[17] See Constitution of the Federation (Act No. 20 of 1963). ss. 117 and 127.
[18] Federal Revenue Court Decree 1973 (No. 13 of 1973).
[19] See Constitution (Basic Provisions) Decree 1975 (No. 32 of 1975), s. 14(2); Constitution (Suspension and Modification) Decree 1966 (No. 1 of 1966), s. 3; Constitution of the Federation, Schedule.
[20] See s. 8(1) of the Federal Revenue Court Decree 1973.

federal law but also courts established by State law and given jurisdiction in federal matters by federal law.

The following charts illustrate the hierarchy of courts in the various jurisdictions in the country:

COURTS EXERCISING JURISDICTION IN FEDERAL MATTERS

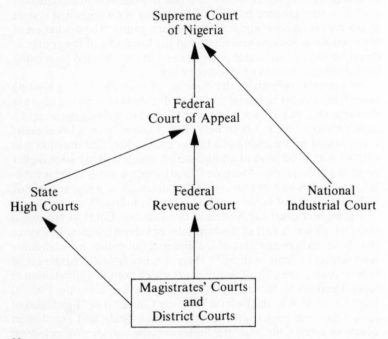

Note

1. The above chart omits several courts and "tribunals" exercising special jurisdiction.

2. The District Courts mentioned in the above chart are district courts of the northern States. It is expressly stated in the Federal Revenue Court Decree 1973 that appeals lie to the Federal Revenue Court from magistrates' courts in civil and criminal cases transferred to those courts by the Federal Revenue Court. Although no mention is made of district courts in the Decree, it seems that it is the intention of the legislature that the words "Magistrates' courts" in the relevant provision of the Decree (s. 27) should be construed to include district courts of the northern States for magistrates' courts of those States exercise criminal jurisdiction only and district courts of the States are courts of civil jurisdiction. See ss. 26 and 27(c) of the Decree.

THE COURT SYSTEMS OF THE STATES

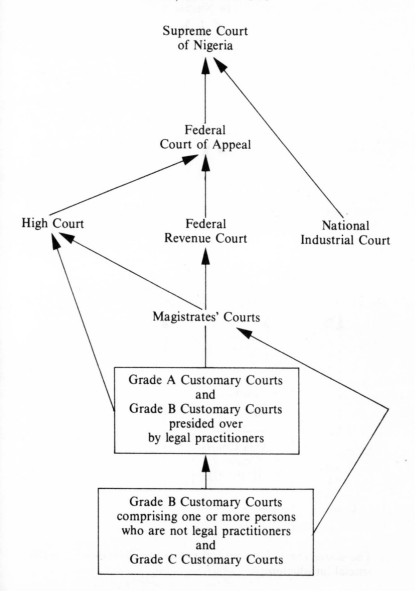

EACH OF THE STATES OF
OGUN, ONDO AND OYO

Supreme Court
of Nigeria

Federal
Court of Appeal

High Court   Federal   National
Revenue Court   Industrial Court

Magistrates' Courts

Grade A Customary Courts
and
Grade B Customary Courts
presided over
by legal practitioners

Grade B Customary Courts
comprising one or more persons
who are not legal practitioners
and
Grade C Customary Courts

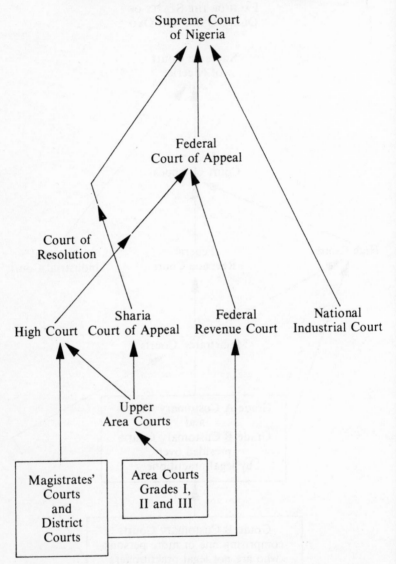

EACH OF THE STATES OF
BAUCHI, BENUE, BORNO, GONGOLA, KADUNA,
KANO, KWARA, NIGER, PLATEAU, AND SOKOTO

Supreme Court
of Nigeria

Federal
Court of Appeal

Court of
Resolution

High Court   Sharia
Court of Appeal

Federal
Revenue Court

National
Industrial Court

Upper
Area Courts

Magistrates'
Courts
and
District
Courts

Area Courts
Grades I,
II and III

Note

The above charts omit several courts and "tribunals" exercising special jurisdiction.

EACH OF THE STATES OF
LAGOS AND ANAMBRA

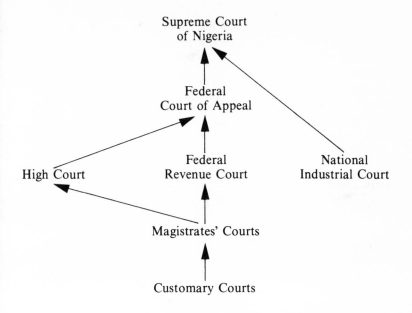

BENDEL

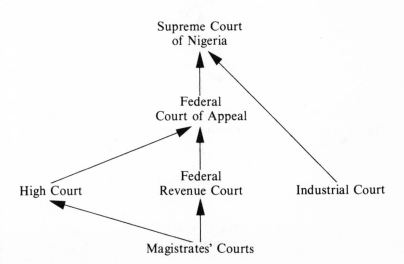

IMO

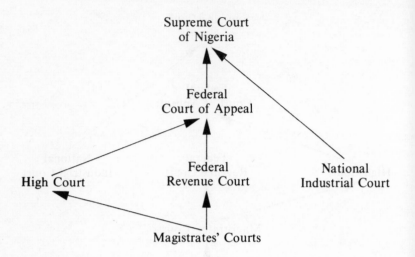

CROSS RIVER

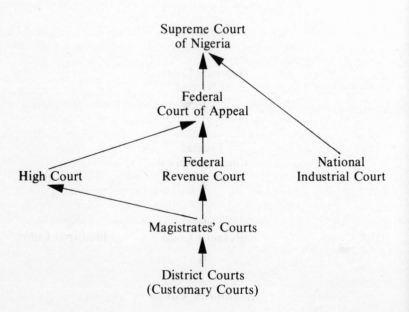

RIVERS

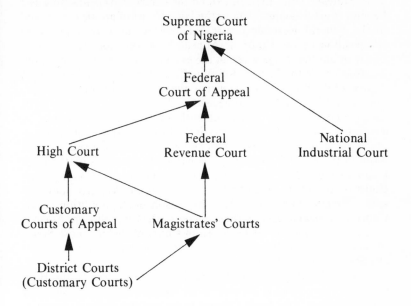

D. JUDICIAL PRECEDENT AND JURISDICTION IN FEDERAL MATTERS

Regular courts exercising jurisdiction in Federal matters consist mainly of the Supreme Court of Nigeria, the Federal Court of Appeal, the Federal Revenue Court, the High Court of each State, the magistrates' courts of each State and the district courts of each of the northern States.[21] Under the common law doctrine of binding precedent, the decisions of the Supreme Court and the Federal Court of Appeal are binding on all other courts to which the doctrine applies whether those other courts sit as Federal courts or as State courts.

An anomalous situation was caused by the establishment in 1967 of the Court of Appeal of the Western State which functioned until the creation of States in 1976.[22] Although the court heard appeals from decisions of the High Court of the State, by virtue of section 127 of the Constitution of the Federation,[23] it exercised such original

[21] In special circumstances, jurisdiction is conferred by or under Federal law on other courts. See *e.g.* the repealed Price Control Decree 1970 (No. 33 of 1970), s. 10(5).

[22] See States (Creation and Transitional Provisions) Decree 1976 (No. 12 of 1976); Constitution (Amendment) (No. 2) Decree 1976 (No. 42 of 1976), s. 3(1).

[23] Act No. 20 of 1963.

jurisdiction in certain cases as was exercised by the High Courts of other States.[24] Thus, to some extent, the Court of Appeal sitting as a Federal court was equivalent to the High Court of another State and to the Federal Revenue Court.[25] Therefore, notwithstanding the composition of the Court of Appeal,[26] the decisions of the High Court of another State given in the exercise of Federal jurisdiction, the decisions of the Federal Revenue Court and those of the Court of Appeal of the Western State given in the exercise of Federal jurisdiction should be considered as decisions of courts of co-ordinate jurisdiction. The decisions of any one of those courts are not binding on any of the others.[27] The decisions of the Court of Appeal of the Western State whether given in the exercise of Federal jurisdiction or given in the exercise of State jurisdiction were binding on the High Court of the State.[28] Those decisions are not binding on the High Court of any of the three States into which the Western State was split — Ogun, Ondo and Oyo. By reason of the abolition of the Court of Appeal of each of those States by the Constitution (Amendment) (No. 2) Decree 1976, the High Court of each of those States should be regarded as a court equivalent in status to the former Western State Court of Appeal.

Clearly, the High Court of each State is equivalent to the High Court of every other State and to the Federal Revenue Court. The decisions of all the High Courts, including the Federal Revenue Court, given in the exercise of Federal jurisdiction are, therefore, to be treated as decisions of courts of co-ordinate jurisdiction. Such decisions of any of the High Courts are not binding on any other High Court. In the exercise of Federal jurisidiction, magistrates' courts of all the States and district courts of the northern States are obviously bound by the decisions of the Federal Revenue Court. They are clearly lower in the hierarchy of Federal courts than the Federal High Court. It is submitted that a magistrate's court or a district court of a State sitting as a Federal court is bound not only by the decisions of the High Court of the State but also by the decisions of the High Courts of all the other States given in the exercise of Federal jurisdiction. Similarly, magistrates' courts of each State and district courts of each of the northern States are bound by the decisions of the defunct Court of Appeal of the Western State given in the exercise of Federal jurisdiction. Magistrates' courts of a State sitting as

[24] See *e.g.* Constitution of the Federation, ss. 115 and 117.
[25] See Constitution of the Federation, s. 127; Federal Revenue Court Decree 1973 (No. 13 of 1973), s. 31.
[26] See Court of Appeal Edict 1967 (No. 15 of 1967), s. 12.
[27] See pp. 129–133, below.
[28] Appeals lay from the High Court to the Court of Appeal. See s. 53 of the Constitution of Western Nigeria (W.N. No. 26 of 1963).

Federal courts and magistrates' courts of other States are all courts of co-ordinate jurisdiction within the same hierarchy. Such decisions of a magistrate's court of a State are not binding on any other magistrate's court of the State; nor are they binding on a magistrate's court of any other State. Similarly, the decisions of a district court of a northern State are not binding on another district court of the State nor are they binding on a district court of any other northern State.

E. The Supreme Court of Nigeria

The decisions of the Supreme Court of Nigeria are binding on all other courts to which the common law doctrine of binding precedent applies. Although the doctrine does not apply to customary courts, area courts or Sharia Courts of Appeal, in principle, by virtue of the appellate systems whereby decisions of these courts can ultimately reach the Supreme Court, the courts should follow decisions of the Supreme Court.

The Supreme Court replaced the Judicial Committee of the Privy Council as the highest court for Nigeria.[29] It should therefore treat the decisions of the Privy Council given before the abolition of appeals to the Council as it would treat its own decision. That was, indeed, the attitude adopted by the Supreme Court in the case of *Johnson* v. *Lawanson.*[30] In that case, a full court of the Supreme Court overruled a Privy Council decision, *Maurice Goualin Ltd.* v. *Aminu.*[31] It is clear from this Supreme Court decision that the Supreme Court does not regard Privy Council decisions as binding upon it. The Court in the same case overruled three of its previous decisions[32] without distinguishing between the authority of its previous decisions and the authority of Privy Council decisions. Although it is clear from the decision in *Johnson* v. *Lawanson* that the Supreme Court is not bound by its previous decisions, the reasoning of the court in that case in relation to its attitude towards its previous decisions is not quite clear. In order to facilitate an analysis of the reasoning it is considered necessary to set out the reasoning in full. It is as follows[33]:

> "We are now faced with this situation in which the decisions to which we have referred have created a conflict of such a serious

---

[29] Constitution of the Federation, s. 120.
[30] [1971] 1 All N.L.R. 56.
[31] Privy Council Appeal No. 17 of 1957 (unreported).
[32] *Odeneye* v. *Savage* 1964 N.M.L.R. 115; *Williams* v. *Akinwumi* [1966] 1 All N.L.R. 115; *John* v. *Adebayo* S.C. 46/66 of June 6, 1969 (unreported).
[33] *Nigeria Lawyers' Quarterly*, Vol. VI, Nos. 1-4, 147 at pp. 156-157; [1971] 1 All N.L.R. 56 at pp. 66-68.

nature as to confuse practitioners and introduce a serious element
of uncertainty into our law. We find that we must and we do come
to the conclusion that the decisions which had equated the 'date of
the contract' appearing in section 129 of the Evidence Act, Cap. 62
with the date of the proceedings in hand are manifestly unsuppor-
table for even if there be no other reason they have failed not only
to give the material words of the statute their ordinary and natural
meaning and import, but also to explain why those plain and
unambiguous words of the statute should be discarded. We have
already pointed out that those decisions in the fashion of *Maurice
Goualin Ltd. & Anor.* v. *Wahabi Atanda Aminu* (*supra*) had been
followed for some twelve years or more. Within those twelve years
the authority of those decisions has certainly been challenged as
we have shown by at least a single decision of the Federal Supreme
Court running the other way. Our system of law reporting in this
country is anything but perfect and we cannot but see the unwhole-
some effect of a serious conflict in a most frequently used area of
our law. The course open to this full court is clear and we would in
this respect refer to the observations, to the following effect, of Verity C.J., delivering the judgment of the West African Court of
Appeal in *Re Sarah I. Adadevoh & Ors. and in the matter of the
estate of Samuel Herbert Macaulay (deceased)* (1951) 13
W.A.C.A. 304 at p. 310:
> 'I am fully alive to the fact that grave inconvenience may arise
> from a judgment of this Court in such a matter which reverses a
> view of the law which has been held for upwards of ten years,
> but when the Court is faced with the alternative of perpetuating
> what it is satisfied is an erroneous decision which was reached
> *per incuriam* and will, if it be followed, inflict hardship and injus-
> tice upon generations in the future or of causing temporary dis-
> turbance of rights acquired under such a decision, I do not think
> we should hesitate to declare the law as we find it.'

We hold, therefore, that a deed to be competent for the presumption contemplated by section 129 of the Evidence Act must be 20
years old 'at the date of the contract' in which the deed is sought to
be relied upon and not 20 years old at the date of the proceedings
at which such a deed is being offered in evidence. We have come to
the conclusion that the decision in *Maurice Goualin Ltd. & Anor.*
v. *Wahabi Atanda* (*supra*) and the other decisions based on it in so
far as they have measured the age of the deed relied upon for secur-
ing the benefit of the presumption created by section 129 of the Evidence Act by reference to the date of the proceedings at which such
deed is being offered in evidence, were wrongly decided and we
over-rule them. They are obviously steering a course which may be
at present uneventful but which ultimately, when pursued to the

logical conclusion, would be disastrous and an owner of property would find himself one day confronted with a deed of sale prepared by a stranger some twenty years back on his property and would be obliged to defend his title in the face of such a deed stored away all the time and which may well prove to be bogus."

The reference to the imperfect system of law reporting read in the context tends to support the view that the court considered the previous decision of the Privy Council and the previous decisions of the Supreme Court as given *per incuriam*. But, in fact, none of the decisions was given in ignorance of the existence of, or by an oversight of, any relevant statute or case law. Rather, it was the case followed by the Supreme Court, *Omosanya* v. *Anifowoshe*,[34] a decision of the Federal Supreme Court given in 1959 after the decision of a higher court (the Privy Council) to the contrary that was given *per incuriam*.[35] The question whether a previous decision was given *per incuriam* was, therefore, irrelevant to the decision of the court.

Furthermore, it should be pointed out that it is difficult to agree with the Supreme Court that it was faced with a situation "in which the decisions to which we have referred have created a conflict of such a serious nature as to confuse practitioners and introduce a serious element of uncertainty into our law." There was a conflict between a decision of the Federal Supreme Court, *Omosanya* v. *Anifowoshe*, on the one hand and three decisions of the Supreme Court and one decision of the Privy Council on the other. It is elementary knowledge that the decisions of the Privy Council were binding on the Federal Supreme Court, a lower court. The decision in *Omosanya* v. *Anifowoshe* in which attention was not drawn to the Privy Council decision was, therefore, given *per incuriam*. Thus, no conflict of a serious nature arose. By virtue of the doctrine of precedent, the position of the law on and immediately after the date of the Federal Supreme Court decision was as stated by the Privy Council in *Maurice Goualin Ltd.* v. *Aminu*.[36] Of course, there was no conflict between the three Supreme Court decisions cited on the one hand and the decision of the Privy Council on the other. Therefore, no element of uncertainty of law was introduced by any of the previous decisions cited. Thus, the element of resolving a serious conflict likely to confuse practitioners or the element of introducing uncertainty into the law was irrelevant to the decision of the Supreme Court to overrule the previous decisions.

[34] (1959) 4 F.S.C. 94.
[35] See D. A. Ijalaye, "Case Comment: The Supreme Court's Power to Overrule Its Earlier Decisions — A Bold Legislative Act!", *Nigeria Lawyers' Quarterly*, Vol. VI, Nos. 1-4, p. 158.
[36] Privy Council Appeal No. 17 of 1957 (unreported).

Reading the judgment in *Johnson* v. *Lawanson* in the light of this observation strongly suggests that the Supreme Court was of opinion that it could overrule its own previous decision or that of the Privy Council in order to avoid perpetuating an error which if not corrected would result in injustice. It may be concluded, therefore, that the Supreme Court would normally treat its previous decisions and those of the Privy Council with great respect but it would depart from a previous decision if it is of opinion that the decision was wrong and that following it would lead to injustice.

This attitude is similar to that of the House of Lords, the highest court for England (except in cases involving the law of the European Economic Community), as stated in a practice direction of 1966. The direction is as follows[37]:

"Their lordships regard the use of precedent ... as an indispensable foundation upon which to decide what is the law and its application to individual cases. It provides at least some degree of certainty upon which individuals can rely in the conduct of their affairs, as well as a basis for orderly development of legal rules.

Their lordships nevertheless recognise that too rigid adherence to precedent may lead to injustice in a particular case and also unduly restrict the proper development of the law. They propose therefore to modify their present practice and, while treating former decisions of this House as normally binding, to depart from a previous decision when it appears right to do so.

In this connexion they will bear in mind the danger of disturbing retrospectively the basis on which contracts, settlements of property and fiscal arrangements have been entered into and also the especial need for certainty as to the criminal law.

This announcement is not intended to affect the use of precedent elsewhere than in this House."

This is a proper attitude of the highest court in a hierarchy. Notwithstanding the need for certainty of the law, it is clear that adhering slavishly to precedent would in certain cases result in perpetuating errors and injustice.

It is submitted that this practice of the Supreme Court applies even where the court is a court of three or four judges rather than a full court. Although the Supreme Court sitting as a three-member or four-member court would treat with very great respect a decision given by a full court constituted by five judges,[38] it would depart

[37] [1966] 3 All E.R. 77.
[38] A full court of the Supreme Court is usually constituted by five judges and not all the judges of the court. See *e.g. Johnson* v. *Lawanson* [1971] 1 All N.L.R. 56 where Coker J.S.C., delivering the judgment of the court, referred to the five-member court as "this full Court."

from such a decision whenever necessary in the interest of justice.[39]

F. The Federal Court of Appeal

The Federal Court of Appeal is bound by the decisions of the Supreme Court of Nigeria. In determining the attitude of this new court towards its previous decisions, mention should be made of section 8(1) of the Federal Court of Appeal Decree 1976[40] which provides that the practice and procedure of the court are to be in accordance with the Decree and, subject to the Decree, in accordance with rules of court. It is provided that until rules of court are made under the Decree the rules in force in the Supreme Court on the date of commencement of the Decree (October 1, 1976) are to apply with respect to practice and procedure to the Federal Court of Appeal, subject to such modifications as may be necessary to bring them into conformity with the Decree and the Constitution of the Federation.[41] Rules of court have not yet been made for the new court. Accordingly, the Supreme Court Rules of 1961,[42] applicable to the Supreme Court on October 1, 1976 apply to the new court subject to necessary modifications. Rule 36 of Order VII of the Rules provides with respect to civil appeals that where "no other provision is made by these Rules the procedure and practice for the time being in force in the Court of Appeal in England shall apply in so far as it is not inconsistent with these Rules . . . " There is no provision in the Rules governing precedent. Accordingly, the practice of the Court of Appeal of England is to be adopted. That practice is stated in the English case of *Young* v. *Bristol Aeroplane Co.*,[43] and in its application to the Federal Court of Appeal is as follows:

The Federal Court of Appeal is bound by its previous decisions subject to the following exceptions:

   (a) The court is entitled and bound to decide which of two conflicting decisions of its own it will follow.
   (b) The court is bound to refuse to follow a decision of its own which though not expressly overruled cannot, in its opinion, stand with a decision of the Supreme Court of Nigeria.

---

[39] Compare the attitude of the former West African Court of Appeal as stated in *Motayo* v. *Commissioner of Police* 13 W.A.C.A. 114 at p. 116: "In local conditions, it would be impracticable to hold a court of more than five judges, but the practice will be that no previous decision of the court will be reviewed save by a full court constituted by that number."; D.A. Ijalaye, "Case Comment: The Supreme Court's Power to Overrule Its Earlier Decisions — A Bold Legislative Act!," *Nigeria Lawyers' Quarterly*, Vol. VI, Nos. 1-4, p. 158.
[40] No. 43 of 1976.
[41] *Ibid.* s. 8(3).
[42] Supreme Court Rules 1961 (L.N. 96 of 1961).
[43] [1944] K.B. 718.

(c) The court is not bound to follow a decision of its own if it is satisfied that the decision was given *per incuriam*.

With respect to criminal appeals, in principle, the Federal Court of Appeal should follow the practice of the Criminal Division of the Court of Appeal of England. That Division is not bound by its previous decisions in criminal appeals but it would normally feel reluctant to refuse to follow such decisions.[44]

It is suggested that when the court is exercising original jurisdiction it should not be bound by its previous decisions given in the exercise of its original jurisdiction. Thus, in this case, the court should, with respect to practice, be in the same position as a High Court.[45] The Federal Court of Appeal sitting as an appellate court is of the same status as the same court sitting as a court of original jurisdiction. It is true that the law prescribes a minimum number of three judges as judges who could constitute the court in the exercise of its appellate jurisdiction[46] and that no minimum number of judges is prescribed with respect to the court sitting as a court of original jurisdiction. But in practice, having regard to the importance of the cases within the original jurisdiction of the court,[47] it is suggested that at least three judges would be sitting to hear and determine such cases. It is further suggested that when the court is exercising original jurisdiction it should not be bound by its previous decisions given in the exercise of its appellate jurisdiction.

The Federal Court of Appeal is bound by the decisions of the Judicial Committee of the Privy Council given before the abolition of appeals to the Committee since the Committee was the highest court for Nigeria. By virtue of its position (second from the top) in the hierarchy, the court is higher in status than the former Supreme Court[48] and is therefore not bound by the decisions of that Supreme Court. The position of the Federal Court of Appeal is similar to that of the Federal Supreme Court or the West African Court of Appeal.[49] Accordingly, the Federal Court of Appeal would treat the previous decisions of the Federal Supreme Court and the West African Court of Appeal as its own previous decisions.

---

[44] *R.* v. *Taylor* [1950] 2 K.B. 368 decided by the Court of Criminal Appeal. The practice of the court as stated in the case has been adopted by the Criminal Division of the Court of Appeal.

[45] See pp. 131-132, below.

[46] Federal Court of Appeal Decree 1976 (No. 43 of 1976), s. 9.

[47] See Constitution of the Federation (Act No. 20 of 1963), s. 121F inserted by the Constitution (Amendment) (No. 2) Decree 1976 (No. 42 of 1976). Under the section, the court has original jurisdiction in disputes between the Federation and a State or between States.

[48] See Chap. 2, above.

[49] *Ibid.*

G. THE HIGH COURTS

All the High Courts including the Federal Revenue Court are bound by the decisions of the Supreme Court of Nigeria and the Federal Court of Appeal. With respect to State matters (that is, matters within the legislative competence of a State), the High Court of a State does not form part of the hierarchy of courts for any other State. Accordingly, the decisions of the High Court of a State given in the exercise of its jurisdiction in State matters are not binding on any court in another State.[50] On the other hand, every High Court in the exercise of Federal jurisdiction binds all magistrates' courts in the country and all district courts in the northern States.[51]

Local legislation has received into Nigerian law rules of practice observed by the High Court of Justice in England, with respect to matters for which no other provision is made in any enactment. One of such matters is practice in relation to precedent. For instance, section 35 of the High Court Law[52] in force in the northern States provides as follows:

"Subject to the other provisions of this Law the jurisdiction vested in the High Court shall be exercised, so far as regards practice and procedure, in the manner provided by this Law, by the Criminal Procedure Code or by any other written law including such rules and orders of court as may be made pursuant to this Law or any other written law and, in civil causes and matters in so far as any such provisions shall not extend, in conformity *mutatis mutandis* with the practice and procedure for the time being of the High Court of Justice in England."

This provision does not receive the practice of the English court in criminal cases. But, with respect to civil cases, it has received the practice in so far as no other local enactment[53] prescribes rules of precedent to be applied by the local High Courts. Similar provisions are contained in rule 10 of Order 35 of the High Court (Civil Procedure) Rules of Ogun, Ondo and Oyo States[54] and in section 12 of the High Court Law of Lagos State[55] but the latter provision is not expressly limited to civil cases. Section 16 of the High Court Law of the eastern

---

[50] See the charts of courts at pp. 117-121, above.
[51] See the chart of courts exercising Federal jurisdiction p. 116, above.
[52] N.N. Laws 1963, Cap. 49.
[53] The term "written law" in s. 35 of the High Court Law of the northern States means, roughly, local enactment. See s. 3 of the Interpretation Law (N.N. Laws 1963, Cap. 52).
[54] W.R.N. Laws 1959, Cap. 44. The Rules apply in Bendel State by virtue of s. 53 of the High Court Law 1964 (No. 9 of 1964) (M.W.N.).
[55] Lagos Laws 1973, Cap. 52.

States[56] is similar to section 12 of the High Court Law of Lagos State, except that the former receives the practice "observed in England in the High Court of Justice on the thirtieth day of September, 1960" and not the practice for the time being of the High Court of England. It should be pointed out, however, that the practice of the English Court with respect to judicial precedent has not changed since that date. In effect, at present, the same rules of precedent apply to all the State High Courts in civil cases, subject to local legislation, and the position is the same with respect to criminal cases where the relevant law-receiving local statute is not confined to civil cases.

Section 9 of the Federal Revenue Court Decree 1973[57] provides that in the absence of provisions in the Decree or in any other legislation in respect of practice, the practice for the time being in force in the High Court of Lagos State is to be applied by the Federal Revenue Court. Rules governing civil procedure in the court are contained in the Federal Revenue Court (Civil Procedure) Rules 1976[58] but none of the rules deals with precedent. Moreover, no legislation prescribes any particular rules relating to precedent in criminal cases with respect to the Federal Revenue Court. Accordingly, the rules of precedent applied by the High Court of Lagos State are to be applied by the Federal Revenue Court. Therefore, the Federal Revenue Court is required to apply the rules of precedent applied by the High Court of England, subject to Nigerian legislation. It is suggested that with respect to criminal cases, even where rules of practice of English courts do not apply by virtue of local enactments, the local High Court should, in principle, adopt the practice of the High Court of England.

The various local High Court enactments which receive the English rules of practice provide that the practice of the local High Courts is to be in substantial conformity with the practice of the High Court of Justice of England. The High Court of Justice of England is normally constituted by a single judge who can exercise original or appellate jurisdiction in civil or criminal cases. But in certain cases, the court must sit as a Divisional Court constituted by two or more judges. Therefore, in applying substantially the practice of the High Court of England, a High Court in Nigeria when constituted by a single judge whether as a court of first instance or as a court of appeal should adopt the practice of a judge of the High Court of England, and when constituted by two or more judges, whether in the exercise of its original jurisdiction or in the exercise of its appellate

---

[56] E.N. Laws 1963, Cap. 61.
[57] No. 13 of 1973.
[58] L.N. 34 of 1976.

jurisdiction, it should adopt the practice of the Divisional Courts of England.[59]

The practice of the High Court of England when constituted by a single judge was stated by Lord Goddard in *Police Authority for Huddersfield* v. *Watson*[60] as follows:

"I think the modern practice, and the modern view of the subject, is that a judge of first instance, though he would always follow the decision of another judge of first instance unless he is convinced the judgment is wrong, would follow it as a matter of judicial comity. He certainly is not bound to follow the decision of a judge of equal jurisdiction. He is only bound to follow the decisions which are binding on him, which, in the case of a judge of first instance, are the decisions of the Court of Appeal,[61] the House of Lords and the Divisional Court."

Accordingly, a judge of a High Court[62] in Nigeria sitting as a court of first instance is not bound by the decisions of another judge of the High Court sitting as a court of first instance.[63] It would appear that he is also not bound by the decisions of another judge of the High Court sitting as a court of appeal for the two judges are judges "of equal jurisdiction."[64] But when a local High Court sitting as a court of appeal is constituted by two or more judges, as it is in the northern States,[65] it is equivalent to a Divisional Court of the High Court of

---

[59] Compare *Olawoyin* v. *Attorney-General of the Northern Region* 1960 N.R.N.L.R. 53 in which Brown C.J. in interpreting s. 35 of the High Court Law (N.N. Laws 1963, Cap. 49) equated, in an *obiter dictum*, the local High Court sitting in its appellate jurisdiction with the Court of Appeal of England and, accordingly, said that the principle in *Young* v. *Bristol Aeroplane Co.* [1944] K.B. 718 applied. It is submitted that this is not a correct interpretation of the section. The Court of Appeal is not part of the High Court of Justice of England.

[60] [1947] K.B. 842 at p. 848.

[61] Although the Court of Appeal mentioned was the former Court of Appeal, a court of civil jurisdiction, the decisions of the former Court of Criminal Appeal certainly bound a High Court judge. Obviously, today, a High Court judge is bound by the decisions of the Court of Appeal (Civil Division and Criminal Division).

[62] Including the Federal Revenue Court.

[63] See *Obeya* v. *Soluade* 1969 N.N.L.R. 17; 1969(1) N.M.L.R. 112.

[64] But in *Agbalaya* v. *Bello* 1960 L.L.R. 109, the High Court of Lagos held that the decisions of the court given in the exercise of its appellate jurisdiction were binding on the court when sitting as a court of first instance. It is submitted that the decision is wrong for the High Court sitting as a court of appeal was constituted by one judge.

[65] See High Court Law (N.N. Laws 1963, Cap. 49), ss. 40(1) and 63(1). S. 29(1) of the High Court Law of Lagos State provides that in any particular case the High Court of the State is to be constituted by three Judges where the Chief Judge of the State so directs. Similarly, s. 33A of the High Court Law of Rivers State (E.N. Laws 1963, Cap. 61), inserted by the High Court Law (Amendment) Law 1974 (No. 1 of 1974) (Rivers State), provides that the High Court of the State is to be constituted by two or three Judges where the Chief Judge of the State so directs.

England. Its decisions, therefore, bind a judge of the High Court sitting as a court of first instance. Clearly, of course, a judge of a High Court sitting in his original jurisdiction is not bound by his previous decisions whether given in the exercise of original jurisdiction or given in the exercise of appellate jurisdiction.

A judge of a local High Court sitting as a court of appeal is not equivalent to a Divisional Court of the High Court of England. His position is similar to that of a judge of the English High Court exercising appellate jurisdiction. He is not bound by his own previous decisions, nor is he bound by the decisions of another judge of the court. But he is bound by the decisions of the court when constituted by two or more judges sitting as a court of appeal.[66]

When a High Court in Nigeria sitting as a court of appeal is constituted by two or more judges, it is equivalent to a Divisional Court of the High Court of England. A Divisional Court whether exercising civil jurisdiction or criminal jurisdiction adopts the principle in *Young* v. *Bristol Aeroplane Co.*[67] Thus, subject to the exceptions mentioned in that case, in civil cases, Divisional Courts are bound by their previous decisions given in the exercise of civil jurisdiction[68] and in criminal cases they are bound by their previous decisions given in the exercise of criminal jurisdiction.[69] Accordingly, a High Court in Nigeria sitting as a court of appeal and constituted by two or more judges is bound by its previous decisions subject to the following exceptions:

(a) The court is entitled and bound to decide which of two conflicting decisions of its own it will follow.

(b) The court is bound to refuse to follow a decision of its own which though not expressly overruled cannot, in its opinion, stand with a decision of the Supreme Court of Nigeria.

(c) The court is not bound to follow a decision of its own if it is satisfied that the decision was given *per incuriam*.[70]

It is now intended to examine the attitude of the High Courts towards decisions of the former Supreme Court,[71] the West African

[66] The decisions of a Divisional Court of the High Court of England bind a judge of the High Court. See *Police Authority for Huddersfield* v. *Watson* [1947] K.B. 842 at 848.

[67] [1944] K.B. 718. *Police Authority for Huddersfield* v. *Watson* [1947] K.B. 842 at p. 847; *Younghusband* v. *Luftig* [1949] 2 K.B. 354 at pp. 361-362. Compare *Kruse* v. *Johnson* [1898] 2 Q.B. 91.

[68] *Police Authority for Huddersfield* v. *Watson* [1947] K.B. 842 at p. 847.

[69] *Younghusband* v. *Luftig* [1949] 2 K.B. 354 at pp. 361-362.

[70] Brown C.J. in an *obiter dictum* in *Olawoyin* v. *Attorney-General of the Northern Region* 1960 N.R.N.L.R. 53 reached the same conclusion by equating the Court of Appeal in England with the High Court of the Northern Region of Nigeria exercising appellate jurisdiction. See n. 59, above.

[71] See pp. 28-29, above.

Court of Appeal and the Federal Supreme Court. The former Supreme Court was equivalent to a High Court[72] although the full court of the Supreme Court was normally constituted by three judges. Indeed, by virtue of the establishment of the Federal Court of Appeal, the position of the High Courts in the hierarchy of courts is equivalent to that of the former Supreme Court. Accordingly, the High Courts should treat the decisions of the former Supreme Court as they treat their own decisions.[73] The West African Court of Appeal was the second court in the hierarchy of courts, a position now held by the Federal Court of Appeal.[74] A similar position was held by the Federal Supreme Court.[75] Therefore, the High Courts, now ranking third in the hierarchy, are bound by the decisions of the West African Court of Appeal and those of the Federal Supreme Court. Clearly, of course, the decision of the Privy Council[76] given when that court was in the hierarchy of courts in Nigeria are binding on the High Courts for the Privy Council was the highest court in the hierarchy.[77]

H. MAGISTRATES' COURTS AND DISTRICT COURTS

Magistrates' courts of a State are bound by the decisions of the High Court of the State by virtue of their position in the hierarchy of courts to which the doctrine of judicial precedent applies. Similarly, district courts of each of the northern States are bound by the decisions of the High Court of the State. Magistrates' courts and district courts are not bound by their previous decisions.

I. COURTS TO WHICH THE COMMON LAW DOCTRINE OF JUDICIAL PRECEDENT DOES NOT APPLY

As already stated,[78] the common law doctrine of judicial precedent does not apply to customary or area courts. Similarly, the doctrine does not apply to the Sharia Court of Appeal of any of the northern States because the court is not empowered to administer adjective

---

[72] See *Ope* v. *Ope* (1959) 4 F.S.C. 208 where Mbanefo F.J. said that the former Supreme Court was replaced by the High Court of Lagos.

[73] See however *Onwudinjoh* v. *Onwudinjoh* (1957) II E.R.L.R. 1 decided by a High Court which ranked third in the hierarchy of courts.

[74] See Constitution (Amendment) (No. 2) Decree 1976 (No. 42 of 1976), s. 1.

[75] See p. 34, above.

[76] See p. 30, above.

[77] s. 158(3) of the Constitution of the Federation abolished appeals to the Judicial Committee of the Privy Council with effect from October 1, 1963, subject to provisions relating to pending appeals. With respect to pending appeals, the jurisdiction of the Privy Council ceased on September 30, 1964.

[78] See p. 114, above.

common law.[79] In principle, however, by virtue of the appellate systems,[80] the Sharia Court of Appeal should follow the decisions of the Supreme Court of Nigeria. Similarly, customary courts and area courts should follow the decisions of higher courts.

J. English Courts

Although the courts in England do not form part of the court systems in Nigeria, it has been argued that by virtue of the reception of the common law of England and the English doctrines of equity into Nigerian law, the decisions of certain English courts, particularly those of the House of Lords, are binding on Nigerian courts.[81] Obviously, the common law of England and the English doctrines of equity are found in judicial decisions and in England the "supreme tribunal to settle" the common law of England and the English doctrines of equity is the House of Lords.[82] But a decision of the House of Lords on the existence of a rule of the common law, for example, binds all other English courts because the House of Lords is the highest court for England in cases involving that law and under the doctrine of judicial precedent a court is bound by the decision of a higher court in the hierarchy.[83] No English court forms part of any Nigerian court hierarchy. Therefore, no Nigerian court is bound by a decision of any English Court under the doctrine.[84] Clearly, of course, the local law-reception enactments nowhere provide that the Nigerian courts are to apply the common law of England or the English doctrines of equity as stated by the English courts.[85] Nigerian courts are to apply rules which in their opinion constitute the correct rules of the common law or of equity, not necessarily rules stated as common law or equity rules by any particular English court. A Nigerian court may state that the correct common law or equity rule on a particular matter is that stated in the decision of a lower English court which has been overruled by the House of Lords. Thus, decisions of Eng-

---

[79] The court is empowered to administer Moslem law of the Maliki School as customarily interpreted at the place where the trial at first instance took place. See Sharia Court of Appeal Law (N.N. Laws 1963, Cap. 122), s. 14.

[80] Appeals lie from a Sharia Court of Appeal to the Supreme Court in certain cases. See Constitution of the Federation (Act No. 20 of 1963), s. 119.

[81] See A. E. W. Park, *The Sources of Nigerian Law* (1963), pp. 62-64; D.A. Ijalaye, "Precedent in the Nigerian Courts" [1965] Nig. L.J. 287.

[82] See *Robins* v. *National Trust Company* [1927] A.C. 515.

[83] The Judicial Committee of the Privy Council does not form part of the hierarchy of courts for England.

[84] See *Alli* v. *Okulaja* [1970] 2 All N.L.R. 35.

[85] Compare s. 14 of the Sharia Court of Appeal Law (N.N. Laws 1963, Cap. 122) which empowers a Sharia Court of Appeal to apply Moslem law of the Maliki School as customarily interpreted at the place where the trial at first instance took place.

lish courts on the received English law are of persuasive authority only. Accordingly, although Nigerian courts should, in principle, treat the decisions of the House of Lords and those of the Court of Appeal in England with great respect, Nigerian courts are free to depart from the decisions of those English courts. For example, the High Court of the Western State held in *Alli* v. *Okulaja*[86] that it was not bound by the decisions of the English Court of Appeal. Beckley J. said in that case that the judgment of an eminent judge in England "would certainly be of the most persuasive authority and would be followed except the court feels otherwise strongly about the *ratio decidendi* of such decision."[87]

K. OTHER FOREIGN COURTS

In general, there is a measure of similarity between the laws of a Commonwealth country and the laws of other Commonwealth countries. This is due to the fact that English law applied in the former dependencies of Britain most of which on becoming independent joined the Commonwealth of Nations and retained generally the pre-existing laws as well as the pre-existing pattern of legislation. Notable examples of such Commonwealth countries are Australia and India. One of Britain's former dependencies outside the Commonwealth is the United States of America which became independent of Britain in 1776. By virtue of its former relationship with Britain, its laws are in some respects similar to English law and therefore also similar to Nigerian law.

Thus, cases on rules similar to rules of Nigerian law can be found in several foreign jurisdictions. Indeed, in some cases particular foreign statutory rules are identical in wording with corresponding rules in force in Nigeria. For example, the Criminal Code of Queensland,[88] Australia, was based on a draft intended to replace the common law of crime in England. The Criminal Codes in force in Nigeria[89] were in turn based on the Queensland Code. Accordingly, many of the sections of the Queensland Code are identical in wording with sections of the Nigerian Criminal Codes.[90] Cases decided by Queensland courts on the interpretation of the sections are therefore of persuasive authority in Nigerian courts. Similarly, decisions of foreign courts on the common law, equity or statutes are of persuasive authority in Nigerian courts.[91]

[86] [1970] 2 All N.L.R. 35.
[87] *Ibid.* See Jill Cottrell, "An End to Slavishness? A Note on *Alli* v. *Okulaja*" [1973] J.A.L. 247.
[88] Criminal Code Act 1899, Sched. 1.
[89] See *e.g.* Criminal Code (Lagos Laws 1973, Cap. 31).
[90] See *e.g.* s. 23 of the Criminal Code of Queensland and s. 24 of the Criminal Code of Lagos State.
[91] See *D.P.P.* v. *Obi* [1961] 1 All N.L.R. 186.

CHAPTER 8

LAW REPORTING

As already stated,[1] in addition to a settled hierarchy of courts, an efficient system of law reporting is essential to the proper operation of the doctrine of judicial precedent.

A case report published or edited in Nigeria usually begins with the title of the case. This is followed by the name of the court and the names of the judges constituting the court. Next are catchwords. Catchwords indicate the subject matter of the case and, sometimes, the issues to be determined. The headnote appears immediately after the catchwords. It is a summary report of the case. It includes what the reporter considers to be the *ratio decidendi* of the case. It lists cases referred to in the case and states how they were dealt with. For example, it states whether a case was distinguished, followed, not followed or overruled. Where a case is on appeal, the headnote states, as appropriate, that the judgment of the lower court was affirmed or reversed or that it was set aside and a retrial ordered; it also states whether an appeal was allowed or dismissed. The headnote is usually followed immediately by a statement of the nature of the proceedings, an account of how the case reached the court including (sometimes) the essential facts[2] and the names of counsel who appeared for the parties and counsel who appeared as friends of the court. Then follows the actual judgment usually reported verbatim. Where a court is constituted by three or more judges and there is a dissenting judgment, the dissenting judgment is reported after the majority judgment or judgments. The actual judgment or judgments are followed by a brief statement of the court's decision in the case, for example, "judgment for the defendant."

Regular law reporting started in Nigeria in 1916 with the establishment of the Nigeria Law Reports series by the Judicial Department. Today, there are official law reporting bodies for most of the jurisdictions.[3] Law reports published or edited by these bodies are, therefore, official law reports. Indeed, the 1967/68 issue of the Midwestern State of Nigeria Law Reports published by the State Committee on Law Reporting is called "Official Document No. 1:

---

[1] See p. 111, above.

[2] In England, the account of the history of the case is usually followed immediately by a summary of counsel's arguments.

[3] The bodies include the Law Reporting Committee of the northern States; the Law Revision, Reporting and Research Division of the Ministry of Justice of Rivers State; the Committee on Law Reporting of Bendel State and the Law Reporting Section of the Federal Ministry of Justice. The former Western State and the former East-Central State each had a Law reporting committee.

Ministry of Justice." Law Reports currently published by the authority of the courts are official law reports, all the authorised publishers being government officials who publish the reports as part of their official duties.

A. NIGERIAN LAW REPORTS

Nigerian law reports are reports of cases, wherever published or edited, decided by Nigerian courts. They include "English law reports" containing decisions of the Judicial Committee of the Privy Council given on appeal from Nigeria,[4] a number of local and foreign periodicals containing case reports, and various cyclostyled reports including loose-sheet (unbound) series.[5]

Before the Nigerian law reports are discussed in some detail, it should be pointed out that the only cases reported in the law reports are selections from cases decided by the superior courts, for example, the Supreme Court of Nigeria and the High Courts. Cases decided by inferior courts, for example, magistrates' courts, are not reported.

1. *Official Law Reports*

Nigeria Law Reports (about 1881 to 1955)
The Nigeria Law Reports series was the first case report series published by the Government of Nigeria. It consists of 21 volumes of reports and one volume of index. The series contains selected decisions of the Divisonal Courts of the former Supreme Court and those of the Full Court of the former Supreme Court together with a few decisions of the Privy Council given in cases on appeal from Nigeria. The decisions reported in the series were given during the period, about 1881 to 1955. The series is cited in the form "4 N.L.R. . . ."[6]

Selected Judgments of the West African Court of Appeal (1930 to 1955)
This series consists of 15 volumes of reports and one volume of index. The reports cover decisions of the West African Court of Appeal given on appeal from the Supreme Court in Nigeria and

---

[4] *e.g.* the Appeal case volumes of the *English Law Reports* series, and the *Weekly Law Reports* series.

[5] Owing to the difficulty encountered in stating the citation of cases reported only in loose-sheet (unbound) series, such cases are sometimes regarded as unreported cases.

[6] It should be pointed out that a writer need not follow the mode of citation prescribed or suggested by the law report publisher.

from the respective Supreme Courts of the Gold Coast, Sierra Leone and Gambia. The series is cited in the form "7 W.A.C.A. . . ." Some of the volumes were published by the Government of Nigeria, others by the Government of the Gold Coast and some others by the Crown Agents for Overseas Governments and Administrations, in England, on behalf of the Governments of Nigeria, the Gold Coast, Sierra Leone and Gambia.

Selected Judgments of the Federal Supreme Court of Nigeria (1956 to 1960)

This report series contains decisions of the Federal Supreme Court given during the period 1956 to 1960. It comprises five volumes, one for each year. It is cited in the form "5 F.S.C. . . . "

All Nigeria Law Reports (from 1961)

This series contains reports of decisions of the Federal Supreme Court from 1961 to 1963, decisions of the Supreme Court of Nigeria as from 1963 and decisions of the High Courts of the various jurisdictions in Nigeria as from 1961. There are now two volumes for each year, the first volume containing decisions of the Supreme Court of Nigeria and the second volume containing decisions of the High Courts. The series is cited in the form "[1972] 1 All N.L.R. . . . ," except that when a volume consists of more than one part cases in the volume are cited in the form "[1973] 1 All N.L.R. (Part 2) . . ."

Law Reports of the High Court of the Federal Territory of Lagos (1956 to 1966)

This report series contains decisions of the High Court of Lagos. There is one volume for each of the years 1956 to 1966. The 1966 volume is the last volume in the series. The series is cited in the form "1965 L.L.R. . . . "

Law Reports of the High Court of Lagos State (from 1967)

The maiden issue of this series is the 1967 issue. The series contains decisions of the High Court of Lagos State. It is cited like the Law Reports of the Federal Territory of Lagos in the form "1967 L.L.R. . . . "

Western Region of Nigeria Law Reports (1957 to 1959)

This series contains reports of cases decided by the Federal Supreme Court (on appeal from the High Court of the Western Region) and those decided by the High Court of the Western Region. The publishers have not adopted a uniform method of citation of cases reported in the series. For instance, they state that the 1957 volume is to be cited without brackets thus, "1957 W.R.N.L.R.

... ," the 1958 volume in a similar form, but the 1959 volume with round brackets thus, "(1959) W.R.N.L.R. ... " The series was replaced by the Western Nigeria Law Reports in 1960.

Western Nigeria Law Reports (from 1960)

This series which started in 1960 contains reports of cases decided by the Federal Supreme Court from 1960 to 1963 on appeal from the High Court of the Western Region, cases decided by the Supreme Court of Nigeria as from 1963 on appeal from the High Court of the Region and cases decided by the High Court of the Region as from 1960. The 1963 volume was published in 1974. The 1966 volume has been published. As a result of the creation of States in 1967, the series will likely be replaced by a new series to be named "Western State of Nigeria Law Reports," covering the period of existence of the Western State, May 1967 to February 1976. The publishers say that the 1960 and 1961 volumes are to be cited with the date in round brackets thus, "(1960) W.N.L.R. ..." and that the 1962 and 1963 volumes are to be cited with the date in square brackets, for example, "[1963] W.N.L.R. ..." Thus, they have not adopted a uniform method of citation.

Law Reports of the Eastern Region of Nigeria (1956 to 1958)

This series contains reports of decisions of the Federal Supreme Court given on appeal from the High Court of the Eastern Region during the period 1956 to 1958 and decisions of the High Court of the Region during the same period. Cases reported in the series are cited in the form "1 E.R.L.R. ..." The series was replaced in 1959 by the Law Reports of Eastern Nigeria.

Law Reports of Eastern Nigeria (1959 to 1967)

This series contains reports of cases decided by the Federal Supreme Court on appeal from the High Court of the Eastern Region from 1959 to 1963, cases decided by the Supreme Court of Nigeria on appeal from the High Court of the Region from 1963 to May 26, 1967 and cases decided from the High Court of the Region from 1959 to May 26, 1967. The final volume, Volume X, was published in 1972 by the Committee for Law Reporting of the East-Central State. The series is cited in the form "10 E.N.L.R. ..."

Law Reports of East-Central State (from 1970)

The maiden volume (Volume 1) of this law report series is the 1970-71 volume. The series contains decisions of the Supreme Court of Nigeria given on appeal from the High Court of the East-Central State as from 1970 and decisions of the High Court of the State given as from 1970. A few decisions of the High Courts of other States in

Nigeria and some Supreme Court decisions given on appeal from those courts are also contained in this series. The series is cited by volume number and without a date thus, "2 E.C.S.L.R. . . ."

Law Reports of the Northern Region of the Federation of Nigeria (1956 to 1961)

This series contains reports of cases decided by the Federal Supreme Court during the period 1956 to 1961 on appeal from the High Court of the Northern Region and cases decided during that period by the High Court of the Region. The publishers are not consistent in prescribing the mode of citation. For instance, they state that the 1956 volume is to be cited as "1956 N.R.L.R. . . ." and the 1961 volume as "1961 N.R.N.L.R. . . ." The series was replaced in 1962 by the Law Reports of Northern Nigeria.

Law Reports of Northern Nigeria (from 1962)

This report series which started in 1962 contains reports of cases decided by the Federal Supreme Court in 1962 and 1963 on appeal from the High Court of the Northern Region, cases decided by the Supreme Court of Nigeria during the period 1963 to 1967 on appeal from the High Court of the Region, cases decided by the Supreme Court of Nigeria as from 1967 on appeal from the respective High Courts of the northern States, cases decided from the High Court of the Northern Region during the period 1962 to 1967 and cases decided by the respective High Courts of the northern States as from 1967. The 1974 volume of the series has been published. The series is cited in the form "1969 N.N.L.R. . . ."

Mid-Western Nigeria Law Reports (1963 to 1966)

This series started in 1963 on the creation of the Mid-Western Region. It contains reports of cases decided by the High Court of the Region during the period 1963 to 1966. It is cited in the form "(1964) M.N.L.R. . . ." The series has bee replaced by the Mid-Western State of Nigeria Law Reports.

Mid-Western State of Nigeria Law Reports (from 1967)

This law report series started with the publication in February 1974 of the 1967-68 volume containing selected decisions of the High Court of the Midwestern State during the period 1967 to 1968. It is hoped that subsequent volumes will contain not only decisions of the High Court of the State but also decisions of the Supreme Court of Nigeria given on appeal from the High Court. Cases reported in the series are cited in the form "(1967/68) M.S.N.L.R. . . ."

Judgments of the High Court of Midwestern State — Annual Law Reports (from 1968)

This series began with the publication of the 1968 volume which is a cyclostyled volume. As its title clearly indicates, the series contains reports of cases decided by the High Court of the Midwestern State. The series is cited in the form "(1968) M.N.A.L.R. ... " It is published by the authority of the High Court of the State.

Law Reports of Rivers State of Nigeria (from 1970)

The maiden issue (Volume 1) of this report series was published in 1973. The series contains reports of selected judgments of the High Court of Rivers State as well as selected judgments of the Supreme Court given in cases on appeal from the High Court of Rivers State. The cases reported in the maiden issue were decided during the period 1970 to 1972. The series is published by the Ministry of Justice of the State. The mode of citation prescribed by the publisher is not uniform. According to the publisher Volume 1 is to be cited by Volume number without the date thus, "1 R.S.L.R. ...," and Volume 2 is to be cited by volume number and date thus, "2 R.S.L.R (1973) ..."

Judgments of the Supreme Court of Nigeria (from 1972)

This new series containing reports of cases decided by the Supreme Court of Nigeria is published by the authority of the Court. It is published monthly, normally, but where the cases decided in a particular month are very few (for instance, where part of the month falls within the court's vacation period) judgments for two months are combined in a single volume. The series started in January 1972. It appears in a cyclostyled form and is cited in the form "(1974) 4 S.C. ....," the number indicating the month of the year covered by the volume. The series was renamed "Reserved Judgments of the Supreme Court of Nigeria" in December 1975.

Selected Judgments of the High Court of Lagos State (from 1972)

This series, too, started in January 1972. It is published monthly by the authority of the Chief Judge of Lagos State. It contains reports of cases decided by the High Court of Lagos State. It appears in cyclostyled form. Issues for the period January 1972 to June 1972 are cited in the form "C.C.C.H.C.J/6/72" standing for certified cyclostyled copies of High Court Judgments (June 1972). Issues for the period July 1972 to December 1974 are cited in the form "C.C.H.C.J/4/74" meaning certified copies of High Court Judgments (April 1974). Beginning with the January 1975 issue, the publisher has been prescribing, with respect to each issue, two modes of citation, apparently by mistake, thus, "(1975) 1 C.C.H.C.J" and

"(1975) 1/C.C.H.C.J." for the January 1975 issue, "C.C.H.C.J/4/75" and "(1975) 4/C.C.H.C.J." for the April 1975 issue, "(1976) 1 C.C.H.C.J." and "(1976) 1/C.C.H.C.J." for the January 1976 issue. In all these cases, one method of citation is prescribed at the front cover and the other at the title page.

Judgments of the Court of Appeal Western State (1973 to 1975)

The series contains reports of decisions of the Court of Appeal of the Western State given during the period 1973 to 1975. It is cited in the form "(1975) 1 W.S.C.A. . . ." The date is an indispensable part of the reference for the first volume for each year is numbered "1." The series is in cyclostyled form.

Loose-leaf cyclostyled reports

The cyclostyled reports already discussed appear in bound volumes. Some States publish cyclostyled reports in loose sheets. The include Kaduna, Kano, Plateau, Rivers and Sokoto States. The Kaduna loose-leaf series is called "Kaduna Reports." The loose-leaf series should be distinguished from mere cyclostyled copies of judgments.

The loose-leaf series, like the bound volume series, contains reports of cases including with respect to each case catchwords, what the reporter considers to be the *ratio decidendi*, a headnote and the actual judgment. But mere cyclostyled copies of judgments are only copies of actual judgments.

2. *Other Law Reports*

There are a number of law reports series containing reports of Nigerian cases and published by non-governmental bodies. Notable among such reports are the Nigerian Monthly Law Reports, the University of Ife (Nigeria) Law Reports and reports contained in legal periodicals.

Nigerian Monthly Law Reports (from 1964)

This series started with the publication of monthly issues for 1964. It contains reports of cases decided by the High Courts of the various jurisdictions, cases decided by the Court of Appeal of the Western State and cases decided by the Supreme Court of Nigeria. The series is now published annually. The mode of citation stated by the publishers is not uniform. The commonest form stated is "1968 N.M.L.R. . . ." But the first volume for 1971 is cited as "(1971) 1 N.M.L.R. . . ." and the first volume for 1973 is cited as "1973 (1) N.M.L.R. . . ." The series is published by Associated Publishers (Nigeria) Limited.

University of Ife (Nigeria) Law Reports (from 1971)
The maiden volume published in this series is part 1 of the 1971 volume. The series contains reports of cases decided by the High Courts of the various jurisdictions, cases decided by the Court of Appeal of the Western State and cases decided by the Supreme Court of Nigeria. The 1971 volume includes reports of cases decided before 1971. The series is edited by the Faculty of Law of the University of Ife, Ile-Ife and published by the University of Ife Press, Ile-Ife. It is cited by volume number, thus, "1 U.I.L.R. . . ."

Federal Law Reports (from 1967)
This new law report series started with the publication of the 1967 volume. The series is published by Sinapis Publishing Company whose head office is at Enugu, Anambra State. It contains reports of cases decided by superior courts in the various jurisdictions in Nigeria. Cases reported in the series are cited in the form "(1967) F.N.L.R. . . ."

Renner's Reports
The Renner's series is an old series of private reports containing decisions of the Supreme Court of the Gold Coast Colony given during the period 1874 to 1886 when Lagos was administered as part of the Colony.

English Law Reports
Reports of cases decided by the Judicial Committee of the Privy Council on appeal from Nigeria are contained in some Appeal case volumes of the *Law Reports* series of England and in the *Weekly Law Reports* series. The *Law Reports* series started in 1865. Before 1891 Appeal case volumes were cited by their number, thus, "4 App. Cas. 1." Since 1891 such volume are cited by date and volume number thus, "[1926] 1 A.C. . . ." The *Weekly Law Reports* series is published in weekly parts. The first volume for each year contains reports of cases which are not intended for publication in the *Law Reports* series but the second and third volumes contain reports of cases to be published in the series. Cases reported in the *Weekly Law Reports* are cited by date and volume number thus "[1962] 1 W.L.R. . . ." Both the *Law Reports* series and the *Weekly Law Reports* series are published by the Incorporated Council for Law Reporting for England and Wales.[7]

---

[7] It should be mentioned that by virtue of the reception of English Law into Nigerian law even those English law reports which do not contain reports of Nigerian cases are, generally, very useful to Nigerian courts and to researchers working on Nigerian law.

African Law Reports (Commercial Law Series)

The Commercial Law series of the African Law Reports contains reports of decisions of Nigerian courts. The series is cited by year and volume number thus, "1964(1) A.L.R. Comm. . . ."

Nigerian Bar Journal

The *Nigerian Bar Journal* sometimes contains reports of cases decided by superior courts in Nigeria. The journal is published by the Nigerian Bar Association, usually once a year.

Nigeria Lawyers' Quarterly

This journal often contains reports of cases decided by superior courts in Nigeria.

Journal of African Law

This journal, too, sometimes contains reports of cases decided by superior courts in Nigeria. The journal is published three times a year, in England.

Newspapers

A few newspapers published in Nigeria sometimes have law reports columns which contain reports of a few of the cases decided by the superior courts in Nigeria. The newspapers include *Sunday Sketch, Daily Sketch, Headlines* and *Business Times*.

CHAPTER 9

INTERNAL CONFLICTS

LOCAL statutes provide for the application of English law and customary law without stating expressly that one is to apply subject to the other.[1]

There are, however, statutory choice-of-law rules for determining in appropriate cases whether it is customary or non-customary law (for example, English law or French law) that governs a particular set of circumstances. But the commonest type of conflict-of-law problem involving both customary law and another system of law is that concerning English law and customary law as alternatives. By reason of the test of incompatibility of customary law with local enactments,[2] a choice-of-law problem would not normally involve customary law and a local enactment as alternatives, for customary law is void if it is inconsistent with a local enactment, and, in such circumstances, no proper choice-of-law problem arises. But a choice-of-law problem arises, where, for example, a local enactment expressly preserves the application of the rules of customary law on the subject-matter of the enactment.

By reason of the preservation, such rules of customary law are not incompatible with the local enactment. For instance, the Property and Conveyancing Law[3] of Bendel, Ogun, Ondo and Oyo States exempts transactions under customary law from the ambit of the Law.[4] Customary land law in the States is, thus, not incompatible with the law and the problem may arise whether it is the law or customary law that applies to a transaction involving land.

Of all the State High Court enactments, only that of the northern States[5] expressly mentions "English law" as an alternative to customary law. In place of "English law," the other State High Court enact-

---

[1] See however *Adesubokan* v. *Yinusa, Nigerian Lawyers' Quarterly*, Vol. VI. Nos. 1-4, 186 at p. 192, where a full court of the Supreme Court of Nigeria (Ademola, C.J. N.; Coker, Lewis, Madarikan and Udoma, JJ.SC) expressed the view that "any law for the time being in force" within the meaning of s. 34(1) of the High Court Law of the northern States included the received English law. According to the court, therefore, where a rule of customary law is inconsistent with the received English law, the rule is void. The relationship between English law and customary law is, thus, expressed in terms of validity of customary law and would, therefore, according to this view, not involve a conflict-of-law problem. It is submitted that the Supreme Court's view on the meaning of the expression "any law for the time being in force" is wrong. See pp. 104-107, above.
[2] See pp. 104-109, above.
[3] W.R.N. Laws 1959, Cap. 100, s. 1(2).
[4] See also *e.g.* the Prescription Law (W.R.N. Laws 1959, Cap. 95), s. 1(2).
[5] The northern States are Bauchi, Benue, Borno, Gongola, Kaduna, Kano, Kwara, Niger, Plateau and Sokoto.

ments mention "rules of" law other than customary law. However, for the purpose of internal conflicts between customary law and non-customary law, English law is the only non-customary law that should be further considered.

Where the choice-of-law rules provide that the applicable law is customary law, the question of choice of a particular system of customary law arises. There are statutory rules for determining this question, too.

A few general remarks on internal conflicts should now be made. First, it should be pointed out that by virtue of the abolition of customary criminal law, internal conflicts involving customary law can arise only in civil proceedings, except in a few cases where the penal code defines particular offences by reference to customary law.[6] Secondly, it is clear that in general the statutory rules are couched in wording dealing apparently only with contractual agreements as if it is only in the area of contract that a problem of choice of law involving customary law can arise. But there are disputes which do not involve any agreement at all, for instance cases in tort and succession. The position of conflict rules governing such cases is not clear, except in the northern States whose High Court enactment contains a provision which may be construed as applicable to disputes not based on agreements.[7]

A. CONFLICTS BETWEEN ENGLISH LAW
AND CUSTOMARY LAW

Rules governing internal conflicts between English law and customary law are contained in the various State High Court enactments.[8] All the rules are similar in wording but there is a difference in the classification of parties for the purpose of applying the rules. The High Court Law of Lagos State and the High Court Law of the northern States classify parties as natives and non-natives; the High Court Law of Bendel and that of Ogun, Ondo and Oyo States classify parties as Nigerians and non-Nigerians; and the High Court Law of the eastern States[9] deals with "persons of Nigerian descent" and "per-

---

[6] See *e.g.* Penal Code (N.N. Laws 1963, Cap. 89), s. 387 (which punishes adultery when committed by a man "subject to any native law or custom in which extra-marital sexual intercourse is recognised as a criminal offence"), s. 388 (which deals with adultery by a woman) and s. 403 (which punishes drinking of alcohol by a person "of the Moslem faith.")

[7] See High Court Law (N.N. Laws 1963, Cap. 49), s. 34(4).

[8] High Court Law (Lagos Laws 1973, Cap. 52), s. 26; High Court Law (E.N. Laws 1963, Cap. 61), s. 20; High Court Law (W.R.N. Laws 1959, Cap. 44), s. 12; High Court Law (N.N. Laws 1963, Cap. 49), s. 34; High Court Law 1964 (No. 9 of 1964) (M.W.M.), s. 13.

[9] The eastern States are Anambra, Cross River, Imo and Rivers.

sons who are not of Nigerian descent."[10] On this question of conflict of law, the High Court Law of the northern States is different in wording from the other High Court enactments in one important respect. It alone contains a residuary provision stating that where no express rule in the preceding subsections of the conflict-of-law section applies, "the court shall be governed by the principles of justice, equity and good conscience."

The relevant provisions of the High Court enactments will now be examined in some detail.

Section 26 of the High Court Law of Lagos State[11] provides as follows:

> "26(1) The High Court shall observe and enforce the observance of every customary law which is applicable and is not repugnant to natural justice, equity and good conscience, nor incompatible either directly or by implication with any law for the time being in force, and nothing in this law shall deprive any person of the benefit of customary law.
>
> (2) Customary law shall be deemed applicable in causes and matters where the parties thereto are natives and also in causes and matters between natives and non-natives, where it may appear to the court that substantial injustice would be done to either party by a strict adherence to any rules of law which would otherwise be applicable.
>
> (3) No party shall be entitled to claim the benefit of any customary law, if it shall appear either from express contract or from the nature of the transactions out of which any suit or question may have arisen, that such party agreed that his obligations in connection with such transactions should be exclusively regulated otherwise than by customary law or that such transactions are transactions unknown to customary law."

In interpreting the provision "nothing in this law shall deprive any person of the benefit of any such native law or custom" contained in section 34(1) of the High Court Law of the northern States (the equivalent of section 26(1) of the High Court Law of Lagos State) Bello J. (as he then was) in *Yinusa* v. *Adesubokan*[12] said,

> "It is clear that this injunction limits the operation of any law for the time being in force to the extent of preserving any of the benefits of every native law and custom which is incompatible with that law in force, to which any person is entitled."

Thus construed, the provisions would negative the application of the

---

[10] See n. 8, above.
[11] Lagos Laws 1973, Cap. 52.
[12] 1968 N.N.L.R. 97 at p. 104.

incompatibility test. In the opinion of the learned judge, in spite of the incompatibility test, where a rule of customary law is incompatible with "any law for the time being in force" the rule of customary law prevails over that law in force in so far as the rule confers a benefit on a person. Clearly such a strained interpretation is wrong. The words "such native law or custom" indicate that it is only those rules of customary law that have passed the tests of validity contained in the subsection — the repugnancy and incompatibility tests — that are referred to; and it would seem absurd to say in another breath that customary law is to be applied notwithstanding its incompatibility with "any law for the time being in force."[13] The Supreme Court of Nigeria disagreed with the judge and correctly explained the provision in the following words[14]:

> "Thus, the legislature, having provided for the type of native law or custom which the High Court should enforce in the exercise of its jurisdiction, went on to provide for the avoidance of doubt, that no person should be deprived of the benefit of that particular native law or custom."

But it should be pointed out that it does not follow from the provision in each of the High Court enactments stating that nothing in the enactment "shall deprive any person of the benefit" of valid customary law that any person whatsoever is entitled to the benefit of customary law.[15] The effect of the provision is that no provision of the enactment is to be construed as depriving any person of the benefit of customary law where such person would normally have been entitled to the benefit of customary law, subject to subsection (3) of the relevant section of each High Court enactment which provides that in specified circumstances a party is not entitled to claim the benefit of customary law. It would be recalled that the High Court Law of Lagos State and the High Court Law of the northern States classify parties for the purpose of internal conflicts between customary law and English law as natives and non-natives. The word "native" is defined in section 3 of the former Interpretation Act.[16] But that section was repealed by the Interpretation Act 1964[17] which contains no

---

[13] Having wrongly assumed that "any law for the time being in force" included the Wills Act 1837, a received English statute, the learned judge had to adopt a strained interpretation in order to hold that notwithstanding the reception of the statute, customary law applied.

[14] *Adesubokan* v. *Yinusa, Nigeria Lawyers' Quarterly*, Vol. VI, Nos 1-4, p. 186, *sub nom. Adesubokun* v. *Yunusa* 1971 N.N.L.R. 77.

[15] See *Savage* v. *MacFoy* (1909) Ren. 504; *Fonseca* v. *Passman* [1958] W.R.N.L.R. 41.

[16] Fed. and Lagos Laws 1958, Cap. 89.

[17] No. 1 of 1964. The Act applies throughout the country as Federal law.

definition of the word. The Interpretation Law of Lagos State,[18] too, published in the 1973 revised edition of the laws of the State, contains no definition of the word. The absence of the term in the 1964 Act or in the Interpretation Law is attributable to an oversight on the part of the Legislature. It is suggested that the definition contained in the repealed section is intended to be adopted by the Legislature. One reason in support of this view is that the Interpretation Laws of the other jurisdictions still contain the definition of "native" in terms identical with the definition of the word in the repealed section of the 1964 Act. The repealed section provided as follows:

"'native' includes a native of Nigeria and a native foreigner; 'native of Nigeria' means any person whose parents were members of any tribe or tribes indigenous to Nigeria and the descendants of such persons; and includes any person one of whose parents was a member of such tribe; 'native foreigner' means any person (not being a native of Nigeria) whose parents were members of a tribe or tribes indigenous to some part of Africa and the descendants of such persons; and includes any person one of whose parents was a member of such a tribe."

1. *Cases between Nigerians*

It is clear from the definition of "native" that a Nigerian is a native within the meaning of the High Court Law of Lagos and the High Court Law of the northern States. Furthermore, Nigerians are clearly "persons of Nigerian descent" within the meaning of the High Court Law of the eastern States.

The High Court enactments provide as a general rule that in cases between natives or between Nigerians or between persons of Nigerian descent, customary law is deemed to be applicable. It follows that in every jurisdiction in the country the general rule is that customary law is the law applicable in cases between Nigerians.[19] This rule is subject to the exceptions contained in subsection (3) of the relevant section of each of the High Court enactments.

(a) Agreement to be bound by English law

The first exception is that if it appears "either from express contract or from the nature of the transactions out of which any suit or question may have arisen, that a party agreed that his obligations in connection with such transactions" should be exclusively regulated otherwise than by customary law, customary law is not applicable. Thus, if a party contending that customary law applies had

[18] Lagos Laws 1973, Cap. 57.
[19] See *Labinjoh* v. *Abake* (1924) 5 N.L.R. 33, *Alfa* v. *Arepo* [1963] W.N.L.R. 95.

agreed that the transaction was to be governed by English law, customary law is not applicable. Even where there is no such express agreement the court can infer from the nature of the transaction that the party had agreed that customary law was to apply. For example, in *Okolie* v. *Ibo*,[20] the court had to determine what law governed a dispute on petrol supply between two Ibos resident in Jos in Northern Nigeria. One of the parties was a transport owner and the other operated a petrol-filling station. The court expressed the view that having regard to "their respective occupations and the nature of the transaction between them and the commodity in which they dealt" the parties did not intend that either Moslem law or Ibo law should apply. According to the court, "the only presumption which it seems open to a court to make is that the parties intended that their relations should be regulated by the principles of English law." Similarly, where a party who purchased a piece of land obtained a receipt mentioning the willingness of the vendors to "convey unto the said purchaser the land aforesaid at any time that we may be called upon so to do and that without delay," the court observed that the parties were both aware that the document was couched in English form and that they intended that it be so couched. Accordingly, the court was of opinion that the purchaser could not claim the benefit of customary law and, therefore his successor in title, too, could not.[21] On the other hand, in *Nelson* v. *Nelson*,[22] a piece of land held under customary law by three brothers as tenants-in-common was acquired compulsorily by the Government. The compensation money was paid to the eldest brother who, to the knowledge of the other two, bought another piece of land and obtained, in respect of the purchase, a conveyance in English law form. The three brothers intended that the newly-bought piece of land be held under customary law like the land acquired. The eldest brother later conveyed the land to another person without the consent of his brothers. His brothers brought an action contending that under customary law their consent was essential to such conveyance. The eldest brother in turn contended that because his brothers had agreed that the land be conveyed to him in English law form, it must be held that they had agreed that all their rights in relation to the land should be governed by English law. The West African Court of Appeal rejected the eldest brother's contention on the ground that the whole set of circumstances indicated that the brothers had agreed that customary law should govern their rights in relation to the land.

Where a party has agreed to be bound by English law in relation to

[20] 1958 N.R.N.L.R. 89.
[21] *Griffin* v. *Talabi* (1948) 12 W.A.C.A. 371.
[22] (1951) 13 W.A.C.A. 248.

property, that agreement necessarily binds his successors in title,[23] but it does not bind any other person who was not a party to the agreement. Thus, in *Villars* v. *Baffoe*,[24] a Gold Coast case, where the plaintiff claiming possession of certain goods which were part of the estate of a deceased person took out letters of administration in the English law form in respect of the estate the court held that the rights of the defendants (who were members of the family of the deceased) in relation to the estate were governed by customary law and not by English law. The court explained that the act of the plaintiff in choosing to be bound by English law could not affect the customary law rights of the family.

On the other hand, where a party had agreed to be bound by English law in relation to a transaction, he cannot claim the benefit of customary law in a dispute concerning the transaction between him and another person who was not a party to the agreement. Thus, in *Green* v. *Owo*[25] the plaintiff brought an action claiming possession of a piece of land. He had bought the land at a public auction and having intended that the purchase be governed by English law he had obtained in relation to the purchase documents of title couched in English law form. But the defendant who had openly occupied the land for 20 years without any interruption or challenge from anyone contended that an English statute of limitation, the Real Property Limitation Act 1833,[26] applied to the action. But the plaintiff argued that English law could not apply as there was no agreement between him and the defendant to be bound by that law. Rejecting the argument, the court explained that it was clear that the plaintiff had agreed that his rights in relation to the property should be governed by English law and that notwithstanding the fact that that agreement was not entered into with the defendant, the plaintiff remained bound by English law.

(b) Transactions unknown to customary law

The second exception to the general rule that customary law governs disputes between Nigerians is that no party is "entitled to claim the benefit" of customary law if it appears that the transactions involved are unknown to customary law. In such circumstances, customary law is not applicable. Clearly, where a transaction is unknown to customary law, customary law cannot govern it and, obviously, customary law has no benefit of its own to bestow upon any person in relation to the transaction. Thus, it appears that this provision is a mere truism and is thus redundant. But Charles J. in

---

[23] (1948) 12 W.A.C.A. 371.
[24] (1909) Ren. 549.
[25] (1936) 13 N.L.R. 43.
[26] 3 & 4 Will. 4, c. 27.

Salau v. *Aderibigbe*,[27] a case involving the question whether a hire-purchase agreement in respect of a motor lorry was governed by customary law, warned that the rejection "of a statutory provision as being redundant or inoperative however is only justified when all efforts have failed to find a manifest object of the provision and to give an intelligent meaning to the words in it, so as to achieve that object." The learned judge then interpreted the provision dealing with the exception, "transactions unknown to customary law" as follows[28]:

> "The words 'to claim the benefit of any customary law' with reference to transactions which appear from their nature to be unknown to that law show, I think, that the object of the Legislature was to prevent the extension of existing rules of customary law in respect of familiar transactions by logic and analogy to transactions which are essentially different either because of their inherent novelty or of the novelty of their subject matter."

Thus, this exception provision does more than stating a truism. It is intended to prevent the application of existing rules of customary law by adaptation to transactions for which customary law does not provide. In discussing the nature of transactions unknown to customary law, Charles J. in the same case[29] expressed the view that customary law related to and therefore governed those things "which were closely connected with the customary way of life and which existed or were usually kept in the locality in which their owners or possessors lived, such as land and simple chattels of a domestic or agricultural use which were normally confined to the area in which the customary law was operative."[30] He added that "it must be assumed that the Legislature intended to allow the extension and application of existing customary law rules to transactions relating to new chattels of the kind mentioned, such as sewing machines, but not to transactions relating to new chattels of a different kind which would not normally be confined in their use in the customary law locality, and the use of which, because of their nature, should be regulated by the general law. If customary law rules were permitted to be applied and adopted to transactions in relation to such new chattels, there would be a danger that the common law in respect of them would be replaced by a number of customary laws varying their contents and incidents from locality to locality — a reversal of one of the processes by which the common law itself developed from local custom."[31] The

[27] [1963] W.N.L.R. 80 at p. 86.
[28] *Ibid.*
[29] *Salau* v. *Aderibigbe* [1963] W.N.L.R. 80.
[30] *Ibid* at p. 86.
[31] *Ibid.*

judge concluded, "As a motor vehicle is a chattel of the new kind mentioned, so far as customary law is concerned, the extension of customary law to transactions in respect of it is forbidden by the disentitling provision,[32] in my judgment, and such transactions must remain outside the cognisance of that law."[33]

This reasoning in the judgment with respect to the nature of transactions unknown to customary law seems faulty. It fails to consider flexibility as a characteristic of customary law. Customary law changes from time to time as it reflects the rapid development of social and economic conditions.[34] It is not correct that what determines whether a transaction is known to customary law is the question whether the chattels to which the transaction relates were of a kind normally confined in their use to a "customary law locality." The use of writing, for example, is not confined to any customary law locality. Indeed, it is comparably new. Yet, it was clearly stated in *Rotibi* v. *Savage*[35] that the use of writing did not necessarily indicate that the transaction in question was governed by English law.

With respect to the question of multiplicity of customary law rules applicable in a jurisdiction, obviously this is not relevant to the determination of the question whether a transaction is unknown to customary law. Acceptance by the local community is a feature of customary law. The smaller each customary law community in a jurisdiction is, the greater the number of customary law systems in the jurisdiction. Hence, multiplicity of customary law systems is unavoidable in the absence of any local enactment purporting to effect uniformity of customary law systems.

Clearly, the provision that no party is entitled to claim the benefit of customary law in relation to a transaction unknown to customary law forbids the adaptation of an existing rule of customary law to circumstances which are not accepted by the members of the community concerned as being governed by the rule at any particular time in question, but once the rule in its accepted form extends to a new set of circumstances, it is to be applied so long as it passes the tests of validity, namely, repugnancy, incompatibility and public policy.[36] A transaction is unknown to customary law where the transaction is of such a nature that the members of the community concerned do not consider it to be subject to any of the existing customs accepted as

---

[32] The provision that no "party shall be entitled to claim the benefit of any customary law, if it shall appear . . . that such transactions are transactions unknown to customary law."

[33] *Salau* v. *Aderibigbe* [1963] W.N.L.R. 80 at p. 87.

[34] *Alfa* v. *Arepo* [1963] W.N.L.R. 95.

[35] (1944) 17 N.L.R. 77.

[36] See pp. 100-110, above.

binding upon them. Thus, where the essential element of a transaction is a promissory note, the courts would hold that the transaction is unknown to customary law.[37] Similarly, where a conveyance in English law form constitutes an essential part of a transaction, the transaction is unknown to customary law.[38] But a transaction involving the use of writing is not necessarily unknown to customary law.[39] The crucial question to be answered in determining whether a transaction is unknown to customary law is not whether the subject-matter or its type was known to the local community in the olden days but whether at any particular time in question there is an existing custom accepted as binding and governing dealings with the subject-matter or with that type of subject-matter. Where neither the particular subject-matter nor its type is known to the local community a transaction based on the subject-matter is unknown to customary law. But the fact that the subject-matter or its type is known to the local community does not necessarily mean that a transaction involving it is known to customary law.

In determining whether a transaction is unknown to customary law, the courts can play a seemingly creative role by stating the subject-matter of the transaction broadly. For instance, the subject-matter of a transaction of sale of mechanised farming equipment in an agrarian locality may be stated simply as farming equipment. Thus, the transaction (sale of farming equipment) is known to the community.

2. *Cases between Nigerians and Non-Nigerians*

(a) Lagos State and northern States

For the purposes of the law governing conflicts between English law and customary law in Lagos State and the northern States, cases between Nigerians and non-Nigerians may be divided into two classes, namely, cases between Nigerians and indigenous non-Nigerian Africans (that is, cases between natives who are natives of Nigeria and natives who are native foreigners) and cases between Nigerians and non-Nigerians other than indigenous Africans (that is, cases between natives and non-natives).

(i) *Cases between Nigerians and indigenous non-Nigerian Africans*

Indigenous non-Nigerian Africans are native foreigners within the meaning of the High Court enactment of Lagos State and that of the northern States; and native foreigners are natives within the mean-

---

[37] See *Bakare* v. *Coker* (1935) 12 N.L.R. 31.
[38] See *Green* v. *Owo* (1936) 13 N.L.R. 43.
[39] *Alfa* v. *Arepo* [1963] W.N.L.R. 95, *Rotibi* v. *Savage* (1944) 17 N.L.R. 77.

ing of the enactments.[40] It follows that under the enactments cases between Nigerians and indigenous non-Nigerian Africans are cases between natives. All cases between natives, whether Nigerians or not, are governed by the same rules. Accordingly, the rules governing cases between Nigerians explained above[41] govern cases between Nigerians and indigenous non-Nigerian Africans.

(ii) *Cases between Nigerians and non-Nigerians other than indigenous Africans*

Non-Nigerians other than indigenous Africans are non-natives within the meaning of the High Court Law of Lagos State and the High Court Law of the northern States.[42] Cases between Nigerians and non-Nigerians other than indigenous Africans are, therefore, cases between natives and non-natives under the enactments.

According to section 26(2) of the High Court Law of Lagos State, customary law applies in cases between natives and non-natives "where it may appear to the court that substantial injustice would be done to either party by a strict adherence to any rules of law which would otherwise be applicable." Such rules of law include, of course, rules of English law. Section 34(2) of the High Court Law of the northern States is similar to this provision except that the Law of the northern States mentions "rules of English law" in place of "any rules of law which would otherwise be applicable." Accordingly, it is implied that the general rule is that English law applies and cases of "substantial injustice" constitute an exception to the rule.[43] Under section 26(3) of the High Court Law of Lagos State and section 34(3) of the High Court Law of the northern States, no party is entitled to claim the benefit of customary law if it appears that he had agreed to be bound by English law in respect of the transaction in question or that the transaction is unknown to customary law. Accordingly, in such circumstances, a dispute between a native and a non-native on whether it is English law or customary law that applies would be resolved in favour of English law.

An illustration of the general rule that in cases between natives and non-natives English law applies is found in *Koney* v. *Union Trading Company*,[44] a Gold Coast case between a native and a non-native, a company being a non-native, where the West African Court of Appeal held that English law applied. Another Gold Coast case,

---

[40] See Interpretation Law (N.N. Laws 1963, Cap. 52), s. 3; pp. 148-149, above.

[41] See pp. 149-154, above.

[42] See High Court Law (N.N. Laws 1963, Cap. 49) s. 3, pp. 148-149, above.

[43] Compare *Osuro* v. *Anjorin* (1946) 18 N.L.R. 45 where the court wrongly construed the "substantial injustice" provision as a provision applicable to cases between "natives," *Ajayi* v. *White* (1946) 18 N.L.R. 41.

[44] (1934) 2 W.A.C.A. 188.

Nelson v. *Nelson*,[45] a case between two natives on the one hand and a native and two non-natives on the other illustrates the exception to the rule. In that case, the West African Court of Appeal expressed the view that substantial injustice would be caused by the application of English law which would have resulted in denying the plaintiffs of their customary law rights. The exception is expressed to relate to cases in which substantial injustice would be done to "either party" by the application of English law. But the application of customary law by reason of this exception is subject to the capacity of the non-native to be subject to customary law.[46] In most cases, however, the operation of the exception would be in favour of the native for it is he, rather than the non-native, who is more likely to contend that customary law should apply on the ground that the operation of English law would result in substantial injustice to him. It is arguable that under the High Court Law of Lagos State and the High Court Law of the northern States, the court is required to apply substantial injustice in cases between natives and non-natives where the native had agreed to be bound by English law and it is found that the application of English law would result in substantial injustice to him, for under section 26(3) of the High Court Law of Lagos State and section 34(3) of the High Court Law of the northern States no party is entitled to claim the benefit of customary law if it appears that he had agreed that English law should govern the transaction in question.[47]

(iii) *Principles of justice, equity and good conscience*

Section 34 of the High Court Law of the northern States has a fourth subsection whose provision has no equivalent in the High Court Law of Lagos State.

The subsection reads:

"In cases where no express rule is applicable to any matter in controversy, the court shall be governed by the principles of justice, equity and good conscience."

The provisons of the first three subsections of section 34 of the High Court Law of the northern States (like the entire provisions of section 26 of the High Court Law of Lagos State) prescribe choice-of-law rules which are generally couched in terms of contractual obligation. They are inappropriate in such cases as succession and tort cases. Section 34(4) of the High Court Law of the northern States therefore, fills the gap with respect to the northern States. Under the subsection, in all situations not relating to agreements, irrespective

---

[45] (1951) 13 W.A.C.A. 248.
[46] See *Fonseca* v. *Passman* [1958] W.R.N.L.R. 41, *Savage* v. *MacFoy* (1909) Ren. 504.
[47] See A. E. W. Park, *The Sources of Nigerian Law* (1963), p. 118.

of the status of any of the parties, the court is to apply the principles of justice, equity and good conscience. It was under such provision as section 34(4) of the Law that the court in *Cole* v. *Cole*[48] applied English law in a case of succession.

(b) Other States

Under the laws of the other States, cases between Nigerians and non-Nigerians are governed by rules substantially the same in wording as those governing cases between natives and non-natives under the High Court Law of Lagos State and the High Court Law of the northern States. The rules governing cases between natives and non-natives under both Laws have been discussed under the subhead "Cases between Nigerians and indigenous non-Nigerian Africans."[49] The rules are the same as those governing cases between Nigerians and non-Nigerians under the laws of the other States, by virtue of the wording of the relevant enactments.[50]

There is no provision equivalent to section 34(4) of the High Court Law of the northern States (which provides for the application of principles of justice, equity and good conscience in cases not involving contractual obligation) in the law of any of the remaining nine States. Under the law in force in any of the remaining nine States, the entire provisions specifically governing internal conflicts between laws prescribe rules which are, in general, couched in terms of contractual obligation and are inappropriate in cases not involving agreements, for example, succession and tort cases. A specific provision on matters not involving agreements which should be more detailed than section 34(4) of the High Court Law of the northern States is suggested for each jurisdiction.

B. Conflicts Between Different Systems of Customary Law

When it is determined that customary law governs a case the question of choosing the appropriate system of customary law arises. Various statutes deal with the determination of this question.

Eastern States

In the four eastern states — Anambra, Cross River, Imo and Rivers States — the courts are required to administer the customary law prevailing in the area of jurisdiction of the court or binding between the

---

[48] (1898) 1 N.L.R. 15.
[49] See p. 154, above.
[50] See *e.g.* High Court Law (W.R.N. Laws, 1959, Cap. 44).

parties.[51] There is nothing in the law of any of the four States to indicate when the law prevailing in the area of the jurisdiction of the court rather than the law binding between the parties is to be applied, and *vice versa*.

The expression, "law prevailing in the area of jurisdiction of the court" was interpreted in *R.* v. *Ilorin Native Court ex p. Aremu*[52] where Ademola J. rejected the view that there could be more than one system of customary law prevailing in the area of jurisdiction of a court and said that the law prevailing in an area was the law predominant in the area. According to the case, therefore, the customary law of a minority group within the area of jurisdiction of a court cannot be the customary law prevailing in the area.

There is nothing in the relevant statute or statutes[53] applicable in any of the four States to indicate what in any particular situation is to be considered as the law binding between the parties. Presumably, with respect to contractual relations the law binding between the parties is that law which is expressly or impliedly agreed upon by the parties for the purpose of governing their relations. It is not easy to determine the law binding between the parties with respect to non-contractual relations.

Succession Cases

It is suggested that in cases of succession to property the applicable law should, in general, be the law binding between the parties rather than the law of the area of jurisdiction of the court where the two laws are different. The personal customary law of the deceased, that is, the customary law to which the deceased was normally subject, should, in general be regarded as the law binding between the parties[54]; for persons claiming through a deceased person should be subject to the law which governed the deceased. But where the personal law of the deceased is unknown or is not established before the court, the law prevailing in the area of jurisdiction of the court should be applied.[55]

Land Cases

With respect to cases involving land other than cases of succession to land, it is suggested that the law prevailing in the area of the juris-

---

[51] Magistrates' Courts Law (E.N. Laws 1963, Cap. 82), s. 43(1) as amended by the Magistrates' Courts Law (Amendment) Edict 1971 (No. 23 of 1971) (E.C.S.), Customary Courts Edict 1969 (No. 9 of 1969), s. 15(*a*) (S.E.S), Customary Courts (No. 2) Edict 1968 (No. 38 of 1966) (E.N.) (Rivers State), s. 15(*a*).

[52] (1950) 20 N.L.R. 144.

[53] See n. 26, above.

[54] See *Tapa* v. *Kuka* (1945) 18 N.L.R. 5; *Ghamson* v. *Wobill* (1947) 12 W.A.C.A. 181, a Gold Coast case.

[55] See *Ekem* v. *Nerba* (1947) 12 W.A.C.A. 258, a Gold Coast case.

diction of the court should be applied. This would ensure that the disposition *inter vivos* of a piece of land is always subject to the same system of customary law.

2. *Bendel, Ogun, Ondo and Oyo States*

The wording of the law governing internal conflicts between different systems of customary law in Bendel is virtually the same as that in Ogun, Ondo and Oyo States.[56] The High Court Law of Ogun, Ondo and Oyo States[57] provides that whenever the High Court determines that customary law is applicable in a case before it, the court is to apply the particular system of customary law which is appropriate under the Customary Courts Law[58] of the State which deals in detail with internal conflicts between different systems of customary law. Similarly, the High Court Law 1964[59] of Bendel State contains provisions directing the High Court of the State to apply systems of customary law appropriate under the provisions of the repealed Customary Courts legislation[60] of Bendel State.

Land Cases

In both laws, it is provided that, as a general rule, in Land Cases the appropriate customary law is "the customary law of the place where the land is situated" (*lex situs*). One advantage of this rule is that in general a particular piece of land is always subject to the same system of customary law. This law is more appropriate than the law prevailing in the area of jurisdiction of the court for the two laws may be different and people having dealings in land would usually consider the land to be subject to the customary law of the place where the land is situated. The general rule is subject to the exception that —

"where the customary law applying to land prohibits, restricts or regulates the devolution on death to any particular class of persons of the right to occupy such land it shall not operate to deprive any person of the beneficial interest in such land (other than the right to occupy the same) or in the proceeds of sale thereof to

---

[56] See High Court Law (W.R.N. Laws 1959, Cap. 44), s. 12(4); High Court Law 1964 (No. 9 of 1964) (M.W.N.), s. 13(4); Customary Courts Law (W.R.N. Laws 1959, Cap. 31), ss. 19 and 20, Customary Courts Edict 1966 (No. 29 of 1966) (M.W.N.), ss. 22 and 23.

[57] W.R.N. Laws 1959, Cap. 44.

[58] W.R.N. Laws 1959, Cap. 31.

[59] No. 9 of 1964.

[60] See Customary Courts (Abolition) Edict 1973 (No. 18 of 1973).

which he may be entitled under the rules of inheritance of any other customary law."[61]

It is suggested that the words "any other customary law" in this provision mean any other customary law to which the party in question is subject. The words could not have been intended to mean "any other customary law whatsoever." The effect of the exception is that where under the *lex situs* a party's right to occupy land by devolution on death is affected, but under the rules of inheritance of any other customary law to which the party in question is subject he would have been entitled to beneficial interest in the land or in the proceeds of the sale of the land, the *lex situs* cannot deprive him of any such beneficial interest except the right to occupy the land. This is very strange for the buyer of the land would, under the provision, have greater rights in the land than the seller, such rights including the right to occupy the land.

Succession

Section 20(2) of the Customary Courts Law of Ogun, Ondo and Oyo States which is the same in wording as section 23(2) of the repealed Customary Courts Edict 1966 of the Midwestern State provides as follows:

"(2) In causes and matters arising from inheritance the appropriate customary law shall, subject to sub-sections (1) and (4) of this section be the customary law applying to the deceased."

Thus, as a general rule, in cases of succession to property, the appropriate Customary Law is the customary law to which the deceased was subject. The exceptions to this rule are found in subsections (1) and (4) of the relevant section of each of the two customary courts enactments. Subsection (1) provides that as a general rule land matters are governed by the customary law of the place where the land is situated and subsection (4) provides for the situation where the application of this customary law would have deprived a party of a beneficial interest which he is entitled to under his own personal (customary) law.[62]

Other civil cases

Subsection (3) of section 20 of the Customary Courts Law of Ogun, Ondo and Oyo States which is identical with subsection (3) of section 23 of the repealed Customary Courts Edict 1966 of the Midwestern State provides as follows:

[61] Customary Courts Law (W.R.N. Laws 1959, Cap. 31), s. 20(4); Customary Courts Edict 1966 (No. 29 of 1966) (M.W.N.), s. 23(4).
[62] See p. 158, above.

"(3) Subject to the provisions of sub-sections (1) and (2) of this section:
  (a) in civil causes or matters where —
      (i) both parties are not natives of the area of jurisdiction of the court; or
      (ii) the transaction the subject of the cause or matter was not entered into in the area of the jurisdiction of the court; or
      (iii) one of the parties is not a native of the area of jurisdiction of the court and the parties agreed or may be presumed to have agreed that their obligations should be regulated, wholly or partly, by the customary law applying to that party,
the appropriate customary law shall be the customary law binding between the parties;
  (b) in all other civil causes and matters the appropriate customary law shall be the law of the area of jurisdiction of the court."

Thus, in civil cases (excluding land and succession cases to which subsections (1) and (2) of the relevant sections of each of the Customary Courts enactments relate), with respect to three specific situations the applicable customary law is the customary law binding between the parties. It should be pointed out, however, that in any of the two situations stated in sub-paragraphs (i) and (ii) of paragraph (a) of each relevant subsection, the law binding between the parties may be the law of the area of jurisdiction of the court. This would be the position in contractual relations where the parties have agreed that the law of the area of jurisdiction of the court is to govern their relations. The two situations are, however, situations in which the parties may not wish to be governed by the law of the area of jurisdiction of the court. For example, in the first situation, because both parties are not natives of the area of the jurisdiction of the court they may prefer another system of customary law, to which one or both of them are subject, to the customary law of the area of jurisdiction of the court.

With respect to civil cases which are not land or succession cases and which are outside sub-paragraphs (i) to (iii) of paragraph (a) of each relevant subsection, the appropriate customary law is the law of the area of jurisdiction of the court.[63]

3. *Lagos State*

In Lagos State, sections 19 and 20 of the Customary Courts Edict[64]

---

[63] Customary Courts Law (W.R.N. Laws 1959, Cap. 31), s. 20(3)(*b*); Customary Courts Edict 1966 (No. 38 of 1966) (M.W.N.), s. 23(3)(*b*).
[64] Lagos Laws 1973, Cap. 33.

govern conflicts between different systems of customary law. The sections are respectively similar to sections 19 and 20 of the Customary Courts Law of Ogun, Ondo and Oyo States except that land cases are not specifically provided for in the Customary Courts legislation of Lagos State.

Succession Cases

The general rule governing choice of law in succession cases is the same as that applicable in Ogun, Ondo and Oyo States. Thus, the customary law applying to the deceased is the appropriate law. The only exception to the rule is found in section 20(4) of the enactment which is identical with section 20(4) of the Customary Courts Law of Ogun, Ondo and Oyo States already discussed in some detail.[65] Thus, the general rule applies subject to the provisions relating to any beneficial interest to which a party is entitled under his personal (customary) law.[66]

Other Civil Cases

In Lagos State, the choice-of-law rules governing cases other than succession cases are the same as the choice-of-law rules of Ogun, Ondo and Oyo States governing civil cases other than land and succession cases and discussed under the sub-heading "Other Civil Cases" in respect of Bendel, Ogun, Ondo and Oyo States.[67]

4. *Northern States*

The Area Courts Edict of each of the northern States contains rules governing conflicts between different systems of customary law. The relevant provisions of the Edicts are identical in wording. They are sections 20 and 21 of each of the Edicts.[68] Section 20(1)(*a*) of the Area Courts Edict 1968[69] of Plateau State, for example, provides as follows:

"20(1) Subject to the provisions of this Edict, and in particular of section 21, an area court shall administer —
    (a) the native law and custom prevailing in the area of jurisdiction of the court or binding between the parties;"

---

[65] See pp. 159-160, above.
[66] See p. 158, above.
[67] See p. 160, above.
[68] Area Courts Edict 1967 (No. 2 of 1967) (Kwara); Area Courts Edict 1967 (No. 2 of 1967) (N.C.S.); Area Courts Edict 1967 (No. 1 of 1967) (N.W.S.); Area Courts Edict 1968 (No. 4 of 1968) (B.P.S.); Area Courts Edict 1967 (No. 1 of 1967) (Kano); Area Courts Edict 1968 (No. 1 of 1968) (N.E.S.).
[69] No. 4 of 1968 (B.P.S.).

This paragraph contains the general rule which applies subject to detailed provisions contained in section 21 of the Edict. Section 21 specifies the law governing various classes of mixed civil causes. A mixed civil cause is a cause in which two or more of the parties are normally subject to different systems of customary law, for example, a cause to which an Igbirra man and an Abeokuta (Yoruba) man are parties. It follows that unmixed civil causes are governed by the general rule contained in section 20(1)(*a*) of the Edict.

Succession Cases

Section 21(1) of the Edict deals with mixed civil causes other than land causes. The last paragraph of the subsection governs mixed succession causes other than land causes. It provides as follows:

"but if in the opinion of the court, none of the paragraphs of this sub-section is applicable to any particular matter in controversy, the court shall be governed by the principles of natural justice, equity and good conscience."

Clearly, the paragraphs referred to in this provision are paragraphs (*a*) to (*c*) of subsection (1) of section 21. Paragraphs (*a*) and (*b*) appear to be couched in terms of contractual relations and are thus inappropriate in relation to succession cases, succession cases being obviously cases not based on any agreement between the parties to the case. Moreover, the three paragraphs mention "obligations in connection with the transactions which are in controversy before the court." The word "transactions" is inappropriate in relation to succession cases for such cases are not based on any transaction involving the parties. Accordingly, in mixed succession cases, the court is to apply the principles of natural justice, equity and good conscience. It is consistent with those principles to apply the personal (customary) law of the deceased.[70]

The general rule that the customary law prevailing in the area of jurisdiction of the court or binding between the parties is to be administered by the court governs unmixed succession cases other than land cases. It is suggested that the law binding between the parties as more appropriate for succession cases could involve non-natives of the area of jurisdiction of the court. It is further suggested that the law binding between the parties is the personal (customary) law of the deceased for any person claiming property by devolution on death should be subject to the law to which the deceased was subject.

Land Cases

All land causes or matters whether mixed or unmixed are

---

[70] See *Tapa* v. *Kuka* (1945) 18 N.L.R. 5; *Ghamson* v. *Wobill* (1947) 12 W.A.C.A. 181, a Gold Coast case.

governed by section 21(2) of the Edict which provides as follows:

"(2) In land causes or matters the native law and custom to be applied by an area court shall be the native law and custom in force in relation to land in the place where the land is situated.

Provided that no tavie law or custom prohibiting, restricting or regulating the devolution on death to any particular class of persons of the right to occupy any land shall operate to deprive any person of the beneficial interest in such land (other than the right to occupy the same) or in the proceeds of sale thereof to which he may be entitled under the rules of inheritance of any other native law and custom."

Thus, the *lex situs* applies as a general rule. The rule is subject to the proviso to section 21(2) which is similar in wording to section 20(4) of the Customary Courts Law[71] of Ogun, Ondo and Oyo States already considered.[72]

Other Civil Cases

It has already been pointed out that the last paragraph of section 21(1) of the Edict deals with succession cases. The rest of the subsection governs civil cases other than land and succession cases. The subsection (excluding its last paragraph) provides as follows:

"21(1) In mixed civil causes other than land causes, the native law and custom to be applied by an area court shall be —

(a) the particular native law and custom which the parties agreed or intended or may be presumed to have agreed or intended, should regulate their obligations in connection with the transactions which are in controversy before the court;

(b) that combination of any two or more native laws or customs which the parties agreed or intended, or may be presumed to have agreed or intended, should regulate their obligations as aforesaid; or

(c) in the absence of any agreement or intention or presumption thereof —
  (i) the particular native law or custom; or
  (ii) such combination of any two or more native laws or customs, which it appears to the court, ought having regard to the nature of the transaction and to the circumstances of the case, to regulate the obligations of the parties as aforesaid."

---

[71] W.R.N. Laws 1959, Cap. 31.
[72] See pp. 159-160, above.

Unmixed cases other than land and succession cases are governed by the general rule contained in section 20(1)(*a*) of the Edict. The court is to choose one of the two alternatives mentioned in that paragraph, namely, the customary law prevailing in the area of jurisdiction of the court and the customary law binding between the parties. In principle, where the law binding between the parties can be ascertained, that law rather than the law of the area of jurisdiction of the court should be applied, where the two laws are different from each other.[73] This view is consistent with that expressed by Brown C.J. in *Osuagwu* v. *Soldier*[74] in the following words:

"We suggest that when the law of the court is the law prevailing in the area but a different law binds the parties, as when two Ibos appear as parties in a Moslem court in an area where Moslem law prevails, the native court will — in the interests of justice — be reluctant to administer the law prevailing in the area, and if it tries the case at all, it will — in the interests of justice — choose to administer the law which is binding between the parties."

It has been suggested that in determining the law governing an unmixed civil cause, guidance may be sought from the provisions relating to mixed civil causes.[75]

Sharia Courts of Appeal

Under section 11(*e*) of the Sharia Court of Appeal Law[76] of each of the northern States, the Sharia Court of Appeal of the State is empowered to determine certain classes of cases in accordance with Moslem law "where all the parties to the proceedings (whether or not they are Moslems) have by writing under their hand requested the court that hears the case in the first instance to determine that case in accordance with Moslem law." This provision is substantially the same in wording as section 53(5) of the Constitution of Northern Nigeria[77] which is in force in each of the northern States. For this reason, it prevails over the choice-of-law rules contained in the Area Courts Edicts. Thus the rules apply subject to this provision. It is unfortunate that parties who had agreed to be bound by a particular law or who are otherwise bound by that law could be held at their instance to be bound by a different law when a dispute arises after the conclusion of the transaction involved.

---

[73] See *Osuagwu* v. *Soldier* 1959 N.R.N.L.R. 39.
[74] 1959 N.R.N.L.R. 39.
[75] *Osuagwu* v. *Soldier* 1959 N.R.N.L.R. 39.
[76] N.N. Laws 1963, Cap. 122.
[77] N.N. Laws 1963, Cap. 1.

Part 4

THE ADMINISTRATION OF JUSTICE

CHAPTER 10

THE COURTS

A. INTRODUCTION

COURTS in Nigeria may be classified in several ways. But the most important forms of classification are, first, classification into superior courts and inferior courts and, second, classification into courts of record and courts other than courts of record.

1. *Superior and Inferior Courts*

Superior courts are usually described as courts of unlimited jurisdiction. In the strict sense of the term "unlimited jurisdiction," no court in Nigeria has such jurisdiction. But superior courts are so described because the limits to their jurisdiction are minimal. They have minimal jurisdictional limits with respect to the type of subject-matter but they are not limited in jurisdiction with respect to the mere value of the subject-matter of a case. Thus, the High Court of a State is a superior court for it has unlimited jurisdiction throughout the State with respect to the value of the subject-matter.

On the other hand, inferior courts are courts which have jurisdictional limits with respect to the type and value of subject-matter. Magistrates' courts are examples of inferior courts. Inferior courts are normally subject to the supervisory jurisdiction of High Courts.[1]

2. *Courts of Record and Courts other than Courts of Record*

Formerly, a court of record was a court which kept a record of its acts and judicial proceedings and had power to punish a person for contempt. Today, the only essential feature of a court of record is its power to punish contempt. Any court which has power to punish contempt is a court of record and any court which does not have such power is not a court of record.

A court of record may be a superior court or an inferior court. For example, the High Court of a State is a superior court of record[2] and a magistrate's court is an inferior court of record.[3]

At common law, a superior court of record has power to punish a person summarily for contempt whether the offence is committed in

---

[1] See pp. 191-192, below.
[2] See *e.g.* Constitution of Western Nigeria (W.N. No. 26 of 1963), s. 48(3).
[3] See *Nunku* v. *Police* (1955) 15 W.A.C.A. 23.

the face of the court or out of court. But an inferior court of record has power at common law to punish contempt summarily only where the offence is committed in the face of the court. Thus, where the offence of contempt is committed in the face of a court of record, whether superior or inferior, the court can punish the offender by imposing a sentence of fine or imprisonment immediately; but where the offence is committed out of court only a superior court of record can impose punishment summarily. Punishing contempt summarily should be distinguished from imposing punishment on a person formally charged with the offence of contempt. An inferior court of record, for example a magistrates' court, may have jurisdiction to try a person on a charge of contempt under the appropriate criminal code[4] or the penal code[5] where the offence was committed out of court, and power to impose punishment in accordance with the code but the court cannot punish the offender in the absence of such a charge. In other words, the court cannot punish the offender summarily. The common law power of a court of record to punish a person summarily for contempt committed in the face of the court has been preserved by the proviso to section 22(10) of the Constitution of the Federation.[6]

B. SUPREME COURT OF NIGERIA

The Supreme Court of Nigeria was established in 1963 by the Constitution of the Federation[7] which provides that the judges of the court are the Chief Justice of Nigeria and such number of other judges known as Justices of the Supreme Court, not being less than five, as may be prescribed by law.[8] The present number of Justices of the Supreme Court as prescribed by law is ten.[9] The power to appoint a person to the office of Chief Justice of Nigeria and to dismiss the holder of the office is vested in the Head of the Federal Military Government.[10] The Supreme Military Council is empowered to appoint and dismiss Justices of the Supreme Court.[11]

---

[4] See *e.g.* Criminal Code (Lagos Laws 1973, Cap. 31), s. 133.

[5] N.N. Laws 1963, Cap. 89.

[6] Act No. 20 of 1963.

[7] *Ibid.*

[8] *Ibid.* s. 111(2) as amended by the Constitution (Suspension and Modification) Decree 1966 (No. 1 of 1966). See Constitution (Basic Provisions) Decree 1975 (No. 32 of 1975).

[9] Supreme Court Act 1960 (No. 12 of 1960), s. 3(1) as amended by the Supreme Court (Amendment) Decree 1977 (No. 72 of 1977).

[10] Constitution of the Federation (Act No. 20 of 1963), s. 112(1) as amended by the Constitution (Amendment) Decree 1972 (No. 5 of 1972).

[11] Constitution of the Federation (Act No. 20 of 1963), s. 112(1) as amended by (a) the Constitution (Suspension and Modification) Decree 1966 (No. 1 of 1966) and (b) ss. 13(3) and 14(2) of the Constitution (Basic Provisions) Decree 1975 (No. 32 of 1975).

For the purpose of the final determination of a case, the court is constituted by a minimum number of three judges of the court.[12] The Court usually consists of this number but a five-member panel sometimes sits to hear and determine very important cases.[13] In general, a single judge of the Supreme Court is empowered to exercise any power vested in the court other than the final determination of a cause[14] or matter[15] but in criminal cases if a judge of the court refuses an application for the exercise of any such power, the applicant is entitled to have his application determined by the Supreme Court, and in civil cases any order, direction or decision made or given by a single judge of the court in the exercise of any such power may be varied, discharged or reversed by the Supreme Court.[16] At present, the court sits in Lagos and a number of State capitals.

The court is a superior court of record. It has appellate jurisdiction in civil and criminal cases. It has no original jurisdiction except in the case of any question referred to it under section 115 of the Constitution of the Federation[17] and in the case of contempt of itself under the proviso to section 22(10) of the same constitution — the proviso which preserves the common law power of a court of record to punish contempt of itself. Under the proviso the court may deal summarily with a case of contempt of itself.

The Supreme Court hears appeals from the Federal Court of Appeal. Section 117(5) of the Constitution of the Federation as amended by the Constitution (Amendment) (No. 2) Decree 1976[18] prescribes a limitation with respect to such appeals. According to the subsection, in general, no appeal lies to the Supreme Court from a decision of the Federal Court of Appeal on an appeal from a decision of a High Court (a State High Court or the Federal Revenue Court), sitting as a court of appeal. But this limitation does not apply to a criminal case where the Attorney-General of the Federation has certified that the decision of the Federal Court of Appeal involves a point of exceptional importance and that it is desirable in the public interest that a further appeal should lie to the Supreme Court.

---

[12] Supreme Court Act 1960 (No. 12 of 1960), s. 9.
[13] See *e.g. National Employers Mutual General Insurance Association Ltd* v. *Uchay* (1973) 4 S.C. 1, 1973 (1) N.M.L.R. 170.
[14] "Cause" includes any action, suit or other original proceeding between a plaintiff and a defendant: Supreme Court Act 1960, s. 2(1).
[15] "matter" includes every proceeding in court not in a cause: Supreme Court Act 1960, s. 2(1).
[16] Supreme Court Act 1960, s. 10.
[17] Act No. 20 of 1963. See *Obeya* v. *Soluade (No. 1)*, 1969 N.N.L.R. 17.
[18] No. 42 of 1976.

Subject to the limitation, section 117(2) of the Constitution of the Federation provides that an appeal lies from the decisions of the Federal Court of Appeal to the Supreme Court as of right in the following cases:

(a) decisions in any civil or criminal proceedings on questions as to the interpretation of the Constitution of the Federation or the Constitution of a State;

(b) decisions in any civil or criminal proceedings on questions as to whether any of the provisions of Chapter III of the Constitution of the Federation (the Chapter on fundamental rights) has been contravened in relation to any person;

(c) decisions in any criminal proceedings in which the Federal Court of Appeal has affirmed a sentence of death imposed by another court or tribunal;

(d) decisions given in the exercise of the original jurisdiction of the Federal Court of Appeal under section 121F of the Constitution of the Federation which relates to disputes between the Federation and a State or between States; and

(e) such other cases as may be prescribed by any enactment.

Subject to the limitation prescribed by section 117(5) of the Constitution of the Federation, subsections (3) and (4) of section 117 of the Constitution state the circumstances in which an appeal lies from a decision of the Federal Court of Appeal to the Supreme Court with the leave of either court. The subsections provide as follows:

"(3) An appeal shall lie from decisions of the Federal Court of Appeal to the Supreme Court with the leave of the Federal Court of Appeal or the Supreme Court in the following cases —

(a) any decision of the Federal Court of Appeal on an appeal from a final decision in any civil proceedings before the High Court or the Federal Revenue Court sitting at first instance; and

(b) where the ground of appeal involves questions of law alone, any decision of the Federal Court of Appeal on an appeal from a decision in any criminal proceedings before the High Court or the Federal Revenue Court sitting at first instance: Provided that nothing in paragraph (a) of this subsection shall confer any right of appeal —

(i) from any order made ex parte;

(ii) from an order relating only to costs;

(iii) from an order made with the consent of the parties; or

(iv) in the case of a party to proceedings for dissolution or nullity of marriage who, having had time and opportunity to appeal from any decree nisi in such proceedings, has not so appealed, from any decree absolute founded upon such a decree nisi.

(4) Without prejudice to the foregoing provisions of this section, an appeal shall lie to the Supreme Court from any other decision of the Federal Court of Appeal only with the leave of the Supreme Court."

The difference between leave to appeal under subsection (3) and leave to appeal under subsection (4) is that under subsection (3) leave to appeal may be granted either by the Supreme Court or by the Federal Court of Appeal but under subsection (4) only the Supreme Court may grant leave to appeal. It should also be pointed out that subject to the limitation contained in section 117(5) of the Constitution, by virtue of the provisions of subsection (4) in any case in which an appeal does not lie as of right from the Federal Court of Appeal appeal lies with leave, except that no appeal lies whether as of right or with leave in any case within the proviso to subsection (3). Further remarks may now be made about the proviso.

It should be noted that the proviso excludes the orders mentioned in its paragraphs (i) to (iii) and a decree absolute within its paragraph (iv) from the ambit of paragraph (a) of subsection (3). By doing so, the proviso indicates that a decree absolute for dissolution or nullity of marriage is a final decision. The wording of paragraph (iv) of the proviso raises the question whether a decree nisi on which such decree absolute is founded is also a final decision. Paragraph (iv) mentions "a party . . . who, having had time and opportunity to appeal from any decree nisi in such proceedings." There could be no opportunity to appeal from such decree nisi unless it is a final decision within the meaning of section 117(3) (*a*). This is because of all the five categories of cases in which an appeal lies as of right to the Supreme Court as stated in section 117(2) the first four categories are inapplicable to such decree nisi and the fifth category, "such other cases as may be prescribed by any enactment" is also inapplicable to such decree nisi, for no enactment has provided that an appeal lies as of right from such decree nisi to the Supreme Court. On reading subsections (2) and (3) of section 117 of the Constitution together, therefore, it is clear that a decree nisi for dissolution or nullity of marriage is a final decision within the meaning of section 117(2)(*a*).[19] Thus, an appeal lies from a decree nisi for dissolution or nullity of marriage issued by the Federal Court of Appeal to the Supreme Court with the leave of either Court. It should also be pointed out that since a decree absolute for the dissolution or nullity of marriage is a final decision

---

[19] See *Nabhan* v. *Nabhan* [1967] 1 All N.L.R. 47 based on the former s. 117(2)(*a*) of the Constitution of the Federation.

within the meaning of section 117(2)(*a*) an appeal lies from such decree absolute issued by the Federal Court of Appeal to the Supreme Court with the leave of either court.

Neither in the case of a decree nisi for the dissolution or nullity of marriage nor in the case of a decree absolute founded upon such decree nisi does the limitation stated in section 117(5) of the Constitution prohibit an appeal to the Supreme Court for that limitation applies only to cases heard by a High Court sitting as a court of appeal and a High Court pronounces a decree nisi or decree absolute for the dissolution of marriage only in its original jurisdiction.[20]

The Supreme Court hears appeals from the National Industrial Court (a newly-established court).[21]

The Supreme Court also hears appeals from the Sharia Court of Appeal of each of the northern States.[22] The circumstances in which such appeals lie as of right are stated in section 119(1) of the Constitution of the Federation. The subsection reads:

"119 — (1) An appeal shall lie from decisions of the Sharia Court of Appeal [of a State] to the Supreme Court as of right in the following cases —
　　(a) decisions on questions as to the interpretation of this Constitution or the constitution of a State;
　　(b) decisions on questions as to whether any of the provisions of Chapter III of this Constitution has been contravened in relation to any person;
　　(c) such other cases as may be prescribed by any law in force in the State:
Provided that nothing in paragraph (a) or (b) of this subsection (in so far as it applies to civil proceedings) shall confer any right of appeal with respect to any question relating to the respective jurisdiction of the High Court [of the State] and the Sharia Court of Appeal that the Court of Resolution [of the State] is competent to determine."

The effect of the proviso is that the right of appeal granted by the subsection does not apply to any question within paragraph (*a*) or (*b*) of the subsection involving a determination of the issue whether it is the High Court or the Sharia Court of Appeal that has jurisdiction in a case.[23]

---

[20] See Matrimonial Causes Decree 1970 (No. 18 of 1970).

[21] Trade Disputes Decree 1976 (No. 7 of 1976), s. 15.

[22] The northern States, that is, the States in the northern part of the country are Bauchi, Benue, Borno, Gongola, Kaduna, Kano, Kwara, Niger, Plateau and Sokoto. See States (Creation and Transitional Provisions) Decree 1976 (No. 12 of 1976), s. 1 and Schedule.

[23] See Court of Resolution Law (N.N. Laws 1963, Cap. 28), s. 5.

It is provided in section 119(2) of the Constitution that subject to section 119(1) of the Constitution, an appeal lies from the Sharia Court of Appeal of a State to the Supreme Court with the leave of the Supreme Court in such cases as may be prescribed by any law in force in the State. Thus, where an appeal does not lie as of right from a decision of the Sharia Court of Appeal of a State, leave to appeal from the decision is obtainable from the Supreme Court provided that a law in force in the State has so provided. No law in force in any of the northern States has specified any case or class of cases from which appeal lies with leave to the Supreme Court. It should also be mentioned that section 119(2) does not provide for leave of the Sharia Court of Appeal.[24]

There is no appeal as of right from the decisions of the Court of Resolution of a State. Section 119(2) of the Constitution provides that subject to section 119(1) of the Constitution an appeal lies from decisions of the Court of Resolution of a State with the leave of the Supreme Court "in such cases as may be prescribed by any law in force" in the State. But section 7 of the Court of Resolution Law[25] applicable in the six northern States provides that the "decision of the Court of Resolution in any matter referred to it in accordance with the provisions of this Law shall be final." It is arguable that this provision is unconstitutional and, therefore, void. Although no Federal law in force in any of the northern States has invoked the provisions of section 119(1) of the Constitution of the Federation, there is no doubt that the words "any law in force" in that subsection include Federal law having regard, in particular to the power of the Federal Military Government to make laws for any part of the country on any matter whatsoever.[26] However, in practice the subsection is not likely to be invoked by the Federal Military Government. Moreover, no Court of Resolution has ever had cause to sit. The question of the constitutionality of section 7 of the Court of Resolution Law is therefore, at present, purely academic.

The Impact of the Supreme Court of Nigeria on the Legal System

The Supreme Court of Nigeria as the highest court for Nigeria has contributed in some measure to the development of the law. Since its establishment in 1963, the court has made some effort to play the role of moulder of the law, notably in the fields of criminal law and constitutional law. Thus, in *Obaji* v. *State*,[27] by seemingly creative

[24] Compare Constitution of the Federation, s. 117(3) as amended by the Constitution (Amendment) (No. 2) Decree 1976.

[25] N.N. Laws 1963, Cap. 28.

[26] See Constitution (Basic Provisions) Decree 1975 (No. 32 of 1975) s. 1(1).

[27] [1965] 1 All N.L.R. 269. See, generally, A. B. Kasunmu (ed.), *The Supreme Court of Nigeria 1956-1970* (1977).

interpretation, the Supreme Court explained the law of provocation under section 318 of the Criminal Code of Eastern Nigeria.[28] A similar attitude was adopted by the Court in *Adams* v. *D.P.P.*[29] in interpreting section 229 of the Criminal Procedure Act.[30] Amending legislation was later made for Lagos in respect of each of the two cases along the line of interpretation given by the Supreme Court.[31] Other cases in which the court appears to have played the role of law-moulder include *Council of the University of Ibadan* v. *Adamolekun*,[32] a case involving the validity of an Edict and thus, the interpretation of section 6 of the Constitution (Suspension and Modification) Decree 1966[33] which provided in clear terms without any exceptions (in the section) that no question as to the validity of an Edict was to be inquired into in a court; *Ereku* v. *The Military Governor, Midwestern State*[34] in which the Supreme Court held than an Edict was void by reason of its inconsistency with the Constitution of the Federation[35]; *Onubogu* v. *The State* where the Supreme Court held that a procedure in a criminal trial whereby an accused person adopted as part of his defence the statement made by him to the Police was irregular, and *Esan* v. *Oluwa*[36] where the court held that if the plaintiff adduced evidence constituting the plea of *res judicata*, a defendant in the case who did not specially plead that defence could rely on it.

C. THE FEDERAL COURT OF APPEAL

The Federal Court of Appeal is a superior court of record established on October 1, 1976 by the Constitution of the Federation as amended by the Constitution (Amendment) (No. 2) Decree 1976.[37] Section 121A(2) of the Constitution provides that the judges of the court consist of the President of the court and at least 21 other judges styled "Justices of Appeal," the actual number of other judges being that prescribed by law. The present prescribed number of Justices of Appeal is 21.

[28] E.N. Laws 1963, Cap. 30. The provision was identical with s. 318 of the Criminal Code of Lagos State (Lagos Laws 1973, Cap. 31).

[29] [1966] 1 All N.L.R. 12.

[30] Fed. and Lagos Laws 1958, Cap. 43.

[31] See Criminal Justice (Miscellaneous Provisions) Decree 1966 (No. 84 of 1966). See now Criminal Code (Lagos Laws 1973, Cap. 31), s. 229.

[32] [1967] 1 All N.L.R. 213. Compare *Lakanmi* v. *Attorney-General (West)* (1971) 1 U.I.L.R. 201. See p. 47, above.

[33] No. 1 of 1966.

[34] (1974) 10 S.C. 59.

[35] Act No. 20 of 1963. See also *Onyiuke* v. *Eastern States Interim Assets Agency* (1974) 10 S.C. 77.

[36] (1974) 3 S.C. 125.

[37] No. 42 of 1976.

Judges of the court (including the President) are appointed by the Supreme Military Council acting after consultation with the Advisory Judicial Committee.[38] With respect to qualification for appointment to the office of President of the court or Justice of Appeal, section 121C(2) of the Constitution provides as follows:

"(2) A person shall not be qualified to hold the office of a Justice [a judge] of the Federal Court of Appeal unless —
  (a) he is or has been a judge of a court having unlimited jurisdiction in civil and criminal matters in Nigeria or a court having jurisdiction in appeals from any such court; or
  (b) he is qualified to practise as a legal practitioner in Nigeria and has been so qualified for not less than 10 years; provided that in computing the period during which any person has been qualified to practise as a legal practitioner any period during which he held office as judge or magistrate after becoming so qualified shall be included."

The court is mainly a court of appeal. It has exclusive jurisdiction to hear appeals from State High Courts, the Federal Revenue Court and such other courts or tribunals as may be specified by law.[39] Formerly, "tribunals" from which appeals lay to the Federal Court of Appeal were tribunals established under the Robbery and Firearms (Special Provisions) Decree 1970,[40] tribunals established under the Offences Against the Person (Special Provisions) Decree 1974[41] and Currency Offences tribunals.[42]

The court has jurisdiction throughout the country. Accordingly, section 121B of the Constitution empowers the Supreme Military Council to divide the whole country, excluding the city of Lagos, into at least three judicial districts for the purpose of the exercise of the court's jurisdiction, provided that no two of the following towns should fall within the same district: Benin, Enugu, Ibadan and Kaduna. Thus, in fact, there should be at least four judicial districts, each of the four towns mentioned falling within a district. The court sits in Lagos. Outside Lagos, the court now sits in the four towns mentioned (Benin, Enugu, Ibadan and Kaduna).

The Federal Court of Appeal has original jurisdiction in addition to its appellate jurisdiction. Its original jurisdiction is provided for

---

[38] Constitution of the Federation (Act No. 20 of 1963), s. 121C(1); Constitution (Basic Provisions) Decree 1975 (No. 32 of 1975), s. 13(3)(a).
[39] Constitution of the Federation (Act No. 20 of 1963), s. 121E(1).
[40] No. 47 of 1970. The Robbery and Firearms (Special Provisions) (Amendment) Decree 1977 (No. 39 of 1977) abolished appeals from the decisions of robbery and firearms tribunals.
[41] No. 20 of 1974.
[42] See Counterfeit Currency (Special Provisions) Decree 1974 (No. 22 of 1974).

by section 121F of the Constitution. The section gives the court exclusive original jurisdiction in any dispute between the Federation and a State or between States to the extent that the dispute involves any question of law or fact provided the existence or extent of a legal right depends on that question.

It is worthy of note that unlike the Court of Appeal of the Western State the Federal Court of Appeal does not replace any High Court for the purpose of the exercise of original jurisdiction under section 115 of the Constitution of the Federation.[43] The section as amended by the Constitution (Amendment) (No. 2) Decree 1976 provides as follows:

"115 — (1) Where any question as to the interpretation of this Constitution or the constitution of a State arises in any proceedings in any court of law in any part of Nigeria (other than the Supreme Court, the Federal Court of Appeal, the High Court of a territory or a court-martial) and the court is of opinion that the question involves a substantial question of law, the court may, and shall if any party to the proceedings so requests, refer the question to the High Court having jurisdiction in that part of Nigeria; and the High Court shall —

(a) if it is of opinion that the question involves a substantial question of law, refer the question to the Supreme Court; or

(b) if it is of opinion that the question does not involve a substantial question of law, remit the question to the court that made the reference to be disposed of in accordance with such directions as the High Court may think fit to give.

(2) Where any question as to the interpretation of this Constitution or the constitution of a State arises in any proceedings in the Federal Court of Appeal or in the High Court of a territory and the Court is of opinion that the question involves a substantial question of law, the court may, and shall if any party to the proceedings so requests, refer the question to the Supreme Court.

(3) Where any question is referred to the Supreme Court in pursuance of this section, the Supreme Court shall give its decision upon the question and the court in which the question arose shall dispose of the case in accordance with that decision."

The circumstances in which appeals lie as of right from the High Court of a State or the Federal Revenue Court to the Federal Court

---

[43] See *Obeya* v. *Soluade (No. 1)*, 1969 N.N.L.R. 17. *Contra Olowosoke* v. *Oke* (1972) 11 S.C. 1 at p. 5 where Elias C.J.N. delivering the judgment of the court said *obiter* that the jurisdiction exercised by a court under the former section 115 of the Constitution of the Federation (a provision similar to the present section 115 of the Constitution) in determining whether a case "involves a substantial question of law" was neither "first instance" jurisdiction nor appellate jurisdiction.

of Appeal are stated in section 121E(2) of the Constitution. The provision reads:

"(2) An appeal shall lie from decisions of the High Court of a State or of the Federal Revenue Court to the Federal Court of Appeal as of right in the following cases —
  (a) final decisions in any civil proceedings before the High Court or the Federal Revenue Court sitting at first instance;
  (b) where the ground of appeal involves questions of law alone, decisions in any criminal proceedings before the High Court or the Federal Revenue Court sitting at first instance;
  (c) decisions in any civil or criminal proceedings on questions as to the interpretation of this Constitution or the constitution of a State;
  (d) decisions in any civil or criminal proceedings on questions as to whether any of the provisions of Chapter III of this Constitution has been contravened in relation to any person;
  (e) decisions in any criminal proceedings in which any person has been sentenced to death by the High Court or the Federal Revenue Court; and
  (f) such other cases as may from time to time be prescribed by any enactment:
Provided that nothing in paragraph (a) of this subsection shall confer any right of appeal —
  (i) from any order made *ex parte*;
  (ii) from any order relating only to costs;
  (iii) from any order made with the consent of the parties, or
  (iv) in the case of a party to proceedings for dissolution or nullity of marriage who, having had time and opportunity to appeal from any decree nisi in such proceedings, has not so appealed, from any decree absolute founded upon such a decree nisi.

It should be noted that the proviso to paragraph (*a*) of section 121E(2) is the same in wording as the proviso to section 117(3)(*a*) of the Constitution already considered in discussing the Supreme Court.[44] In accordance with the argument adduced with respect to section 117(3)(*a*), both a decree nisi for dissolution or nullity of marriage and a decree absolute founded upon such decree are final decisions within the meaning of section 121E(2)(*a*).

With respect to appeals with leave to the Federal Court of Appeal, section 121E(3) of the Constitution provides as follows:

"(3) Subject to the provisions of subsection (2) of this section, an appeal shall lie from decisions of the High Court of a State or

[44] See pp. 173-174, above.

the Federal Revenue Court with the leave of the High Court or, as the case may be, the Federal Revenue Court, or with the leave of the Federal Court of Appeal in the following cases —

(a) where the ground of appeal involves a question of fact, mixed law and fact or quantum of sentence, decisions in any criminal proceedings before the High Court or the Federal Revenue Court sitting at first instance;

(b) any case in which, but for the terms of the proviso to subsection (2) of this section, an appeal would lie as of right to the Federal Court of Appeal by virtue of paragraph (a) of that subsection;

(c) decisions in any civil or criminal proceedings in which an appeal has been brought to the High Court or the Federal Revenue Court from some other court;

(d) any interlocutory decision of the High Court or the Federal Revenue Court; and

(e) such other cases as may be prescribed by any enactment."

Thus, under section 121E(3)(*b*), appeals lie from a High Court (State High Court or Federal Revenue Court) to the Federal Court of Appeal with the leave of the High Court or with the leave of the Federal Court of Appeal in all cases within the proviso to section 121E(2)(*a*). Such cases include any final decision which is: (a) an order made *ex parte*; (b) an order relating to costs only; or (c) an order made with the consent of the parties.

But section 15(1) of the Federal Court of Appeal Decree 1976[45] provides as follows:

"Where in the exercise by the High Court of a State or, as the case may be, by the Federal Revenue Court of its original jurisdiction an interlocutory order or decision is made in the course of any suit or matter, an appeal shall, by leave of that court or of the Court of Appeal, lie to the Court of Appeal; but no appeal shall lie from any order made *ex parte*, or by consent of the parties, or relating only to costs."

There is no conflict between these two provisions — section 121E(3)(*b*) of the Constitution and section 15(1) of the Federal Court of Appeal Decree 1976. The provision of the Constitution says that appeals lie with leave from orders made *ex parte*, orders made with the consent of the parties and orders relating only to costs where those orders are final decisions in civil proceedings before a State High Court or the Federal Revenue Court. On reading the provision of section 15(1) of the Federal Court of Appeal Decree 1976 as a whole, it is clear that it deals not with final decisions but with interloc-

[45] No. 43 of 1976.

utory orders or decisions. It says that where any of the three types of order is an interlocutory order no appeal lies. But section 121E(3)(*d*) of the Constitution provides that subject to the provisions of section 121E(2) of the Constitution, an appeal lies from any interlocutory decisions of the High Court or the Federal Revenue Court with leave. Accordingly, under section 121E(3)(*d*), where an order made by a State High Court or the Federal Revenue Court is an order made *ex parte*, an order relating only to costs or an order made with the consent of the parties, and is an interlocutory decision, an appeal lies, with leave, from that order to the Federal Court of Appeal. There is, therefore, a conflict between section 121E(3)(*d*) of the Constitution and section 15(1) of the Federal Court of Appeal Decree 1976. The fact that the provision for appeal under section 121E(3) of the Constitution is made subject to section 121E(2) does not avoid such conflict for there is nothing in section 121E(2) that can reasonably be construed as excluding an interlocutory order which is an order made *ex parte*, an order relating only to costs or an order made with the consent of the parties from the ambit of interlocutory decisions which can go on appeal, with leave, to the Federal Court of Appeal. Although section 121E(3)(*d*) of the Constitution was inserted by a Decree, it forms part of the Constitution and since a Decree prevails over the Constitution, section 15(1) of the Federal Court of Appeal Decree 1976 prevails over section 121E(3)(*d*) of the Constitution. The question of a later Decree prevailing over an earlier Decree does not apply here. In any case, both the Constitution (Amendment) (No. 2) Decree 1976 (which made the provision of section 121E(3)(*d*) part of the Constitution) and the Federal Court of Appeal Decree 1976 came into operation on the same day. It may be that the conflict in question is a result of a drafting error.

For the purpose of final determination of an appeal, the Federal Court of Appeal is constituted by at least three judges, except that any one of the judges sitting who disagrees with the majority may deliver a dissenting judgment.[46] Any one of the judges who have sat as the court and fully heard an appeal before the court may deliver a reserved judgment on behalf of any of the others who is absent at the time of delivery of the judgment.[47] Section 10 of the Federal Court of Appeal Decree 1976 provides that in general a single judge of the court may exercise any power vested in the court except the power of final determination of a case. But where in a criminal appeal a single judge acting under this provision rejects an application, the applicant is entitled to bring the application before the court. Similarly, in a civil appeal, any order, direction or decision made or given by a

---

[46] Federal Court of Appeal Decree 1976 (No. 43 of 1976), s. 9.
[47] *Ibid.* s. 11.

single judge acting under this provision may be varied, discharged or reversed by the court. It would be recalled that under section 117(5) of the Constitution of the Federation no criminal appeal lies from a decision of the Federal Court of Appeal on appeal to the court from a decision of a High Court (State High Court or Federal Revenue Court) sitting as a court of appeal unless the Attorney-General of the Federation has issued a certificate to the effect that the decision involves a point of law of exceptional public importance and that it is desirable in the public interest that a further appeal should lie to the Supreme Court. Section 31(2) of the Federal Court of Appeal Decree 1976 provides that where the Federal Court of Appeal has allowed an appeal against a conviction and the prosecutor notifies the court immediately after the decision of the court has been given that he intends to apply to the Attorney-General of the Federation for a certificate under section 117(5) of the Constitution, the court may make an order providing for the detention of the defendant, or directing that the defendant must not be released except on bail, until either the Attorney-General has rejected the application for the certificate or (where the application is granted) a decision on the appeal has been given by the Supreme Court.

There is no provision prescribing the minimum number of judges that would constitute the court when it is sitting as a court of first instance. Section 10 of the Federal Court of Appeal Decree 1976 which vests power on a single judge does not confer on him the power of final determination of a case. Having regard to the importance of the cases within the original jurisdiction of the court,[48] it is suggested that whenever it is sitting as a court of first instance, it will be constituted by at least three judges — the same minimum number constituting the court as a court of appeal.

It is provided in section 8 of the Federal Court of Appeal Decree 1976 that the practice and procedure of the court are to be in accordance with the Decree and, subject to the Decree, in accordance with rules of court. The section empowers the President of the court to makes rules of practice and procedure for the court with the approval of the Federal Executive Council. No such rules have yet been made. Pending the making of such rules, the rules of practice and procedure in force in the Supreme Court on October 1, 1976 (the date of commencement of the Federal Court of Appeal Decree 1976) are to apply to the Federal Court of Appeal with such modifications as may be necessary to bring them into conformity with the Federal Court of Appeal Decree 1976 and the Constitution of the Federation.[49]

---

[48] See Constitution of the Federation (Act No. 20 of 1963), ss. 115 and 121F.
[49] Federal Court of Appeal Decree 1976, s. 8(3).

Section 26 of the Federal Court of Appeal Decree 1976 provides for legal assistance. It states that in any appeal or proceedings preliminary or incidental to an appeal the Federal Court of Appeal may assign counsel to an appellant or prospective appellant[50] where in the opinion of the court it appears desirable in the interest of justice that the appellant or prospective appellant should have legal assistance and that he does not have sufficient means to enable him to obtain that assistance. The provision covers application for leave to appeal to the Federal Court of Appeal.

D. COURTS OF RESOLUTION

The Court of Resolution of each of the 10 northern States is governed by the Court of Resolution Law.[51]

It consists of the Chief Judge of the State as President, the Grand Kadi, one judge of the High Court nominated by the Chief Judge and one judge of the Sharia Court of Appeal nominated by the Grand Kadi.[52] Where the opinions of the members of the court are evenly divided on a matter before it, the opinion supported by the Chief Judge is to be declared the opinion of the court.[53] The court has jurisdiction to resolve conflicts of jurisdiction arising between the High Court and the Sharia Court of Appeal.[54] In cases where there is no such conflict between the two courts but each of them decides that it has no jurisdiction, the Court of Resolution is empowered to determine which of the two courts has jurisdiction.[55] Section 7 of the Court of Resolution Law provides that the decision of the court in any matter referred to it in accordance with the provision of the Law is final.[56]

No occasion has ever arisen for the convening of any of the Courts of Resolution.

E. SHARIA COURTS OF APPEAL

The Sharia Court of Appeal of each of the 10 northern States is a superior customary court of record which hears appeals from the Upper

---

[50] See Federal Court of Appeal Decree 1976, s. 32. Compare Legal Aid Decree 1976 (No. 56 of 1976), ss. 6 and 8.

[51] N.N. Laws 1963, Cap. 28. See States (Creation and Transitional Provisions) Decree 1976 (No. 12 of 1976).

[52] Court of Resolution Law, s. 3(1) as amended by the Chief Justice of a State (Change of Title) Decree 1976 (No. 41 of 1976).

[53] *Ibid.* s. 3(2).

[54] *Ibid.* s. 5(1).

[55] *Ibid.* s. 5(2).

[56] See pp. 34-35, above.

Area Courts in cases involving Moslem personal law.[57] "Moslem personal law" consists of Moslem law of the Maliki school governing the following matters:

"(a) any question of Moslem law regarding a marriage concluded in accordance with that law, including a question relating to the dissolution of such marriage or a question that depends on such a marriage relating to family relationship or the guardianship of an infant";

(b) where all the parties to the proceedings are Moslems, any question of Moslem law regarding a marriage, including the dissolution of that marriage, or regarding family relationship, a foundling or the guardianship of an infant;

(c) any question of Moslem law regarding a wakf, gift, will or succession where the endower, donor, testator or deceased person is a Moslem;

(d) any question of Moslem law regarding an infant, prodigal or person of unsound mind who is a Moslem or the maintenance or guardianship of a Moslem who is physically or mentally infirm": and

(e) any other question "where all the parties to the proceedings (whether or not they are Moslems) have by writing under their hand requested the court that hears the case in the first instance to determine that case in accordance with Moslem law."[58]

The only criminal jurisdiction given to the court is summary jurisdiction with respect to contempt of the court.[59] Accordingly, jurisdiction in cases involving Moslem personal law including "any other question" in category (*e*) under the definition of Moslem personal law is limited to civil jurisdiction.[60]

The court consists of a Grand Kadi and two other judges learned in the Sharia.[61] The quorum for a sitting of the court is two judges.[62]

In order to be eligible for appointment as a judge of the court a person must be —

(a) a Moslem;

(b) not less than thirty-five years of age; and

---

[57] Sharia Court of Appeal Law (N.N. Laws 1963, Cap. 122), s. 3.

[58] *Ibid.* s. 2.

[59] Sharia Court of Appeal Law, s. 3(2).

[60] In view of the abolition of customary criminal law (see p. 38, above), criminal cases involving Moslem personal law would rarely arise. See however pp. 34-36 above.

[61] See *e.g.* Sharia Court of Appeal Law (N.N. Laws 1963, Cap. 122), s. 4(1) as amended by the Sharia Court of Appeal Law (Amendment) Edict 1970 (No. 4 of 1970) (B.P.S.).

[62] See *e.g.* Sharia Court of Appeal Law, s. 4(3) as amended by the Sharia Court of Appeal (Amendment) Edict 1970 (No. 4 of 1970) (B.P.S.).

(c) (i) one who has been an alkali or adviser on Moslem law in the service of a native authority for not less than ten years; or
(ii) the holder of a certificate showing that he has satisfactorily completed a recognised course of study in Sharia law at a university college or school approved by the Military Governor;
(iii) a distinguished scholar in Islamic studies.[63]

Judges of the court are appointed by the Supreme Military Council acting after consultation with the Advisory Judicial Committee.[64]

Legal practitioners are not permitted to appear for any party before the court.[65]

F. FEDERAL REVENUE COURT

The Federal Revenue Court was established by the Federal Revenue Court Decree 1973[66] as a Federal High Court of Justice.[67] The court consists of a President and such number of other judges (four being the minimum) as the Head of the Federal Military Government may prescribe by order.[68] It is to operate in at least four Judicial Divisions altogether covering the entire country, the area of each Division being determined by the President of the court.[69] A single judge duly appointed constitutes the court.[70] Judges of the court are appointed by the Supreme Military Council acting after consultation with the Advisory Judicial Committee.[71] A person is not eligible for appointment to the office of a judge of the court unless —

"(a) he is or has been a Judge of a court having unlimited jurisdiction in civil and criminal matters in Nigeria or a court having jurisdiction in appeals from any such court; or
(b) he is qualified for admission as a legal practitioner in Nigeria and has been so qualified for not less than 10 years:
Provided that in computing the period during which any person has been qualified for admission as a legal practitioner any period during which he has held office as a judge or magistrate after becoming so qualified shall be included."[72]

---

[63] *Ibid.* s. 5. See Sharia Court of Appeal Law (Amendment) Edict 1977 (No. 8 of 1977) (Kano).
[64] Constitution of Northern Nigeria (N.N. Laws 1963, Cap. 1), s. 54(1) as amended by the Constitution (Basic Provisions) Decree 1975 (No. 32 of 1975), s. 13(3)(*b*).
[65] Sharia Court of Appeal Law, s. 20(1).
[66] No. 13 of 1973.
[67] *Ibid.* s. 1(1).
[68] *Ibid.* s. 1(2).
[69] *Ibid.* s. 19(1)
[70] *Ibid.* s. 19.
[71] *Ibid.* s. 2(1).
[72] *Ibid.* s. 2(2).

Although alternative (*b*) of the eligibility test mentions "legal practitioner" in place of the word "advocate" used in similar provisions governing appointments to State High Courts and the Supreme Court of Nigeria, the difference in wording has no significant practical effect, for every legal practitioner is entitled to practise as an advocate (a barrister).[73] There is a clear distinction between "qualified for admission as a legal practitioner" and "admitted as a legal practitioner." Accordingly, on a strict interpretation of test (*a*), a person who satisfied the requirements for admission as a legal practitioner 10 years ago, for example, one who was then called to the Bar and at the time produced his certificate of call to the Bar to the Chief Registrar of the Supreme Court[74] but has not in fact been enrolled as a legal practitioner is eligible for appointment to the office of Judge of the Court. It may be that there is a mistake of drafting in the provision prescribing the tests, for no person who has not in fact been enrolled as a legal practitioner has been appointed a judge of the court; nor has any person who has not had his name on the roll for at least 10 years been so appointed.

The court has civil and criminal jurisdiction in cases —

"(a) relating to the revenue of the Government of the Federation in which the said Government or any organ thereof or a person suing or being sued on behalf of the said Government is a party;

(b) connected with or pertaining to —
   (i) the taxation of companies and of other bodies established or carrying on business in Nigeria and all other persons subject to Federal taxation,
   (ii) customs and excise duties,
   (iii) banking, foreign exchange, currency or other fiscal measures;

(c) arising from —
   (i) the operation of the Companies Decree 1968 or any other enactment regulating the operation of companies incorporated under the Companies Decree 1968,
   (ii) any enactment relating to copyright, patents, designs, trade marks and merchandise marks;

(d) of Admiralty jurisdiction."[75]

Before the creation of the Federal Revenue Court the jurisdiction conferred on it had been exercised by the State High Courts acting as

---

[73] A legal practitioner is a person entitled in accordance with the law to practise as a barrister or a barrister and solicitor. See Legal Practitioners Decree 1975 (No. 15 of 1975) s. 23, Interpretation Act 1964 (No. 1 of 1964), ss. 18(1) and 4(2)(*b*).

[74] See Legal Practitioners Decree 1975, s. 6.

[75] Federal Revenue Court Decree 1973, s. 7(1)(2).

Federal courts under the authority of Federal legislation.[76] Now, State High Courts have no jurisdiction in any matter with respect to which jurisdiction is conferred on the Federal Revenue Court.[77]

There has been a controversy as to the ambit of the jurisdiction conferred on the court. The Supreme Court in *Jammal Steel Structures Ltd.* v. *African Continental Bank Ltd.*[78] had to determine whether jurisdiction in civil causes and matters connected with or pertaining to "banking, foreign exchange, currency or other fiscal measures" conferred on the court by section 7(1)(*b*)(iii) of the Federal Revenue Court Decree 1973 included, with respect to banking, ordinary banker-customer cases. If it did the jurisdiction of the State High Courts was ousted by virtue of section 8(1) of the Decree. Purporting to apply the *ejusdem generis* rule, the court by a majority of 2 to 1 rejected the view that "banking" in section 7(1)(*b*)(iii) of the Decree meant all banking transactions and accordingly included ordinary banker-customer transactions. The majority expressed the view that the words "other fiscal measures" in that paragraph must be construed *ejusdem generis* with the words "banking," "foreign exchange" and "currency" notwithstanding argument by counsel that "banking" in the context was a noun and had no relationship with "measures." The majority held that "banking" in the paragraph meant banking measures the word "or" having been construed as implying similarity and not disjunctively. Accordingly, the court held that the High Court and not the Federal Revenue Court had jurisdiction in ordinary banker-customer transactions, that is, disputes between a bank and its customer in the ordinary course of banking business or transaction. The Court explained the law as follows[79]:

> "[T]he true object and purpose of the Federal Revenue Court Decree as can be gathered from the four corners of it, is the more expeditious despatch of revenue cases, particularly those relating to personal income tax, company tax, customs and excise duties, illegal currency deals, exchange control measures and the like which the State High Courts were supposed to have been too tardy to dispose of especially in recent years. It does not seem to us that the legislative intention behind the Decree was to clutter up the

---

[76] See State Courts (Federal Jurisdiction) Act (Fed. and Lagos Laws 1958, Cap. 177). All such enactments have been repealed by s. 63(4) of the Federal Revenue Court Decree 1973.

[77] Federal Revenue Court Decree 1973, s. 8(1). But s. 8(2) of the Decree empowers the Head of the Federal Military Government to confer Federal jurisdiction in any case on the High Court of a State or any other State court.

[78] [1973] 1 All N.L.R. (Part 2) 208; (1973) 11 S.C. 77.

[79] [1973] All N.L.R. (Part 2) 208 at p. 222.

new Revenue Court with ordinary cases involving banker-customer relationship, such as disputes in respect of an over-draft, or the negligent payment of a forged cheque or negligent dishonouring of a customer's cheques — all 'banking transactions' having nothing to do with Federal revenue concern. All the State High Courts and other appropriate courts must continue to exercise their jurisdiction in these and similar matters if the Federal Revenue Court must be allowed to concentrate on its essentially revenue protection functions."

The court is normally a court of original jurisdiction.[80] But section 27 of the Federal Revenue Court Decree 1973 empowers the court to hear appeals from —

"(a) the decision of Appeal Commissioners established under the Companies Income Tax Act 1961 and the Personal Income Tax Act 1961 in so far as applicable as Federal law;
(b) the decisions of the Board of Customs and Excise established under the Customs and Excise Management Act 1958;
(c) the decisions of Magistrates' courts in respect of civil or criminal causes or matters transferred to such courts pursuant to this Decree; and
(d) the decisions of any other body established by or under any other Federal enactment or law in respect of matters concerning which jurisdiction is conferred by this Decree."

Rules of civil procedure applicable in the court are contained in the Federal Revenue Court (Civil Procedure) Rules 1976.[81] Section 32 of the Federal Revenue Court Decree 1973 expressly provides that in general the Criminal Procedure Act[82] is to apply substantially in criminal proceedings. But all criminal cases before the court are to be tried summarily.[83]

The Court is required as far as practicable to try revenue causes or matters in priority to any other business.[84] It is empowered to try cases with the assistance of assessors.[85]

G. State High Courts

On the creation of Lagos State in 1967, a High Court was established

[80] See section 1(3) of the Federal Revenue Court Decree 1973.
[81] L.N. 34 of 1976.
[82] Lagos Laws 1973, Cap. 32.
[83] Federal Revenue Court Decree 1973, s. 32(2).
[84] *Ibid.* s. 33(1). S. 33(2) defines "revenue causes or matters" as causes or matters concerned with, involving or pertaining to the revenue of the Government of the Federation in respect of which jurisdiction is conferred upon the Federal Revenue Court by or under the provisions of this Decree.
[85] Federal Revenue Court Decree 1973, s. 34(1).

for the State by the Constitution of the Federation [86] as amended by the States (Creation and Transitional Provisions) Decree 1967.[87] Similarly, the Constitution of Northern Nigeria[88] as amended by the 1967 Decree established a High Court for Kano State and another for Kwara State; and the Constitution of Eastern Nigeria[89] as amended by the same Decree established a High Court for Rivers State. On the creation of States in 1976, a High Court for Bendel was established by the Constitution of Midwestern Nigeria[90] as amended by the States (Creation and Transitional Provisions) Decree 1976,[91] a High Court for each of the States of Ogun, Ondo and Oyo was established by the Constitution of Western Nigeria[92] as amended by the 1976 Decree, a High Court for each of the States of Anambra, Cross River, Imo and Rivers was established by the Constitution of Eastern Nigeria[93] as amended by the 1976 Decree, and a High Court for each of the States of Bauchi, Benue, Borno, Gongola, Kaduna, Kano, Kwara, Niger, Plateau and Sokoto was established by the Constitution of Northern Nigeria[94] as amended by the same Decree.

The structure, organisation and jurisdiction of the State High Courts are generally uniform. The High Court of each of the northern States consists of the Chief Judge of the State and at least two other Judges.[95] The High Court of Lagos State consists of the Chief Judge of the State and at least five other Judges.[96] The High Court of each of the States of Anambra, Bendel, Cross River, Imo, Ogun, Ondo, Oyo and Rivers consists of the Chief Judge of the State and at least six other Judges.[97]

With respect to jurisdiction, it should be noted that the High Court of each of the northern States is not empowered to issue in relation to any proceedings in any area court or in the Sharia Court of Appeal an order of *mandamus*, *certiorari* or prohibition, or an injunction in lieu of *quo warranto*.[98] There is no such prohibition in

[86] Act No. 20 of 1963.   [87] No. 14 of 1967.
[88] N.N. Laws 1963, Cap. 1, s. 50(1).
[89] E.N. Laws 1963, Cap. 25, s. 50(1).
[90] Constitution of Midwestern Nigeria Act 1964 (No. 3 of 1964), Schedule, s. 48(1).
[91] No. 12 of 1976.
[92] W.N. No. 26 of 1963, s. 48(1).
[93] E.N. Laws 1963, Cap. 25, s. 50(1).
[94] N.N. Laws 1963, Cap. 1, s. 50(1).
[95] Constitution of Northern Nigeria, s. 51(1) as amended by the Constitution (Suspension and Modification) Decree 1966 (No. 1 of 1966) and also by the Constitution (Northern States) (Amendment) Decree 1969 (No. 40 of 1969).
[96] Constitution of the Federation (Act No. 20 of 1963), s. 122(2).
[97] See *e.g.* Constitution of Western Nigeria (W.N. No. 26 of 1963), s. 48(2) as amended by the Constitution (Suspension and Modification) Decree 1966.
[98] See High Court Law (N.N. Laws 1963, Cap. 49), s. 27. An injunction in lieu of *quo warranto* restrains a person acting in an office in which he is not entitled to act from so acting. (See s. 25(2) of the High Court Law of the Northern States.)

any of the southern States.[99] Of course, this question does not arise
with respect to Bendel and Imo for customary courts do not exist in
either of those States.[1] But there are plans to re-establish customary
courts in both States.

In all the States where customary or area courts exist, the High
Courts have no original jurisdiction in specified customary law
cases.[2] Such jurisdiction is reserved for customary or area courts
which, presumably, are considered to be versed in the applicable law.

There is provision for dividing each State into two or more judicial
Divisions of the High Court of the State.[3]

The judges of each High Court are appointed by the Supreme Military Council acting after consultation with the Advisory Judicial
Committee.[4]

In each State, the High Court in the exercise of its original jurisdiction is constituted by a single judge.[5] In each of the northern States,
the High Court sitting as a court of appeal is constituted by two
judges[6] except when it sits in its Native (Customary) Appellate Division in which case it is constituted by three judges including a judge
of the Sharia Court of Appeal.[7] In each of the southern States, the
High Court in the exercise of its appellate jurisdiction is normally
constituted by a single judge but in Lagos State the High Court in its
appeallate jurisdiction may be constituted by tree judges in any particular case where the Chief Judge of the State so directs[8] and in Rivers State, the High Court sitting as a court of appeal may be
constituted by two or three judges in any particular case where the
Chief Judge of the State so directs.[9]

The High Courts are generally courts of unlimited jurisdiction[10]
— their jurisdiction being unlimited with respect to the monetary
value of the subject-matter of a case.

[99] See *e.g.* High Court Law (Lagos Laws 1973, Cap. 52), s. 19(2).
[1] See Customary Courts (Abolition) Edict 1973 (No. 18 of 1973) (M.W.S.), s. 2;
   Magistrates' Courts Law (Amendment) Edict 1971 (No. 5 of 1971) (E.C.S.), s. 16(1).
[2] See *e.g.* High Court Law (W.R.N. Laws 1959, Cap. 49), s. 9, Proviso. For a critique
   of this jurisdictional limitation, see A. Obilade, "Jurisdiction in Customary Law
   Matters in Nigeria: A Critical Examination" [1973] J.A.L. 227.
[3] See *e.g.* High Court Law (Lagos Laws 1973, Cap. 52), s. 53(1).
[4] See *e.g.* s. 51(1) of the Constitution of Northern Nigeria as modified by the Constitution (Suspension and Modification) Decree 1966 (No. 1 of 1966) and also by the
   States (Creation and Transitional Provisions) Decree 1976 (No. 12 of 1976). See
   also Constitution (Basic Provisions) Decree 1975, s. 13(3)(*b*).
[5] See *e.g.* High Court Law (Lagos Laws 1973, Cap. 52), s. 6(2).
[6] High Court Law (1963 N.N. Laws, Cap. 49), s. 40(1).
[7] *Ibid.* s. 63(1).
[8] High Court Law (Lagos Laws 1973, Cap. 52), s. 29(1).
[9] See High Court Law (E.N. Laws 1963, Cap. 61), s. 33A(1), inserted by the High
   Court Law (Amendment) Law 1974 (No. 1 of 1974) (Rivers State).
[10] See *e.g.* High Court (Lagos Laws 1973, Cap. 52), s. 10.

Their jurisdiction and powers include such jurisdiction and powers as "are vested in or capable of being exercised by the High Court of Justice in England."[11]

The High Courts hear appeals from the lower courts.[12] They also exercise supervisory jurisdiction over inferior courts by orders of *mandamus*, prohibition and *certiorari*. Section 24(4)(*a*) of the High Court Law 1964[13] in force in Bendel State provides with respect to the orders of *mandamus*, prohibition and *certiorari* as follows:

"The court shall have all the jurisdiction of the High Court of Justice in England to make an Order of *Mandamus* requiring any act to be done, or an Order of *Prohibition* prohibiting any proceedings or matter, or an Order of *Certiorari*[14] removing any proceedings, cause or matter into the High Court for any purpose."

In general, similar provisions are contained in all the other High Court enactments in force in the country.[15] Accordingly, in general, a High Court in Nigeria has power to issue orders of *mandamus*, prohibition and *certiorari* in circumstances in which the High Court of Justice in England would grant such orders.

An order of *mandamus* is an order requiring a person or an inferior court to do a thing specified in the order being a thing relating to his or its office and in the nature of a public duty. In general, the High Court does not issue the order where another legal remedy is open to the applicant, but it is open to the court to issue the order notwithstanding the availability of an alternative remedy if that alternative is less convenient, less beneficial and less effectual than the remedy of *mandamus*.[16] The grant of the order is discretionary. Where an inferior court refuses or neglects to exercise its jurisdiction, the High Court may grant the order to command the inferior court to exercise the jurisdiction.

An order of prohibition directed to an inferior court prohibits the continuance of specified proceedings before the inferior court in excess of its jurisdiction. It thus forbids the inferior court to continue to exceed its jurisdiction.

Where an inferior court has exceeded its jurisdiction with respect to proceedings before the court, an order of *certiorari* directed to the

---

[11] *Ibid.*
[12] See pp. 116-121, above.
[13] No. 9 of 1964 (M.W.N.).
[14] Originally, in England, *mandamus*, prohibition and *certiorari* were prerogative writs. The Administration of Justice (Miscellaneous Provisions) Act 1938 (1 & 2 Geo. 6, c. 63) substituted orders of the same names for the writs.
[15] See *e.g.* High Court Law (Lagos Laws 1973, Cap. 52), s. 19(2).
[16] See *R.* v. *Thomas* [1892] 1 Q.B. 426; *Stepney Borough Council* v. *John Walker & Sons Ltd.* [1934] A.C. 365 at p. 395; *Lasisi* v. *Registrar of Companies* (1976) 7 S.C. 73.

court by the High Court removes the proceedings to the High Court
in order that the proceedings may be dealt with by the High Court.

On the removal of the proceedings to the High court, the proceedings including the decision of the inferior court, if it has already been
given, are quashed. In general, the order of *certiorari* is not issued
where there is an alternative remedy. But sometimes, in the interest
of justice the order is issued even where there is an alternative
remedy.[17]

H. Magistrates' Courts

There are magistrates' courts in every State in Nigeria.[18] A magistrate's court is constituted by a single magistrate.[19] In each State,
magistrates are divided into a number of classes, the classification
being, in general, the basis of defining the jurisdiction and powers of
each magistrate.[20] The classes of magistrates in the States mentioned
below are as follows:

Anambra: Chief Magistrate, Senior Magistrate Grade I, Senior
Magistrate Grade II, Magistrate Grade I, Magistrate Grade II and
Magistrate Grade III.[21]

*Bauchi, Benue, Borno, Gongola, Kaduna, Kano, Kwara, Niger,
Plateau and Sokoto*: Chief Magistrate, Magistrate Grade I, Magistrate Grade II and Magistrate Grade III.[22]

Bendel: Chief Magistrate, Senior Magistrate Grade I, Senior
Magistrate Grade II, Magistrate Grade I, Magistrate Grade II and
Magistrate Grade III.[23]

Cross River: Chief Magistrate, Senior Magistrate Grade I, Senior
Magistrate Grade II, Magistrate Grade I, Magistrate Grade II and
Magistrate Grade III.[24]

Lagos: Chief Magistrate, Senior Magistrate, Magistrate Grade I,

---

[17] See *R.* v. *District Officer* [1961] 1 All N.L.R. 51.

[18] Magistrates' Courts Law (Lagos Laws 1973, Cap. 82); Magistrates' Courts Law
(W.R.N. Laws 1959, Cap. 74) in force in Bendel, Ogun, Ondo and Oyo States;
Magistrates Courts Law (E.N. Laws 1963, Cap. 82) in force in Anambra, Cross
River, Imo and Rivers States; Criminal Procedure Code (N.N. Laws 1963, Cap. 30)
in force in the 10 northern States.

[19] See *e.g.* s. 6 of the Magistrates' Courts Law of Lagos State.

[20] There is provision for increasing the jurisdiction and powers of any particular magistrate, irrespective of his actual class. See *e.g.* s. 20 of the Magistrates' Court Law of
Lagos State; s. 24 of the Magistrates' Courts Law of Bendel, Ogun, Ondo and Oyo
States (W.R.N. Laws 1959, Cap. 74); Magistrates (Increased Jurisdiction) Order
1968 (M.N.L.N. 5 of 1968).

[21] Magistrates' Courts Law (E.N. Laws 1963, Cap. 82), s. 6 as amended by s. 4 of the
Magistrates' Courts Law (Amendment) Edict 1977 (No. 16 of 1977). See States
(Creation and Transitional Provisions) Decree 1976 (No. 12 of 1976).

[22] Criminal Procedure Code (N.N. Laws 1963, Cap. 30), s. 4. See States (Creation and
Transitional Provisions) Decree 1976 (No. 12 of 1976).

[23] Magistrates' Courts Law (W.R.N. Laws 1959, Cap. 74), s. 7(1) as amended by s. 2 of
the Magistrates' Courts (Amendment) Edict 1977 (No. 14 of 1977) (Bendel).

Magistrate Grade II and Magistrate Grade III.[25]

Oyo: Chief Magistrate, Senior Magistrate Grade I, Senior Magistrate Grade II, Magistrate Grade I, Magistrate Grade II and Magistrate Grade III.[26]

Rivers: Chief Magistrate, Senior Magistrate, Magistrate.[27]

In some States, some persons are designated magistrates of specified classes which classes are not provided for under the law. For example, some magistrates in Lagos State are styled "Senior Magistrates Grade I" even though there is only one class of senior magistrates under the Magistrates' Courts Law of the State. Similarly, although there is no provision for any class of magistrates known as Associate Magistrates under the Criminal Procedure Code of the northern States, persons are appointed associate magistrates in some of those States. Obviously, appointments to grades of magistrates that are, legally, non-existent are irregular and do not confer any jurisdiction on the appointee. A distinction should, however, be made between a person who was a magistrate under the law immediately before his appointment to the non-existent grade of magistrate and one who was not a magistrate at all before such irregular appointment. The former is a magistrate having the jurisdiction of the grade to which he was lawfully appointed originally. But the latter is not a magistrate at all.[28]

In each State, a person is appointed Magistrate, other than Magistrate Grade III, by the Interim Judicial Committee established for the State and the power to appoint a person Magistrate Grade III is vested in the Chief Judge of the State.[29] Every magistrate in each of the southern States is *ex officio* a justice of the peace for the State.[30]

Under the law in force in some of the States a person is not eligible for appointment as a magistrate unless he is qualified to practise as a barrister and solicitor in a court of unlimited jurisdiction in civil and criminal matters in a part of the Commonwealth and he has attained a specified minimum of post-qualification experience expressed in terms of years. Such law is in force in Anambra, Bendel, Cross River,

---

[24] Magistrates' Courts Law (E.N. Laws, Cap. 82), s. 6(1) as amended by s. 2 of the Magistrates' Courts Law (Amendment) Edict 1974 (No. 18 of 1974)(S.E.S.).

[25] Magistrates' Courts Law (Lagos Laws 1973, Cap. 82), s. 7(1).

[26] Magistrates' Courts Law (W.R.N. Laws 1959, Cap. 74), s. 7(1) as amended by s. 2 of the Magistrates' Courts (Amendment) Edict 1977 (No. 21 of 1977) (Oyo). See States (Creation and Transitional Provisions) Decree 1976 (No. 12 of 1976).

[27] Magistrates' Courts Law (E.N. Laws 1963, Cap. 82), s. 6(1) as amended by s. 3 of the Magistrates' Courts Law (Amendment) Edict 1969 (No. 7 of 1969) (Rivers State).

[28] See *Oluokun* v. *C.O.P.* 1974 N.N.L.R. 111.

[29] Interim Judicial Committees (Establishment, etc.) Decree 1977 (No. 66 of 1977), s. 2. The Decree came into force on October 27, 1977.

[30] See *e.g.* s. 9 of the Magistrates' Courts Law (Lagos Laws 1973, Cap. 82).

Imo, Ogun, Ondo, Oyo and Rivers States. The prescribed post-qualification experience is as follows:

Ogun, Ondo and Oyo: Chief Magistrates and Senior Magistrates
Grades I and II — Seven years; Magistrates — four years.[31]

Bendel: Chief Magistrates and Senior Magistrates Grades I and II
— seven years; Magistrate Grade I — five years; Magistrate Grade II
— two years.[32]

Imo: Chief Magistrates — seven years; all other Magistrates —
three years.[33]

Cross River: Chief Magistrates — seven years; Senior Magistrates
Grade I — five years; Senior Magistrates Grade II — four years;
Magistrates Grade I — three years; Magistrates Grade II — two
years; Magistrates Grade III — one year.[34]

Rivers: Chief Magistrates — seven years; Senior Magistrates —
six years; Magistrates — three years.[35]

Each State is divided into a number of magisterial districts[36] and
although a magistrate has jurisdiction throughout a State,[37] he normally exercises his jurisdiction only within a magisterial district.

Magistrates' courts in the southern States have civil and criminal
jurisdiction.[38] Those in the northern States have criminal jurisdiction only.

CIVIL JURISDICTION

The civil jurisdiction of magistrates (that is, magistrates in the southern States) is generally uniform. In Lagos State, in general, a magistrate has civil jurisdiction:

(a) "in all personal actions, whether arising from contract, or from
tort or from both, where the debt or damage claimed, whether as
balance or otherwise" does not exceed ₦1,000 in the case of a
Chief Magistrate, ₦600 in the case of a Senior Magistrate, ₦400
in the case of a Magistrate Grade I, ₦200 in the case of a Magis-

---

[31] Magistrates' Courts Law (W.R.N. Laws 1959, Cap. 74), s. 7(2) as amended by s. 2 of
the Magistrates' Courts (Amendment) Edict 1968 (No. 20 of 1968) and by the Magistrates' Courts (Amendment) Edict 1971 (No. 5 of 1971) (W.S.).

[32] Magistrates' Courts Law (W.R.N. Laws 1959, Cap. 74), s. 7(2) as amended by s. 2 of
the Magistrates' Courts (Amendment) Edict 1972 (No. 26 of 1972) (M.W.S.).

[33] Magistrates' Courts Law (E.N. Laws 1963, Cap. 82), s. 6(2), and s. 22A(1) as
inserted by s. 9 of the Magistrates' Courts Law (Amendment) Edict 1971 (No. 23 of
1971) (E.C.S.).

[34] Magistrates' Courts Law (1963 E.N. Laws, Cap. 82), s. 6(2) and (3) as inserted by s. 2
of the Magistrates' Courts Law (Amendment) Edict 1974 (No. 18 of 1974) (S.E.S.).

[35] Magistrates' Courts Law (E.N. Laws 1963, Cap. 82), s. 6(2) as amended by s. 3 of the
Magistrates' Courts Law (Amendment) Edict 1969 (No. 7 of 1969) (Rivers State).

[36] See *e.g.* Magistrates' Courts Law (Lagos Laws 1973, Cap. 82), s. 3.

[37] *Ibid.* s. 8.

[38] *Ibid.* ss. 17 and 18.

trate Grade II, and ₦50 in the case of a Magistrate Grade III.

(b) "in all actions for the recovery of any penalty, rates, expenses, contribution or other like demand which is recoverable by virtue of any enactment for the time being in force, if —

    (i) it is not expressly provided by that or any other enactment that the demand shall be recoverable only in some other court;" and

    (ii) the amount claimed in the action does not exceed ₦1,000 in the case of a Chief Magistrate, ₦600 in the case of Senior Magistrate, ₦400 in the case of a Magistrate Grade I, ₦200 in the case of a Magistrate Grade II, and ₦50 in the case of a Magistrate Grade III.

(c) "to appoint guardians *ad litem* and to make orders and issue and give directions relating thereto;" and

(d) "to grant in any action instituted in the court injunctions or orders to stay waste or alienation or for the detention and preservation of any property the subject of such action or to restrain breaches of contract or torts."[39]

But, as a general rule, a magistrate in the State has no original jurisdiction in any civil case which raises any issue as to the title to land, or to any interest in land; or raises any issue as to the validity of any devise, bequest or limitation under any will or settlement.[40]

Magistrates in Anambra, Bendel, Cross River, Imo, Ogun, Ondo, Oyo and Rivers States have jurisdiction in all cases falling within categories (a) to (d) just listed in respect of Lagos State except that where the subject-matter is capable of estimation in terms of monetary value (categories (a) to (b)), the monetary value limits prescribed vary from State to State. The maximum monetary value prescribed for the various jurisdictions is as follows:

Bendel[41] *and Oyo*: Chief Magistrate — ₦5,000; Senior Magistrate Grade I — ₦3,000; Senior Magistrate Grade II — ₦2,000; Magistrate Grade I — ₦1,000, Magistrate Grade II — ₦500, Magistrate Grade III — ₦200.[42]

Imo: Chief Magistrate — ₦2,000; Senior Magistrate Grade I — ₦1,500; Senior Magistrate Grade II — ₦1,000; Magistrate Grade I or II — ₦600.[43]

[39] Magistrates' Courts Law (Lagos Laws 1973, Cap. 82), s. 17(1) and (3).

[40] *Ibid.* s. 17(2).

[41] Magistrates' Courts Law (W.R.N. Laws 1959, Cap. 74), s. 19 as amended by the Magistrates' Courts (Amendment) Edict 1977 (No. 14 of 1977) (Bendel). By virtue of s. 1(1) of the Decimal Currency Decree 1971 (No. 21 of 1971), the unit of currency in Nigeria is now the naira (₦).

[42] Magistrates' Courts Law (W.R.N. Laws 1959, Cap. 74), s. 19 as amended by the Magistrates' Courts (Amendment) Edict 1977 (No. 21 of 1977) (Oyo).

[43] Magistrates' Courts Law (E.N. Laws 1963, Cap. 82), ss. 17 and 18 as amended by the Magistrates' Courts Law (Amendment) Edict 1971 (No. 23 of 1971) (E.C.S.).

Cross River: Chief Magistrate — ₦1,000; Senior Magistrate Grade I or II — ₦600; Magistrate Grade I or II — ₦400; Magistrate Grade III — ₦200.[44]

Rivers: Chief Magistrate — ₦1,000; Senior Magistrate ₦600; Magistrate — ₦400.[45]

As a result of the abolition of customary courts in the East-Central State,[46] magistrates in Imo have civil jurisdiction in the following customary law cases:

(a) cases under customary law involving a debt, demand or damage not exceeding the prescribed monetary value limit[47];

(b) matrimonial cases between persons married under customary law;

(c) cases relating to custody of children and obligations of maintenance of certain classes of people under customary law;

(d) cases relating to established customary institutions and practices; and

(e) cases relating to succession in respect of property under customary law or to the administration of estates or grant of letters of administration under customary law, where the value of the property, or in the case of cash, the amount of such cash, does not exceed the prescribed monetary value limit, provided the case is not one in which any will or settlement is or may be disputed.[48]

In addition, Chief Magistrates and Senior Magistrates Grades I and II in Imo have unlimited jurisdiction in civil cases relating to title to or interest in land.[49] Magistrates Grades I and II in those States have jurisdiction in suits relating to trespass to land so long as the

---

[44] Magistrates' Courts Law (E.N. Laws 1963, Cap. 82), ss. 17 and 18 as amended by the Magistrates' Courts (Amendment) Edict 1969 (No. 11 of 1969) (S.E.S.), and ss. 17A and 18A as inserted by the Edict.

[45] Magistrates Courts Law (E.N. Laws 1963, Cap. 82) ss. 17 and 18 as amended by the Magistrates' Courts Law (Amendment) Edict 1969 (No. 7 of 1969) (Rivers State).

[46] See s. 16(1) of the Magistrates' Courts Law (Amendment) Edict 1971 (No. 23 of 1971) (E.C.S.); States (Creation and Transitional Provisions) Decree 1976, s. 5(1).

[47] Magistrates' Courts Law (E.N. Laws 1963, Cap. 82), ss. 17 and 18 as amended by the Magistrates' Courts Law (Amendment) Edict 1971 (No. 23 of 1971) (E.C.S.).

[48] Magistrates' Courts Law (E.N. Laws, 1963, Cap. 82), ss. 17 and 18 as amended by the Magistrates' Courts Law (Amendment) Edict 1971 and by the Magistrates' Courts Law (Amendment) Edict 1974 (No. 18 of 1974) (E.C.S.). The position was the same in Anambra until customary courts were re-established there in 1978.

[49] Magistrates' Courts Law (Amendment) Edict 1974 (No. 18 of 1974) (E.C.S.), s. 3. This amending law provides, however, that the defendant is entitled to apply *ex parte* to the High Court for a transfer of the case to that court.

suit does not raise any issue as to the title to or interest in the land.[50]

As a result of the abolition of customary courts in the Midwestern State,[51] magistrates' courts in Bendel have original jurisdiction in those classes of customary law cases with respect to which, as a general rule, customary courts had had exclusive original civil jurisdiction.[52] But unless the Military Governor otherwise directs a magistrate in Bendel has no original jurisdiction in any of the following cases: suits which raise an issue as to the title to land or as to the title to any interests in land and suits in which the validity of a devise, bequest or limitation under a will or settlement is or may be disputed.[53] Similarly, magistrates' courts in Cross River, Ogun, Ondo, Oyo and Rivers States are prohibited from exercising original civil jurisdiction in any case falling within any of those two categories in the absence of an order made by the Military Governor of the State concerned directing the exercise of such jurisdiction, except that in the case of Rivers State a Magistrates' Court has such jurisdiction where the case has been transferred to it under the Customary Courts (No. 2) Edict 1966.[54] Furthermore, as a general rule, Magistrates' Courts in those five States have no original civil jurisdiction in the classes of customary law cases with respect to which Magistrates' Courts of Bendel State have jurisdiction by virtue of the non-existence of customary courts in that State.[55]

[50] Magistrates' Courts Law (Amendment) Edict 1974 (E.C.S.), s. 3.

[51] Customary Courts (Abolition) Edict 1973 (No. 18 of 1973), s. 2(a). See States (Creation and Transitional Provisions) Decree 1976, s. 5(1).

[52] See s. 19(4) of the Magistrates' Courts Law (W.R.N. Laws 1959, Cap. 74). The cases are listed in s. 20(c)-(e) of the Laws as follows: suits relating to the custody of children under customary law, causes and matters relating to inheritance upon intestacy under customary law and the administration of intestate estates under customary law, matrimonial causes and matters between persons married under customary law or arising from or connected with a union contracted under customary law.

[53] Magistrates' Courts Law (W.R.N. Laws 1959, Cap. 74) ss. 19(4) and 20(a)-(b).

[54] No. 29 of 1966 (E.N.). See Magistrates' Courts Law (W.R.N. Laws 1959, Cap. 74), ss. 19(4) and 20; Magistrates' Courts Law (E.N. Laws 1963, Cap. 82), s. 17 and s. 18 as amended by s. 4 of the Magistrates' Courts Law (Amendment) Edict 1969 (No. 7 of 1969) (Rivers State); Magistrates' Courts Law (E.N. Laws 1963, Cap. 82), ss. 17 and 18 as amended by the Magistrates' Courts (Amendment) Edict 1969 (No. 11 of 1969) (S.E.S.) and s. 17A as inserted by the same Edict. The customary courts of Rivers State do not function. (See *Rivers State at a Glance* (1971) published by the Government of Rivers State, p. 11.)

[55] See n. 54, above. The magistrates' courts in those States exercise jurisdiction in such customary law cases where the Military Governor so directs or, as an alternative in the case of Rivers State, where the cases are transferred to the courts under the Customary Courts (No. 2) Edict 1966. For a critique of similar jurisdictional limitations in respect of the High Courts, see A. Obilade, "Jurisdiction in Customary Law Matters in Nigeria: A Critical Examination" [1973] J.A.L. 227.

CRIMINAL JURISDICTION

The term "jurisdiction" in relation to criminal cases may be used to denote authority to deal with criminal cases excluding authority to impose a sentence. In this sense, it refers, for example, to authority to try cases, to hold preliminary inquiries into criminal charges or to prepare proofs of evidence. In a wider sense the term is used to denote authority to deal with criminal cases including authority to impose a sentence. The word "power" is sometimes used to denote the authority of a court to impose a sentence. Thus, in the expression "jurisdiction and power," the word, "jurisdiction" is used in the narrow sense.[56]

Magistrates' courts are essentially courts of summary jurisdiction; they have jurisdiction to deal with criminal cases summarily. In the southern States, for the purpose of jurisdiction of magistrates in criminal cases, offences are divided roughly into two classes, namely, indictable offences and offences other than indictable offences (non-indictable offences). An indictable offence is an offence which on conviction may be punished by a term of imprisonment exceeding two years, or which on conviction may be punished by imposition of a fine exceeding 400 naira, not being an offence declared by the law creating it to be punishable on summary conviction.[57] In the northern States there is no such express classification of offences. The jurisdiction and powers of magistrates' courts in the southern States will now be examined.

Southern States

All magistrates in the southern States have jurisdiction to try summarily offences other than indictable offences and they have power to impose the punishment prescribed for any such offence to the extent of their power of punishment.

The maximum fine and maximum term of imprisonment which magistrates' courts of the following southern States are normally empowered to impose in respect of an offence are as follows:

Imo: Chief Magistrate — ₦2,000, 14 years; Senior Magistrate Grade I — ₦1,500, 12 years; Senior Magistrate Grade II — ₦1,000,

---

[56] Of course, "jurisdiction" is also used to denote a geographical area of authority.

[57] See *e.g.* s. 2 of the Criminal Procedure Law (Lagos Laws 1973, Cap. 32). An offence other than an indictable offence is a summary conviction offence. But, curiously, a summary conviction offence under the Criminal Procedure enactments of the southern States is not necessarily a non-indictable offence. It includes an indictable offence punishable by a magistrate on summary conviction. See *e.g.* s. 2 of the Criminal Procedure Law of Lagos State.

10 years; Magistrate Grade I or II — ₦400, 5 years.[58]

Bendel: Chief Magistrate — ₦5,000, 6 years; Senior Magistrate Grade I — ₦3,000, 4 years; Senior Magistrate Grade II — ₦2,000, 3 years; Magistrate Grade I — ₦1,000, 2 years; Magistrate Grade II — ₦500, 18 months; Magistrate Grade III — ₦200, 6 months.[59]

Cross River: Chief Magistrate — ₦1,000, 5 years; Senior Magistrate Grade I or II — ₦600, 3 years; Magistrate Grade I or II — ₦400, 2 years; Magistrate Grade III — ₦200, 1 year.[60]

Lagos State: Chief Magistrate — ₦1,000, 5 years; Senior Magistrate — ₦600, 3 years; Magistrate Grade I — ₦400, 2 years; Magistrate Grade II — ₦200, 1 year; Magistrate Grade III — ₦50, 3 months.[61]

Ogun and Ondo: Chief Magistrate — ₦1,000, 5 years; Senior Magistrate Grade I — ₦600, 3 years; Senior Magistrate Grade II — ₦400, 2 years; Magistrate — ₦200, 1 year.[62]

Rivers: Chief Magistrate — ₦1,000, 5 years; Senior Magistrate — ₦600, 3 years; Magistrate — ₦400, 2 years.[63]

In each of the six States, there is provision for authorising any magistrate to impose punishment greater than the maximum prescribed in relation to his grade.[64]

In Lagos State, all magistrates other than Magistrates Grade III have jurisdiction to try any indictable offence other than a capital offence summarily subject to the provisions of section 304 of the Criminal Procedure Law.[65] That section provides that where an

[58] Magistrates' Courts Law (E.N. Laws 1963, Cap. 82), s. 22 as amended by the Magistrates' Courts Law (Amendment) Edict 1971 (No. 23 of 1971) (E.C.S.), s.20 and s. 22A(2) (as amended by the Magistrates' Courts Law (Amendment) Edict 1974 (No. 18 of 1974) (E.C.S.)).

[59] Magistrates' Courts Law (W.R.N. Laws 1963, Cap. 74), s. 21, and s. 22 as amended by the Magistrates' Courts (Amendment) Edict 1977 (Bendel).

[60] Magistrates' Courts Law (E.N. Laws 1963, Cap. 82), s. 20, s. 20A as amended by the Magistrates' Courts Law (Amendment) Edict 1974 (No. 18 of 1974)(S.E.S.), s. 22 as amended by the Magistrates' Courts (Amendment) Edict 1969 (No. 11 of 1969) (S.E.S.), and s. 22A inserted by the Magistrates' Courts Law (Amendment) Edict 1974.

[61] Magistrates' Courts Law (Lagos Laws 1973, Cap. 82), s. 18(4) and s. 18(5).

[62] Magistrates' Courts Law (W.R.N. Laws 1959, Cap. 74), s. 21, and s. 22 as amended by the Magistrates' Courts (Amendment) Edict 1968 (No. 20 of 1968) (W.S.).

[63] Magistrates' Courts Law (E.N. Laws 1963, Cap. 82), s. 20 and s. 22 as amended by the Magistrates' Courts Law (Amendment) Edict 1969 (No. 7 of 1969) (Rivers).

[64] See *e.g.* Magistrates' Courts Law (Lagos Laws 1973, Cap. 82), s. 20(2).

[65] Lagos Laws 1973, Cap. 32. See s. 18(3) of the Magistrates' Courts Law (Lagos Laws 1973, Cap. 82). That subsection provides that the jurisdiction is to be exercised in accordance with Pts. 34 and 35 of the Criminal Procedure Law. S. 304 forms part of Pt. 35. The reference to Pt. 34 which consists of ss. 302 and 303, in s. 18(3) of the Magistrates' Courts Law as published in the 1973 revised edition of the laws of Lagos State is obviously a mistake for that Part had been repealed in 1972 by the Lagos State (Adaptation of Laws) (Miscellaneous Provisions) Order 1972 (L.S.L.N. 16 of 1972).

adult is charged with an indictable offence other than a capital offence, a magistrate may deal summarily with the case provided the accused, who is required to be informed by the magistrate of his right to be tried by the High Court, consents before he is called upon to make his defence to summary trial by the magistrate, and, where the prosecution is conducted by a law officer, the law officer consents to the summary trial of the case by the magistrate. The magistrate may impose the punishment provided by law for the offence, subject to the maximum punishment prescribed in relation to his grade.[66]

In all the other southern States where the maximum punishment prescribed for an offence is within the power of punishment of the magistrate, he has jurisdiction for the summary trial of the case subject in all cases (except in the case of Chief Magistrates in Anambra, Cross River, Imo States) to section 304 of the Criminal Procedure enactment in force in the State in question. Section 304 of each such enactment provides that where an adult is charged with an indictable offence other than a capital offence the magistrate may deal summarily with the offence provided that the accused consents to the summary trial of the case by the magistrate before he is called upon to make his defence and where the prosecution is conducted by a law officer the law officer consents to the summary trial of the case by the magistrate.

Furthermore, in Rivers State, magistrates of the lowest grade, that is, magistrates styled simply "Magistrates" have jurisdiction to deal summarily with indictable offences where the maximum punishment prescribed for the offence exceeds the maximum punishment which Magistrates are empowered to impose but does not exceed the maximum punishment which Senior Magistrates are empowered to impose, subject to the application of section 304 of the Criminal Procedure Law[67] of the State which is identical with section 304 of the Criminal Procedure enactment in force in any of the other southern States. Of course, Magistrates in the State are not thereby empowered to exceed the power of punishment prescribed in relation to their grade.

In Anambra, Bendel, Cross River, Imo, Ogun, Ondo and Oyo States, where an indictable offence is declared by the enactment creating it to be punishable by a fine or a term of imprisonment or both such fine and imprisonment, the fine or term exceeding the maximum which a magistrate is empowered to impose in respect of an offence the magistrate has jurisdiction to deal summarily with the

---

[66] Magistrates' Courts Law (Lagos Laws 1973, Cap. 82), s. 18(3). The power to impose the punishment prescribed by law is stated in this subsection to be subject to s. 302 of the Criminal Procedure Law, a section which was repealed in 1972. See n. 65, above.

[67] E.N. Laws 1963, Cap. 31.

case where, having regard to the circumstances of the particular offence with which the accused is charged and the character and antecedents of the accused, the magistrate is of opinion that the charge appears to be of such a nature that if proved it would be adequately punished by any of the following punishments:

(a) imprisonment for a term not exceeding the maximum which the magistrate is empowered to impose in respect of an offence;

(b) a fine not exceeding the maximum which the magistrate is empowered to impose in respect of an offence to be enforced in default of payment by distress or by imprisonment for a term not exceeding the maximum which the magistrate is empowered to impose in respect of an offence;

(c) the punishment stated in (a) and (b) above with or without any additional or alternative punishment in respect of the offences for which such punishment may be legally inflicted;

(d) in the case of a juvenile offender, the punishment stated in (a) or (b) above with or without whipping in respect of offences for which a whipping may be legally inflicted;

(e) any lesser penalty or order which the magistrate in the exercise of his summary jurisdiction may impose or make;

provided that where the person charged is an adult there is compliance with section 304 of the Criminal Procedure enactment and where he is a juvenile he is informed by the magistrate, before any evidence is taken, of his right to be tried in the High Court and he consents to summary trial by the magistrate before he is called upon to make his defence.[68]

In Cross River State, the same adequate punishment principle applies except that it is expressly provided that a Chief Magistrate has jurisdiction to try summarily burglary, house-breaking and stealing involving in each case or in a combination of any two or more of the offences property not exceeding ₦3,000 in value. The maximum punishment which the Chief Magistrate may impose in such circumstances is the normal maximum that he is empowered to impose under the Magistrates' Courts Law.[69]

In Rivers State, the adequate punishment principle as stated in respect of Anambra, Bendel, Imo, Ogun, Ondo and Oyo States applies where the charge is brought before a Chief Magistrate or a Senior Magistrate. Where the charge is brought before a Magistrate in the State the same principle applies provided that the law creating the offence declares it to be punishable by a fine or a term of imprisonment or both such fine and imprisonment, the fine or term exceeding the maximum which a Senior Magistrate (not a Magistrate) is

[68] See *e.g.* Magistrates' Courts Law (E.N. Laws 1963, Cap. 82), s. 20.
[69] Criminal Justice (Miscellaneous Provisions) Edict 1973 (No. 4 of 1973).

empowered to impose. But the maximum fine or term of imprisonment which a Magistrate may impose in respect of the offence does not by reason of this provision exceed the maximum prescribed in respect of Magistrates.[70] It is difficult to understand the reason behind this departure from the usual adequate punishment formula which is used in relation to Chief Magistrates and Senior Magistrates in the State.

It should be noted that the adequate punishment provisions cover only cases punishable with fine or imprisonment or both with or without whipping or less penalty. They do not cover capital offences. Thus, magistrates have no jurisdiction for the summary trial of capital offences.

In general, Chief Magistrates in Rivers State and all magistrates in Bendel, Lagos, Ogun, Ondo and Oyo States have jurisdiction to hold preliminary inquiries into all charges of indictable offences in accordance with the provisions of the applicable Criminal Procedure enactment.[71] In Anambra, Cross River and Imo States, there are no preliminary inquiries into charges of indictable offences. But in general, all magistrates in Anambra and Imo States have jurisdiction to prepare proofs of evidence in accordance with the provisions of the Criminal Procedure (Miscellaneous Provisions) Edict 1974[72] in respect of all charges of indictable offences for the purpose of determining whether an information may be preferred.[73] Similarly, in Cross River State, in place of the procedure of preliminary inquiry there is a procedure whereby magistrates prepare proofs of evidence taken from witnesses for the prosecution for the purpose of determining whether an information may be filed.[74]

Northern States

The jurisdiction of magistrates' courts in the northern States is governed by the Criminal Procedure Code,[75] section 12(1) of which provides in respect of offences under the Penal Code[76] as follows:

---

[70] S. 22 of the Magistrates' Courts Law (E.N. Laws 1963, Cap. 82) as amended by s. 6 of the Magistrates' Courts Law (Amendment) Edict 1969 (No. 7 of 1969) (Rivers).

[71] See Magistrates' Courts Law (Lagos Laws 1973, Cap. 82) s. 19; Magistrates' Courts Law (W.R.N. Laws 1959, Cap. 74), s. 22; Magistrates' Courts Law (E.N. Laws 1963, Cap. 82), s. 21.

[72] No. 19 of 1974.

[73] Magistrates' Courts Law (E.N. Laws 1963, Cap. 82), s. 21 as amended by s. 6 of the Magistrates' Courts Law (Amendment) Edict 1974 (No. 18 of 1974). S. 3(1) of the Criminal Procedure (Miscellaneous Provisions) Edict 1974 abolished preliminary inquiries into indictable offences.

[74] Criminal Justice (Miscellaneous Provisions) Edict 1973 (No. 4 of 1973), s. 2. S. 2(1) of the Edict abolished preliminary inquiries into indictable offences.

[75] N.N. Laws 1963, Cap. 30.

[76] N.N. Laws 1963, Cap. 89.

"Subject to the other provisions of this Criminal Procedure Code, any offence under the Penal Code may be tried by any court by which such offence is shown in the sixth column of Appendix A to be triable or by any court other than a native court[77] with greater powers."

Thus, the words "Magistrate of the Third Grade" appear in the Sixth Column of Appendix A against the offence of theft under section 287 of the Penal Code. Accordingly, all grades of magistrates (Chief Magistrate and Magistrates Grades I to III) have jurisdiction to try the offence. But the words "Magistrate of the First Grade" appear in the column against the offence of robbery under section 298 of the Penal Code and accordingly the only magistrates who have jurisdiction to deal with the offence are Chief Magistrates and Magistrates Grade I.

The jurisdiction of magistrates' courts in respect of an offence under a law other than the Penal Code is governed by section 13 of the Criminal Procedure Code which provides that in general any such offence may be tried by any court given jurisdiction in such offence by such law or by any court with greater powers but where the law does not mention any court the offence may be tried by the High Court or any court constituted under the Criminal Procedure Code.[78] This general provision is subject to the following limitations:

(a) A Chief Magistrate is not empowered to try an offence punishable with imprisonment for a term exceeding 10 years or with a fine exceeding ₦1,000.
(b) Magistrates of other grades are not empowered to try an offence punishable with terms of imprisonment or with a fine exceeding respectively the terms or amount indicated below against their grades:

> Magistrate Grade I   - five years, ₦400
> Magistrate Grade II - two years, ₦200
> Magistrate Grade III - three months, ₦50.[79]

The maximum term of imprisonment or maximum fine which a magistrate is empowered to impose in respect of an offence is as follows:

Chief Magistrate   - five years, ₦1,000
Magistrate Grade I   - three years, ₦600

---

[77] The expression "native court" should now be construed as area court in view of the replacement of the native court systems under the Native Courts Law (N.N. Laws 1963, Cap. 78), with area court systems under the various Area Courts Edicts. See *e.g.* Area Courts Edict 1968 (No. 4 of 1968) (B.P.S.).

[78] Magistrates' Courts in the northern States are constituted under the Criminal Procedure Code (see s. 4 of the Code).

[79] Criminal Procedure Code, s. 13(2).

Magistrate Grade II - 18 months, ₦400
Magistrate Grade III - 9 months, ₦200.[80]

All magistrates other than Magistrates Grade III are empowered to impose a sentence of detention under section 71 of the Penal Code which relates to treatment of juveniles in accordance with the provisions of the Children and Young Persons Law.[81] Similarly, all magistrates other than Magistrates Grade III may impose a sentence of caning.[82]

There is provision in section 19 of the Criminal Procedure Code whereby "an increased jurisdiction in criminal matters," to be exercised by any magistrate specified in an order made under the section, may be authorised. It appears that the word "jurisdiction" is used here to mean authority to deal with a case including the power to impose punishment. This wide sense seems to be the sense in which the word is used in section 13(3) of the Criminal Procedure Code, too, for that subsection provides that section 13(2) which only prescribes offences which various classes of courts are authorised to try is not to be deemed to confer upon any court any "jurisdiction" in excess of that conferred upon that court by sections 15 to 25 of the Code. But sections 15 to 25 merely prescribe punishment — they do not deal with authority to try cases.[83]

Magistrates in the northern States have jurisdiction to hold preliminary inquiries into offences.[84]

I. DISTRICT COURTS
(*Northern States*)

On the creation of States in 1967, each of the then six northern States had district courts established by the District Courts Law[85] as modified by the States (Creation and Transitional Provisions) Decree 1967.[86] Similarly, by virtue of the States (Creation and Transitional Provisions) Decree 1976,[87] each of the present 10 northern States has district courts established by the District Courts Law. A district court is constituted by a single judge. District court judges are divided into four classes, namely, Senior District Judge, District Judge Grade I, District Judge Grade II and District Judge Grade

---

[80] *Ibid.* ss. 15-18.
[81] N.N. Laws 1963, Cap. 21. See ss. 15-18 of the Criminal Procedure Code.
[82] See ss. 15-18 of the Criminal Procedure Code.
[83] Compare *e.g.* s. 24(1) of the Magistrates' Courts Law (W.R.N. Laws 1959, Cap. 74) which relates to increase of power of punishment only.
[84] See Criminal Procedure Code (N.N. Laws 1963, Cap. 30), ss. 167-184.
[85] N.N. Laws 1963, Cap. 33.
[86] No. 14 of 1967.
[87] No. 12 of 1976.

III.[88] District Court judges, other than District Judges Grade III, are appointed by the Interim Judicial Committee established for the State and District Judges Grade III are appointed by the Chief Judge of the State.[89]

A district court is a court of civil jurisdiction.[90] It is the equivalent of a magistrate's court in any of the southern States sitting in the exercise of its civil jurisdiction. Accordingly, its jurisdiction is similar to the civil jurisdiction of a magistrate's court in each of the southern States. Thus, in general, a district court has jurisdiction, subject to prescribed monetary value limits where the subject matter is money or is capable of estimation in terms of money:

(a) in personal suits;

(b) in suits between landlord and tenant;

(c) in civil proceedings for the recovery of money recoverable under a local enactment where it is not expressly stated in the enactment that the money is recoverable only in some other court;

(d) in civil proceedings in which jurisdiction has been conferred on a district court by the Land Tenure Law[91];

(e) in civil proceedings outside (c) and (d) in respect of which jurisdiction has been conferred on a District Court by a local enactment;

(f) to appoint guardians *ad litem* and issue orders and directions relating to such appointment;

(g) to grant in any suit within (a) to (f) above instituted in the court injunctions or order to stay waste or stay alienation or for the detention and preservation of any property which is the subject of such suit before the court or to restrain breaches of contracts or torts.

But, subject to any local enactment, the jurisdiction conferred on a district court in any of the above cases, except (d) excludes original jurisdiction in any suit or matter which:

(i) raises any issue as to the title to land, or to any interest in land;

(ii) raises any issue as to the validity of any devise, bequest or limitation under any will or settlement; or

(iii) is subject to the jurisdiction of an area court relating to marriage, family status, guardianship of children, inheritance or disposition of property on death;

---

[88] District Courts Law, s. 7.

[89] Interim Judicial Committees (Establishment, etc.) Decree 1977 (No. 66 of 1977), ss. 2 and 3.

[90] District Courts Law, s. 4.

[91] N.N. Laws 1963, Cap. 59.

unless the Military Governor otherwise orders or the suit is one transferred to the district court under the provisions of the Area Courts
Edict in force in the State.[92]

The prescribed monetary value limits in respect of the various
classes of district court judges where the subject matter is money or is
capable of estimation in terms of money are as follows:

Senior District Judge   - ₦1,000
District Judge Grade I   - ₦400
District Judge Grade II   - ₦200
District Judge Grade III - ₦50.[93]

J. CUSTOMARY AND AREA COURTS

Courts established essentially for the administration of customary
law exist in the following 17 States: Anambra, Bauchi, Benue,
Borno, Cross River, Gongola, Kaduna, Kano, Kwara, Lagos, Niger,
Ogun, Ondo, Oyo, Plateau, Rivers and Sokoto. They are designated
"customary courts" in Anambra, Cross River, Lagos, Ogun, Ondo,
Oyo and Rivers States, and "Area Courts" in Bauchi, Benue, Borno,
Gongola, Kaduna, Kano, Kwara, Niger, Plateau and Sokoto. Such
courts do not exist in Bendel and Imo.[94] But arrangements are being
made to re-establish customary courts in the two States.

Customary Courts in Lagos State

Customary Courts in Lagos State are governed by the Customary
Courts Law.[95] Under the Law, the Attorney-General for the State is
empowered to establish by warrant customary courts of a single
grade outside the city of Lagos.[96] There is no provision for the establishment of customary courts in the city of Lagos. With respect to the
composition of the court, section 2 of the Law provides:

"A Customary Court shall consist of a President and at least two
or other four members as the case may be."

It seems clear that the words "at least two or other four members
as the case may be" suggest that a customary court may consist of the

---

[92] District Courts Law, s. 13.
[93] District Courts Law, ss. 13 and 14.
[94] See Customary Courts (Abolition) Edict 1973 (No. 18 of 1973)(M.W.S.) applicable
in Bendel by virtue of s. 5(1) of the States (Creation and Transitional Provisions)
Decree 1976 (No. 12 of 1976); Magistrates' Courts Law (Amendment) Edict 1971
(No. 23 of 1971) (E.C.S.), s. 16(1) applicable in Imo by virtue of s. 5(1) of the States
(Creation and Transitional Provisions) Decree 1976.
[95] Lagos Laws 1973, Cap. 33.
[96] *Ibid.* s. 1(1).

President and three other members (a total of four members). But section 6(1) of the law — the only provision on quorum — provides, "For the purpose of hearing any case in a Customary Court, two or three members shall form a quorum *where the court consists of three or five members* respectively."[97] Thus, a quorum is prescribed only where the court consists of three members (the President and two other members) or five members (the President and four other members). It would appear therefore, that the words "at least" in section 2 of the Law were inserted there by mistake and that a customary court consists of a President and two other members or a President and four other members.

Customary court members including Court Presidents are appointed by the Interim Customary Courts Judicial Service Committee for the State. Qualifications for appointment to the membership of a customary court are similar to qualifications for appointment to membership of customary courts in the Midwestern State under the Customary Courts Edict 1966[98] of that State. A person is not eligible for appointment unless: (a) he is literate in English language, (b) he possesses at least the Primary or Standard VI Certificate, or its equivalent and suitable experience, and (c) he is a native of the area of jurisdiction of the customary court.[99]

A customary court in the State has civil and criminal jurisdiction.[1] It has unlimited civil jurisdiction in two classes of cases, namely:

    (a) matrimonial causes and other matters between persons married under customary law or arising from or connected with a union contracted under customary law, that is matrimonial causes and related matters under customary law, and

    (b) suits relating to the guardianship and custody of children under customary law.[2]

It has jurisdiction in the following two classes of cases provided that the money claimed or the subject-matter of the case does not exceed ₦100:

    (a) causes and matters relating to inheritance upon intestacy and the administration of intestate estates under customary law, and

    (b) other cases under customary law.[3]

In general, a customary court in the State has criminal jurisdiction in the following cases:

---

[97] Emphasis supplied.
[98] No. 38 of 1966.
[99] Customary Courts Law (Lagos Laws 1973, Cap. 33) s. 4(1).
[1] *Ibid.* ss. 15 and 16 and Sched. 2.
[2] *Ibid.* s. 15 and Sched. 2. (Pt. I).
[3] *Ibid.*

"(a) any offences against the provisions of an enactment which expressly confers jurisdiction on the court;

(b) offences against rules and bye-laws made by a local government council or having effect as if so made, under the provisions of any enactment and in force in the area of jurisdiction of the court;

(c) contempt of court committed in the face of the court."[4]

But it has no jurisdiction in the following cases: homicide, treason; any other capital offence; sedition; rape; procuration; defilement of girls and offences against the enactments relating to official secrets.[5]

The maximum punishment which a customary court in the State is empowered to impose is as follows:

Imprisonment - a term of one month
Fine   - ₦20[6]

With respect to jurisdiction over persons, a customary court in the State has jurisdiction over all Nigerians.[7]

Customary courts in the State are under the general supervision and control of the Ministry of Justice of the State.[8] An official of the Ministry in his capacity as Inspector for Customary Courts acts as the supervising authority. He is empowered to supervise any specified customary courts. He has access to such courts and to their records and proceedings.

Appeals lie from the decisions of a customary court to a magistrate's court.[9] Section 42 of the Customary Courts Law provides that appeals from a magistrate's court thus sitting as a court of appeal lie to the High Court provided that in a criminal case the term of imprisonment or the fine imposed by the magistrate's court exceeds ₦10 and that in a civil case "the subject matter is of the value of one hundred Naira." Probably, the words "at least one hundred Naira" rather than just "one hundred Naira" were intended.

The Customary Courts Rules[10] contain rules of practice and procedure in the customary courts.

Customary Courts in Ogun, Ondo and Oyo States

The Customary Courts Law applicable in the Western State[11] contin-

---

[4] Customary Courts Law (Lagos Laws 1973, Cap. 33), s. 16 and Sched. 2. (Pt. II).
[5] *Ibid.*
[6] *Ibid.*
[7] *Ibid.* s. 14.
[8] *Ibid.* s. 38.
[9] *Ibid.* s. 41.
[10] Lagos Laws 1973, Cap. 33.
[11] Customary Courts Law (W.R.N. Laws 1959, Cap. 31).

ues to apply in the entire territory formerly constituting the State and now comprising the three States of Ogun, Ondo and Oyo.[12]

In each of the three States, customary courts are divided into three classes, namely, Grade A Customary Courts, Grade B Customary Courts and Grade C Customary Courts.[13] All Grade A courts are presided over by legal practitioners.[14] Such Grade B courts as are specified by a direction in writing issued by the Commissioner for Justice are presided over by legal practitioners.[15] All other Grade B courts and all Grade C courts are presided over by lay persons. But a person is not eligible for appointment as president or vice-president of a Grade B court or of a customary court of appeal unless he is literate in the English language.[16] Except with respect to Grade C customary courts, jurisdiction is conferred on the customary courts by reference not only to the grade of the court but also to the status of the person or persons constituting the court. There is a similarity between this principle of determining jurisdiction and the jurisdictional principle applicable to magistrates' courts. A Grade A court is constituted by a Chief Customary Court President or Senior Customary Court President Grade I. A Grade B court is constituted by *either*: (a) a legal practitioner who is styled (i) Senior Customary Court President Grade II; or (ii) Customary Court President Grade I; or (iii) Customary Court President Grade II; *or* (b) a person or persons who are not legal practitioners.[17] Customary Courts not to be presided over by legal practitioners are established by the Commissioner for Justice by warrant.[18] Those to be presided over by legal practitioners are established by the Chief Judge of the State.[19]

Members of customary courts in each State are appointed by the Interim Customary Courts Judicial Service Committee for the State.[20]

A customary court administers:

(a) customary law (in civil cases only);
(b) the provisions of any written law which it may be authorised to enforce by an order made under section 24 of the Customary Courts Law;

[12] See States (Creation and Transitional Provisions) Decree 1976 (No. 12 of 1976), s. 5(1).
[13] Customary Courts Law (W.R.N. Laws 1959, Cap. 31), s. 18.
[14] *Ibid.* s. 6(1).   [15] *Ibid.* s. 6(2).
[16] *Ibid.* s. 6(3). With respct to customary courts of appeal, see p. 212, below.
[17] Customary Courts Law (W.R.N. Laws 1959, Cap. 31), s. 2 as amended by s. 2 of the Customary Courts (Amendment) Edict 1972 (No. 15 of 1972) (W.S.).
[18] Customary Courts Law (W.R.N. Laws 1959, Cap. 31), s. 3 as amended by the Customary Courts (Amendment) Edict 1972 (No. 15 of 1972) (W.S.).
[19] *Ibid.*
[20] Local Courts Interim Judicial Service Bodies (Establishment, etc.) Decree 1978 (No. 3 of 1978). The Decree came into force on March 1, 1978.

(c) the provisions of any enactment which confers jurisdiction on the court with respect to the enactment;

(d) the provisions of rules and bye-laws made by a local government council, or having effect as if made by the council under the provisions of an enactment where those provisions are in force in the area of jurisdiction of the court.[21]

Customary courts in each of the States have civil and criminal jurisdiction. Subject to limits prescribed by reference to the amount of money involved or the monetary value of the subject-matter involved, a customary court in each of the States has civil jurisdiction in —

(a) land cases under customary law;

(b) matrimonial causes and matters between persons married under customary law or arising from or connected with a union contracted under customary law (excluding any such cause or matter relating to, arising from or connected with a Christian marriage as defined in section 1 of the Criminal Code)[22];

(c) cases relating to custody of children under customary law;

(d) cases relating to inheritance upon intestacy under customary law;

(e) administering or granting power or authority to any person to administer the estate of an intestate under customary law;

(f) other cases under customary law.[23]

The jurisdictional monetary value limits prescribed for the various grades of courts with respect to the cases just listed under categories (a) to (f) are as follows:

Grade A
Chief Customary Court President
   (a) to (d) - None (No limit)
   (e)   - ₦1,000 (gross capital value of the estate)
   (f)   - ₦1,000
Senior Customary Court President, Grade I
   (a) - (d) - None (No limit)
   (e)   - ₦600 (gross capital value of the estate)
   (f)   - ₦600

[21] Customary Courts Law (W.R.N. Laws 1959, Cap. 31), s. 19.

[22] "Christian marriage" under the Criminal Code (W.R.N. Laws 1959, Cap. 28) means a marriage which is recognised by the law of the place where it is contracted as the voluntary union for life of one man and one woman to the exclusion of all others. A marriage under the Marriage Act (Fed. and Lagos Laws 1958, Cap. 115) is a Christian marriage within the meaning of the Code.

[23] Customary Courts Law (W.R.N. Laws 1959, Cap. 31), s. 18 and Sched. 2. (Pts. I-III) as amended by s. 16 of the Customary Courts (Amendment) Edict 1972 (W.S.).

Senior Customary Court President, Grade II
  (a) - (c) - None (No limit)
  (d)   - ₦400 (gross capital value of the estate)
  (e)   - ₦400 (gross capital value of the estate)
  (f)   - ₦400

Customary Court President, Grade I or II, or Grade B Court comprising a person or persons who are not legal practitioners
  (a)- ₦200
  (b)- ₦200
  (c)- None (No limit)
  (d)- ₦200 (gross capital value of the estate)
  (e)- ₦200 (gross capital value of the estate)
  (f) - ₦200

Grade C
  (a)- ₦100
  (b)- ₦100
  (c)- None (No limit)
  (d)- ₦100 (gross capital value of the estate)
  (e)- ₦100 (gross capital value of the estate)
  (f) - ₦100[24]

Customary Courts in the States have jurisdiction in criminal cases where such jurisdiction is conferred on them by an enactment.

The maximum terms of imprisonment and the maximum fines which the various classes of customary court are empowered to impose are as follows:

A Grade A Customary Court presided over by a Chief Customary Court President — imprisonment for a term of five years, a fine of ₦1,000.

A Grade A Customary Court presided over by a Senior Customary Court President Grade I — imprisonment for a term of three years, a fine of ₦600.

A Grade B Customary Court presided over by a Senior Customary Court President Grade II — imprisonment for a term of two years, a fine of ₦400.

A Grade B Customary Court presided over by a Customary Court President Grade I or Grade II, or comprising a person or persons who are not legal practitioners — imprisonment for a term of one year, a fine of ₦200.

A Grade C Customary Court — imprisonment for a term of six months, a fine of ₦100.[25]

---

[24] *Ibid.*
[25] Customary Courts Law (W.R.N. Laws 1959, Cap. 31), s. 18, and Sched. 2. (Pt. IV) as amended by s. 16 of the Customary Courts (Amendment) Edict 1972 (W.S.).

The jurisdiction of customary courts in the States over persons is limited to Nigerians.[26]

Appeals from a Grade C Customary Court and a Grade B Customary Court not presided over by a legal practitioner lie to a customary court (normally a Grade A Court) designated a court of appeal for them, the Grades C and B courts being within its area of jurisdiction.[27] Where no customary court is so designated, appeals from Grade C courts and Grade B courts not presided over by legal practitioners,[28] lie to the magistrates' courts. Appeals from a Grade B court presided over by a legal practitioner and from a Grade A court lie to the High Court.[29]

There are provisions in the Customary Courts Law for the supervision of the customary courts.[30] For this purpose, there is a supervising authority who has access to any customary court with respect to which the authority is appointed. The authority also has access to the records and proceedings of such customary courts.[31] A customary court under the control of a supervising authority must submit to the authority a report of any cases tried by the court whenever it is required to do so by the authority. The supervising authority has powers to review the decisions of customary courts under its control.[32]

Moreover, under section 44F of the Customary Courts Law, the Chief Judge may require the president of any customary court in the State presided over by a legal practitioner to send every month to him or to another judge of the High Court specified by him a list of all criminal or specified criminal cases decided or brought before the customary court. The Chief Judge or the judge is empowered to review any such cases.

Customary Courts in Cross River State

The Customary Courts Edict 1969 [33] provides for the establishment in Cross River State[34] of customary courts known as district courts. A district court is established by warrant by the Military Governor of the State. It consists of a President and four other members. The quorum for the purpose of hearing any case is three members including the President or another member presiding in the President's

[26] Customary Courts Law (W.R.N. Laws 1959, Cap. 31), s. 17.
[27] Customary Courts Law (W.R.N. Laws 1959, Cap. 31), s. 17.
[28] *Ibid.* s. 47.
[29] *Ibid.* s. 48.
[30] *Ibid.* ss. 44A-44F.
[31] *Ibid.* s. 44C.
[32] *Ibid.* ss. 44D and 44E.
[33] No. 9 of 1969 (S.E.S.).
[34] See the States (Creation and Transitional Provisions) Decree 1976 (No. 12 of 1976).

absence. Members of the court including the President are appointed by the Interim Customary Courts Judicial Service Committee for the State.[35] Appointment is for a term of three years but a member may be reappointed for one or more terms.[36]

A district court is a court of record having original jurisdiction in civil and criminal cases.[37] It exercises civil jurisdiction in the following cases:

(a) Cases of debt, demand or damages under customary law where the amount involved does not exceed ₦100;

(b) Cases of debt, demand or damages under any written law where the Governor has conferred jurisdiction on the court with respect to such cases;

(c) Cases concerning ownership, possession, occupation or alienation of land, the jurisdiction being unlimited where there is no claim for damages and being limited to cases in which the claim does not exceed ₦100 where there is a claim for damages;

(d) Cases relating to succession of property and administration of estates under customary law where the value of the property involved does not exceed ₦100;

(e) Matrimonial causes and matters between persons married under customary law or arising from or connected with a union contracted under customary law, the jurisdiction being unlimited; and

(f) Cases relating to the custody of children under customary law, the jurisdiction being unlimited.[38]

The court has jurisdiction in criminal cases under any written law which it may be authorised by the Governor to administer where the punishment prescribed for the offence is: (a) a fine not exceeding ₦80 or imprisonment for a term not exceeding three months, or both such fine and imprisonment; or (b) in the case of juvenile offenders, a punishment not exceeding 12 strokes of the cane.[39] The court may impose the maximum fine or the maximum sentence of imprisonment in any criminal case within its jurisdiction.[40] But the court must grant bail to any person convicted of an offence by it if that person lodges an appeal, pending the determination of the appeal.

With respect to jurisdiction over persons, section 11 of the Customary Courts Edict[41] provides that the court has jurisdiction over the following persons or classes of persons:

[35] Local Courts Interim Judicial Service Bodies (Establishment, etc.) Decree 1978.
[36] *Ibid.* ss. 3 and 12(1).
[37] *Ibid.* s. 14 and Sched. 1 (para. 2).
[38] *Ibid.* s. 12(1) and Sched. 1 (para. 2).
[39] *Ibid.* s. 12(1) and Sched.1 (para. 1).
[40] *Ibid.* s. 12(1).
[41] No. 9 of 1969.

(a) all Nigerians;

(b) persons or classes of persons other than Nigerians whom or which the Governor directs to be subject to the jurisdiction of any particular customary court or to be subject to such jurisdiction in certain cases or in certain classes of cases only; and

(c) persons other than Nigerians who have at any time instituted proceedings in any customary court or have by their conduct submitted to the jurisdiction of a customary court.

Appeals lie from the decisions of a district court to a magistrate's court.[42] From the decisions of the magistrate sitting as a court of appeal, appeals lie to the High Court.

District courts, and magistrates' courts acting as Customary Courts of Appeal[43] are subject to the supervision of the Chief Judge of the State.

Customary Courts in Rivers State

Customary Courts of Rivers State are still governed by the Customary Courts (No. 2) Edict 1966[44] of Eastern Nigeria. They have not functioned at all since the end of the civil war in Nigeria in 1970.[45]

Area Courts

In all the States where Area Courts exist — Bauchi, Benue, Borno, Gongola, Kaduna, Kano, Kwara, Niger, Plateau and Sokoto — the area courts legislation is in general uniform. The principal legislative enactments governing area courts are as follows:
Area Courts Edict 1967[46] in force in Kwara, Area Courts Edict 1967[47] in force in Niger and Sokoto States, Area Courts Edict 1967[48] in force in Kaduna State, Area Courts Edict 1967[49] in force in Kano State, Area Courts Edict 1968[50] in force in Bauchi, Borno and Gongola States and Area Courts Edict 1968[51] in force in Benue and Plateau States.

---

[42] *Ibid.* s. 50(1) as amended by the Customary Courts (Miscellaneous Provisions) Edict 1971 (No. 6 of 1971) (S.E.S.).

[43] The Customary Courts (Miscellaneous Provisions) Edict 1971 suspended certain provisions of the Customary Courts Edict relating to a customary court of appeal and modified other provisions relating to such appellate court to enable Magistrates' Courts to serve as courts of appeal.

[44] No. 29 of 1966.

[45] See Chap. 2, above.

[46] No. 2 of 1967 (Kwara State).

[47] No. 2 of 1967 (N.W.S.).

[48] No. 2 of 1967 (N.C.S.).

[49] No. 2 of 1967 (Kano State).

[50] No. 1 of 1968 (N.E.S.).

[51] No. 4 of 1968 (B.P.S.).

An area court in a State is established by warrant by the Chief Judge of the State.[52] It is constituted by a judge, designated area judge, sitting alone or an area judge sitting with one or more members.[53] All members of area courts including area judges are public officers in the public service of the State.[54] They are appointed by the Interim Area Courts Judicial Service Board for the State.

Area courts are divided into the following four classes: Upper Area Courts, Area Courts Grade I, Area Courts Grade II and Area Courts Grade III.[55] Every area court normally has civil and criminal jurisdiction under the appropriate Area Courts Edict but a particular area court may be required to exercise only civil or only criminal jurisdiction if the warrant establishing it so specifies.[56] Part II of the First Schedule to each Area Courts Edict states the jurisdiction of the various grades of area courts with respect to subject matter, the monetary value limits being specified in appropriate cases.[57] But the Chief Judge may give any area court of any particular grade such additional jurisdiction as he considers proper.[58] All grades of area courts have unlimited jurisdiction in the following cases:

(a) Matrimonial causes and matters between persons married under customary law or arising from or connected with a union contracted by customary law other than those arising from or connected with a Christian marriage as defined in section 1 of the Criminal Code[59]; and

(b) Suits relating to the custody of children under customary law.

In civil actions involving a debt, demand or damages, the jurisdiction of an Upper Area Court is unlimited but the jurisdiction of area courts Grades I, II and III is limited to cases where the sums of money involved do not exceed ₦1,000, ₦400 and ₦100 respectively.

In civil cases relating to succession to property and the administration of estates under customary law, an Upper Area Court and an Area Court Grade I have unlimited jurisdiction. The jurisdiction of an Area Court Grade II in such cases is limited to cases in which the value of the property involved does not exceed ₦500. The monetary

[52] See *e.g.* Area Courts Edict 1968 (No. 4 of 1968) (B.P.S.), s. 3(1).

[53] *Ibid.* s. 4(1).

[54] *Ibid.* s. 4(4).

[55] *Ibid.* s. 17.

[56] See *e.g.* Area Courts Edict 1968 (No. 4 of 1968) (B.P.S.), s. 3(2) and Area Courts Jurisdiction Notice 1968 (Kano State L.N. 6 of 1968).

[57] See *e.g.* Area Courts Edict 1968 (B.P.S.), s. 17 (1).

[58] *Ibid.* s. 17(2).

[59] Fed. and Lagos Laws 1958, Cap. 42. "Christian marriage" is defined in the Code as a marriage which is recognised by the law of the place where it is contracted as the voluntary union for life of one man and one woman to the exclusion of all others. A marriage under the Marriage Act (Fed. and Lagos Laws 1958, Cap. 115) is a Christian marriage within the meaning of the Code.

value limit prescribed for an Area Court Grade II in such cases is ₦200.

An Upper Area Court has unlimited jurisdiction in cases relating to the ownership, possession or occupation of land, Area Courts Grade I, II and III have jurisdiction in such cases where the value of the subject-matter does not exceed ₦2,000, ₦500 and ₦200, respectively.[60]

Area courts have jurisdiction to try criminal cases in accordance with the provisions of the Criminal Procedure Code.[61] No area court has jurisdiction in homicide cases. With respect to power of punishment, an Upper Area Court is empowered to impose the maximum punishment for any offence which it has jurisdiction to try. The maximum sentences of imprisonment and fines which the other grades of area courts are empowered to impose are as follows:

Area Court Grade I   - 5 years' term, ₦1,000 fine
Area Court Grade II   - 3 years' term, ₦600 fine
Area Court Grade III - 9 months' term, ₦100 fine.[62]

Appeals lie from an Area Court Grade I, II or III to the Upper Area Court within whose area of jurisdiction the lower court is situated,[63] an Upper Area Court thus having original and appellate jurisdiction. Appeals from the decisions of an Upper Area Court lie to the Sharia Court of Appeal in cases involving Moslem personal law and to the High Court in other cases.[64]

Area courts are in general subject to the general supervision of the High Court.[65] But the High Court is not empowered to issue orders of mandamus, certiorari and prohibition, or to grant an injunction in lieu of *quo warranto* in respect of area courts.[66]

K. JUVENILE COURTS

Juvenile courts are special courts established for the trial of young offenders and for the welfare of the young. Such courts exist in Anambra, Bendel, Cross River, Imo, Lagos, Ogun, Ondo, Oyo and Rivers States. In each of those States, the courts are established by the Children and Young Persons Law.[67] Although juvenile courts do

---

[60] See *e.g.* Area Courts Edict 1968 (B.P.S.), s. 17 and Sched. (Pt. II).
[61] N.N. Laws 1963, Cap. 30.
[62] See *e.g.* Area Courts Edict 1968 (B.P.S.), s. 17 and Sched. (Pt. I).
[63] *Ibid.* s. 53.
[64] *Ibid.* s. 54.
[65] *Ibid.* s. 43(1).
[66] See High Court Law (N.N. Laws 1963, Cap. 49), s. 27.
[67] Lagos Laws 1973, Cap. 26; W.R.N. Laws 1959, Cap. 20 in force in Bendel, Ogun, Ondo and Oyo; E.N. Laws 1963, Cap. 19 in force in Anambra, Cross River, Imo and Rivers States. See States (Creation and Transitional Provisions) Decree 1976 (No. 12 of 1976).

not exist in any of the other 10 States — Bauchi, Benue, Borno, Gongola, Kaduna, Kano, Kwara, Niger, Plateau and Sokoto — the Children and Young Persons Law[68] of Northern Nigeria which is in force in the 10 States is in general similar in wording to the Children and Young Persons legislation of the other nine States. All the enactments contain provisions relating to special treatment of juvenile offenders and welfare of juveniles. Each enactment defines a "child" as a person who has not attained the age of 14 years.[69] The Northern Nigeria enactment[70] defines a "young person" as a person who has attained the age of 14 years but has not attained the age of 18 years. The other enactments[71] define the term "young person" as a person who has attained the age of 14 years but has not attained the age of 17 years.

A juvenile court is constituted by a magistrate sitting with other members appointed by an appropriate authority.[72] In Lagos State the appointing authority is the Chief Judge. As a general rule, whenever a court (whether a juvenile court or not) in any State is to hear charges against children or young persons, the court must sit either in a different building or room from that in which the ordinary sittings are held, or on different days or at different times from those at which the ordinary sittings are held.[73] Accordingly, a magistrate who when sitting alone may constitute a magistrate's court must, when sitting with other persons to constitute a juvenile court, sit in a place different from that in which he sits as a magistrate's court or on different days or at different times from those at which he sits as a magistrate's court. This provision is apparently aimed at preventing children and young persons from associating with adults charged with offences. Even when juveniles are in custody or are being taken to or from court arrangements are normally required by law to be made to prevent them from associating with adults charged with offences.[74] Furthermore, the law emphasises the welfare and protection of the juvenile by providing that in general nobody is to publish

---

[68] N.N. Laws 1963, Cap. 21.

[69] See *e.g.* Children and Young Persons Law (Lagos Laws 1973, Cap. 26), s. 2.

[70] Children and Young Persons Law (N.N. Laws 1963, Cap. 21).

[71] Children and Young Persons Law (Lagos Laws 1973, Cap. 26); Children and Young Persons Law (W.R.N. Laws 1959, Cap, 20); Children and Young Persons Law (E.N. Laws 1963, Cap. 19).

[72] See *e.g.* Children and Young Persons Law (Lagos Laws 1973, Cap. 26), s. 6(1).

[73] s. 6(2) of the Children and Young Persons Law of Lagos State provides: "A court when hearing charges against children or young persons shall, unless the child or young person is charged jointly with any other person not being a child or young person, sit either in a different building or room from that in which the ordinary sittings of the court are held, or on different days or at different times from those at which the ordinary sittings are held."

[74] See *e.g.* Children and Young Persons Law (Lagos Laws 1973, Cap. 26), ss. 5 and 6(4).

anything likely to lead to the identification of a juvenile brought before a juvenile court except with the permission of the court.[75] It should also be mentioned that hearings in juvenile courts are normally closed to the public. Section 6(5) of the Children and Young Persons Law of Lagos State provides, for example that in general no person other than the members and officers of a juvenile court, the parties to the case, their solicitors and counsel and other persons directly concerned in the case is to be allowed to attend the court without the leave of the court, the only exception being *bona fide* representatives of a newspaper or newsagency who may attend without such leave unless a special order of the court forbids their attendance.

The law provides for preferential treatment for the young in respect of punishment. For example, it is provided that an order for imprisonment of a child must not be made.[76] Furthermore, a sentence of imprisonment must not be imposed on a young person if he can be suitably dealt with in any other way. A person who was under the age of 17 years at the time he committed an offence must not be sentenced to death.[77] Where the normal punishment for the offence is a death sentence, the court must order that the young offender be detained at the pleasure of the Governor.

When a child or young person is found guilty of an offence the court must consider the appropriate method of dealing with him. The Children and Young Persons Law of Lagos State lists the various methods as follows:

(a) dismissing the charge;
(b) discharging the offender on his entering into a recognisance;
(c) discharging the offender and placing him under the supervision of a probation officer[78];
(d) committing the offender by means of a corrective order[79] to the care of a relative or other fit person;
(e) sending the offender by means of a corrective order to an approved institution;
(f) ordering the offender to be caned;
(g) ordering the offender to pay a fine, damages or costs;
(h) ordering the parent or guardian of the offender to pay a fine, damages or costs;
(i) ordering the parent or guardian of the offender to give security for his good behaviour;

[75] *Ibid.* s. 6(6).
[76] *Ibid.* s. 11(1). See also s. 16 of the Law which forbids the use of the words "conviction" and "sentence" in relation to children and young persons.
[77] *Ibid.* s. 12.
[78] See Children and Young Persons Law (Lagos Laws 1973, Cap. 26), s. 17.
[79] See Children and Young Persons Law (Lagos Laws 1973, Cap. 26), s. 19.

(j) committing the offender to custody in a place of detention provided under the Children and Young Persons Law;

(k) ordering the offender, if he is a young person, to be imprisoned; and

(l) any other method under the law.[80]

Mention should be made of the provisions of the Children and Young Persons enactments relating to juveniles in need of care. A child or young person may be brought before a Juvenile Court by a police officer or any other authorised person having a reasonable ground for believing that the child or young person falls within any of certain specified categories. The categories include orphans, persons who are deserted by their relations, those found destitute, persons found wandering and having no home or settled place of abode or visible means of subsistence and those found begging or receiving alms.[81] Where the court finds that the child or young person comes within any of the categories, it may make an order, for example, a corrective order, under the Children and Young Persons enactment.[82]

L. CORONERS

There is provision in the law of each State for coroners' inquests. A coroner is a person empowered to hold inquests on the body of a deceased person who appears to have died a violent or an unnatural death, or on the body of a deceased person belonging to any other class specified by the appropriate Coroners Law.

Every magistrate is a coroner.[83] In addition, other fit persons may be appointed coroners. A coroner's inquest must normally be held where it appears that a deceased person has died a violent or unnatural death, where the deceased has died a sudden death of which the cause is unknown, where the deceased has died while confined in a lunatic asylum or in any place or circumstances which in the coroner's opinion makes the holding of an inquest necessary or desirable[84] and where a prisoner or any person in police custody has died.[85] But

---

[80] Children and Young Persons Law (Lagos Laws 1973, Cap. 26), s. 14. The sanctions prescribed by the other Children and Young Persons Laws are generally the same as those listed. But in place of the term "corrective order" the Eastern Nigeria enactment uses the term "committal order" and the Northern Nigeria Law uses the term "mandate."

[81] Children and Young Persons Law (Lagos Laws 1973, Cap. 26).

[82] See Coroners Law (Lagos Laws 1973, Cap. 30); Coroners Law (W.R.N. Laws 1959, Cap. 27); Coroners Law (N.N. Laws 1963, Cap. 27); Coroners Law (E.N. Laws 1963, Cap. 29).

[83] See *e.g.* Coroners Law (Lagos Laws 1973, Cap. 30), s. 3(1).

[84] *Ibid.* s. 4.

[85] *Ibid.* s. 6.

whenever it appears to the coroner that the death in question is due to natural causes and that there is nothing in the form of the body to suggest that the death is attributable to or has been accelerated by violence or by any culpable or negligent conduct of the deceased or of any other person the coroner is not bound to hold an inquest unless the death in question is that of a prisoner or of a person in police custody.[86] Furthermore, whenever a coroner holding an inquest is informed that criminal proceedings have been or are about to be instituted against any person already in custody or about to be arrested in respect of the death, he must stop the inquest and must not resume it until the completion of the criminal proceedings. Similarly, where a coroner who has not started an inquest is so informed, he must not start an inquest until the conclusion of the criminal proceedings.

‘A coroner at an inquest must take on oath evidence available with respect to the identity of the deceased, and the time, place and manner of his death.[87] In general, the rules of evidence applicable in civil or criminal proceedings are not binding on a coroner.[88] A coroner holding an inquest has the same powers as those of a magistrate with respect to summoning witnesses.[89] Where a coroner has concluded an inquest, he must send to the judicial division of the High Court in which the inquest has been held a report of his findings.[90]

M. NATIONAL INDUSTRIAL COURT

The National Industrial Court was established by section 14 of the Trade Disputes Decree 1976[91] for the purpose of dealing with trade disputes and collective agreements. The Decree defines "trade dispute" as any dispute between "employers and workers or between workers, which is connected with the employment or non-employment, or the terms of employment and physical conditions of work of any person."[92] The term "collective agreement" is defined by the Decree as any agreement in writing between "(a) an employer, a group of employers or one or more organisations representative of employers, on the one hand, and (b) one or more organisations representative of workers, or the lawfully appointed representatives of any body of workers on the other hand."[93]

[86] *Ibid.* s. 4.
[87] *Ibid.* s. 14.
[88] *Ibid.* s. 17.
[89] *Ibid.* s. 16(1).
[90] See *e.g.* Coroners Law (Lagos Laws 1973, Cap. 30), ss. 25 and 28.
[91] No. 7 of 1976.
[92] *Ibid.* s. 37(1).
[93] *Ibid.*

In general, the court has exclusive original jurisdiction to make awards for the purpose of settling trade disputes.[94] It also has exclusive jurisdiction to determine questions concerning the interpretation of:

(a) a collective agreement;
(b) an award made by an arbitration tribunal or by the court itself under the Decree;
(c) the terms of settlement of a trade dispute as stated in a memorandum, in cases where a conciliator is appointed under the Trade Disputes Decree 1976 to deal with a trade dispute.[95]

But where a question before the court involves an allegation that a provision of Chapter III of the Constitution of the Federation[96] (the chapter on fundamental rights) has been contravened in a territory in Nigeria, that person may seek redress in the High Court of the territory.[97] Moreover, the Supreme Court has original jurisdiction under section 115 of the Constitution of the Federation to determine questions as to the interpretation of the Constitution of the Federation or of a State notwithstanding the fact that the questions relate to trade disputes or collective agreements.[98] In general, decisions of the National Industrial Court are final. But appeals lie to the Supreme Court from its decisions on questions as to whether any of the provisions of Chapter III of the Constitution of the Federation has been contravened in relation to a person.[99]

The court consists of a President and four other members. The Decree provides that all the four other members (referred to in the Decree as "ordinary members") must be persons of good standing who to the knowledge of the Federal Commissioner charged with responsibility for matters relating to the welfare of labour are well acquainted with employment conditions in Nigeria.[1] Curiously, no such provision is made with respect to the President. At least one of the ordinary members must to the satisfaction of the Federal Commissioner have a competent knowledge of economics, industry or trade.[2]

Section 16(2) of the Trade Disputes Decree 1976 provides that a person is not qualified to hold the office of President of the court unless:

---

[94] Trade Disputes Decree 1976, s. 15(1).
[95] *Ibid.*
[96] Act No. 20 of 1963.
[97] See Trade Disputes Decree 1976, s. 15(3).
[98] *Ibid.*
[99] See Trade Disputes Decree 1976, s. 15(2) and s. 15(3).
[1] See Trade Disputes Decree 1976, s. 14(2).
[2] Trade Disputes Decree 1976, s. 14(2)(*b*).

"(a) he has been a judge of a court of unlimited jurisdiction in civil and criminal matters in some part of the Commonwealth or a court having jurisdiction in appeals from any such court; or

(b) he is qualified for admission as an advocate in Nigeria and has been so qualified for not less than ten years. Provided that, in computing the period during which any person has been qualified for admission as an advocate any period during which he has been in office as judge or magistrate after becoming so qualified shall be included."[3]

A person is appointed to the office of President of the court by the Supreme Military Council after consultation with the Advisory Judicial Committee.[4] The same Council appoints ordinary members of the Court. But in appointing ordinary members, it is not required to consult the Advisory Judicial Committee.[5]

For the purpose of dealing with any case, the court is duly constituted, at the discretion of the President, by either all the five members or the President and two ordinary members.[6] The court may be assisted by assessors appointed under the Decree at the discretion of the President.[7]

N. MILITARY COURTS

There are military courts in the country.[8] Normally, only members of the Armed Forces — the Nigeria Army, the Nigerian Navy and the Nigerian Air Force — are subject to the jurisdiction of military courts.[9]

O. TRIBUNALS

Many bodies not designated "courts" under the law perform judicial or quasi-judicial functions. They are usually designated "tribunals" by the law establishing them. A tribunal performing judicial or quasi-judicial functions may be regarded as a court having special jurisdiction. A body performing such functions may be called "a tribunal" rather than "a court" by the legislature merely because the legislature

[3] See p. 186, above.
[4] Trade Disputes Decree 1976, s. 16(1).
[5] *Ibid.*
[6] Trade Disputes Decree 1976, s. 14(3).
[7] *Ibid.* s. 14(4).
[8] See Nigerian Army Act 1960 (No. 26 of 1960), Air Force Act 1964 (No. 11 of 1964), Navy Act 1964 (No. 21 of 1964), Military Courts (Special Powers) Decree 1977 (No. 4 of 1977), Forces Acts (Amendment) Decree 1974 (No. 3 of 1974).
[9] Non-members of the Armed Forces are subject to the jurisdiction of the special military tribunal established by the Treason and Other Offences (Special Tribunal) Decree 1976 (No. 8 of 1976).

requires the body to consist of experts in a particular area of the law or to deal with a particular area of the law, or to deal speedily with certain aspects of the law, or to adopt a procedure different from the usual court procedure, or for any two or more of those reasons.

Tribunals include Robbery and Firearms tribunals established under the Robbery and Firearms (Special Provisions) Decree 1970,[10] special tribunals for the trial of kidnapping and lynching cases established under the Offences Against the Person (Special Provisions) Decree 1974,[11] Currency Offences tribunals established under the Counterfeit Currency (Special Provisions) Decree 1974[12] and Rent tribunals.[13]

Other bodies exercising judicial or quasi-judicial functions include the Joint Tax Board established by section 27(1) of the Income Tax Management Act 1961,[14] the Body of Appeal Commissioners established under section 55 of the Companies Income Tax Act 1961,[15] tribunals of inquiry established under the Tribunals of Inquiry Decree 1966,[16] the Medical and Dental Practitioners Disciplinary Committee established by section 12(1) of the Medical and Dental Practitioners Act 1963,[17] the Pharmacists Act 1964,[18] the Architects Disciplinary Tribunal established by section 12 of the Architects (Registration, etc.) Decree 1969,[19] arbitration tribunals established under the Trade Disputes Decree 1976,[20] the Legal Practitioners Disciplinary Committee established under section 9 of the Legal Practitioners Decree 1975[21] and the Appeal Committee of the Body of Benchers established under section 11 of the Legal Practitioners Decree 1975.

[10] No. 47 of 1970.
[11] No. 20 of 1974.
[12] No. 22 of 1974. See also Exchange Control (Anti-Sabotage) Decree 1977 (No. 57 of 1977) under which special tribunals are constituted.
[13] See *e.g.* Rent Control and Recovery of Residential Premises Edict 1976 (No. 9 of 1976) (Lagos State).
[14] No. 21 of 1961.
[15] No. 22 of 1961.
[16] No. 41 of 1966.
[17] No. 9 of 1963.
[18] No. 22 of 1964.
[19] No. 10 of 1969.
[20] No. 7 of 1976.
[21] No. 15 of 1975.

CHAPTER 11

AN OUTLINE OF CIVIL PROCEDURE

A. INTRODUCTION

THE sources of the law of civil procedure consist of statutes[1] and subsidiary legislation. The subsidiary legislation forms a larger body of that law than the statutes. It may be divided into two classes, namely,

(a) rules of practice and procedure (rules of court) made under Nigerian statutes,
(b) received English rules of practice and procedure.

Statutes establishing the courts usually contain a few rules of procedure and provide that in general where there are no provisions on any particular matter in the rules of court made under those statutes, appropriate English rules of court are to apply in so far as the English rules are not inconsistent with the statutes. Thus, generally, Rules of the Supreme Court of England apply in all jurisdictions in Nigeria with respect to matters not dealt with by local enactments containing rules of court.

The main local enactments containing rules of court applicable in the various courts are as follows:

Supreme Court of Nigeria
Supreme Court Rules 1977.[2]
Federal Court of Appeal
Supreme Court Rules 1961.[3]
High Courts
Federal Revenue Court (Civil Procedure) Rules 1976[4] applicable in the Federal Revenue Court.

High Court (Civil Procedure) Rules[5] of Lagos State applicable in the High Court of Lagos State.

High Court (Civil Procedure) Rules[6] of the former Western Region of Nigeria applicable in the High Courts of Bendel, Ogun, Ondo and Oyo States.

High Court (Civil Procedure) Rules[7] of the former Eastern Nigeria applicable in the High Courts of Anambra, Cross River, Imo and Rivers States.

[1] See *e.g.* Federal Court of Appeal Decree 1976 (No. 43 of 1976), ss. 8(1) and 30.
[2] L.N. 48 of 1977.
[3] See Federal Court of Appeal Decree 1976 (No. 43 of 1976), s. 8.
[4] L.N. 34 of 1976.
[5] Lagos Laws 1973, Cap. 52.
[6] W.R.N. Laws 1959, Cap. 44.
[7] E.N. Laws 1963, Cap. 61.

High Court (Civil Procedure) Rules 1977[8] in force in Kaduna State and similar Rules in force in the other northern States.

Magistrates' courts

Magistrates' Courts (Civil Procedure) Rules[9] of Lagos State applicable in Lagos State.

Magistrates' Courts (Civil Procedure) Rules[10] 1958 of the former Western Region applicable in Bendel, Ogun, Ondo and Oyo States.

Magistrates' Courts (Civil Procedure) Rules[11] of the former Eastern Nigeria applicable in Anambra, Cross River, Imo and Rivers.

District Courts[12]

District Courts Rules[13] of the former Northern Nigeria applicable in Bauchi, Benue, Borno, Gongola, Kaduna, Kano, Kwara, Niger, Plateau and Sokoto States.

Customary Courts

Customary Courts Rules[14] of Lagos State in force in Lagos State.

Customary Courts Rules[15] of the former Western Region of Nigeria applicable in Ogun, Ondo and Oyo States.

South-Eastern State Customary Courts Rules 1969[16] applicable in Cross River State.

Customary Courts Rules[17] of the former Eastern Nigeria applicable in Rivers State.

Area courts

Area Courts (Civil Procedure) Rules 1971[18] in force in Niger and Sokoto States, and similar Rules in force in the other northern States.

B. Civil Procedure in the High Court of Lagos State

In general, civil procedure in the various High Courts is uniform but there are some important differences. It is intended to discuss here the rules of civil procedure in the High Court of Lagos State.

---

[8] Kaduna State Legal Notice No. 7 of 1977. See also High Court (Civil Procedure) Rules 1976 (Kano State Legal Notice No. 6 of 1976). Formerly, the Supreme Court Rules (Nigeria Laws 1948, Cap. 211) applied in all the northern States.

[9] Lagos Laws 1973, Cap. 82.

[10] W.L.R.N. 292 of 1958.

[11] E.N. Laws 1963, Cap. 82.

[12] Established under the District Courts Law (N.N. Laws 1963, Cap. 33).

[13] N.N. Laws 1963, Cap. 33.

[14] Lagos Laws 1973, Cap. 33.

[15] W.R.N. Laws 1959, Cap. 31.

[16] S.E.S.L.N. No. 6 of 1969.

[17] E.N. Laws 1963, Cap. 32.

[18] N.W.S.L.N. 5 of 1971. See also Area Courts (Civil Procedure) Rules 1971 (Kano State).

1. *Parties*

As a general rule, every entity recognised as a person by the law can sue and be sued and any entity not recognised by the law as a person can neither sue nor be sued. But there are certain classes of persons under disability, for example, infants and lunatics. It is intended now to deal with those classes and also with other special classes of persons such as corporations.

Infants

An infant may sue by his "next friend" and may defend by his "guardian *ad litem*."[19] His next friend is usually his father or a person *in loco parentis*. No person is to act as next friend unless: (a) he has signed a written authority for the purpose; (b) the authority has been filed in the High Court Registry; and (c) he gives his own written consent to act in that capacity.[20] An infant is not entitled to enter an appearance personally; he appears by his guardian *ad litem* (usually his father or a person *in loco parentis*).[21] It is unnecessary to apply for an order for the appointment of a person as guardian *ad litem* where a legal practitioner has filed an affidavit for entry of appearance whereby he swears that a named person is, or is believed by him to be, a fit and proper person to act as guardian *ad litem* and that the named person has no interest in the matters in question adverse to that of the infant.[22]

Lunatics, and persons of unsound mind not adjudged lunatics

Lunatics may sue and defend an action by their committees. Persons of unsound mind may sue by their next friends with the consent of the next friends and defend an action by guardians appointed for that purpose.[23]

Trustees, executors and administrators

Trustees, executors and administrators of an estate may sue on behalf of the estate and may be sued as representatives of the estate.[24]

Incorporated associations

An incorporated association is a person under the law. It may sue and be sued in its corporate name.

---

[19] High Court (Civil Procedure) Rules (Lagos Laws 1973, Cap. 52), Order 13, r. 8.
[20] *Ibid.* Order 13, rr. 11 and 19.
[21] *Ibid.* Order 13, r. 10.
[22] *Ibid.*
[23] High Court (Civil Procedure) Rules (Lagos Laws 1973, Cap. 52), Ord. 13 r. 9.
[24] *Ibid.* Ord. 13, r. 13.

Unincorporated associations

An unincorporated association is not a person under the law. It has no legal existence distinct from its members. One of such associations is a partnership. Partners may sue and be sued in the name of the firm. But if they are sued in the firm name they must enter an appearance individually in their own names.[25] Some unincorporated associations are required to be registered under statute, for example, trade unions and, generally, associations having business names. They do not thereby acquire the right to sue or become liable to be sued in the registered name. Under rule 42 of Order 13 of the High Court (Civil Procedure) Rules of Lagos State, any person carrying on business within the jurisdiction of the High Court in a name or style other than his own name may be sued in the name or style as if it were a firm name.

Representative actions in which one or more members of a group represent the whole group may be taken in cases where the group is an unincorporated association.[26]

2. *Commencement of Proceedings*

Proceedings in the High Court of Lagos State may commence by:
(a) writ of summons;
(b) originating summons;
(c) originating notice of motion;
(d) petition.

(a) Writ of summons

A writ of summons usually called "a writ" is a command to the defendant to enter an appearance in an action brought by the plaintiff. It contains the name of the High Court, the judicial division and the names of the parties to the case. It commands the defendant to enter an appearance personally or by a solicitor and states that in case of default of appearance the plaintiff may proceed with the action and judgment may be given in the defendant's absence. A writ also contains certain indorsements — indorsement of claim and formal indorsement. The indorsement may be a special indorsement (of claim) or a general indorsement (of claim). A special indorsement is a statement of claim appearing on the writ, which statement serves as the statement of claim in the action.[27] Where a writ is so indorsed, it is unnecessary to serve another statement of claim unless an amendment is desired. When a writ is so indorsed, it is said to be specially

25 Ord. 13, r. 35.
26 *Ibid.* Ord. 13, r. 15.
27 *Ibid.* Ord. 3, r. 4.

indorsed. One advantage of the indorsement is that it saves time. Under Order 10 of the High Court (Civil Procedure) Rules[28] of Lagos State, once the defendant has entered an appearance, the plaintiff may apply to the court for summary judgment. A writ not specially indorsed but accompanied with a statement of claim serves the same purpose as a specially indorsed writ.

A general indorsement states in a summary form the nature of the claim made, or the nature of the remedy requested. In this case, the plaintiff has to serve not only the writ but also the statement of claim which contains the details of the claim.

Formal indorsements

A writ whether specially indorsed or not must contain formal indorsements. For example, if the action is for a debt or liquidated demand (a specific sum of money already ascertained) only, the writ must be indorsed with a statement of the amount of money claimed as debt or demand and the amount of costs demanded; it must also state that the defendant can pay the amount claimed including costs. Other formal indorsements include, in the case of a plaintiff suing in person, the plaintiff's address for service (an address within the jurisdiction of the High Court)[29] and in the case of a person suing by a legal practitioner the name and address of the legal practitioner which address must be the address for service within the jurisdiction of the High Court. Another formal indorsement relates to cases in which the plaintiff sues or the defendant is sued in a representative capacity. In such cases, the writ must be indorsed to indicate the capacity.[30]

(b) Originating summons

An originating summons is a summons other than a summons in a pending cause or matter.[31] It is a summons (a writ of summons) which originates an action.

It is expressly provided in the High Court rules that any person who claims to be interested under a deed, will or other written instrument may apply by originating summons for the determination of any question of construction arising under the instrument, and for a declaration of the rights of the persons interested.[32] Similarly, where a person claims any legal or equitable right and the determination of the question whether he is entitled to the right depends upon a con-

---

[28] Lagos Laws 1973, Cap. 52.
[29] *Ibid.* Ord. 3, rr. 9 and 10.
[30] *Ibid.* Ord. 3, r. 2.
[31] *Ibid.* Ord. 1, r. 2(2).
[32] See *e.g.* High Court (Civil Procedure) Rules (Lagos Laws 1973, Cap. 52), Ord. 44, r. 1.

struction of an enactment, he may apply by originating summons for the determination of the question of construction and for a declaration as to the right which he claims.[33] But where a case concerning the construction of a document or statute is commenced by originating summons the court or judge in chambers is not bound to determine the question of construction if the court or judge in chambers is of opinion that an originating summons procedure is not appropriate for the purpose of determining the question.[34] Interpleader proceedings are commenced by originating summons where the applicant is not a defendant in a pending action on the subject matter of the proceedings.[35]

Proceedings in the High Court of Lagos State must be commenced by writ unless otherwise expressly provided.[36]

An originating summons procedure is appropriate where the main or only point in dispute is the construction of a statute or other enactment or the construction of a document or where the main or only point in dispute is some other question of law. It is not appropriate where a substantial dispute of fact is likely to arise.[37] An originating summons dispenses with the need for pleadings.

(c) Originating notice of motion

An originating notice of motion is a notice of motion by which an action commences. In general, where leave to apply for an order of *mandamus*, prohibition or *certiorari* has been granted, the application must be made by notice of motion.[38]

(d) Petition

An action may be commenced by petition. For example, divorce proceedings are commenced by petition.

3. *Life of a Writ*

Normally, a writ of summons is valid for a period of twelve months from the date of issue.[39] But where the defendant has not been served it may be renewed from time to time for a period of six months on each occasion from the date of renewal if the court or judge in chambers is satisfied that a good reason has been given for failure to effect

---

[33] High Court (Civil Procedure) Rules (Lagos Laws 1973, Cap. 52), Ord. 44, r. 2.
[34] *Ibid.* Ord. 44, r. 5.
[35] *Ibid.*
[36] High Court (Civil Procedure) Rules, Ord. 2, r. 1.
[37] *Odgers on Pleading and Practice* (21st ed., by D. B. Casson and I. H. Dennis, 1975), p. 314.
[38] See Ords. 40 and 53 of the High Court (Civil Procedure) Rules of Lagos State.
[39] High Court (Civil Procedure) Rules (Lagos Laws 1973, Cap. 52), Ord. 5, r. 5.

service. Every renewal must take place during the currency of the writ or the renewed writ. In other words, the first renewal must be effected within 12 months from the date of issue of the writ. Any subsequent renewal must be effected within six months from the date of the latest renewal.

4. *Service of Writ and other Originating Processes*

As a general rule, under the rules of court in force in Lagos State, a writ of summons, an originating notice of motion and a petition by which an action is commenced are to be served personally by delivering to the person to be served a copy of the document duly certified by the Registrar.[40] But service of a writ of summons is not required where the defendant by his legal practitioner undertakes to accept service, and enters an appearance.[41] Where prompt personal service is impossible, the party seeking to effect service may apply to the court or a judge in chambers for an order for substituted service which may take the form of advertisement or other just means, the application being supported by an affidavit stating the grounds on which the application is based.[42]

5. *Appearance*

A defendant may enter an appearance to a writ by sending by post to the Registrar a memorandum of appearance together with a copy of the memorandum. Where the defendant appears in person the memorandum must be signed by him and must contain an address for service, which address must be within the jurisdiction of the High Court.[43] The following special cases should be noted:

(a) Where the defendant is a firm, the appearance is to be entered by the individual partners by name with the description "Partner in the firm of . . . "

(b) Where the defendant is an individual trading in the name other than his own, the appearance is to be entered by him in his own name with the addition of the description "Trading as . . ."

(c) Where the defendant is a limited liability company, the appearance is to be entered by a legal practitioner.

(d) Where the appearance is being entered by leave of the Court, a

---

[40] *Ibid.* Ord. 6, r. 2.
[41] *Ibid.* Ord. 6, r. 3.
[42] *Ibid.* Ord. 6, r. 6.
[43] *Ibid.* Ord. 8, rr. 1 and 2.

copy of the order granting leave is to accompany the Form of Entry of Appearance.

(e) Where the defendant has no defence or admits the plaintiff's claim the entry of appearance delays judgment and may increase the costs payable by the defendant.[44]

Although a defendant is commanded by a writ to cause an appearance to be entered within eight days after the service of the writ,[45] a defendant may appear at any time before judgment but if his appearance occurs after the expiration of the period specified by the writ for appearance (that is after the expiration of a period of eight days after the service of the writ), he is not entitled to any further time for delivering his defence or for any purpose than if he had appeared in accordance with the writ, unless the court or a judge in chambers otherwise orders.[46]

Default of appearance

As a general rule, where a defendant fails to appear to a writ of summons within the period specified by the writ for appearance, the plaintiff may enter judgment in default of appearance (default judgment). One of the exceptions to this rule relates to infants and persons of unsound mind. Where the defendant is an infant or a person of unsound mind not adjudged a lunatic and no appearance has been entered to the writ, the plaintiff must, before proceeding further with the action, apply to the court or a judge in chambers for an order for the appointment of a proper person as guardian *ad litem*.

A default judgment may be final or interlocutory and the type obtainable by the plaintiff depends on the indorsement on the writ. Where the indorsement on the writ is a claim for a liquidated demand, the judgment entered is a final judgment for any sum of money not exceeding the sum indorsed on the writ together with interest and costs, but notwithstanding the fact that the indorsement is a claim for a liquidated demand, where the action is by a moneylender or an assignee for the recovery of money lent by a moneylender or the enforcement of any agreement or security relating to any such money, leave of the court or of a judge in chambers is required before judgment is entered in default of appearance.[47] As a final judgment, the judgment is final with respect to the liability of the defendant to pay damages as well as with respect to the quantum of damages. In the case of an action for the

---

[44] See High Court (Civil Procedure) Rules (Lagos Laws 1973, Cap. 52), Appendix A, Form No. 11, Notes 1-5.
[45] High Court (Civil Procedure) Rules (Lagos Laws 1973, Cap. 52), Appendix A, Form No. 1.
[46] *Ibid.* Ord. 8, r. 5.
[47] *Ibid.* Ord. 9, r. 3.

recovery of land, where the defendant fails to enter an appearance, a final judgment may be entered by the plaintiff.[48]

Where the writ is indorsed with a claim for unliquidated damages, the plaintiff cannot enter final judgment immediately on default of appearance for the damages have to be assessed. But in specified cases, he is entitled to an interlocutory judgment. For example, where the indorsement on the writ is for a claim for pecuniary damages only, or for detention of goods with or without a claim for pecuniary damages, and the defendant fails to enter an appearance, the plaintiff may enter interlocutory judgment and the damages, or the value of the goods, are to be assessed on the application of either party to the judge in chambers; but where a writ so indorsed is further indorsed for a liquidated demand and the defendant fails to enter an appearance, the plaintiff may enter final judgment for the debt or liquidated demand, interest and costs against the defendant and interlocutory judgment for the value of the goods and damages or damages only, as the case may be.[49] Where a writ is indorsed with a claim for specific performance of a contract in writing for sale or purchase of property with or without alternative claims for damages, the plaintiff may make an affidavit stating that in his belief there is no defence to the action. He may then make an application, supported by the affidavit, to a judge in chambers for an order for specific performance of the contract. The application in made by summons (ordinary summons, an interlocutory step in an action commenced by writ, a summons in a pending cause or matter).[50] The application must be served on the defendant.[51] The defendant may file an affidavit opposing the application,[52] and he may be given leave to defend the action.[53]

Where a writ is indorsed with a claim for an account or where the indorsement on a writ involves taking an account, if the defendant either fails to appear or does not after appearance satisfy the court or a judge in chambers that there is some preliminary question to be tried, the court must make an order for the proper accounts, with all necessary inquiries and directions.[54] An application for the order must be made by summons supported by an affidavit stating concisely the grounds of his claim to an account.[55]

---

[48] *Ibid.* Ord. 9, r. 8.
[49] *Ibid.* Ord. 9, r. 7.
[50] *Ibid.* Ord. 11, r. 11.
[51] *Ibid.* Ord. 11, r. 2.
[52] *Ibid.* Ord. 11, r. 3(1).
[53] *Ibid.* Ord. 11, r. 4.
[54] *Ibid.* Ord. 12, r. 1.
[55] *Ibid.* Ord. 12, r. 2.

Default of appearance to an originating summons

Rule 13 of Order 9 of the High Court (Civil Procedure) Rules[56] of Lagos State deals with cases in which the process by which the action commences is an originating summons. It provides that where a defendant or respondent to an originating summons to which appearance is required to be entered fails to appear within the time specified for appearance by the originating summons, the plaintiff or applicant may apply to the Court or to a judge in chambers for an appointment for the hearing of the summons. Appearance to an originating summons is normally required.[57] But under rule 8 of Order 42 of the High Court (Civil Procedure) Rules of Lagos State, such appearance is not required in certain circumstances including cases where the summons is (a) for a legal practitioner to deliver papers or a cash account or securities, or to pay money and (b) a summons under the Arbitration Law.[58]

6. *Payment into Court and Discontinuance*

In many cases, the next stage in the proceedings immediately after the defendant has entered an appearance to a writ is the stage of filing pleadings. But sometimes the position is different. For example, the defendant may pay money into court in satisfaction of the claim[59] or the plaintiff may discontinue the action.[60]

(a) Payment into court

In an action for debt or damages, the defendant may at any time after entering appearance pay into court a sum of money in satisfaction of the plaintiff's claim. He must give notice of the payment to the plaintiff.[61] The plaintiff must acknowledge the receipt of the notice within three days of receiving the notice. He may within 14 days of receiving the notice of payment accept the sum of money in satisfaction of the claim. He may then take the money from the court.[62] But where the plaintiff has been allowed to sue as a poor person, payment is not to be made except in accordance with the directions of the court or a judge in chambers.[63] When the payment is made to the plaintiff proceedings in the cause of action with respect to which it is made are stayed. The defendant may pay money into court in satis-

---

[56] Lagos Laws 1973, Cap. 52.
[57] *Ibid.* Ord. 42, r. 5.
[58] Lagos Laws 1973, Cap. 10.
[59] High Court (Civil Procedure) Rules (Lagos Laws 1973, Cap. 52), Ord. 19, r. 1.
[60] *Ibid.* Ord. 23, r. 1.
[61] *Ibid.* Ord. 19, r. 1.
[62] *Ibid.* Ord. 19, r. 2(2).
[63] *Ibid.* Ord. 19, r. 2(2), Proviso.

faction of one or more causes of action where several causes of action are joined in one action.[64]

(b) Discontinuance

The plaintiff may (presumably, without leave of court or of a judge in chambers) discontinue his action at any time before receiving the defendant's defence, or after receiving the defence but before taking any other proceeding in the action (except an interlocutory application).[65] In order to discontinue the action, the plaintiff has to serve a written notice to that effect on the defendant.[66] Where the defendant's defence has been served on the plaintiff and a further proceeding other than an interlocutory application has been taken by the plaintiff, leave of the court or of a judge in chambers is required if the plaintiff wishes to discontinue the action without the written consent of the defendant.[67] Similarly, the defendant may after filing his defence make an application to the court or to a judge in chambers for an order that his defence be withdrawn.[68] If the application is granted, the plaintiff may enter judgment in default of defence.

A cause ready for trial may be withdrawn by either the plaintiff or the defendant where a consent in writing signed by both parties is produced to the Registrar.[69] Where an action has been discontinued and a subsequent action in respect of the same, or substantially the same cause of action is brought before payment of the costs of the discontinued action, the court or a judge in chambers may order a stay of the subsequent action until the payment of the costs.[70]

7. Pleadings

Pleadings are written statements served by a party on his opponent and containing the allegations of fact on which the party relies. They enable the parties to determine areas on which they are agreed and areas on which there is a controversy between them. Certain facts stated by a party may be admitted by his opponent; in that case the facts need not be proved. Thus, pleadings enable each party to know what facts he had to prove at the trial and surprise, which might follow from one party raising at the trial facts that his opponent did not anticipate, is avoided. In short, the principal advantage of plead-

---

[64] *Ibid.* Ord. 19, r. 1(1).
[65] *Ibid.* Ord. 23, r. 1.
[66] *Ibid.*
[67] *Ibid.*
[68] *Ibid.*
[69] High Court (Civil Procedure) Rules (Lagos Laws 1973, Cap. 52), Ord. 23, r. 2.
[70] *Ibid.* Ord. 23, r. 4.

ings is that they enable the parties to determine the precise issues in controversy between them. Rule 4 of Order 16 of the High Court (Civil Procedure) Rules[71] of Lagos State provides as follows:

> "Every pleading shall contain and contain only, a statement in a summary form of the material facts on which the party pleading relies for his claim or defence, as the case may be, but not the evidence by which they are to be proved ..."

According to this rule, a pleading must contain facts only.[72] But this does not mean that a point of law cannot be raised in a pleading. It only means that conclusions of law (for example, in an action in negligence, the statement "The defendant owes me a duty of care,") are not to be stated in a pleading. Indeed, rule 2 of Order 22 of the High Court (Civil Procedure) Rules of Lagos State provides that any party is entitled to raise by his pleading any point of law. Thus, the statement "The facts alleged in the statement of claim (the plaintiff's pleading) do not disclose a cause of action" is a point of law and can be raised in a pleading.

All the material facts intended to be relied upon by the party pleading must be raised in the pleading. Facts necessary to establish a cause of action or to establish a defence to a cause of action are material facts. In order to avoid surprise a party is not permitted to raise at the trial any matter which he did not state in his pleading. Immaterial facts are not to be contained in the pleading. Facts merely constituting evidence by which the material facts are to be proved are not to be contained in the pleading. They are to be raised at the trial. The material facts are to be stated briefly.

The main types of pleadings are as follows:

Statement of Claim
Statement of Defence
Reply

A statement of claim is a pleading filed by the plaintiff as the first pleading in an action. The pleading filed in defence by the defendant is the statement of defence. A reply is a pleading filed by the plaintiff in reply to the statement of defence.

The statement of defence may contain a special claim known as set-off. A set-off is essentially a defence. It is a claim whereby a defendant in an action in which the plaintiff claims a sum of money contends that a sum of money is due to him from the plaintiff. The amount claimed by the defendant may thus be set off against the plaintiff's claim. At common law, a set-off could not be pleaded unless: (a) both claims were due between the same parties and in the

---

[71] Lagos Laws 1973, Cap. 52.
[72] See *North Western Salt Co. Ltd.* v. *Electrolytic Alkali Co. Ltd.* [1914] A.C. 461.

same capacity[73]; and (b) both claims were liquidated. Equity intervened; consequently, any claim which a debtor could have raised as a set-off against his creditor, had the common law prohibition never existed, may now be pleaded as a set-off against an assignee of the debt where the set-off arose before the debtor received notice of the assignment. Even where the set-off did not arise before then it could be raised against the assignee if it arose out of the same transaction as the plaintiff's claim.[74] Also in equity a set-off may be pleaded against unliquidated claims.[75]

As a general rule, the amount of money to be set off must have been due before the issue of the writ,[76] but if the amount is due after the issue of the writ but before the defence is delivered, it may be set off if pleaded specifically as a set-off. If the plaintiff's claim is discontinued, the set-off, too, is automatically discontinued; for a set-off is a defence and it exists only if the plaintiff's claim exists. But under rule 16 of Order 18 of the High Court (Civil Procedure) Rules[77] of Lagos State, where a sum of money established as a set-off or counter-claim, against the plaintiff's claim in an action exceeds the plaintiff's claim, the court or judge in chambers may give judgment for the defendant for the balance. Thus, no distinction between a set-off and a counterclaim is made by the rule.

A counterclaim, like a set-off, is filed as part of the defence. It is a cross-action in fact and not a defence. It need not be related to the plaintiff's claim. A counterclaim may be for liquidated or unliqidated damages. If it exceeds the plaintiff's claim judgment may be given to the defendant in respect of the balance.[78] If the plaintiff's action is stayed, discontinued or dismissed, the counterclaim may nevertheless be proceeded with.[79] A party pleading a counterclaim must state specifically that he is doing so.[80]

Plea or defence in abatement

A plea in abatement was a plea contending that an action must abate by reason of a mistake in the statement of claim. Such mistake may be non-joinder of a necessary party or misnomer of a defendant. The plaintiff in such action was non-suited. In 1875, such pleas were abolished in England. Rule 19 of Order 18 of the High Court (Civil Procedure) Rules[81] of Lagos State provides that no plea or defence is to be pleaded in abatement.

[73] See *Reeves* v. *Pope* [1914] 2 K.B. 284.
[74] *Young* v. *Kitchen* (1878) 3 Ex.D. 127.
[75] *Hanak* v. *Green* [1958] 2 Q.B. 9.
[76] *Richard* v. *James* (1848) 2 Exch. 471.
[77] Lagos Laws 1973, Cap. 52.
[78] *Ibid.* Ord. 18, r. 16.
[79] *Ibid.* Ord. 18, r. 15.
[80] *Ibid.* Ord. 18, r. 9.   [81] Lagos Laws 1973, Cap. 52.

8. *Discovery and Inspection*

After the exchange of pleadings, the legal practitioner may require those documents in the possession of his client's opponent that are relevant to the case. The first step taken on this matter is to find out which such documents exist. The procedure whereby a party delivers to the opposite party a list of the documents relevant to the case which documents are or have been in his possession, custody or power is known as discovery of documents.[82] After knowing what documents are in his opponent's possession, a party may seek to inspect such documents by a procedure known as inspection of documents.

9. *Interrogatories*

Interrogatories are questions served by a party to his opponent for the purpose of discovering facts. An application for leave to deliver interrogatories is made to the court or a judge in chambers. The application is to be granted with respect to only those interrogatories that are necessary either for disposing fairly of the case or for saving costs.[83] Interrogatories which do not relate to the matters in question in the case are not allowed.[84] Interrogatories are to be answered by affidavit.[85]

10. *Summons for Directions*

A plaintiff may take out within seven days from the time the pleadings are deemed to be closed a summons under rule 1 of Order 26 of the High Court (Civil Procedure) Rules of Lagos State for the purpose of giving the court or a judge in chambers the chance of considering the preparations for the trial of the action. The court or judge in chambers may thus deal as far as possible with interlocutory applications and he may give such directions with respect to the course of the action as seems best adapted to secure the just, expeditious and economical disposal of the action.[86] This summons is known as summons for directions. Under the High Court (Civil Procedure) Rules of Lagos State as a general rule, the summons for directions must be taken by the plaintiff in an action commenced by writ of summons. The exceptions to the general rule are as follows:

[82] See Ord. 27, r. 12 of the High Court (Civil Procedure) Rules of Lagos State.
[83] High Court (Civil Procedure) Rules (Lagos Laws 1973, Cap. 52), Ord. 27, r. 2.
[84] *Ibid.* Ord. 27, r. 1, Proviso.
[85] *Ibid.* Ord. 27, r. 6.
[86] *Ibid.* Ord. 26, r. 1.

(a) actions in which the plaintiff has applied for judgment in default of appearance under Order 9 or for judgment on a writ specially indorsed with a statement of claim or accompanied by a statement of claim under Order 10 and directions have been given with respect to the application;

(b) actions in which an order for accounts has been made under Order 12;

(c) actions in which an order has been made for the trial of an issue or question before determining a right to discovery or inspection;

(d) actions which have been dealt with under rule 7 of Order 30 (which rule relates to questions of fact without formal pleadings where the parties are agreed as to the questions of fact to be decided between them);

(e) action in which directions have been given on applications for orders of mandamus, for an injunction, for orders for the preservation or inspection of property or for any of the other similar purposes.[87]

Where the plaintiff fails to take out a summons for directions in any of those cases, the defendant may do so or apply for an order to dismiss the action.

11. *Proceedings at the Trial*

Absence of parties

Where a cause on the Weekly Cause List[88] is called and neither of the parties appears the cause must be struck out by the court unless it sees good reason to the contrary. If the plaintiff appears and the defendant does not appear, the plaintiff may prove his claim so far as the burden lies upon him.[89] Where the defendant appears and the plaintiff does not appear, the defendant is entitled to judgment dismissing the action if he has no counterclaim but if he has a counterclaim he may prove the counterclaim so far as the burden of proof lies upon him.[90] Any judgment obtained where one party does not appear at the trial may be set aside by the court on the application of the party absent, on such terms as may seem fit.[91]

---

[87] *Ibid.* Ord. 26, r. 1(2).

[88] The List which is to be posted up on one or more notice boards every Friday must set out the arrangements of fixtures before each of the Judges sitting in court during the following week. See High Court (Civil Procedure) Rules of Lagos State, Ord. 31, r. 3(1).

[89] High Court (Civil Procedure) Rules (Lagos Laws 1973, Cap. 52), Ord. 32, r. 2.

[90] *Ibid.* Ord. 32, r. 3.

[91] *Ibid.* Ord. 32, r. 4.

Order of proceedings at the trial

Where pleadings have been filed, the party on whom the burden of proof lies in respect of the material issues or questions between the parties must begin by stating his case. Then he must produce his evidence and examine his witnesses.[92] When he has concluded his evidence he must ask the other party if he intends to call evidence. If the other party does not intend to call evidence, the party who began is entitled to sum up the evidence already given and comment on it.[93] Then the other party states his case. The case on both sides is then considered closed.[94] But if the other party states that he intends to call evidence when the party beginning has concluded his case, the other party is entitled to state his case, to call evidence, to sum up and comment on the evidence.[95] Then the party beginning may reply generally on the whole case. The case on both sides is then considered closed. Alternatively, the party beginning instead of replying generally at this stage may by leave of the court call fresh evidence in reply to the evidence called by the other party on points material to the determination of any of the issues but not on collateral matters.[96] Then the other party is entitled to address the court.[97] After the address, the party beginning is entitled to reply generally on the whole case[98] and that reply closes the case on both sides. The court then gives judgment and makes an order as to costs.

12. *Third Party Procedure*

The defendant in an action may apply to the court or judge in chambers for leave to issue and serve on a third party a notice known as a "third party notice" where he claims as against that party as follows:

"(a) that he is entitled to contribution or indemnity, or

(b) that he is entitled to any relief or remedy relating to or connected with the original subject matter of the action and substantially the same as some relief or remedy claimed by the plaintiff, or

(c) that any question or issue relating to or connected with the said subject matter is substantially the same as some question or issue arising between the plaintiff and the defendant and should properly be determined not only as between the plaintiff and the

---

[92] *Ibid.* Ord. 32, r. 12.
[93] *Ibid.* Ord. 32, r. 13.
[94] See Ord. 32, rr. 15 and 16 of the High Court (Civil Procedure) Rules of Lagos State.
[95] High Court (Civil Procedure) Rules (Lagos Laws 1973, Cap. 52), Ord. 32, r. 14.
[96] *Ibid.* Ord. 32, r. 17.
[97] *Ibid.* Ord. 32, r. 18.
[98] *Ibid.*

defendant but as between the plaintiff and the defendant and the third party or between any or either of them."[99]

With effect from the time of the service upon him of the notice, the third party becomes a party to the action with the same rights in respect of his defence as if he had been duly sued in the normal way by the defendant.[1]

13. *Interpleader Proceedings*

A person in possession of money and chattels which he does not himself claim personally and with respect to which there are rival claimants may be liable in tort if he delivers the money or chattels to the wrong person. This may arise, for example, in the case of a banker who holds money in respect of which there are rival claimants or in the case of a stakeholder holding lottery or football pools winnings with respect to which there are rival claimants.

If the person in possession of the property is not a sheriff or other person lawfully executing a process, he may obtain a relief by way of interpleader under Order 45 of the High Court (Civil Procedure) Rules of Lagos State. Such relief is usually referred to as a stakeholder's interpleader. If he is a sheriff he may obtain interpleader relief usually known as sheriff's interpleader under the Sheriff and Civil Process Law[2] and the Judgment (Enforcement) Rules.[3]

Stakeholder's interpleader

Where a person who is under a liability in respect of any debt, money, goods or chattels is or expects to be sued by two or more rival claimants in respect of any of those items, he may apply for relief known as relief by way of interpleader.[4]

He may apply by taking out a summons (ordinary summons if he is already sued on the matter, originating summons if no action against him on the matter is pending) calling on the claimants to appear and state the nature and particulars of their claims and either to maintain the claims or relinquish them.[5] The interpleader proceedings commence with the issue of the summons. The applicant must satisfy the court or a judge in chambers by affidavit or by other means that:

(a) he claims no interest in the subject matter in dispute other than charges and costs;

---

[99] High Court (Civil Procedure) Rules (Lagos Laws 1973, Cap. 52), Ord. 13, r. 23.
[1] *Ibid.* Ord. 13, r. 24.
[2] Lagos Laws 1973, Cap. 127.
[3] *Ibid.*
[4] High Court (Civil Procedure) Rules (Lagos Laws 1973, Cap. 52), Ord. 45, r. 1.
[5] *Ibid.* Ord. 45, r. 5.

(b) he does not collude with any of the claimants; and

(c) he is willing to pay or transfer the subject matter into court or to dispose of it as the court or judge in chambers may direct.[6]

If the applicant is a defendant in an action the application for relief may be made at any time after the service of the writ of summons[7] and the court or judge in chambers may stay all further proceedings in the action.[8] If the claimants appear, the court or a judge in chambers may make either: (a) an order that any claimant be made a defendant in an action already commenced in respect of the subject matter in dispute in substitution for or in addition to the applicant; or (b) an order that an issue between the claimants be stated and tried, together with a direction as to which of the claimants is to be defendant.[9]

Sheriff's Interpleader

In Lagos State where a sheriff in the course of executing a judgment under a writ of attachment and sale seizes goods and a third party claims that the goods belong to him and not to the judgment debtor, the sheriff may apply by summons for interpleader relief under the Sheriffs and Civil Process Law[10] of the State and the Judgment (Enforcement) Rules[11] of the State. Before applying for interpleader, he is to serve a notice of the claim on the judgment creditor. If the creditor does not dispute the claim, the sheriff must withdraw from possession and so he need not apply for the relief.[12] But if the creditor disputes the claim, the sheriff is to take out a summons for interpleader relief.[13] The proceedings are similar to interpleader proceedings under Order 45 of the High Court (Civil Procedure) Rules[14] of Lagos State.

14. *Enforcement of Judgments*

A party in whose favour a money judgment is given is known as the judgment creditor and his opponent, the party against whom the judgment is given, is the judgment debtor. The judgment extinguishes the rights of the judgment creditor in respect of the judgment debt. The judgment creditor may enforce the judgment under the Sheriffs

---

[6] *Ibid.* Ord. 45, r. 2.
[7] *Ibid.* Ord. 45, r. 4.
[8] *Ibid.* Ord. 45, r. 6.
[9] *Ibid.* Ord. 45, r. 7.
[10] Lagos Laws 1973, Cap. 127, s. 27.
[11] Lagos Laws 1973, Cap. 127.
[12] *Ibid.* Ord. 6, r. 3.
[13] *Ibid.* Ord. 6, r. 4(1).
[14] Lagos Laws 1973, Cap. 52.

and Civil Process Law[15] and the Judgments (Enforcement) Rules[16] by any of the following methods:

(a) a writ of attachment and sale of property;
(b) garnishee proceedings;
(c) a writ of sequestration;
(d) a writ of possession;
(e) a writ of delivery.[17]

A writ of attachment and sale of property gives the sheriff authority to seize and sell the property of the judgment debtor for the purpose of obtaining money sufficient to satisfy the debt together with the costs of the execution.[18] There are two types of writ of attachment and sale of property. One relates to goods and chattels (movable property) and the other relates to immovable property.[19] In the first instance, a writ of attachment and sale of goods and chattels of the judgment debtor found within the State is issued. Where sufficient movable property of the judgment debtor can be found in the State to satisfy the judgment and costs and the costs of execution, no writ of attachment and sale of immovable property is to issue. But if no movable property of the judgment debtor can with reasonable diligence be found in the State or if such movable property is insufficient to satisfy the judgment and costs and the costs of execution, application may be made to the court by the judgment creditor for a writ of attachment and sale of the judgment debtor's immovable property.[20]

Where a writ is for attachment and sale of goods of a judgment debtor the sheriff or any bailiff executing the writ may attach and sell:

(a) any movable property to which the judgment debtor is entitled but which is not in his possession or subject to a lien or right of some other person to the immediate possession of the property; and
(b) any shares in any public company or corporation to which the judgment debtor is entitled.[21]

The attachment of such movable property or shares is effected under an order of court by delivering an office copy of the order to any person bound by it. The order prohibits:

"(a) the person in possession of, or entitled to a lien or right of

---

[15] *Ibid.* Cap. 127.
[16] *Ibid.*
[17] The list is not exhaustive.
[18] Sheriffs and Civil Process Law (Lagos Laws 1973, Cap. 127), ss. 13, 37, 38 and 39; Judgments (Enforcement) Rules (Lagos Laws 1973, Cap. 127), Ord. 5, r. 1.
[19] *Ibid.*
[20] Sheriffs and Civil Process Law (Lagos Laws 1973, Cap. 127).
[21] Judgments (Enforcement) Rules (Lagos Laws 1973, Cap. 127), Ord. 5, r. 1.

immediate possession over, the property from giving over the property to the judgment debtor, or
(b) the person in whose name the shares may be standing from making any transfer, or receiving payment of any dividends thereof, and the manager, secretary or other proper officer of the corporation from permitting any such payment until further order of the court."[22]

Where a writ is for attachment and sale of immovable property, the sheriff or any bailiff executing the writ may attach and sell any of the immovable property of the judgment debtor.[23] The attachment of the property is effected by delivering to the judgment debtor or leaving at the place where the attachment takes place a notice of attachment in a prescribed form and unless the court otherwise orders by posting in a conspicuous place on the land a prescribed notice prohibiting all persons from receiving the property by purchase, a gift or otherwise; in addition, the sheriff may take and retain actual possession of the land by putting into possession of it a fit person approved by him (the sheriff).[24]

Garnishee proceedings are taken in order that the benefit of a debt owed by a third party to the judgment debtor may be assigned to the judgment creditor.[25]

A writ of sequestration commands and empowers two or more commissioners to be appointed by the court for the purpose to enter upon all the immovable property of the judgment debtor, to collect the rents and profits of the immovable property and also to take possession of all the goods and movable property of the judgment debtor, until the debtor clears his contempt (consisting in his refusal or neglect to comply with the judgment) or the court makes an order to the contrary.[26]

Where a judgment is given or an order is made for the recovery of land or for the delivery of possession of land, in an action other than one between landlord and tenant under the Recovery of Premises Law[27] the judgment or order is enforceable by a writ of possession in a prescribed form addressed to the sheriff.[28] It is provided in rule 6 of Order 11 of the Judgment (Enforcement) Rules of Lagos State that where in an action for recovery of land judgment is given for the recovery of the land (with or without rent or mesne profits) and costs, there may be either one writ or warrant or separate writs or warrants

---

22 *Ibid.* Ord. 5, r. 2.
23 *Ibid.* Ord. 5, r. 1.
24 *Ibid.* Ord. 5, rr. 3 and 4.
25 See Judgment (Enforcement) Rules (Lagos Laws 1973, Cap. 127), Ord. 8.
26 Judgment (Enforcement) Rules (Lagos Laws 1973, Cap. 127), Ord. 11, r. 9.
27 Lagos Laws 1973, Cap. 118.
28 Judgments (Enforcement) Rules (Lagos Laws 1973, Cap. 127), Ord. 11, r. 5.

for possession of the land and for rent and mesne profits and for costs, and after the execution of the writ the sheriff must file a certificate in a prescribed form.

A judgment for the delivery of goods is enforceable by writ of delivery. The judgment creditor is either by the writ or by a separate writ of execution entitled to execution against the judgment debtor's property for any sum of money and costs awarded.[29]

It should also be mentioned that the court may make an order for the commitment of a judgment debtor to prison in accordance with the provisions of the Sheriffs and Civil Process Law[30] for refusal or neglect on the part of the judgment debtor to comply with the judgment.[31]

[29] *Ibid.* Ord. 11, r. 4.
[30] Lagos Laws 1973, Cap. 127.
[31] See Sheriffs and Civil Process Law (Lagos Laws 1973, Cap. 127), ss. 55 and 56; Judgments (Enforcement) Rules (Lagos Laws 1973, Cap. 127), Ord. 10.

CHAPTER 12

AN OUTLINE OF CRIMINAL PROCEDURE

A. Introduction

THE main sources of the law of criminal procedure are the Criminal Procedure Ordinance[1] (in force in Ogun, Ondo and Oyo States), the Criminal Procedure Act[2] (in force throughout the country as Federal law with respect to Federal matters and in force in Bendel State as State Law[3]), the Criminal Procedure Law of Eastern Nigeria[4] in force in Anambra, Cross River, Imo and Rivers States, the Criminal Procedure Law of Lagos State,[5] and the Criminal Procedure Code[6] in force in Bauchi, Benue, Borno, Gongola, Kaduna, Kano, Kwara, Niger, Plateau and Sokoto States.

B. Classification of Offences

Offences may be classified in two ways as follows:
  (a) indictable and non-indictable offences;
  (b) felonies, misdemeanours and simple offences.
Both types of classification are important for the purpose of the law of criminal procedure in the southern States. Neither type of classification exists in the law of criminal procedure in the northern States.
  An indictable offence is an offence:

  "(a) which on conviction may be punished by a term of imprisonment exceeding two years, or
  (b) which on conviction may be punished by imposition of a fine exceeding four hundred naira;
  not being an offence declared by the law creating it to be punishable on summary conviction."[7]

An offence other than an indictable offence is a non-indictable offence.
  The importance of the division of offences into indictable and non-indictable offences lies in the method of trial and in the power of arrest for an offence.
  Indictable offences are triable on information but they may be

[1] Nigeria Laws 1948, Cap. 43.
[2] Fed. and Lagos Laws 1958, Cap. 43.
[3] See High Court Law 1964 (No. 9 of 1964) (M.W.N.), s. 12.
[4] E.N. Laws 1963, Cap. 31.
[5] Lagos Laws 1973, Cap. 32.
[6] N.N. Laws 1963, Cap. 30.
[7] Criminal Procedure Law (Lagos Laws 1973, Cap. 32), s. 2(1).

tried summarily in certain circumstances.[8] Non-indictable offences are triable summarily and normally not on information. The power to arrest a person without warrant for an offence depends in part on whether the offence is an indictable offence.[9]

A felony is any offence which is declared by law to be a felony, or is punishable, without proof of previous conviction, with death or with imprisonment for three years or more. A misdemeanour is any offence which is declared by law to be a misdemeanour, or is punishable by imprisonment for not less than six months, but less than three years. Any offence which is neither a felony nor a misdemeanour is a simple offence.[10] The classifications of offences into felonies, misdemeanours and simple offences is important first of all for the purpose of determining the power of arrest for the offence[11]; secondly for the purpose of determining criminal liability or punishment with respect to attempt to commit an offence, preparation to commit an offence, neglect to prevent the commission of an offence, conspiracy to commit an offence and being an accessory after the fact to an offence[12]; and thirdly for the purpose of determining the ambit of the power of the court to grant bail to an accused person with respect to an offence.[13]

C. COMMENCEMENT OF PROCEEDINGS

Criminal proceedings in the southern States may commence by:

(a) a complaint whether on oath or not to the court;

(b) information (filed in the High Court) of the Attorney-General of the State in the case of a State offence or of the Attorney-General of the Federation in the case of a federal offence in accordance with the provisions of section 72 of the Criminal Procedure Law[14] of Lagos State or its equivalent;

(c) information filed in the High Court after the accused has been summarily committed for perjury by a judge or magistrate under the appropriate Criminal Procedure enactment;

(d) information filed in the High Court after the accused has been committed for trial by a magistrate under the provisions of the Criminal Procedure enactments in force in Lagos, Ogun, Oyo, Ondo, Rivers and Bendel States;

(e) information filed in a High Court after the preparation of

---

[8] See *e.g.* Criminal Procedure Law (Lagos Laws 1973, Cap. 32), s. 304.

[9] See *e.g.* Criminal Procedure Law (Lagos Laws 1973, Cap. 32), ss. 10 and 12.

[10] Criminal Code (Lagos Laws 1973, Cap. 31), s. 3.

[11] See *e.g.* Criminal Procedure Law (Lagos Laws 1973, Cap. 32), s. 12.

[12] Criminal Code (Lagos Laws 1973, Cap. 31), ss. 508-521.

[13] See *e.g.* Criminal Procedure Law (Lagos Laws 1973, Cap. 32), s. 118.

[14] Lagos Laws 1973, Cap. 32.

proofs of evidence in Anambra, Imo and Cross Rivers States;
(f) information filed in a High Court by the direction or with the consent of a judge, except in Anambra and Imo States[15];
(g) bringing a person arrested without a warrant before the court upon a charge in accordance with the appropriate criminal procedure enactment, in the case of proceedings before a magistrate's court.[16]

Where a complaint has been made to a magistrate's court that a person has committed an offence, and an application has been made to the magistrate for the issue of either a summons commanding the person to appear before the court for the purpose of the complaint or a warrant for the arrest of the person, the magistrate may issue a summons or warrant to compel the appearance of that person before him.[17] The summons is directed to the person accused of having committed the offence. It must state concisely the substance of the complaint and require him to appear at a certain time and place being, normally, not less than 48 hours after the service of the summons before the court to answer to the complaint and to be further dealt with according to law.[18] In certain circumstances, notwithstanding the issue of a summons, the presence of the accused may be dispensed with. For example, under section 100 of the Criminal Procedure Law of Lagos State where a magistrate issues a summons in respect of an offence punishable by a fine not exceeding ₦100 or by imprisonment for a term not exceeding six months or by both such fine and imprisonment, the magistrate may, on the application of the accused if he sees reasons to do so dispense with the personal attendance of the accused provided that the accused pleads guilty in writing or appears by a legal practitioner and pleads guilty by the legal practitioner. Where such application is made by an accused with respect to an offence punishable by only a fine not exceeding ₦100, the magistrate must grant the application provided the accused himself pleads guilty in writing or appears and so pleads by a legal practitioner.

A warrant of arrest is not to be issued in consequence of a complaint unless the complaint is one made on oath by the complainant himself or by a material witness.[19]

An information filed in a High Court contains essentially a statement that a person is charged before the High Court with a specified

---

[15] See *e.g.* Criminal Procedure Law (Lagos Laws 1973, Cap. 32), ss. 77 and 340(2)(*b*); Criminal Procedure (Miscellaneous Provisions) Edict 1974 (No. 19 of 1974) (E.C.S.), s. 18.
[16] See *e.g.* Criminal Procedure Law (Lagos Laws 1973, Cap. 32), s. 78(*b*).
[17] See *e.g.* Criminal Procedure Law (Lagos Laws 1973, Cap. 32), ss. 78 and 79.
[18] See *e.g.* Criminal Procedure Law (Lagos Laws 1973, Cap. 32), ss. 83 and 85.
[19] Criminal Procedure Law (Lagos Laws 1973, Cap. 32), s. 23.

offence. An information begins with a number (the number of the information) followed by the following items in the order in which they are set forth:

    (a) the title of the case, *e.g.* "The *State* v. *John Aketoz*";
    (b) the name of the High Court preceded by the preposition "In" *e.g.* "In the High Court of Lagos State";
    (c) the name of the judicial Division, *e.g.* "The Ikeja Judicial Division";
    (d) the date of preparation of the information, *e.g.* "The 28th day of June, 1976";
    (e) a statement of information to the effect that the accused is charged with a specified offence before the court on a specified date, *e.g.* "At the sessions holden at Ikeja, Lagos State, on the 27th day of June, 1976, the court is informed by the Attorney-General on behalf of the State that John Aketoz is charged with the following offence:"

Under section 337 of the Criminal Procedure Law of Lagos State the commencement part of an information may be in the form just stated in (a) to (e) with such modifications as are necessary to adapt it to the circumstances of each case.

An information must contain a description of the offence charged or where there are more than one offence charged in the same information, a description of each offence in a separate paragraph called "a count." A count of an information must begin with a statement of the offence charged, called "the statement of offence," which statement must describe the offence briefly in ordinary language, avoiding as far as possible the use of technical terms, and without necessarily stating all the essential elements of the offence. If the offence is one created by a written law, the statement must contain a reference to that law. Particulars of the offence must be set out in ordinary language after the statement of offence. Where any written law prescribes limits to the particulars of an offence which are required to be given in an information particulars given need not exceed those limits. Where an information contains more than one count, the counts must be numbered consecutively.[20] The Third Schedule to the Criminal Procedure Law of Lagos State sets out forms of statements of offences and particulars of offences and section 338(2) of the Law provides that those forms or forms conforming to them as nearly as possible must be used in appropriate cases, the statement of offence and the particulars of offence being varied according to the circumstances of each case. Thus, immediately, after the commencement

---

[20] See *e.g.* Criminal Procedure Law (Lagos Laws 1973, Cap. 32), s. 338(1).

part of an information, the following form, may be used in an appropriate case:

Statement of Offence — First Count
Wounding with intent, contrary to section 332, subsection (1), of the Criminal Code.

Particulars of Offence

John Aketoz, on the 25th day of June, 1976, in the Ikeja Judicial Division of Lagos State, wounded Jack Ojapix with intent to maim, disfigure or disable, or to do some grievous harm.
—Statement of Offence — Second Count
Wounding, contrary to section 338, subsection (2), of the Criminal Code.

Particulars of Offence

John Aketoz, on the 25th day of June, 1976, in the Ikeja Judicial Division unlawfully wounded Jack Ojapix.[21]

As a general rule, every information must be signed by a law officer. But it may be signed by any other officer or person designated by the appropriate Commissioner for Justice where the Commissioner for reasons of public convenience thinks fit.[22] Moreover, under section 343 of the Criminal Procedure Law of Lagos State where a private person desires to prosecute an offence on information, the information must be signed by him and not by any other person. A registrar must receive an information from a private person and the private person is entitled to prosecute the offence stated in the information where:

(a) there is endorsed on the information a certificate by a law officer stating that he has seen the information and he declines to prosecute at the public instance the offence stated in the information; and

(b) the private person has entered into a recognisance in the sum of 100 naira together with one surety approved by the registrar in the like sum, to prosecute the information to conclusion at the times at which the accused is required to appear and to pay such costs as may be ordered by the court, or, in lieu of entering into such recognisance has deposited 100 naira in court to abide the same conditions.[23]

---

[21] See Criminal Procedure Law (Lagos Laws 1973, Cap. 32), Sched. 3, Form 6.
[22] See *e.g.* Criminal Procedure Law (Lagos Laws 1973, Cap. 32), s. 341.
[23] See Criminal Procedure Law (Lagos Laws 1973, Cap. 32), ss. 342 and 343.

D. Preliminary Inquiry into an Indictable Offence

There are provisions for a preliminary inquiry into an indictable offence in Lagos, Ogun, Ondo, Bendel and Rivers States.

A preliminary inquiry is not a trial at all. It is simply an inquiry aimed at determining whether there is sufficient evidence to justify a trial of the accused.

The inquiry is conducted by a magistrate. The proceedings open with the magistrate causing the substance of the complaint to be stated to the accused. The accused is not required to make any reply to the complaint and if he does, the reply must not be recorded by the magistrate. The next stage is the examination by the magistrate of witnesses for the prosecution. When any one of the witnesses is being examined, no other witness should be present unless the magistrate is of opinion that it is necessary or conducive to the ends of justice that any particular witness should be permitted or required to be present during the whole or any part of the examination of any other of the witnesses. The evidence of the witnesses must be given in the presence of the accused. The accused is entitled to cross-examine the witnesses and if he is not represented by a legal practitioner, he must be informed of his right to cross-examine the witnesses. The magistrate must take down in writing in the form of a deposition the evidence of every witness. The deposition must be read over to the witness in the presence and hearing of the accused. It must be signed normally by the witness and the magistrate and by the interpreter, if any. But if the witness refuses to sign or is incapable of signing, the deposition must be signed by the magistrate alone. After the signing of the deposition, the magistrate must as soon as practicable bind over the witness by a recognisance entered into before the magistrate to attend the trial to give evidence. Any witness who refuses, without reasonable excuse, to sign his deposition or to enter into a recognisance for the purpose of attending the trial to give evidence may be committed by the magistrate by warrant to prison or other place of safe custody. Such committal is to last, normally, until after the trial or until the witness signs the deposition before the magistrate or enters into such recognisance before the magistrate, as the case may be. But if the accused is later discharged the magistrate (in the case of refusal to sign) or any magistrate (in the case of refusal to enter into a recognisance) may order the release of the witness.[24]

If at the close of the evidence for the prosecution the magistrate is of opinion that a *prima facie* case has been established against the accused, immediately after the last witness for the prosecution has been bound over to attend the trial the magistrate must read the

[24] See Criminal Procedure Law (Lagos Laws 1973, Cap. 32), ss. 312 and 313.

charge or read the amended or substituted charge to the accused and explain the nature of it to him in ordinary language and inform him that he has the right to call witnesses, and, if he so desires, to give evidence on his own behalf.[25] After this, 'the magistrate must ask the accused whether he wishes to say anything in answer to the charge. He must tell the accused that he is not obliged to say anything unless he desires to do so but that whatever he says will be taken down in writing and may be given in evidence at his trial.[26] Before any statement is made by the accused in answer to the charge, the magistrate must clearly inform the accused and let him understand that he has nothing to hope from any promise of favour and nothing to fear from any threat which may have been held out to him to induce him to make any admission or confession of his guilt, but that whatever he then says may be given in evidence at his trial notwithstanding the promise or threat.[27] Anything that the accused then says in answer to the charge must be written down in full and must be read over to him. He must be permitted to explain or add to his statement. The statement must be signed by the magistrate. If the accused desires, he must be permitted to sign the statement. The statement must be sent to the trial court with the depositions. It may be given in evidence at the trial without further proof of it unless it is proved that the magistrate did not in fact sign it.

Whether the accused has made a statement or not immediately after informing the accused that anything he says may be given in evidence against him, the magistrate must ask the accused whether he desires to give evidence for himself and whether he desires to call witnesses. If the accused replies that he wishes to give evidence but not to call witnesses the magistrate must proceed at once to take the evidence of the accused. After the evidence, the magistrate must give a hearing to the legal practitioner, if any, appearing for the accused if the legal practitioner so desires. If the accused replies that he desires to give evidence for himself and to call witnesses or to call witnesses without giving evidence for himself, the magistrate must take either immediately or, if an address is to be made by a legal practitioner on behalf of the accused, after the address, the evidence of the accused, if he desires to give evidence himself, and of any witness called by him who knows anything relating to the facts and circumstances of the case or anything tending to prove the innocence of the accused. All statements which the accused makes must be taken down in writing and all the evidence given by him or by any of his witnesses must be taken down in writing in the form of a deposition. The deposition

---

[25] Criminal Procedure Law (Lagos Laws 1973, Cap. 32), s. 314(1).
[26] *Ibid.* s. 314(2).
[27] See Criminal Procedure Law (Lagos Laws 1973, Cap. 32), s. 314(3).

including evidence given by the accused on his own behalf, if any, must be read over to the witness, in the presence and hearing of the accused. It must be signed by the magistrate and, normally, by the interpreter, if any. It must also, normally, be signed by the witness but if he refuses to sign or is incapable of signing, the magistrate alone must sign. The magistrate must as soon as practicable afterwards bind over the witness by a recognisance to attend the trial to give evidence. Statements made by the accused and the depositions of the witnesses for the accused must be sent to the court of trial together with the depositions of the witnesses for the prosecution.[28]

The magistrate must take into consideration the statement made by the accused and any evidence given by him or his witnesses before deciding whether to commit the accused for trial.[29] Where there is a conflict between the evidence for the accused and the evidence against him, the magistrate must consider the evidence against the accused to be sufficient to put the accused on his trial if that evidence is such as, if uncontradicted, would raise a probable presumption of the guilt of the accused.[30]

If the magistrate considers the evidence against the accused insufficient to put him on his trial, the magistrate must immediately order that the accused be discharged with respect to the charge under inquiry but the discharge is not a bar to any subsequent charge in respect of the same facts.[31] If the magistrate considers the evidence sufficient to put the accused on his trial, he must commit him for trial before the High Court. In that case, the magistrate must until the trial, either admit the accused to bail or send him to prison for safe keeping.[32]

It is provided in section 332 of the Criminal Procedure Law of Lagos State that if it appears to the magistrate in the course of a preliminary inquiry that the court has jurisdiction to try the offence summarily and the offence is of such a nature that it can be suitably dealt with under the powers of the court with respect to criminal cases, the magistrate may, subject to the provisions of the law relating to summary trial hear and finally determine the case and either convict the accused or dismiss the charge. But in every such case the accused is entitled to have recalled for cross-examination all witnesses for the prosecution whom he had not cross-examined or fully cross-examined.[33]

---

[28] Criminal Procedure Law (Lagos Laws 1973, Cap. 32), s. 314.
[29] *Ibid.* s. 323.
[30] *Ibid.* s. 324.
[31] *Ibid.* s. 325.
[32] *Ibid.* s. 326.
[33] *Ibid.* s. 332. The Criminal Justice Edict 1977 (No. 8 of 1977) abolished preliminary inquiries in Oyo.

E. PREPARATION OF PROOFS OF EVIDENCE

In Anambra, Cross River and Imo States the procedure of preliminary inquiry into an indictable offence has been replaced by a procedure whereby proofs of evidence are prepared with a view to determining whether there is sufficient evidence to put the accused on trial.[34] The Criminal Justice (Miscellaneous Provisions) Edict 1973[35] of the South-Eastern State[36] which abolished the procedure of preliminary inquiry in the State and provides for the procedure of preparation of proofs of evidence does not contain detailed provisions on the new procedure. It amended section 340(2) of the Criminal Procedure Law[37] of Eastern Nigeria by providing that no information charging any person with an indictable offence should be preferred unless:

"(a) the information is supported by statements from witnesses for the prosecution verified on oath before a Magistrate; or
(b) the information is preferred by the direction or with the consent of a Judge or pursuant to an order made under Part XXXI to prosecute the person charged for perjury ... "

The law is in force in Cross River State by virtue of section 5(1) of the States (Creation and Transitional Provisions) Decree 1976.

On the other hand, the Criminal Procedure (Miscellaneous Provisions) Edict 1974[38] of the East Central State in force in Anambra and Imo States by virtue of section 5(1) of the States (Creation and Transitional Provisions) Decree 1976 contains detailed provisions on the procedure of preparation of proofs of evidence. According to the Edict, proofs of evidence in respect of a criminal charge are to be prepared by law officers in the Ministry of Justice in the case of a public prosecution. In the case of a private prosecution, proofs of evidence are to be prepared by the private prosecutor. The preparation of proofs of evidence in respect of any criminal charge is subject to the direction and control of the Attorney-General.[39]

The charges in respect of which proofs of evidence must be prepared under the Edict are as follows:

---

[34] See Criminal Justice (Miscellaneous Provisions) Edict 1973 (No. 4 of 1973) (S.E.S.), s. 2; Criminal Procedure (Miscellaneous Provisions) Edict 1974 (No. 19 of 1974) (E.C.S.), s. 3.
[35] No. 4 of 1973.
[36] See States (Creation and Transitional Provisions) Decree 1976 (No. 12 of 1976), s. 1.
[37] E.N. Laws 1963, Cap. 31.
[38] No. 19 of 1974.
[39] See Criminal Procedure (Miscellaneous Provisions) Edict 1974 (No. 19 of 1974) (E.C.S.), s. 4.

(a) capital offences;
(b) offences punishable with imprisonment for life; and
(c) any indictable offence in respect of which the accused person has elected to be tried by the High Court.[40]

Proofs of evidence are to be prepared after the charge has been read (in cases under (a) or (b)) or after the accused person has elected to be tried by the High Court (in cases under (c)).[41] Section 7(1) of the Edict provides that after the charge has been read in a case under (a) or (b) or after the accused person has elected to be tried by the High Court in a case under (c), the magistrate before whom the charge is pending must record:

(i) the charge against the accused;
(ii) the fact that the accused has elected to be tried by the High Court;
(iii) whether bail was granted or refused to the accused and, where bail was refused, the fact that the accused was informed of his right to apply to the High Court for bail; and
(iv) any other fact or matter relevant to the charge which arose in the proceedings before the magistrate.

Then, the magistrate must direct the prosecuting police officer to send immediately to the Attorney-General:

(a) the police case file relating to the charge; and
(b) an inventory of all exhibits relating to the charge.

As soon as possible after recording the matters stated in paragraphs (i) to (iv), the magistrate must send a copy of the record to the Attorney-General.[42] The prosecuting police officer given a direction by the magistrate with respect to the police case file and an inventory of exhibits, or any other police officer acting under the general or special instruction of the State Commissioner of Police must send the file and the inventory.[43] Once the Attorney-General has received the records prepared by the magistrate, the police case file and the inventory of all exhibits rlating to the charge, the Director of Public Prosecutions of the State and other law officers in the Public Prosecution Division of the Ministry of Justice of the State, acting under and in accordance with the general or special instructions of the Attorney-General, must prepare proofs of evidence in respect of the charge.[44] Section 9(2) of the Edict provides that proofs of evidence must consist of:

[40] *Ibid.* s. 5.
[41] *Ibid.* s. 6.
[42] *Ibid.* s. 7(2).
[43] *Ibid.* s. 8.
[44] *Ibid.* s. 9(1).

(a) a statement of the charge against the accused person;

(b) a statement that the accused elected to be tried by the High Court, where he has a right of election;

(c) the name, address and statement of any material witness whom the prosecution intends to call;

(d) the name, address and statement of any material witness whom the prosecution does not intend to call; provided that the submission of the names does not prevent the prosecution from calling any such witness at the trial if the prosecution later desires to call him;

(e) the copy of any report, if available, made by a doctor about the state of mind of an accused person in custody;

(f) records of convictions, if any, affecting the credibility of any witness for the prosecution;

(g) statements of the accused person;

(h) an inventory of all the exhibits to be produced to the court at the trial; and

(i) any other statement or document which the prosecution may consider relevant to the case.

It is provided in section 10(1) of the Edict that after the preparation of the proofs of evidence the Attorney-General may if he deems it necessary or expedient to do so remit or cause to be remitted to the magistrate before whom the charge was laid, or to any other magistrate, the statement of any witness for the purpose of verification.[45] Where the statement of a witness is sent to a magistrate under this provision, the magistrate must fix a date when the witness and the accused must be summoned before him for the purpose of the verification of the statement. On the date the clerk of court must read out the statement of the witness in the presence of the witness and the accused person. The witness must then verify the statement on oath.[46] After that, the magistrate must inform the accused of his right to cross-examine the witness and must give him the opportunity to do so.[47] The accused person or his counsel may then cross-examine the witness if he desires to do so. The magistrate must record as part of the proofs of evidence:

(a) the answers of the witness to the cross-examination;

(b) the fact that the accused was informed of his right to cross-examine the witness;

[45] In Cross River State, statements taken from witnesses for the prosecution must be verified on oath before a magistrate. See s. 340(2)(*a*) of the Criminal Procedure Law (E.N. Laws 1963, Cap. 31) as amended by s. 2 of the Criminal Justice (Miscellaneous Provisions) Law 1973 (No. 4 of 1973) (S.E.S.).

[46] Criminal Procedure (Miscellaneous Provisions) Law 1974 (No. 19 of 1974) (E.C.S.), s. 10(2) and s. 10(3).

[47] *Ibid.* s. 10(4).

(c) the fact that the accused was given the opportunity to cross-examine (where he or his counsel did not elect to do so).[48]

The verified proofs of evidence including (a), (b) and (c) must then be sent back to the Attorney-General.

When a charge with respect to which proofs of evidence are to be prepared is laid before a magistrate, the magistrate must after the charge has been read or after the accused person has elected to be tried by the High Court, as the case may be, or at any time thereafter bind over, by a recognisance, every witness present in court or brought before him subsequently to attend the trial of the accused person before the High Court to give evidence.[49] The recognisance must be acknowledged by the witness and be signed by the magistrate before whom it is acknowledged.[50] Where a witness refuses, without reasonable excuse, to enter into such recognisance he may, by a warrant made by the magistrate, be committed to prison or to another place of safe custody. The witness is normally to be kept there until after the trial or until he enters into the recognisance before a magistrate. But if the accused person is afterwards discharged, any magistrate may order any such witness to be released immediately.[51]

If at the conclusion of the taking of the proofs of evidence the Attorney-General is satisfied that there is *prima facie* evidence from the record to put the accused person on trial on all or any of the charges against him, he must prefer an information against the accused person in respect of such charge or charges.[52] If the Attorney-General is of opinion that the record of the proofs of evidence does not disclose sufficient evidence to support the charge or charges against the accused person, the Attorney-General must so inform the magistrate in writing, and the magistrate must as soon as possible after receiving the information summon the accused person to the court and discharge him.[53]

F. SUMMARY TRIAL

All trials before magistrates' courts are summary trials. In the High Courts, most trials on information, that is trials other than summary trials; a few are summary trials.

Under the Criminal Procedure Law[54] of Lagos State, there are

[48] *Ibid.* s. 10(5).
[49] *Ibid.* s. 11(1)(3).
[50] *Ibid.* s. 11(4).
[51] *Ibid.* s. 11(5).
[52] *Ibid.* s. 13(1).
[53] *Ibid.* s. 13(2).
[54] Lagos Laws 1973, Cap. 32.

roughly uniform rules of procedure for the summary trial of:

(a) indictable and non-indictable offences in the High Court; and

(b) non-indictable offences in the magistrates' courts.[55]

The procedure for the summary trial by the High Court of indictable offences with respect to which there has been a committal for trial in the High Court is, in general, similar to the procedure for the summary trial of non-indictable offences in magistrates' courts.[56] But the procedure for the summary trial of indictable offences in magistrates' courts is different.[57]

Summary trial by the High Court
after committal for trial

Normally, when an accused person is committed, by a magistrate, for trial in the High Court, the trial is on information. But under section 364 of the Criminal Procedure Law of Lagos State, where after such committal an information against the accused is not filed on or before the day fixed for the trial or no duly authorised person appears before the High Court to prosecute the case on behalf of the State, the court must try the case summarily. The court must direct the registrar to charge the accused with the offence in respect of which he has been committed for trial. It is open to the court to direct the registrar to charge the accused with any other offence which in the opinion of the court is founded on the facts disclosed in the depositions. The court must then explain the substance of the charge or charges to the accused and require him to plead to the charge or charges. If the accused pleads guilty, the court may convict him and impose a sentence. If the accused pleads not guilty, the court must proceed to hear the witnesses and to determine the case.[58] It should be pointed out that the summary trial of an accused committed for trial is in accordance with the provisions of the rules governing summary trials in cases in which there is no committal in so far as those rules are in the opinion of the High Court applicable.[59]

Summary trial of offences by the High Court
(excluding cases in which there has been a
committal) and summary trial of non-indictable offences by
magistrates' courts

Where a charge, not being one with respect to which there is a committal for trial in the High Court, is to be tried summarily by the High

---

[55] See Criminal Procedure Law (Lagos Laws 1973, Cap. 32), s. 277.

[56] See Criminal Procedure Law (Lagos Laws 1973, Cap. 32), s. 364.

[57] See Criminal Procedure Law (Lagos Laws 1973, Cap. 32), ss. 304 to 309.

[58] Criminal Procedure Law (Lagos Laws 1973, Cap. 32), s. 364.

[59] *Ibid.* s. 365.

Court of Lagos State or a non-indictable offence is to be tried by a magistrate's court in the State, the first stage at the hearing is the calling of the case for hearing.[60] If the defendant appears and the complainant does not appear, the court must, as a general rule, dismiss the complaint, provided that it is satisfied that the prosecution had had due notice of the time and place of hearing. There are two exceptions to this rule. First, where the personal attendance of the defendant has been dispensed with under section 100 of the Criminal Procedure Law of Lagos State, it is that section and not this rule that applies. Second, where the court has received a reasonable excuse for the non-appearance of the complainant or his representative and for that reason or for other sufficient reason thinks fit to adjourn the hearing of the case to a future day upon such terms as it thinks just, the rule does not apply.[61] When a defendant to whom a summons is directed fails to appear or plead guilty under section 100 of the Criminal Procedure Law of Lagos State (which relates to dispensing with the personal attendance of the defendant) and no sufficient excuse is offered for his absence the court, if satisfied that the summons has been duly served, may issue a warrant known as a bench warrant for his arrest or if not satisfied that the summons has been duly served may adjourn the hearing of the case to a future day in order that proper service may be effected. Similarly, where a warrant has been issued for the apprehension of a defendant and the defendant fails to appear by reason of failure to apprehend him, the court may adjourn the hearing of the case until the defendant is apprehended.[62] Where the defendant is apprehended on the bench warrant or on another warrant, he must be brought before the magistrate who must then commit him by warrant to prison or to such other place of safe custody as he may think fit, and order him to be brought at a certain time and place before the court. The complainant must by direction of the magistrate be served with due notice of such time and place.[63]

Where neither the complainant nor the defendant appears, the court is required to make such order as the justice of the case requires.[64]

Where both the complainant and the defendant appear the court must proceed to hear and determine the case.[65] After the case has been called for hearing and both parties have appeared, the court must state or cause to be stated to the defendant the substance of the complaint, and must ask him whether he is guilty or not guilty. If he

[60] Criminal Procedure Law (Lagos Laws 1973, Cap. 32), s. 279.
[61] *Ibid.* s. 280.
[62] *Ibid.* s. 281(1).
[63] *Ibid.* s. 281(2).
[64] *Ibid.* s. 282(1).
[65] *Ibid.* s. 283.

says that he is guilty and the court is satisfied that he intends to admit the commission of the offence and shows no cause or insufficient cause why sentence should not be passed the court must proceed to pass sentence. If he says that he is not guilty, the court must normally direct that all witnesses must leave the court. But the court may in its discretion permit professional or technical witnesses to remain in court. Failure to direct witnesses to leave court does not invalidate proceedings. After the defendant has pleaded guilty and witnesses have been directed to leave the court, the court must proceed to hear the complainant, the witnesses called by the complainant and other evidence that the complainant may adduce in support of the claim. The court also hears the defendant, the witnesses called by the defendant and other evidence that the defendant may adduce in his defence. Furthermore, the court, if it thinks fit, may hear witnesses that the complainant may call in reply, if the defendant has called any witnesses or given any evidence. The complainant and the defendant may cross-examine each witness called by the other side. If the defendant gives evidence, he may be cross-examined. Where the defendant is not represented by a legal practitioner the court must at the close of the examination of each witness for the prosecution ask whether he wishes to cross-examine the witness, and must record his answer on the minutes.[66]

If at the close of the evidence for the prosecution, it appears to the court that a case is not made out against the defendant sufficiently to require him to make a defence the court must discharge him.[67] If at the close of the evidence for the prosecution it appears to the court that a *prima facie* case is made out against the defendant sufficiently to require him to make a defence the court must ask him to make his defence. In that case, if the defendant is not represented by a legal practitioner, the court must inform him that:

   (a) he may make a statement without being sworn from the place where he is then; in which case he is not liable to cross-examination; or

   (b) he may give evidence in the witness box after being sworn as a witness; in which case he will be liable to cross-examination; or

   (c) he may, if he so wishes, say nothing.

Furthermore, the court must ask him if he has any witnesses to examine or other evidence to adduce in his defence and the court must then hear him and his witnesses and other evidence, if any.[68] Failure to state the three alternatives to the defendant does not vitiate the

[66] *Ibid.* s. 285.
[67] *Ibid.* s. 286.
[68] *Ibid.* s. 287(1)(*a*).

trial in any case in which the court called upon the defendant for his defence, asked him if he had any witnesses, and heard him and his witnesses and other evidence, if any.[69] If the defendant is represented by a legal practitioner, the court must ask the legal practitioner to proceed with the defence.[70]

The court must, at the sitting at which the hearing is concluded or at an adjourned sitting, give its decision on the case either by dismissing or convicting the accused. The court may, in addition, make such other order as may seem just.[71] Whether the complaint is dismissed or not, the court may bind over the complainant or defendant or both of them, with or without a surety or sureties, to be of good behaviour, and may order any person so bound who fails to comply with the order to be imprisoned for a term not exceeding three months with or without hard labour, in addition to any other punishment to which the person is liable.[72]

Where a complaint dismissed is stated by the court to be dismissed on the merits the dismissal has the same effect as an acquittal. Where a complaint is dismissed and the dismissal is stated by the court to be not on the merits or to be without prejudice the dismissal does not have the same effect as an acquittal.[73]

It should be pointed out that if in the course of the hearing of a complaint before a magistrate's court it happens that the court is of opinion that the offence, on account of its aggravated character or other sufficient reason, is not suitable to be disposed of by such court, the magistrate's court may, instead of adjudicating, hold a preliminary inquiry into the charge and commit the accused for trial before the High Court.[74]

Summary trial, by a magistrate, of indictable offences

Section 413 of the Criminal Procedure Law of Lagos State provides that where a child or young person is brought before the High Court or a magistrate's court charged with an offence, the charge must be inquired into in accordance with the provision of the Children and Young Persons Law.[75]

Sections 304 to 309 of the Criminal Procedure Law of Lagos State govern the summary trial by a magistrate of an adult charged with an indictable offence.

---

[69] *Ibid.* s. 288.
[70] *Ibid.* s. 287(1)(*b*).
[71] *Ibid.* s. 299.
[72] *Ibid.* s. 300.
[73] *Ibid.* s. 301.
[74] See Criminal Procedure Law (Lagos Laws 1973, Cap. 32), s. 298.
[75] Lagos Laws 1973, Cap. 26.

A magistrate's court may, normally, with the consent of the accused try summarily an adult accused charged before the court with an indictable offence other than a capital offence. But where the prosecution is conducted by a law officer the magistrate must not deal summarily with the offence without the consent of the law officer.[76] In order to satisfy the requirement of obtaining the consent of the accused to summary trial, the magistrate must inform the accused of his right to be tried by the High Court and he must ask the accused whether he consents to the case being tried summarily by the magistrate's court.[77] If the magistrate fails to inform the accused of his right to be tried by the High Court, the trial is null and void *ab initio* unless the accused consents at any time before he is asked to make his defence to be tried summarily. Where the accused so consents the trial must proceed as if the accused had consented to being tried summarily by the magistrate before the magistrate proceeded to hear evidence in the case.[78] Until a magistrate assumes the power to deal with an indictable offence other than a capital offence summarily, he must deal with it in accordance with the rules governing preliminary inquiry into an indictable offence. He must assume such power if during the hearing of the charge he is satisfied that it is expedient to deal with the case summarily. In that case he must cause the charge to be reduced into writing if it has not been so reduced, and then read to the accused before he asks the accused whether he consents to being tried summarily by the court. Where the accused consents to being tried summarily he must immediately be asked whether he pleads guilty or not guilty.

It is provided in section 309 of the Criminal Procedure Law of Lagos State that a person convicted of an indictable offence tried summarily may, instead of or in addition to any punishment to which he is liable, be ordered to enter into his own recognisance, with or without sureties, in such amount as the court thinks fit that he must keep the peace and be of good behaviour for a period of time to be fixed by the court. The section further provides that the person convicted may be ordered to be imprisoned until such recognisance, with sureties if so directed, is entered into provided that the imprisonment for not entering into the recognisance must not extend for a term longer than one year and must not together with the fixed term of imprisonment, if any, extend for a term longer that the longest term for which he might be sentenced to imprisonment without fine.[79]

[76] Criminal Procedure Law (Lagos Laws 1973, Cap. 32), s. 304.
[77] *Ibid.* s. 304(2).
[78] *Ibid.* s. 304(3).
[79] *Ibid.* s. 309.

G. Sentences and Orders

The various types of punishment which may be imposed in respect of an offence are as follows:

(a) death sentence
(b) imprisonment
(c) fine
(d) caning
(e) deportation.

Orders which may be given in respect of an offence include the following:

(a) binding over order
(b) dismissal order
(c) acquittal order
(d) discharge order
(e) order of committal for trial
(f) order for the recovery of fine by distress
(g) order of detention during the pleasure of a Military Governor or of the Head of the Federal Military Government
(h) order for the disposal of property with respect to which an offence has been or appears to have been committed
(i) order for the payment of costs
(j) order for the payment of compensation
(k) order for the payment of damages
(l) probation
(m) orders other than the above orders made under the Children and Young Persons legislation.

Death Sentence

Under the Criminal Procedure enactments the death penalty is inflicted by hanging the offender by the neck till he dies.[80] Under enactments establishing certain special tribunals the death penalty may be inflicted by causing a firing squad to kill the person sentenced to death.[81]

Where a woman found guilty of a capital offence is found by the court to be pregnant the sentence of death must not be passed on her; she must be sentenced to imprisonment for life.[82] Where an offender who in the opinion of the court had not attained the age of 17 years at

---

[80] See *e.g.* Criminal Procedure Law (Lagos Laws 1973, Cap. 32), s. 367(1).
[81] See *e.g.* Robbery and Firearms (Special Provisions) Decree 1970 (No. 47 of 1970). It may be mentioned in passing that the capital sentence has been abolished in England with respect to all types of murder. See Murder (Abolition of Death Penalty) Act 1965.
[82] Criminal Procedure Law (Lagos Laws 1973, Cap. 32), s. 368(2).

the time the offence was committed is found guilty of a capital offence, he must not be sentenced to death; the court must order that he be detained during the pleasure of the Military Governor in the case of a State offence or during the pleasure of the Head of the Federal Military Government in the case of a Federal offence.[83]

Imprisonment

Where a sentence of imprisonment is imposed the imprisonment may be either with hard labour or without hard labour. Normally, where no specific order is given as to whether it is with hard labour or not, the imprisonment must be with hard labour.[84] In general, where a court is authorised to impose imprisonment for an offence and has no specific authority to impose a fine for the offence, the court may impose a fine instead of imprisonment.[85] This rule does not apply where a written law specifies a minimum period of imprisonment to be imposed for the commission of the offence.[86] Where there is a conviction in the High Court and a fine is imposed instead of imprisonment, any term of imprisonment imposed in default of payment of fine must not exceed two years.[87]

Where the conviction is a conviction in a magistrate's court the amount of fine imposed instead of imprisonment must not exceed the maximum fine authorised to be imposed by the magistrate by or under the law by virtue of which he was appointed a magistrate. Furthermore, a term of imprisonment imposed in default of payment of the fine must normally not exceed the maximum term stated in relation to the amount of the fine in the following scale stated in section 390(2) of the Criminal Procedure Law of Lagos State:

Fine	*Term of Imprisonment*
Not exceeding ₦1	7 days
Exceeding ₦1 but not exceeding ₦2	14 days
Exceeding ₦2 but not exceeding ₦20	1 month
Exceeding ₦20 but not exceeding ₦60	2 months
Exceeding ₦60 but not exceeding ₦100	4 months
Exceeding ₦100 but not exceeding ₦200	6 months
Exceeding ₦200 but not exceeding ₦400	1 year
Exceeding ₦400	2 years[88]

But a magistrate may impose a term of imprisonment longer than two years where the law under which the accused has been convicted prescribes or allows a longer period.[89]

---

[83] See *e.g.* Criminal Procedure Law (Lagos Laws 1973, Cap. 32), s. 368(3).
[84] Criminal Procedure Law (Lagos Laws 1973, Cap. 32), s. 377.
[85] *Ibid.* s. 382(1).   [86] *Ibid.* s. 382(5).
[87] *Ibid.* s. 382(2).   [88] *Ibid.* s. 382(3).
[89] *Ibid.* s. 390(3).

It should be pointed out, however, that the term of imprisonment imposed by a court in default of payment of fine imposed instead of imprisonment must not exceed the maximum term authorised as a punishment for the offence by written law.[90]

Fines

As already noted, a person on whom a fine for an offence is imposed under section 382 of the Criminal Procedure Law of Lagos State may be sentenced to imprisonment in default of payment of the fine. Section 389 of the law provides that a person convicted of an offence punishable by: (a) imprisonment as well as fine, and sentenced to pay a fine whether with or without imprisonment; or (b) imprisonment or fine, and sentenced to pay a fine, may be sentenced to imprisonment in default of payment of the fine for a certain term, such imprisonment being in addition to any other imprisonment to which he may have been sentenced.

Caning

Under the Criminal Procedure Law of Lagos State, caning must be effected with a light rod or cane or birch, the number of strokes must be specified and that number must not exceed 12. Furthermore, where a person is convicted of one or more offences at one trial the total number of strokes awarded must not exceed 12.[91] Under the law no person is to be sentenced to be caned more than once for the same offence.[92] It is also provided in the law that a sentence of caning must not be passed on any female or on any male who in the opinion of the court has attained the age of 45 years.[93]

Deportation

The punishment of deportation under the Criminal Procedure Law of Lagos State means: (a) in the case of a citizen of Nigeria deportation from the place where the offence took place or proceedings which culminated in the recommendation for deportation were heard to any other place in Nigeria; (b) in the case of a person not a citizen of Nigeria to a place outside Nigeria.[94] Under the Law, where a person is convicted of an offence punishable by imprisonment without the option of a fine the court may, in addition to or instead of any other punishment, recommend to the appropriate Commissioner

[90] *Ibid.* s. 382(4).
[91] Criminal Procedure Law (Lagos Laws 1973, Cap. 32), s. 386.
[92] *Ibid.* s. 384.
[93] *Ibid.* s. 385.
[94] *Ibid.* s. 402.

that the person be deported if it appears to the court to be in the interest of peace, order and good government that an order of deportation as a punishment should be made.[95] This is just one of the cases to which the order of deportation applies. Where a recommendation for deportation has been made as stated, the person concerned may be detained in custody pending the decision of the Commissioner and during such time shall be deemed to be in lawful custody.[96]

Binding over

Section 300 of the Criminal Procedure Law of Lagos State provides that on a summary trial, whether the complaint is dismissed or not, the court may bind over the complainant or defendant or both of them, with or without a surety or sureties, to be of good behaviour. The court may order any person so bound, in default of compliance with the order, to be imprisoned for any term not exceeding three months, with or without hard labour, in addition to any other punishment to which such person is liable.

Dismissal order

This is an order dismissing a charge or complaint.[97] Where it is stated to be on the merits it has the same effect as an acquittal but where it is stated to be not on the merits or to be without prejudice, the dismissal order does not have the same effect as an acquittal.[98]

Under section 435(1)(*a*) of the Criminal Procedure Law of Lagos State, where the charge against the accused is proved in the opinion of the court and the court thinks that in view of the character, antecedents, age, health or mental condition of the accused it is inexpedient to impose any punishment the court may, without proceeding to conviction, make an order dismissing the charge.

Acquittal order

An acquittal order is an order issued in favour of an accused person found not guilty of an offence. A result of the order is that he is not liable to be tried for the same offence or for another offence of which he might have been convicted by virtue of being charged with the offence tried.[99]

Order of discharge

An order of discharge may be issued by a magistrate's court at the end of a preliminary inquiry into an indictable offence where the

---

[95] *Ibid.* s. 404. See also ss. 405 and 406 of the Criminal Procedure Law of Lagos State.
[96] Criminal Procedure Law (Lagos Laws 1973, Cap. 32), s. 409.
[97] *Ibid.* s. 301.
[98] *Ibid.*
[99] See Criminal Procedure Law (Lagos Laws 1973, Cap. 32), s. 181.

court considers that the evidence against the accused is not sufficient to put the accused on his trial.[1] Where at the conclusion of a trial, the accused is found not guilty he must be discharged and an order of acquittal must, in addition to an order of discharge, be recorded in his favour.[2]

Order of committal for trial

Where at the end of a preliminary inquiry into an indictable offence, the magistrate is of opinion that the evidence is sufficient to put the accused on his trial, he issues an order sending him for trial to the High Court.[3] That order is an order of committal for trial.

Order for recovery of fine by distress

The court may give an order that a fine be recovered by a process known as distress under section 398 of the Criminal Procedure Law of Lagos State. Under the warrant of distress issued for the purpose of recovering a fine, the property of the person against whom the warrant is issued may be seized and sold by the Sheriff.[4]

Order for the detention of a person during the pleasure of a Military Governor or that of the Head of the Federal Military Government

In certain circumstances, a person may be ordered to be detained at the pleasure of a Military Governor where the offence with respect to which he was charged is a State offence or at the pleasure of the Head of the Federal Military Government in the case of federal offences. Where a person is found not guilty of an offence by reason of insanity and the court finds that he committed the act alleged, the appropriate Military Governor or the Head of the Federal Military Government, as the case may be, may order such person to be confined in a lunatic asylum, prison or other suitable place of safe custody during the pleasure of the Military Governor or that of the Head of the Federal Military Government.[5] A similar order may be made under section 225(2) of the Criminal Procedure Law of Lagos State with respect to an accused person who is found to be of unsound mind and incapable of making his defence.

A person detained during the pleasure of the Military Governor or of the Head of the Federal Military Government may be discharged by him on licence.[6]

---

[1] Criminal Procedure Law (Lagos Laws 1973, Cap. 32), s. 325(1).
[2] See s. 246 of the Criminal Procedure Law of Lagos State.
[3] Criminal Procedure Law (Lagos Laws 1973, Cap. 32), s. 326.
[4] *Ibid.* s. 399.
[5] *Ibid.* ss. 229 and 230.
[6] *Ibid.* s. 401(2).

Order for the Disposal of Property

Section 263(1) of the Criminal Procedure Law of Lagos State provides that during or at the conclusion of any trial or inquiry the court may make such order as it thinks fit for the disposal whether by way of forfeiture, confiscation or otherwise of any property produced before it with respect to which an offence appears to have been committed or which has been used for the commission of the offence. For the purpose of this provision, the term "property" includes, "in the case of property with respect to which an offence appears to have been committed not only such property as has been originally in the possession or under the control of any party, but also any property into or for which the same has been converted or exchanged and anything acquired by such conversion or exchange, whether immediately or otherwise."[7]

Costs

Where a person has been convicted of an offence by the court, the court may order him to pay to the prosecutor in addition to any penalty imposed such reasonable costs as the court may think fit.[8] Where there is a private prosecution and the court acquits or discharges the accused, the court may normally order the private prosecutor to pay to the accused such reasonable costs as the court thinks fit.[9] But no order for the payment of costs may be made where the court is of opinion that the private prosecutor had reasonable grounds for making his complaint. Moreover, the costs awarded must not exceed ₦100 in the case of an award by a judge or ₦50 in the case of an award by a magistrate.[10] For the purpose of this provision, the term "private prosecutor" does not include any person prosecuting on behalf of the State, a public officer prosecuting in his official capacity or a police officer.[11]

Compensation

Where an accused person is discharged or acquitted with respect to an offence by the court which heard the case and the judge or the magistrate presiding over the court is of opinion that the accusation against him was false and either frivolous or vexatious the judge or magistrate may for reasons which are to be recorded, direct that

---

[7] *Ibid.* s. 263A.
[8] *Ibid.* s. 255(1).
[9] *Ibid.* s. 255(2).
[10] *Ibid.* s. 255(3). The provisions of s. 255 of the Law are subject to any express provision made in any written law relating to the procedure to be followed in the awarding of costs in respect of conditions specified in the written law. (See s. 258 of the Law.)
[11] *Ibid.* s. 255(5).

compensation to such an amount not exceeding ₦20 as he may determine, be paid to the accused by the person upon whose complaint the
accused was charged.[12] Such compensation may be awarded in addition to costs awarded under section 255 of the Criminal Procedure
Law of Lagos State.[13] But the award of compensation under section
256 of the Law and of costs under section 255 of the Law are subject
to any express provisions made in any written law relating to the
procedure to be followed in the awarding of costs or compensation
in respect of conditions specified in such written law.[14]

Order awarding Damages

Under section 261 of the Criminal Procedure Law of Lagos State,
where in a charge of stealing or receiving stolen property the court is
of opinion that the evidence is insufficient to support the charge, but
that it establishes wrongful conversion or detention of property, the
court may order that such property be restored, and may also award
damages. But the value of the property and the amount of damages
awarded must not together amount to ₦20 in value. Damages
awarded under this provision are recoverable in the same way as a
penalty is recoverable.[15]

Probation Order

A court may in certain circumstances release conditionally an
accused person charged with an offence before it notwithstanding
the fact that the charge is proved, upon his entering into a recognisance to be of good behaviour, such a recognisance stating that he is
to be under the supervision of a named person during a specified
period not exceeding three years. The order whereby he is placed
under such supervision is known as a probation order. When such an
order is issued in respect of an offender he is said to be placed on probation. Section 435(1) of the Criminal Procedure Law of Lagos
State provides that where a person is charged before a court with an
offence punishable by such court, and the court thinks that the
charge is proved but is of opinion that having regard to the character, antecedents, age, health, or mental condition of the person
charged, or to the trivial nature of the offence or to the extenuating
circumstances under which the offence was committed, it is inexpedient to inflict any punishment or any other than a nominal punishment or that it is expedient to release the offender on probation the
court may without proceeding to conviction make an order either:

[12] *Ibid.* s. 256.
[13] *Ibid.* s. 255(4).
[14] *Ibid.* s. 258.
[15] *Ibid.* s. 261.

(a) dismissing the charge; or (b) discharging the offender conditionally on his entering into a recognisance, with or without sureties, to be of good behaviour and to appear at any time during such period not exceeding three years as may be specified in the order.

Other orders made under the Children and Young Persons enactments

Under the various Children and Young Persons enactments, other orders may be made.[16]

---

[16] See *e.g.* Children and Young Persons Law (Lagos Laws 1973, Cap. 26).

CHAPTER 13

THE LEGAL PROFESSION

A. INTRODUCTION

MEMBERS of the legal profession comprise:
(a) legal practitioners; and
(b) judges and other members of the Bench.
A legal practitioner is a person entitled to practise as a barrister (advocate) or as a barrister and solicitor.[1] In Nigeria (unlike the case in England), in general, every legal practitioner is a barrister and solicitor. But some legal practitioners are not entitled to practise as solicitors. For example, an advocate practising in a country whose legal system is similar to that of Nigeria may be permitted by the Chief Justice of Nigeria to practise as a barrister.[2] The Chief Justice has no power to permit him to practise as a solicitor. Furthermore, a Senior Advocate of Nigeria is not entitled to practise as a solicitor.[3]

All members of the courts as persons administering the law are members of the legal profession. Many members of the Bench are legal practitioners within the meaning of the law.[4]

The history of the legal profession in Nigeria dates back to the period before the arrival of the British at any of the territories which together now constitute Nigeria. But the profession in its present form comprising practitioners of the English type of law came into being in 1863, for in that year English law was introduced into the Colony of Lagos and courts were established there. The Supreme Court Ordinance 1876[5] provided that:

"the Chief Justice shall have power to approve, admit and enrol to practise as barristers and solicitors in the court such persons as shall have been admitted as solicitors . . . in any of the Courts of London, Dublin and Edinburgh; . . ."[6]

Similarly, Order XVI, rule 1 of the Supreme Court (Civil Procedure) Rules[7] made under section 56 of the Supreme Court Ordinance[8] provided that the

"Chief Justice may in his discretion approve, admit and enrol to practise as a barrister and solicitor in the court —

[1] See Legal Practitioners Decree 1975 (No. 15 of 1975), s. 23.
[2] See Legal Practitioners Decree 1975, s. 2(2).
[3] Legal Practitioners Decree 1975, s. 5(6).
[4] See Legal Practitioners Decree 1975, s. 23.
[5] No. 4 of 1876.
[6] *Ibid.* s. 71.
[7] Nigeria Laws 1948, Cap. 211.
[8] *Ibid.*

(a) any person who is entitled to practise as a barrister in England or Ireland or as an advocate in Scotland; and who —
(i) produces testimonials sufficient to satisfy the Chief Justice that he is a man of good character, . . ."

Under Order XVI, rule 6 of the same Rules every person admitted to practise was entitled to practise as barrister and solicitor. Thus, in order to qualify as a legal practitioner in Nigeria, a person had to be called to the English, Scottish or Irish Bar or be a solicitor in England, Scotland Northern Ireland or Eire. Most persons who came to Nigerian to seek enrolment as legal practitioners were persons called to the Bar in Britain or Eire. But on enrolment here, they were entitled to practise as barristers and solicitors. Such practitioners did not, normally, study Nigerian law before seeking enrolment. It was, therefore, not easy for them to render efficient service as legal practitioners.

The need for a better system of legal education was thus felt. Accordingly, in April 1959, the Federal Government appointed a committee known as the Committee on the Future of the Nigeria Legal Profession (the Unsworth Committee) "to consider and make recommendations for the future of the legal profession in Nigeria with particular regard to legal education and admission to practise, the right of audience before the courts and the making of reciprocal arrangements in this connection with other countries, the setting up of a General Council of the Nigeria Bar, the powers and functions of such a Council, the institution of a Code of Conduct, the disciplinary control of the profession's members, and the principles to be applied in determining whether a member of the bar should be prohibited from practising in Nigeria."[9] The Committee was also required to "make suggestions for amending, expanding or improving the Legal Practitioners Ordinance[10] in conformity with present day requirements."

The Government implemented recommendations of the Committee by passing the Legal Education Act 1962[11] and the Legal Practitioners Act 1962.[12]

The Legal Education Act 1962 provided for legal education in Nigeria. The Act established a council known as the Council of Legal Education charged with responsibility for the legal education of persons seeking to become members of the profession. The Council established in 1962 a law school then known as the Federal Law School and later known as the Nigerian Law School, a school which offers a professional course lasting one academic year. The Legal Education

---

[9] Government Notice No. 915 (*Federation of Nigeria Official Gazette*, No. 26, Vol. 46, 1959).
[10] Nigeria Laws 1948, Cap. 110.
[11] No. 12 of 1962.   [12] No. 33 of 1962.

(Consolidation, etc.) Decree 1976,[13] principally a consolidation enactment, repealed the Legal Education Act 1962 and substantially re-enacted the provisions of the Act as amended by various enactments.

The Council of Legal Education established by the Decree consists of —

(a) a Chairman appointed by the Federal Executive Council on the recommendation of the Attorney-General of the Federation;

(b) Attorneys-General of the States, or where there are no Attorneys-General, Solicitors-General of the States;

(c) a representative of the Federal Ministry of Justice appointed by the Attorney-General of the Federation;

(d) the head of the Faculty of Law of any recognised University in Nigeria whose course of legal studies is approved by the Council as sufficient qualification for admission to the Nigerian Law School;

(e) the President of the Nigerian Bar Association;

(f) 15 persons entitled to practise as legal practitioners in Nigeria of not less than 10 years' standing and selected or elected by the Nigerian Bar Association;

(g) the Director of the Nigerian Law School; and

(h) two persons, being authors of published learned works in the field of law, appointed by the Attorney-General of the Federation.[14]

The Council, like that established by the Legal Education Act 1962, is responsible for the legal education of persons seeking to become members of the legal profession.[15] In addition, it is charged with responsibility for continuing legal education.[16] The Nigerian Law School remains in existence. It continues to offer a course of professional training covering not only barrister's work but also that of a solicitor.

In order to be admitted to the Nigerian Law School a person must, normally, have obtained:

(a) a law degree of an approved University; or

(b) a pass in the English, Irish or Scottish Bar Examination; or

---

[13] No. 13 of 1976.

[14] Legal Education (Consolidation, etc.) Decree 1976 (No. 13 of 1976), s. 2(1) as amended by the Legal Education (Consolidation, etc.) (Amendment) Decree 1977 (No. 10 of 1977).

[15] Legal Education (Consolidation, etc.) Decree 1976, s. 1(2).

[16] *Ibid.* s. 3.

(c) a pass in the Solicitors Final Examination of Great Britain and Ireland.[17]

In determining whether to approve a university under alternative (a), the Council considers the content of the law degree course with a view to ascertaining that the course gives the minimum basic knowledge of the law against which background the Nigerian Law School course is designed. A candidate who does not obtain any of the three alternatives may nevertheless be admitted to the school where having regard to the content of the course he has successfully completed he is considered suitable for admission. Thus, the holder of a degree (other than a law degree) of a university in the Commonwealth is likely to be admitted where the content of the degree course covers what the Council considers to be the minimum basic knowledge of the law.

On the successful completion of the course at the Nigerian Law School a person is entitled to the award of a qualifying certificate issued by the Council provided that he is a citizen of Nigeria. The qualifying certificate states that the person is qualified to be called to the Bar.[18]

B. Call to the Bar

There was no provision for the formal call to the Bar until the passing of the Legal Practitioners (Amendment) Decree 1971[19] which came into force on November 27, 1971 and the provisions of which have been incorporated in the Legal Practitioners Decree 1975.[20] Section 3 of the 1975 Decree established a body known as the Body of Benchers and described as a body of legal practitioners of the highest distinction in the legal profession in Nigeria. The body is charged with responsibility for the formal call to the Bar of persons seeking to become legal practitioners. It consists of:

(a) the Chief Justice of Nigeria and all the Justices of the Supreme Court;
(b) the Attorney-General of the Federation;
(c) the President of the Federal Court of Appeal;
(d) the President of the Federal Revenue Court;
(e) the Chairman of the Council of Legal Education;
(f) the Chief Judges of all the States in the Federation;
(g) the Attorneys-General of all the States in the Federation;

---

[17] See Government Notice No. 955 of 1963 (*Federation of Nigeria Official Gazette*, No. 32, Vol. 50, 1963).
[18] Legal Education (Consolidation, etc.) Decree 1976 (No. 13 of 1976), s. 5.
[19] No. 54 of 1971.
[20] No. 15 of 1975.

(h) the President of the Nigerian Bar Association;

(i) 20 members of the Nigerian Bar Association of not less than 15 years' post-call standing, nominated by the association; and

(j) such other persons as may be appointed members pursuant to regulations made by the Body of Benchers under the Decree.[21]

Under section 4 of the Legal Practitioners Decree 1975,[22] in general, a person is entitled to be called to the Bar if, and only if:

(a) he is a citizen of Nigeria; and

(b) he produces a qualifying certificate to the Body of Benchers; and

(c) he satisfies the Body of Benchers that he is of good character.

But the Council of Legal Education may, by regulation, waive the requirement of producing a qualifying certificate in such cases and on such conditions, if any, as may be specified by the regulations.[23] Moreover, the requirement of being a citizen of Nigeria is waived in respect of persons who in the opinion of the Council have completed courses of study approved by the Council and have obtained qualifications approved by the Council for call to the Bar in Nigeria.[24]

The Body of Benchers must issue to every person called to the Bar by the Body in accordance with the Decree a certificate of call to the Bar.[25]

C. PRACTISING AS A LEGAL PRACTITIONER

1. *Enrolment*

There is a roll of legal practitioners kept as a roll of court and maintained by the Chief Registrar of the Supreme Court of Nigeria.[26]

In general, a person is entitled to be enrolled if, and only if:

(a) he has been called to the Bar by the Body of Benchers; and

(b) he produces a certificate of his call to the Bar to the Chief Registrar of the Supreme Court.

---

[21] *Ibid.* s. 3 as amended by: (a) the Legal Practitioners (Amendment) Decree 1976 (No. 29 of 1976); (b) the Legal Practitioners (Amendment) Decree 1977 (No. 40 of 1977); and (c) the Chief Justice of a State (Change of Title) Decree 1976 (No. 41 of 1976). S. 3(5) of the Legal Practitioners Decree 1975 empowers the Body of Benchers to make regulations providing for, *inter alia*, an increase in the membership of the Body.

[22] No. 15 of 1975.

[23] *Ibid.* s. 4(2).

[24] See the Professional Bodies (Legal Profession) (Exemption) Order 1973 (L.N. 52 of 1973) made under the Professional Bodies (Special Provisions) Decree 1972 (No. 3 of 1972).

[25] Legal Practitioners Decree 1975, s. 4(3).

[26] See Legal Practitioners Decree 1975, ss. 23, 22 and 6.

But the Attorney-General of the Federation may, after consultation with the General Council of the Bar[27] make regulations providing for the enrolment of persons who are authorised by law to practise as members of the legal profession in any country other than Nigeria where, in his opinion, legal practitioners in Nigeria are given special facilities for practising as members of the profession.[28] Such regulations may state that persons seeking enrolment by virtue of the regulations must pass such examinations and pay such fees as may be specified by or under the regulations. They may also provide for the cancellation of enrolments secured by virtue of the regulations where the appropriate country has altered or withdrawn the special facilities given to persons enrolled as legal practitioners in Nigeria to practise as members of the legal profession in that country.[29]

2. *Permission to Practise Without being Enrolled*

In general, only persons whose names are on the roll of legal practitioners kept as a roll of court and maintained by the Chief Registrar of the Supreme Court are entitled to practise as barristers and solicitors.[30] But the Chief Justice of Nigeria may, under section 2(2) of the Legal Practitioners Decree 1975, by warrant under his hand authorise a person whose name is not on the roll, on payment to the Chief Registrar of the Supreme Court of such fee not exceeding 50 naira as may be specified in the warrant, to practise as a barrister for the purpose of specified proceedings and of any appeal brought in connection with those proceedings.

The power of the Chief Justice to authorise a person to practise as a barrister under this provision is exercisable where:

(a) an application for permission to practise as a barrister is made to the Chief Justice by or on behalf of any person who in the opinion of the Chief Justice is entitled to practise as an advocate in any country where the legal system is similar to that of Nigeria; and

(b) the Chief Justice is of opinion that it is expedient to permit the person to practise as a barrister for the purposes of proceedings with respect to which the application is brought.

---

[27] A body established by s. 1(1) of the Legal Practitioners Decree 1975 and having responsibility for the general management of the affairs of the Nigerian Bar Association, subject to any limitations for the time being stated in the constitution of the association.

[28] Legal Practitioners Decree 1975, s. 6(2).

[29] *Ibid.*

[30] Legal Practitioners Decree 1975, s. 2(1).

Furthermore, a person for the time being exercising the functions of any of the following offices is entitled to practise as a barrister and solicitor for the purposes of the office:

(a) the office of the Attorney-General, Solicitor-General or Director of Public Prosecutions of the Federation or of a State; and
(b) such offices in the public service of the Federation or of a State as the Attorney-General of the Federation or of the State, as the case may be, may by order specify.[31]

3. *Limitations to the Right to Practise as a Legal Practitioner*

Even though a person has been enrolled as a legal practitioner, his right to practise as a legal practitioner may be limited where:

(a) he is a Senior Advocate of Nigeria; or
(b) he has not paid a practising fee; or
(c) he is a legal practitioner of less than seven years' standing.

(a) Senior Advocate of Nigeria

Section 5 of the Legal Practitioners Decree 1975 established a rank of legal practitioners known as Senior Advocates of Nigeria. The rank is equivalent to that of Queen's Counsel which has been abolished in Nigeria.[32] The section, as amended by the Legal Practitioners (Amendment) Decree 1977,[33] provides that the Legal Practitioners' Privileges Committee (a committee established by subsection (3) of the section) may by instrument confer the rank of Senior Advocate of Nigeria on a legal practitioner who has been qualified to practise as a legal practitioner in Nigeria for not less than 10 years and "who has achieved distinction in the legal profession in such manner as the committee may from time to time determine." According to section 5 of the 1975 Decree, as further amended by the Legal Practitioners (Amendment) (No. 2) Decree 1977, the Committee consists of:

(i) the Chief Justice of Nigeria who is the chairman;
(ii) the Attorney-General of the Federation;
(iii) one Justice of the Supreme Court, appointed by the Chief Justice of Nigeria in consultation with the Attorney-General of the Federation;
(iv) the President of the Federal Court of Appeal;
(v) five of the Chief Judges of the States, appointed by the Chief

---

[31] *Ibid.* s. 2(3).
[32] See Queen's Counsel (Abolition) Act 1964 (No. 12 of 1964).
[33] No. 40 of 1977. The amending Decree came into force on May 18, 1977.

Justice of Nigeria in consultation with the Attorney-General of
the Federation;
(vi) the President of the Federal Revenue Court; and
(vii) five Senior Advocates of Nigeria appointed by the Chief Justice
of Nigeria in consultation with the Attorney-General of the Federation.

Under section 5(5) of the Legal Practitioners Decree 1975 the Committee may, with the approval of the Federal Executive Council,
make rules on the privileges to be accorded to Senior Advocates of
Nigeria, the functions of a legal practitioner which are not to be performed by a Senior Advocate of Nigeria and, generally, ensuring the
dignity of the rank. It is provided that until the first rules made pursuant to this provision come into force, a Senior Advocate of Nigeria is
not entitled to practise as a member of the legal profession except as
a barrister; but he is not precluded from entering into, or continuing
in partnership with a legal practitioner who is not of the rank of
Senior Advocate of Nigeria.[34]

(b) Practising fee

As a general rule, no legal practitioner is to be accorded the right
of audience in any court in Nigeria in any year unless he has paid to
the Chief Registrar of the Supreme Court the practising fee for that
year. A person exercising the functions of any of the following
offices is exempted from the rule:

(a) the office of the Attorney-General, Solicitor-General or Director of Public Prosecutions of the Federation or of a State;
(b) such offices in the public service of the Federation or of a State
as the Attorney-General of the Federation or of the State, as the
case may be, may by order specify.[35]

The practising fees now payable by the various categories of legal
practitioners are as follows:

Senior Advocate of Nigeria	- ₦42.
A person of 10 or more years' standing as a legal practitioner at the beginning of the year, not being a Senior Advocate of Nigeria	- ₦25.
A person of more than five and less than 10 years' standing as a legal practitioner at the beginning of the year	- ₦15

---

[34] *Ibid.* s. 5(6).
[35] See Legal Practitioners Decree 1975, s. 7(2).

A person of not more than five years'
standing as a legal practitioner at the
beginning of the year.   - ₦10[36]

The amount of practising fees payable may be varied by the Attorney-
General of the Federation after consultation with the General Council of the Bar.[37]

(c) Legal practitioners of less than seven years' standing

As a general rule, a legal practitioner of less than seven years'
standing at the Bar is not entitled to appear in any case before the
Supreme Court of Nigeria except as a junior to a legal practitioner of
at least seven years' standing at the Bar.[38] But a legal practitioner of
less than seven years' standing may in special cases be permitted by
the Supreme Court of Nigeria to appear in a case before the Court.[39]
Any such permission must be in writing.[40]

D. The Liability of a Legal Practitioner for Negligence

As a general rule, a person may be liable in negligence for an act done
by him in his capacity as a legal practitioner.[41] Any provisions purporting to exclude or limit such liability in any contract is void,
except in cases in which he gives his services without reward.[42] But a
legal practitioner acting in his capacity as a barrister is not liable in
negligence with respect to the conduct of proceedings in the face of
any court, tribunal or other body. This common law rule[43] is embod-
ied in section 8(3) of the Legal Practitioners Decree 1975. In *Rondel*
v. *Worsley*,[44] Lord Denning M.R., sitting at the Court of Appeal in
England explained the reason for the rule by referring to the need for
the barrister to perform his duty fearlessly and independently, the
barrister's obligation with respect to accepting a brief, the barrister's
duty to the court and the need to avoid protracted litigation that
would arise if a barrister could be sued for negligence.[45] He stated as
follows[46]:

---

[36] *Ibid.*
[37] Legal Practitioners Decree 1975, s. 7(3).
[38] Supreme Court Practice and Procedure Order 1972.
[39] *Ibid.*
[40] *Ibid.*
[41] See Legal Practitioners Decree 1975, s. 8(1).
[42] See Legal Practitioners Decree 1975, s. 8(2).
[43] See *Rondel* v. *Worsley* [1969] 1 A.C. 191.
[44] [1967] 1 Q.B. 443 at pp. 501-504.
[45] See "Rules of Professional Conduct in the Legal Profession," Government Notice
No. 1977, *Federal Republic of Nigeria Official Gazette* No. 107, Vol. 54, 1967.
[46] [1967] 1 Q.B. 443 at pp. 501, 504.

"There is, in my judgment, a sure ground on which to rest the immunity of a barrister. At any rate, so far as concerns his conduct of a case in court. It is so that he may do his duty fearlessly and independently as he ought; and to prevent him being harassed by vexatious actions . . . As an advocate he is a minister of justice equally with the judge . . . A barrister cannot pick or choose his clients. He is bound to accept a brief for any man who comes before the courts. No matter how given to complaining. No matter how undeserving or unpopular his cause. The barrister must defend him to the end. Provided only that he is paid a proper fee, or in the case of a dock brief, a nominal fee. He must accept the brief and do all he honourably can on behalf of his client. I say 'all he *honourably* can' because his duty is not only to his client. He has a duty to the court which is paramount. It is a mistake to suppose that he is the mouthpiece of his client to say what he wants: or his tool to do what he directs. He is none of these things. He owes allegiance to a higher cause. It is the cause of truth and justice . . . If a barrister is to be able to do his duty fearlessly and independently, he must not be subject to the threat of an action for negligence . . . If a barrister could be sued for negligence, it would mean a retrial of the original case . . . Finally, on public policy I would say this: If this action were to be permitted, it would open the door to every disgruntled client . . . Every convicted prisoner who blamed his counsel could at once bring an action for negligence. Rather than open the door to him, I would bolt it."

The House of Lords of England affirmed the decision of the Court of Appeal of England in *Rondel* v. *Worsley* that a barrister could not be liable in negligence with respect to his conduct of a case in Court.[47]

E. REMUNERATION OF LEGAL PRACTITIONERS

Section 14 of the Legal Practitioners Decree 1975 established a committee known as the Legal Practitioners Remuneration Committee and empowered to make orders regulating generally the charges of legal practitioners. The committee consists of:

(a) the Attorney-General of the Federation who is the chairman;
(b) the Attorneys-General of the States; and
(c) the President of the Nigerian Bar Association.

The provision does not affect the continued application of the pre-existing rules governing the remuneration of legal practitioners,

---

[47] [1969] 1 A.C. 191.

until the first order made in pursuance of this provision comes into force.[48]

Under section 15(1) of the Legal Practitioners Decree 1975 a legal practitioner is entitled to recover his charges by action in a court of competent jurisdiction.[49] In general, before a legal practitioner brings such action, a bill for the charges containing particulars of the principal items included in the bill and signed by him, or in the case of a firm by one of the partners or in the name of the firm, must have been served on the client personally or left for him at his last address as known to the practitioner or sent by post addressed to the client at that address. In addition, the period of one month beginning with the date of delivery of the bill must have expired.[50] There are provisions in the Legal Practitioners Decree 1975 for taxation of bills of charges delivered by a legal practitioner to his clients.[51]

F. Clients' Moneys

Sections 19 and 20 of the Legal Practitioners Decree 1975 deal with the keeping of accounts and records of clients' moneys. Section 19 of the Decree provides that in general the General Council of the Bar "may from time to time as the Council considers expedient, make rules —

(a) as to the opening and keeping by legal practitioners of accounts at banks for clients' moneys and
(b) as to the keeping by legal practitioners of records containing particulars and information as to moneys received, held or paid by them for or on account of their clients and
(c) as to the opening and keeping by a legal practitioner who is the sole trustee, or who is a co-trustee only with one or more of his partners, clerks or servants, of an account at a bank for moneys of any trust of which he is the sole trustee or such a co-trustee as aforesaid; and
(d) as to the keeping by such a practitioner as is mentioned in the last foregoing paragraph of records containing particulars and information as to moneys received, held or paid by him for or on account of any such trust as is so mentioned; and
(e) empowering the bar council to take such action as it thinks necessary to enable it to ascertain whether the rules are being complied with."

---

[48] Legal Practitioners Decree 1975, s. 14(5). See Legal Practitioners (Remuneration for Conveyancing Matters) Order 1971 (L.N. 31 of 1971).
[49] Compare the common law rule according to which a barrister cannot sue for his fees. See *Wells* v. *Wells* [1914] P. 157.
[50] Legal Practitioners Decree 1975, s. 15(2).
[51] *Ibid.* ss. 16 and 17.

But rules made by the General Council of the Bar with respect to clients' moneys must not require the keeping of accounts or records by a legal practitioner in respect of moneys received, held or paid by him as a member of the public service of the Federation or a State. Furthermore, in such other circumstances as may be specified by the rules, the keeping of accounts or records of clients' moneys is not to be required by the rules.[52]

Where a legal practitioner keeps an account for clients' moneys with a bank, the bank is not to have or obtain any recourse or right against moneys standing to the credit of that account in respect of any liability of the practitioner to the bank which does not arise in connection with that account.[53] Where a legal practitioner keeps with a bank a client account (other than an account kept by him as a trustee for a specified beneficiary) the bank does not incur any liability in connection with any transaction in respect of that account or in respect of such client account kept with any other bank except that liability it would incur in the case of an account kept by a person entitled absolutely to all the money paid or credited to the account.

G. THE GENERAL COUNCIL OF THE BAR

The General Council of the Bar is a body established by section 1 of the Legal Practitioners Decree 1975. It is responsible for the general management of the affairs of the Nigerian Bar Association (the association of legal practitioners in Nigeria) subject to any limitations for the time being provided by the Constitution of the association. In addition, the body is to perform any functions conferred on it by the association's Constitution and other functions conferred on it by the Decree.

The principal function of the General Council of the Bar (apart from the general management of the affairs of the Nigerian Bar Association) conferred on it by the Decree is the duty of the Council under section 10(4) of the Decree to prepare, and from time to time revise, a statement of the kind of conduct which the Council considers to be infamous conduct in a professional respect. The Council is to be consulted by the Attorney-General of the Federation before making regulations under section 6(2) of the Decree for the enrolment as legal practitioners in Nigeria of members of the legal profession in any other country on a reciprocal basis. The Attorney-General of the Federation is also required to hold consultation with the Council under section 7(3) of the Decree before varying the rates

[52] *Ibid.* s. 19(4).
[53] *Ibid.* s. 20(1).
[54] See Legal Practitioners Decree 1975, s. 20(2).

of practising fees specified by the Decree. The pre-existing General Council of the Bar made a set of rules, known as Rules of Professional Conduct in the Legal Profession, pursuant to provisions of the Legal Practitioners Act 1962.[55] The General Council of the Bar consists of:

(a) the Attorney-General of the Federation who is the president of the Council;

(b) the Attorneys-General of the States; and

(c) 20 members of the Nigerian Bar Association.[56]

H. DISCIPLINE

Section 9 of the Legal Practitioners Decree 1975 established a committee known as the Legal Practitioners Disciplinary Committee and consisting of:

(a) the Attorney-General of the Federation, who is the Chairman of the Committee;

(b) the Attorneys-General of the States in the Federation; and

(c) 12 legal practitioners of at least 10 years' standing appointed by the body of Benchers on the nomination of the Nigerian Bar Association.

The disciplinary committee has the duty of considering and determining any case where it is alleged that a person whose name is on the roll of legal practitioners has misbehaved in his capacity as a legal practitioner or should for any other reason be the subject of proceedings under the Decree.

Section 11 of the Decree established a committee known as the Appeal Committee of the Body of Benchers. The duty of the Committee is to hear appeals from any direction given by the disciplinary committee. The Appeal Committee consists of the following seven persons, being members of the Body of Benchers appointed by the Body of Benchers from time to time:

(a) chairman — a Bencher whose membership of the Body of Benchers is not by virtue of being nominated by the Nigerian Bar Association;

(b) two Attorneys-General in the Federation;

(c) two judges of the High Court or higher court of any State; and

(d) two members of the Nigerian Bar Association.[57]

A person may, if otherwise eligible, be a member of both the disciplinary committee and the appeal committee, but a person who has

[55] No. 33 of 1962.
[56] Legal Practitioners Decree 1975, s. 1(2).
[57] Legal Practitioners Decree 1975, s. 11(2).

acted as a member of the disciplinary committee in a case must not act as a member of the appeal committee with respect to that case.[58]

Under section 10(1) of the Legal Practitioners Decree 1975, where:

(a) the disciplinary committee finds a person whose name is on the roll of legal practitioners guilty of infamous conduct in any professional respect; or

(b) a person whose name is on the roll of legal practitioners is convicted, by any court in Nigeria having power to impose a sentence of imprisonment, of an offence (whether or not an offence punishable with imprisonment) which in the opinion of the disciplinary committee is incompatible with the status of a legal practitioner; or

(c) the disciplinary committee is satisfied that the name of any person has been fraudulently enrolled,

the disciplinary committee may, if it thinks fit, give a direction —

(i) ordering the Chief Registrar of the Supreme Court to strike that person's name off the roll of legal practitioners; or

(ii) suspending that person from practice as a legal practitioner for such period as may be specified in the direction; or

(iii) admonishing that person.

Where appropriate, any such direction may include a provision requiring the refund of moneys paid or the handing over of documents or any other thing as the circumstances of the case may require.

Where the disciplinary committee finds a person whose name is on the roll of legal practitioners guilty of misconduct not amounting to infamous conduct which, in the opinion of the committee, is incompatible with the status of a legal practitioner, the committee may, if it thinks fit, give a direction of suspension from practice or of admonition, and as in the case of a person found guilty of infamous conduct, the direction may in an appropriate case include provision requiring the refund of moneys paid or the handing over of documents or any other thing, as the circumstances of the case may require.[59]

Although the General Council of the Bar has the duty of preparing and, from time to time, revising a statement as to the kind of conduct it considers to be infamous conduct in a professional respect, it is open to the disciplinary committee or the Supreme Court to which appeals from the appeal committee lies to hold that a person is guilty of infamous conduct in a professional respect by reference to a matter not contained in the statement.[60]

It should be noted that the provisions of the Decree on discipline

---

[58] *Ibid.* Sched. 2, para. 4(2).
[59] *Ibid.* s. 10(2).
[60] *Ibid.* s. 10(4).

of legal practitioners do not apply to a class of legal practitioners consisting of persons permitted to practise as barristers under a warrant issued by the Chief Justice of Nigeria.[61] Section 10 of the Decree deals with persons whose names are on the roll. But barristers practising under warrant are not enrolled even though they come within the meaning of legal practitioner under the Decree.[62]

I. RULES OF PROFESSIONAL CONDUCT IN THE LEGAL PROFESSION

Rules of Professional Conduct in the Legal Profession made by the pre-existing General Council of the Bar in pursuance of provisions of the Legal Practitioners Act 1962[63] were stated by the Council to be made "in furtherance of the aims and objects of the Nigerian Bar Association under the Constitution of the association as referred to in section 1 of the Legal Practitioners Act 1962 and for the maintenance of the highest standards of Professional Conduct, etiquette and discipline in terms of that Constitution."

The sub-headings to the various rules are as follows:

Rule 1 - The duty of the lawyer to the court
Rule 2 - Relations with judges
Rule 3 - Conduct towards judges during trial
Rule 4 - Candour and fairness
Rule 5 - Attitude towards jurors
Rule 6 - Courtroom decorum
Rule 7 - Employment in criminal cases
Rule 8 - Counsel for an indigent prisoner
Rule 9 - Conduct of criminal cases
Rule 10 - Adverse influences and conflicting interests
Rule 11 - Professional colleagues and conflicts of opinion
Rule 12 - Advising upon the merits of a client's cause
Rule 13 - Negotiations with opposite party
Rule 14 - How far a lawyer may go in supporting a client's cause
Rule 15 - Restraining clients from improprieties
Rule 16 - Ill-feeling between advocates
Rule 17 - Technical advantage over counsel and enforcement of agreements
Rule 18 - Right of lawyer to control the incidents of the trial
Rule 19 - Lawyer as witness for clients

---

[61] See Legal Practitioners Decree 1975, s. 2(2).
[62] The term "legal practitioner" is defined as a person entitled in accordance with the provisions of this Decree to practise as a barrister or as a barrister and solicitor, either generally or for the purposes of any particular office or proceedings. See Legal Practitioners Decree 1975, s. 23.
[63] No. 33 of 1962.

Rule 20 - Investigation of facts and production of witnesses, etc.
Rule 21 - Upholding the honour of the profession
Rule 22 - Justifiable and unjustifiable litigation
Rule 23 - Responsibility for litigation
Rule 24 - The lawyer's duty in its last analysis
Rule 25 - Instigating litigation either directly or through agents, etc.
Rule 26 - Confidence of a client
Rule 27 - Newspaper comment on pending litigation, etc.
Rule 28 - Discovery of imposition and deception
Rule 29 - Withdrawal from employment
Rule 30 - Engaging in business
Rule 31 - Salaried employment
Rule 32 - Calling at a client's house or place of business
Rule 33 - Advertising, touting and publicity
Rule 34 - Scope of the prohibition of advertisement
Rule 35 - Newspapers and periodicals
Rule 36 - Notice to local lawyers
Rule 37 - Aiding the unauthorised practice of law
Rule 38 - Equality of members
Rule 39 - Retirement from judicial position or public employment
Rule 40 - Fee for each piece of work
Rule 41 - Retainers
Rule 42 - Acquiring interest in litigation
Rule 43 - Expenses
Rule 44 - Fixing the amount of the fee
Rule 45 - Division of fees
Rule 46 - Compensation, commission and rebates
Rule 47 - Suing clients for professional fees
Rule 48 - Intermediaries
Rule 49 - Dealing with trust property
Rule 50 - Partnerships
Rule 51 - Practising fees
Rule 52 - Interpretation

A declaration made pursuant to the provisions of rule 30 forms Appendix I to the Rules.[64]

According to the Rules, it is the duty of the lawyer to maintain a respectful attitude towards the court.[65] It is unprofessional on the part of a member of the Bar to promote a case which to his own knowledge is false, or to file a pleading or other document which he knows

---

[64] See Government Notice No. 1977 (*Federal Republic of Nigeria Gazette*, No. 107, Vol. 54, 1967); Government Notice No. 1550 (*Federal Republic of Nigeria Gazette*, No. 78, Vol. 55 1968); Government Notice No. 1549 (*Federal Republic of Nigeria Gazette*, No. 78, Vol. 55, 1968).
[65] Rules of Professional Conduct in the Legal Profession, r. 1(*a*).

to be false in whole or in part, or which is intended to delay the trial.[66] A lawyer should rise when addressing, or being addressed by the judge.[67] In criminal cases, refusal to undertake a defence may not be justified merely on the ground of belief in the guilt of the accused, or repugnance towards him or to the offence as charged.[68] A member of the Bar who accepts a brief for the defence in a murder trial is deemed to have given a solemn undertaking that he will personally conduct the defence provided his fee is paid.[69] The primary duty of a lawyer engaged in public prosecution is to see that justice is done, not to see that the accused is convicted.[70]

It is unprofessional conduct on the part of a lawyer to represent conflicting interests except by express consent of all concerned given after a full disclosure of the facts.[71] As a general rule, a lawyer is bound to accept any brief in the courts in which he professes to practise at a proper professional fee but special circumstances may justify his refusal, at his discretion to accept a brief.[72] A lawyer must refuse to conduct a civil cause when he is convinced that it is intended merely to harass or to injure the opposite party or to work oppression or wrong.[73] Under rule 25(a) of the Rules, it is unprofessional conduct on the part of a lawyer to offer advice to bring a law suit except in cases where ties of blood relationship or trust may render it necessary. The rule also states that it is unprofessional conduct on the part of a lawyer to foment strife or instigate litigation. It is unprofessional conduct on the part of a lawyer to solicit professional employment by circulars, advertisements, through touts or by personal communications or interviews; but it is not improper for a lawyer to use simple professional cards.[74] It is contrary to the Rules for a member of the Bar to insert in any newspaper, periodical or any other publication an advertisement offering as a member of the Bar, to undertake confidential inquiries; to write for publication or give an interview to the Press or otherwise cause or permit to be published, except in a legal periodical, any particulars of his practice or earnings in the profession or of cases pending in the courts or cases where the time for appeal has not expired on any matter in which he has been engaged as a member of the Bar; to answer questions on legal subjects in the Press or any periodical or in a wireless

---

[66] *Ibid.* r. 4(*e*).
[67] *Ibid.* r. 6(*a*).
[68] *Ibid.* r. 7(*a*).
[69] *Ibid.* r. 7(*b*).
[70] *Ibid.* r. 9(*d*).
[71] *Ibid.* r. 10(*b*).
[72] *Ibid.* r. 23.
[73] *Ibid.* r. 22.
[74] *Ibid.* r. 33.

or television broadcast where his name or initials are directly or indirectly disclosed or likely or be disclosed; or to take steps to procure the publication of his photograph as a member of the Bar in the Press or any periodical.[75] According to rule 35 of the Rules, although a lawyer may write articles for publication in which he gives information on the law he should not accept employment to advise inquirers in respect of their individual rights.

A lawyer should not accept employment as an advocate in a matter upon the merits of which he had previously acted in a judicial capacity.[76] Similarly, a lawyer having once held public office or having been in the public employment should not after his retirement accept employment with respect to any matter which he had advised on or dealt with while in such public office or public employment.[77]

Rule 30 of the Rules states as follows:

"No member of the Bar may practise as a lawyer and be engaged in any trade or business which the Bar Council may declare to be incompatible with practice as a lawyer or tending to undermine the high standing of the profession."

In July 1968, the General Council of the Bar established under the Legal Practitioners Act 1962[78] declared the following trades and businesses to be incompatible with practice as a legal practitioner or as tending to undermine the high standing of the profession:

(i) all forms of trading, the word "trading" including all forms of participation in any trade or business but not including —
    (a) membership of a board of directors of a company which does not involve administrative, executive or clerical duties
    (b) secretaryship of a board of directors of a company or of a general meeting of a company
    (c) being a shareholder in a company
(ii) salaried employment in an exclusively legal capacity in a firm or company other than a law firm or under a person other than a legal practitioner, a public authority, a statutory corporation, or a university
(iii) salaried employment with a law firm or legal practitioner other than in respect of legal practice.[79]

Rule 31 of the Rules provides as follows:

"(a) In general a member of the Bar whilst a servant or in salaried employment of any kind should not appear as an advocate in any

---

[75] *Ibid.* r. 34.
[76] *Ibid.* r. 39(*a*).
[77] *Ibid.* r. 39(*b*).
[78] No. 33 of 1962.
[79] See n. 64, above.

court or tribunal; but the following shall not be deemed to constitute a member of the Bar a servant or in salaried employment:

(i) the receipt of fees as a director of a limited liability company, provided that the recipient of such fees shall not appear as an advocate for his company;

(ii) employment as a legal officer in any Government Department or a Statutory Corporation or a University;

(iii) employment as a pupil at a salary in the chambers of another legal practitioner;

(iv) employment as a lecturer in law.

(b) Legal practitioners holding whole-time legal appointments with local government authorities, nationalised industries or statutory corporations may appear in court as counsel on behalf of their employers.

(c) A non-practising barrister in whole-time salaried employment may represent his employing authority or body as an officer or agent in cases where the authority or body concerned is permitted to appear by an officer or agent; and in such cases robes should not be worn.

(d) An officer in the Armed Forces who is also a member of the Bar is not precluded by reason of his being a barrister from discharging as an officer any duties which may devolve upon him as such and may therefore appear at a court martial, provided he does so in his capacity as an officer and not as a barrister."

There is no doubt that the Rules are consistent with the view that members of the legal profession have a noble role to play in the administration of justice in the country.[80]

---

[80] See "Editorial: The Legal Profession, Social Change and the Independence of the Judiciary," *Nigerian Bar Journal*, Vol. XIII (1976), p. 1.

INDEX